Art Market Research

Art Market Research

A Guide to Methods and Sources

Tom McNulty

McFarland & Company, Inc., Publishers
Jefferson, North Carolina, and London

Library of Congress Cataloguing-in-Publication Data

McNulty, Tom.
Art market research : a guide to methods and sources / Tom McNulty.
p. cm.
Includes bibliographical references and indexes.

ISBN-13: 978-0-7864-2372-9
(softcover : 50# alkaline paper) ∞

1. Art — Collectors and collecting. 2. Art — Economic aspects.
3. Art literature. I. Title.
N5200.M39 2006
702.9 — dc22 2006001522

British Library cataloguing data are available

Manufactured in the United States of America

McFarland & Company, Inc., Publishers
Box 611, Jefferson, North Carolina 28640
www.mcfarlandpub.com

Contents

Preface

In recent years, the market for works of art has undergone some major transformations. Once the exclusive province of a very small and extremely wealthy group, art collecting is becoming increasingly democratized. Of course, the collector of major works of art is still, with very few exceptions,[1] a member of the more privileged class; but increasingly, individual collectors with limited budgets are becoming investors, if only on a small scale.

As the market for fine and decorative art works has grown, so has the number of information sources available to guide collectors, dealers and other art market researchers. The purpose of this book is to organize and evaluate the best of these information tools, and to assist the reader in the selection of the most appropriate sources for the valuation of specific works of art. Much more than an annotated bibliography of print and electronic resources, however, this guide explores in detail the various processes to be undertaken in researching artworks and decorative art objects.

There are three major venues in which art is bought and sold: the gallery (commercial and noncommercial), the auction, and the private sale (artist-to-collector, collector-to-collector, or any other two-party exchange). Chapter One explores these markets, and provides an overview of the contemporary world of fine and decorative art collecting. Here, the reader will learn the basics of auction terminology, including buyer and seller premiums, pre-sale estimates, reserve prices, buy-ins and more. The gallery world is similarly defined, and specific factors to be taken into account in deciding where to sell or buy art are identified.

When we consider the "value" of anything, several factors must be taken into consideration. From cars to clothes, most things that we acquire begin to lose value the minute we buy them; other purchases—like houses, fine furniture and art—while subject to fluctuations in value and marketability, can grow in value over time. The novice art market researcher might be surprised to learn that any given work can have more than one value. We end Chapter One, therefore, with an overview of the concept of value, and consider the factors that contribute to the value assigned to specific objects and artworks. Fair market value and replacement value, the two concepts most important to the collector, are explored here in some detail.

As a first step in exploring the myriad resources available to the art market researcher, some very basic techniques and general resources are introduced in Chapter Two. Here, the basics of artwork analysis and documentation are described, and the reader is guided in formulating a strategy for further research. Of particular value to the novice researcher, Chapter Two also presents a very concise overview of database searching methods, and introduces some of the online tools that can streamline the process of researching works of fine and decorative art. The description and overview of basic features of the many specialized databases of interest to the art researcher precede an exploration of some very important, but often overlooked tools that can be tremendously useful to the market researcher — databases that are intended for the business professional. In addition to these, sources of information unique to the art world are outlined. Some of these sources are, in fact, *people*. Consider, for example, the process of authenticating a silkscreen print presumed to be a Warhol. For recently deceased artists like Andy Warhol, the foundation set up in the artist's name is often the ultimate arbiter of authenticity.[2] Similarly, imagine that you've inherited a painting that certainly looks like a real Marc Chagall — signature and all. You might begin by researching on your own, but only a certificate of authentication will lay to rest any doubts about the work's authenticity.[3] Recognizing the importance of experts, we end Chapter Two with an overview of the role of the art world expert — including tips on how to find them.

In order to research the value of any work of art, it is of course most important to learn as much as possible about the work and who created it. In chapters Three and Four, sources and strategies for researching artworks and decorative arts objects, respectively, are explored in detail. Taken together, these chapters might best be described as a crash course in fine and decorative arts research. Major published sources, including artists' catalogues raisonnés, exhibition catalogues, dictionaries and encyclopedias, are identified and fully annotated.

One of the factors that can affect an artwork's value is its provenance, or record of ownership. Inclusion in a major collection can have a tremendous impact on the value of certain works of art. Perhaps more importantly, provenance research can lay to rest any doubts about rightful ownership.

In recent years, artworks looted during the Nazi era have garnered considerable media attention, and many museums are addressing the issue of rightful ownership by undertaking extensive provenance research on their collections. Chapter Five provides an overview of provenance research, and identifies sources that can assist in determining ownership history.

Numerous print and electronic information sources are available to assist the researcher in establishing the value of both fine and decorative arts objects. The auction market is the best-documented and therefore most trustworthy source of information. Unlike galleries and individuals who buy and sell art, auction houses are required to publicly disclose prices paid for works sold. In chapters Six (Fine Arts) and Seven (Decorative Arts), the auction market is explored in detail. Relevant information sources are identified, described and organized by type and format. These chapters also provide the collector with assistance in researching the retail (commercial gallery) market, identifying gallery representation of specific artists or types of artwork, and using freely available tools on the Internet to establish the probable values of specific works.

The history of the art market has been the subject of considerable research and scholarship in recent years, and the historical researcher has a wide array of sources at his or her disposal. Chapter Eight presents a core bibliography of primary documents and data sources for historical research. Most of the resources included up to this point have been selected both for their quality and because they are widely held in libraries across the nation, but the latter criterion is relaxed here; some of the tools selected for inclusion in the historical overview are, in fact, quite rare, but they are essential for in-depth research of the history of collecting and patronage.

Finally, two appendices identify some important resources touched upon throughout the book. Appendix A is a list of those periodicals (newspapers, magazines, journals) that offer reliable, current coverage of art market issues. Appendix B presents a list of auction houses, and describes how their websites can be used to obtain art market information.

Before we begin, a word of caution. It has often been said that anyone who represents himself in a legal proceeding has a fool for a client; the same could be said of the individual who serves as his own appraiser. An experienced appraiser is familiar with the many factors that affect artwork value, from "big picture" market forces to the nuances of an individual artist's work and market. But with some understanding of the art research process and the vast array of sources available for identifying prices, even novice collectors can establish a price range for the works of art they acquire.

ONE

The Concept of Value and the Markets for Art

The attempt to define the concepts of "value" and "worth" has occupied economists and others for millennia. In the first century B.C., Publius Syrus coined the proverb "Every thing is worth what its purchaser will pay for it." Some important assumptions underlie this simple explanation of worth — assumptions that would, centuries later, be made explicit in the legal definition of "fair market value" (more about this later). Before going on to consider some of the unique factors and forces that work in tandem to create value in works of fine or decorative art, let's consider what we mean by "value" in the first place.

The *Oxford English Dictionary* defines "value" as "the material or monetary worth of a thing; the amount at which it may be estimated in terms of some medium of exchange or other standard of a similar nature." We all comprehend the idea of value in relation to certain materials or commodities. Gold, for example, is universally accepted as precious, so much so that the expression "gold standard" has come to be used synonymously with anything —from objects to actions— that are considered exceptionally fine or valuable.

The assignment of monetary value to any work of art is a complex process. Unlike most of our major acquisitions (like houses and cars), the cost of the raw materials used to create works of fine or decorative art are usually of little or negligible value relative to the value of the work. A major painting by Pablo Picasso, currently valued in the tens-of-millions of dollars, really represents less than one hundred dollars worth of raw material —canvas and paint. What *are* the factors that, taken together, contribute to an artwork's monetary value? Each work of art has unique qualities— and its sale may very well have unique circumstances— that will work in concert to affect its overall valuation. But for most purposes, the following points must be assessed, and related to each other, in the attempt to determine the value of any work of art.

Value Factors

Popularity of the Subject Work's Style

American figurative sculpture, while extremely popular (and abundant) in the 19th century, fell so out of favor among collectors, critics and scholars alike by the mid–20th century that major works could be acquired in the 1950s and '60s for a fraction of their current value adjusted for inflation. Taste evolves over time; some styles or forms fall out of favor rapidly, while others' devaluation occurs more slowly. Myriad factors affect the desirability of certain types of work at any point in time. It is probably safe to say that the vast majority of paintings, drawings, sculpture and prints that are in private hands were acquired for the purpose of display; indeed, they are sometimes simply part of a decorating scheme, and because of this, even trends in design can affect the desirability of any particular period or style.

This aspect of the value equation represents just one of the reasons why a major, historically significant Renaissance bronze sculpture might attain just a fraction of the price garnered by a small painting by one of the most highly sought-after French Impressionists. It also explains how, very recently, two paintings of dogs playing poker, by Cassius Marcellus Coolidge, exceeded their high estimates more than ten-fold when they were sold at auction in New York City for about $600,000; America's appreciation of the iconic imagery of popular culture is at work here. Whether or not the current owner made a wise long-term investment in these kitsch classics remains to be seen.

The Artist's Reputation

The stature of the artwork's creator, if he or she is known, is often the most important factor in the construction of value. But how do we measure an artist's stature? While there is certainly no mathematical formula for determining how popular an artist is, or was, at any point in time, a few measures to consider include:

- Exhibition history. Has the artist been the subject of any major exhibitions? Are there any exhibitions in the planning stages?

- Critical reception. How have the artist's exhibitions been received in the popular and scholarly communications media? Much more about this in later chapters.
- Publication. Has the artist been the subject of any major books? Is the artist included in standard surveys? Encyclopedias of art? Art journals and magazines?
- Inclusion in major public and private collections. Many works accrue additional value simply by their inclusion in a highly regarded collection, whether public or private.

Note that all artists' bodies of work must be further analyzed for the relative importance or popularity of different periods, imagery, styles and other factors. Prolific artists with long careers in particular often have works that sell for anywhere from the low thousands to several millions of dollars, depending upon the unique circumstances surrounding each work, and its place in the artist's oeuvre.

Rarity

Supply and demand economics apply in the art market just as they do in other areas of economic exchange. Consider the housing market, for example. The finite number of housing units in an extremely desirable location — like New York, London or Paris— works to drive prices extremely high. The same is true for works of art by highly sought-after artists. Very strong demand coupled with a small supply of available works equals high — sometimes, as we've seen in recent years, *very* high prices.

Nothing underscores the effect of supply on an artist's market more than the fact that the concept of "blockage" is applied to appraisals that include a very large number of his or her artworks. Once applied exclusively in the world of finance, blockage is essentially a discount that offsets the diminished prices that would certainly occur in a market suddenly flooded with an artist's work. That is, if approximately 10 works by the artist sold annually at auction in the 10-thousand dollar range over the past few years, and suddenly (e.g., upon the artist's death) hundreds or even thousands of comparable works were to become available at once, the supply would have a devastating effect on the values of those works.

Condition

The condition of a work of fine or decorative art can have an enormous impact on its value. Certain types of work are almost expected to be in less than mint condition; indeed, a very, very fresh "Old Master" would be immediately questionable to dealers, collectors, and other art market participants. On the other hand, a chipped piece of 20th century porcelain would certainly attain a significantly lower price than a pristine example of the same piece.

The "loss in value" associated with damage is best determined by a professional appraiser with experience in the world of damage assessment as it relates to value. Most appraisers would probably agree that this is one of the most complex areas of valuation. Generally speaking, "at every rising level of art the associated loss becomes increasingly restricted."[1] In other words, there is an inverse relationship between the original value of a work and the loss in value assigned to it as a result of damage. A very rare painting worth many millions of dollars would lose a far smaller *percentage* of its original value if damaged than would a $2,000 work with the same degree of damage.

Provenance

In a later chapter, we'll discuss provenance — the record of a work's ownership — in much greater detail. But note from the outset that a work's prior ownership can greatly affect its value. This has been demonstrated time and again in recent highly-publicized auction sales of historical and celebrity collections. One of these sales — the April 1996 Jacqueline Kennedy Onassis Estate Sale at Sotheby's — saw a good number of fairly pedestrian items sell for prices that exceeded their high estimates many times over. Buyers at these sorts of sales are, in effect, acquiring a "piece of history," and are advised to keep all paperwork relating to the sale, because they are in fact investing more in provenance than in the object itself. Unless the item at hand is an historical document, its connection to history rests only in its documented provenance.

Other Factors

In addition to the more obvious factors described so far, unique factors sometimes play a major role in bolstering the prices of artworks. In some instances, the buyer might bring a special "need" for a work of art that is on the auction block or in a retail gallery. Consider the case of works produced in series, like a suite of prints. The collector who owns nine of 10 works comprising a series of major lithographs by a popular artist, for example, might so desire a complete set that she or he will be willing to pay more — sometimes, much more — than the individual work is actually worth. The expenditure might actually make sense, since the complete series may have a greater value than its individual parts — especially if the number of extant complete sets is small. There is really no limit to the possible scenarios that can be included in this, the most elusive of the valuation factors.

The Appraisal Process

Some of the factors outlined above are easier than others to assess, and a good deal of expertise is required to assess their effect on value. That's where the professional appraiser's services are most required. How does an appraiser relate one work to another, to arrive at a value? For the most part, the appraiser looks for sales of comparable works—comparable, that is, in terms of medium, dimensions, subject matter, style, date of execution, etc.

The search for true comparables can sometimes be quite straightforward, as in the case of a print or three-dimensional multiple. Indeed, physical condition of the subject work aside, the individual prints that make up a contemporary edition are one and the same, beyond comparable — in this case, they're identical. But identifying comparables for most unique artworks is usually a very challenging task. For some artists— like Mark Rothko— palette is one of the primary factors taken under consideration. The market for the artist's brightly colored works differs markedly from his somber canvases. Knowledge of art is at least as important as understanding of the market in the selection of comparables.

Some artists are so rarely offered for sale at auction that identifying a truly comparable sale is next to impossible. Here, the professional appraiser will apply knowledge of the subject work's style, or period, and possibly even relate it to sales of works by artists of similar stature for whom there *is* some market data. Or the appraiser might extrapolate a value using data from the sale of works that are *somewhat* comparable (e.g., right period, different medium). The nuances in the comparable selection process are very important, because they guide the appraiser in the selection of data that will obviously affect the value assigned to the subject work.

"Fair Market" and "Replacement" Value

Most newcomers to market research are unaware of the many values that might be assigned to the same item or group of items. For most collectors and market researchers, the most commonly sought-after values are "fair market" and "replacement." The remaining classes of value — including wholesale, liquidation and others— are very well defined in *The Appraisal of Personal Property: Principles, Theories, and Practice Methods for the Professional Appraiser*, edited by Patricia C. Soucy and Janella N. Smyth, ASA. (Washington, D.C.: American Society of Appraisers, 1994 [updated version is in press]).

Fair market value is the price at which the property would change hands between a willing buyer and a willing seller, neither being under any compulsion to buy or sell and both having reasonable knowledge of relevant facts.[2] Fair market value relies heavily upon the concept of the "most relevant market"—that is, the market in which such item is most commonly sold to the public.[3] While auction sale might be deemed the "most relevant market" in some circumstances, the specific nature of each piece will be used to determine most relevant market. In the case of a print, for example, that was published just last year, chances are very slim that the work will yet have found its way into the auction market. So, in this case, the most relevant market would likely be either the publisher of the print, or the artist's dealer/representative.

Replacement value, on the other hand, is the value usually applied to a property for insurance purposes; it is, further, "most customarily understood to represent that amount of money required to replace a property with another of similar qualities within a reasonable length of time in an appropriate and relevant market."[4]

The Auction Market

Today, the word "auction" undoubtedly evokes images of paintings, works of sculpture, or other "high-end" collectible object or artwork tastefully presented on a pedestal, with an auctioneer acknowledging bid after bid, each higher by an increment set forth by the auctioneer. "I have $300,000, do I hear $325? I have $325,000 from a telephone bidder, do I hear $350?" In fact, the very word "auction" reflects this procession of successively increasing bids, or offers, as it derives from the Latin word meaning "increase."

While "auction" and "art" go hand-in-hand in the popular imagination, the auction is actually just one of several methods of selling merchandise, and it dates from the time of ancient Babylon.[5] But at one of the earliest auction sales, the successful bidder would be more likely to return home with a new wife, a slave, or a farm animal than with a painting or a piece of sculpture.

Anything from bulk quantities of wheat or corn, to used cars, to the confiscated yachts of convicted drug smugglers can be subject to sale at auction. In the case of consumable and manufactured goods, the auction works so well for certain kinds of commercial transactions because interested parties can dispose of large quantities of material quickly, thus reducing or even eliminating at least some of the "overhead" costs associated with maintaining a large stock of goods. Although many auctions are attended by individuals in search of a single item, very often these kinds of auctions serve to supply retailers with inventory. The used car salesman, for example, might return from a successful auction with five, 10, even 20 cars to add to his lot; in this way, the auction serves as a kind of wholesale outlet, in which the retailer can acquire items for resale at a mark-up. The same held true, until recent decades, for the larger auction houses vis-à-vis fine and decorative artworks; they supplied gallery owners, who in turn offered works of art in their retail galleries, often at a very significant mark-up.

Popular interest in the auction market for works of art peaked in the second half of the 20th century, and two sales in particular seem to have captured the imagination of the general public. The first of these occurred on November 15, 1961, when the Metropolitan Museum of Art in New York paid the then-highest price on record for a work of art — Rembrandt's *Aristotle Contemplating the Bust of Homer*. The sale, at Parke-Bernet, sparked such interest in the popular press that the Metropolitan Museum would soon boast record attendance. A *New York Times* headline of November 19, 1961, reads, "42,000 View $2,300,000 Rembrandt at Metropolitan."[6] The next day, attendance records continued to break and the *Times* reported, "Rembrandt Draws Record of 82,679 to Metropolitan."[7] It seemed that everyone wanted to see the world's (then) most valuable work of art.

A second sale, while certainly less "hyped" than the sale of *Aristotle* to the Metropolitan, had an immediate and lasting effect on the art world and should not go unnoticed here. On October 18, 1973, Robert Scull, owner of a fleet of New York City taxis, offered about one-fifth of his collection for sale at Parke Bernet. The list of artists represented in the Scull Collection and offered for sale at Parke Bernet reads like a "Who's Who of Contemporary Art," and numerous records were set. The sale further served to forever alter the nature of fine art auctions by its inclusion of so many contemporary works by living artists. Today, the major contemporary sales at all of the international houses receive a great deal of attention in the art press, and serve as a kind of bellwether of the market's vigor.

Selling and Buying at Auction

While Sotheby's, Christie's, Bonham and a few others come to mind when most people speak of the auction world, there are in fact many thousands of auction houses worldwide. Some specialize in specific types of material, or represent regional tastes in their offerings. Some hold "cataloged" sales, while others' offerings are sold without the production of an accompanying catalog. In later chapters, we'll talk a great deal about auction catalogs, because these represent one of the most important and reliable of the art market research information sources. Further, in recent years the Internet-based auction has garnered considerable attention in the news, and for a short while some speculated on the demise of the "brick and mortar" auction house. But just as the electronic book doesn't seem to have supplanted the paper volume, so do physical auction houses continue to thrive.

Online auctions, including those on the now famous Internet site eBay, have had a great effect on the markets for certain classes of object. On any given day, collectors can find examples of many thousands of works that would heretofore require a great deal of hunting in shops, showrooms, auction houses and flea markets. Porcelain, ceramics, glass, furniture and every imaginable collectible object can be found on eBay. When such a spectacular volume of items appears at once on an easy-to-navigate site, the element of competition can have a tremendous effect on prices. The volume of Internet commerce, and the resultant competition among sellers, has had a great effect on everything from decorative arts to out-of-print (rare and common) book prices.[8]

This book's Appendix B includes a list of some major auction houses, with their web addresses. Today, even many smaller houses have an Internet presence, if only to advertise their services and to notify potential buyers of forthcoming auctions. The houses included in Appendix B have the added value of providing substantial market information on their sites.

Major auction houses provide estimates to potential sellers upon request. Both Christie's and Sotheby's, for example, offer a number of ways that potential buyers may investigate the probable value of works they hope to sell. It is interesting to note that the online forms provided ask a number of questions that are addressed throughout this book — questions relating to provenance, publication record, exhibition history and the like. Of course, both houses note that they only provide estimates on works of art that they typically handle.

In order to utilize auction sales data effectively, users of many of the valuation sources described throughout this book will require some knowledge of the jargon associated with the auction market. Consider the typical entry in an auction sales catalog. In the vast majority of cases, the catalog will include high and low estimates. These are established by auction house professional staff. In addition to the published estimates, there is an agreed upon "reserve" price which, if not met or exceeded during the bidding period, will result in the subject work being "bought-in." The reserve price is not published or otherwise shared with bidders. The price at which the subject work sells is referred to as the "price realized." The price recorded in the valuation sources may or may not include a "buyer's premium," a percentage established by the auction house. In some cases, the buyer's premium can be as high as 15 percent, and users of auction pricing sources are urged to consult the introductory material to the source at hand to learn if the premium is or is not included in the prices recorded.

Commercial Galleries

Unlike the prices attained by works of art offered for sale at public auction, those paid in the retail gallery world are very difficult, and often impossible to obtain or to verify. Although the list price is almost always available to even the casual gallery visitor, a good deal of bargaining goes on in the art world. Most valuation sources—whether print or electronic—report auction sales, and the very few that offer retail values should be used with caution. We'll discuss this at much greater length in later chapters.

Before going on to survey some of the many sources available to the art and art market researcher, we'll review, in the next chapter, some techniques for conducting research in the library and online.

For Further Reading

The titles listed below offer more information on the history of art collecting. To find additional books of this type, in libraries that utilize the Library of Congress Classification System, conduct a subject search using headings like "Art—Collectors and Collecting"; "Art—Collectors and Collecting—History"; or "Art—Collectors and Collecting—United States."

Alsop, Joseph. *The Rare Art Traditions: The History of Art Collecting and Its Linked Phenomena Wherever These Have Appeared.* New York: Harper & Row, 1982. 691p. (Series: *Bollingen Series*, 35; *A.W. Mellon Lectures in the Fine Arts*, 27.)

This extremely well-researched work provides an in-depth survey of art collecting from its beginning through the 17th century. Most such surveys focus on collecting in the West, but Asian and Middle Eastern areas are included here. This work's extensive bibliography serves as an excellent tool for further historical research on the history of collecting. Prices for many works are included throughout, making it also a good source for the researcher of market history.

The Collector in America. Compiled by Jean Lipman and the editors of *Art in America.* New York: Viking, 1971. 270p.

Well-illustrated survey of major American collectors, including: Nelson A. Rockefeller; Wright S. Ludington; Edgar William and Bernice Chrysler Garbisch; John Hay Whitney; Joseph H. Hirshhorn; William Copley; Mary and Leigh Block; A. James Speyer; Paul and Ruth Tishman; Philip Johnson; Roy Neuberger; Mrs. Albert D. Lasker; James Thrall Soby; Lydia Winston Malbin; Larry Aldrich; Alfonso Ossorio; Paul Bernat; Mr. & Mrs. Jack W. Glenn; Dr. and Mrs. Irving Levitt; Henry P. McIlhenny.

Constable, W.G. *Art Collecting in the United States of America: An Outline of a History.* London; New York: Nelson, [1964]. 210p.

Surveys the history of art collecting in the United States, with the goal of relating "political, economic, social and cultural influences and personal predilections" (pref.) to the development of various private collections.

Gere, Charlotte, and Marina Vaizey. *Great Women Collectors.* New York: Abrams, 1999. 208p.

Fascinating, well-researched and illustrated exploration of major collections of fine and decorative art assembled by women over the last three centuries. Representative collectors include: Catherine the Great; Madame de Pompadour; Madame du Barry; Empress Marie Feodorovna; Empress Josephine; Duchess of Portland; Lady Dorothy Nevill; Lady Charlotte Schreiber; Alice de Rothschild; Queen Mary; Princess Marie Louise; Queen Alexandra; Marjorie Merriweather Post; Isabella Steward Gardner; Louisine Elder Havemeyer; Mary Cassatt; Gertrude Stein; Helena Rubenstein; Coco Chanel; Mrs. Abby Aldrich Rockefeller; Gertrude Vanderbilt Whitney; Dominique de Menil; Peggy Guggenheim.

Herbert, John. *Inside Christie's.* New York: St. Martin's Press, 407p.

John Herbert, public relations director for Christie's from the late 1950s through the mid–1980s, offers a fascinating account of the development of the auction house on the international scene during his tenure.

Herrmann, Frank. *Sotheby's: Portrait of an Auction House.* New York and London: W.W. Norton, 1981.

Scholarly, but very readable history of storied auction house from its earliest days through the 20th century. Well-indexed, the many sales detailed include a good deal of market data, making it a valuable source for the historian of the art market in England and the United States.

Holst, Niels von. *Creators, Collectors and Connoisseurs: The Anatomy of Artistic Taste from Antiquity to the Present Day* [translation of *Künstler, Sammler, Publikum*]. New York: Putnam, [1967].

Encyclopedic survey of the history of collecting, museums, and the concept of connoisseurship and taste from antiquity through the early 20th century.

Norton, Thomas E. *100 Years of Collecting in America: The Story of Sotheby Parke Bernet.* New York: Abrams, 1984. 240p.

Traces the emergence of Sotheby Parke Bernet as one of the most important auction houses in the world. Each year, commencing with 1884, is briefly described and illustrated with notable works of fine and decorative art acquired from the American Art Association, Parke Bernet or Sotheby Parke Bernet. Review ends in 1983.

Rheims, Maurice. *The Strange Life of Objects: 35 Centuries of Art Collecting & Collectors* [translation of *La Vie Étrange des Objets*]. New York: Athenaeum, 1961. 274p.

Very readable overview of the evolution of art collecting over the centuries. Presents the authors musings on collectors' psychology, the development of collections throughout history, the impact of "fashion" on art and vice-versa, and the myriad forces that have affected the value of art — positively and negatively — over the years.

Robson, A. Deirdre. *Prestige, Profit and Pleasure: The Market for Modern Art in New York in the 1940s and 1950s.* New York: Garland, 1995. 375p.

Traces the development of the art world in New York City, including the museums, commercial galleries, and auction houses that fueled the growing market for contemporary art. Very scholarly and well-researched.

Saarinen, Aline B. *The Proud Possessors: The Lives, Times, and Tastes of Some Adventurous American Art Collectors.* New York: Random House, [1958]. 423p.

Profiles the lives of major collectors from the 19th through mid–20th centuries.

Watson, Peter. *From Manet to Manhattan: The Rise of the Modern Art Market.* New York: Random House, 1992. 558p.

Very lively, readable survey of the development of the art market in Europe and the United States; includes a very extensive bibliography. Of particular interest to the art market history researcher: Outroping, sales by candle and Mr. Colnaghi's Levee: the early years of the art market; appendixes: world record prices paid for works of art (with their present-day equivalents); real value of paintings in history: an index to convert prices in the past to present-day values.

TWO

Researching Fine and Decorative Arts: The Library, the Internet, or the Expert?

Confronted with a research question — whether simple or complex — most people today probably turn immediately to the Internet, and hope to find an answer quickly and easily by using their favorite search engine. Sometimes this strategy works, especially for basic, factual questions. But for most art and design research projects of any complexity, the "free" Internet does not currently suffice — nor will it, most likely, in the foreseeable future.

There is, however, an ever-increasing volume of good quality, freely available art and design information on the Internet. In fact, the Internet is indispensable for a great many tasks—finding an artist's current dealer(s), locating basic biographical information on a designer, and the like. But a tremendous amount of popular and scholarly art information continues to appear exclusively in print, and the vast majority of the books, journals, exhibition and other catalogs are simply not available in digital format, nor will they be — at least for a very, very long time. Further, most of the very best Internet-based resources are not available to the public, but are rather subscription-based, and some of those subscriptions can be prohibitively expensive for the individual researcher.

So, where should we begin? For most projects, only the traditional, "brick-and-mortar" library, along with the vast array of Internet-based tools, will provide the breadth and depth of information required to properly research works of art, both fine and decorative.

In this chapter, we'll explore basic library research techniques and survey some of the most important art and design research tools—both print-based and electronic. The information sources included here are general in nature; that is, they may be used to research both fine and decorative arts objects. Note that while the bulk of this chapter deals with sources that provide information on specific works of fine or decorative art, knowledgeable collectors, dealers and other art market researchers often require data and analysis of "big picture" art market issues. With this in mind, we include a discussion of methods and sources of market research, and explore the often-overlooked economics, business and current affairs databases that can be extremely valuable to the art market researcher.

Although a great deal of information about artists and artworks can be found in books, journals, reference works and on the Internet, sometimes *people*—dealers, collectors, curators, scholars and other art world professionals—can be invaluable in the research process. In fact, depending upon the goal of the research project, identifying and consulting the appropriate expert(s) might be absolutely necessary. Faced with doubts about a work's authenticity, for example, the collector/researcher will certainly want to go beyond traditional bibliographic research, and have the work analyzed by one or more experts on the work of the subject artist. With this in mind, the role of the expert on specific artists, styles, or periods, is explored in detail.

Preparing a Research Strategy

In order to research a work of art effectively and efficiently, it is best to begin with a plan of attack and to consider, in broad terms, *what* we're trying to find out, *where* we'll look to find it, and *how* the research will be conducted.

WHAT?

Find out as much as possible about the piece by thoroughly examining it, or its surrogate (reproduction). Tips on proper examination procedures are offered in the next section.

WHERE?

As noted above, the Internet will be of limited value for most art research projects. You'll need access to a library—preferably a large academic or public research library with a strong, historical collection of books, journals and other print materials.

How?

Before delving into books, journals, and Internet sites, think about all of the potential sources of information at your disposal. If you know that your subject artist is a young contemporary painter with few exhibitions to her credit, common sense tells you that you won't find major books on her work. At best, you might find some exhibition reviews in magazines and newspapers, some information on the Internet, etc. At the other end of the spectrum is the artist whose career is well established, and for whom there is, consequently, a vast amount of information in the form of books, exhibition catalogs, magazine and newspaper articles. Pinpointing the few items that relate to the subject artwork can be daunting, but also rewarding, if approached systematically.

Examination and Documentation of the Work

Physical Examination of the Work

Whatever course the research project will take, in the vast majority of cases it will begin with the work itself. If the work of art subject to research is available for inspection, it should be carefully examined on all sides. In the case of a two-dimensional artwork, back, front, and edges of the *unframed* (if possible) piece should be closely inspected for clues to the work's identity, including creator and date (in the form of a mark or signature) and possibly its place of origin. Once unframed, the piece might also provide indications of its appearances in exhibitions or prior ownership in individual or institutional collections. (The process of researching the ownership, or provenance, of a work is explored in much greater detail in chapter five.)

Because a good deal of research on works of art can only be conducted in libraries, it is important to carefully document the work to be studied, and create one or, preferably, a number of reproductions for use in the library. Document anything found in the examination process, including:

- Dimensions (in inches and centimeters. Many indispensable sources record metric values)
- Artist (if signed)
- Date
- Marks on support (e.g., stretcher manufacturer)
- Indications of exhibition
- Indications of ownership, or provenance

Finally, the work should be photographed. If the work is eventually to be offered for sale, this will be required in the vast majority of cases, and so, depending upon the price range of the work, professional photographs might be a worthwhile investment.

In addition to at least one good image of the complete work, several detail shots (e.g., the signature, if present) should be taken. Photograph the back of the work as well (including its support, i.e., canvas stretchers) if it bears any labels, manufacturers' marks or other information. A number of sources noted in the next two chapters can be used to identify marks, which in turn might give clues to date and/or place of execution and other details pertinent to the piece.

Examination of Photographic Reproductions

Sometimes, the researcher does not have access to the actual artwork, but rather has only a bare-bones description and a photographic reproduction. Assemble whatever information is available and be sure to examine the photograph closely and bring it to the library for comparison to other images found during the research process.

A clear traditional photograph (as opposed to a reproduction in a book or a magazine) can be examined very closely, using closed circuit television enlargement systems, or CCTV. These devices, used by people with disabilities to enlarge printed texts, are widely available. Medium-sized and large public libraries, and a great many academic libraries provide access to CCTV systems for their patrons with visual impairments. The basic CCTV allows the user to place an image (photograph, book, or even a small three-dimensional object) on a platform, and a closed-circuit video camera enlarges the item on a traditional television screen. Often, a signature or other mark indiscernible to the naked eye will be visible if enlarged on a CCTV (see illustration). Note, however, that most *published* images do not project as clearly as traditional, emulsion-based photographs do; the benday dots used in print production are often magnified to the point that they obliterate any meaningful imagery. Of course, not everyone will have access to a CCTV, in which case a traditional magnifying glass will have to suffice.

Library Research

Now that we've examined and documented the subject work, it's off to the library! In this section, we'll review the basics of library research.

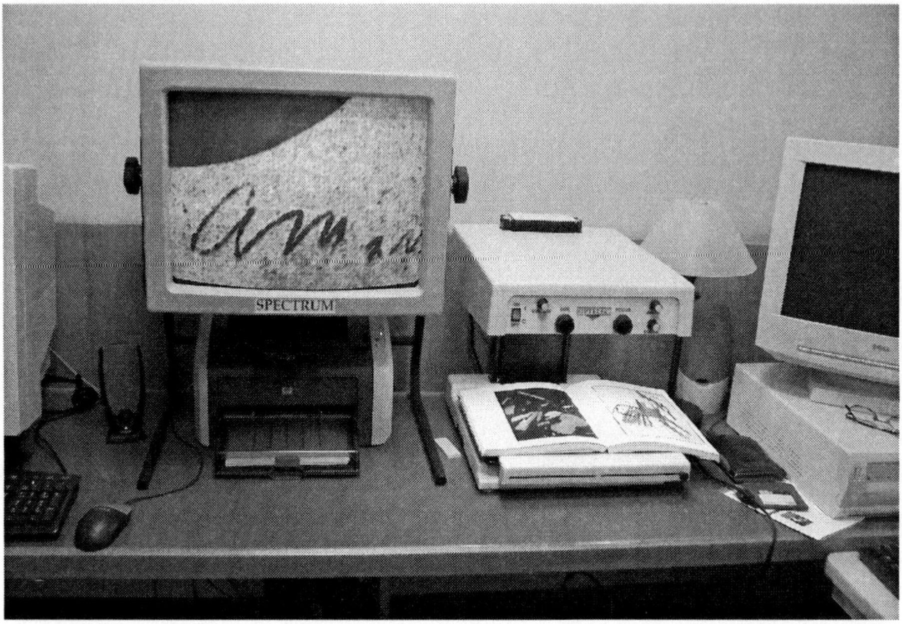

Closed Circuit Video Enlargement (CCTV) system magnifies photographs, printed materials and small three-dimensional objects many times their original size. Note the size and clarity of the signature here (courtesy Ron Milland).

The true novice researcher, as well as those who have not used a research library in some time, will benefit from reviewing the basics of library research. From proper subject searching of books to the selection and use of periodical indexes and databases, this chapter offers practical tips on using the numerous resources available in the contemporary library.

Finding an Appropriate Library

As noted above, few research projects involving art objects can be completed successfully with free-of-charge Internet resources. Many projects require the use of books, journals, magazines and other traditional media that were published long before the advent of Internet-based information delivery. For example, the researcher attempting to identify prior ownership (provenance) of a particular artwork will need to consult all of the catalogues raisonnés, exhibition catalogues, monographs and other books (many dating from the 18th or 19th century) that feature the subject piece. The vast majority of these sources are not digitized.

While art and art history are somewhat "behind the curve" as compared with other disciplines vis-à-vis electronic information, an increasing number of traditional tools— including indexes, journals and electronic books— are beginning to appear on the web. Most of these, however, require subscriptions with their issuing agencies or institutions. Individual user subscriptions are often available, but they can be prohibitively expensive; luckily, many libraries provide access to one or more of the best fee-based resources for art and design research. The three types of libraries that provide the best collections of materials for researching works of art — the public library, the museum-affiliated library, and the academic, or university library — are described below, along with a discussion of some of the access issues involved in each.

The Public Library

Depending upon the size of the municipality it serves, and also upon the complexity of the research endeavor, the public library might suffice for researching many artworks. Larger cities in particular often provide access to a rich array of the kinds of historical materials necessary to research a painting, drawing, or work of decorative art. Most public libraries— even those serving small communities— provide access to interlibrary loan systems, through which (sometimes for a fee) their patrons can borrow books or receive photocopies of journal articles from other libraries. Because it offers (at the very least) free-of-charge access to the materials in its own collection, the public library is the likely first candidate for the beginning researcher.

The Museum Library

Many museums maintain libraries to support the research needs of their curatorial staff members; some of these libraries are available for use by members of the public, either free of charge or as part of a museum membership package. Smaller museum library collections are usually highly focused, but often treat their narrowly defined subject(s) in considerable depth. Large museum libraries, usually concentrated in or near larger cities, often maintain very extensive collections of materials to serve the curators whose interests include various media, periods, styles and geographic foci.

Depending largely upon the source of their operating budgets, some museums offer public access to their often quite strong collections. Sometimes an appointment is required, certain days are set aside for public access, or other access restrictions are in place. In other cases, access to the library is a privilege extended to those who become "members" of the museum. For the researcher lacking access to a large public library, or an affiliation with a university library, participation in a museum membership program might provide relatively inexpensive access to a good art history collection.

The Academic (College, University) Library

There was a time—not so long ago—that just about anyone could enter and use (but not borrow, usually) the collections held in most academic libraries. Depending upon the location of the library (large urban libraries are most restrictive), free access is still sometimes possible. Some libraries require a simple sign-in, or perhaps the presentation of some form of ID. Others are restricted to faculty, students and staff of the library's parent institution.

Like museum libraries, some otherwise restricted, but very strong academic libraries are available to members of the public for a fee. Sometimes referred to as "Friends of the Library" programs, memberships are often available in various categories, allowing the participant on-site access for a modest fee or access with full borrowing privileges (usually much more expensive than on-site access) along with other benefits like invitations to readings, author receptions and exhibition openings. For the infrequent user, some universities even make provisions for short-term (daily, weekly) use of their collections and some facilities.

The benefits of the large academic library are numerous. Throughout this book, we'll be discussing some rather expensive, often impossible to find out-of-print materials. Large universities with good art history programs represent the best sources for these types of materials. Some research projects will also require some prohibitively expensive electronic tools that are usually only available in business libraries. The art market tools that can be found in the academic library—including the business and legal databases discussed later in this chapter—will not be found in even the strongest of museum library collections. The serious art market researcher lacking access to a very large public library should investigate the collections and access policies of the nearest large academic library.

Finding a Library

Several directories can be used to locate the public, college or research, museum and other libraries that are within your area. The best sources are:

International Directory of Art Libraries. International Federation of Library Association and Institutions (IFLA). Section of Art Libraries. http://artlibrary.vassar.edu/ifla-idal

The IFLA *International Directory of Art Libraries* provides information on almost 3,000 libraries with specialized holdings in art, architecture and archaeology. International in scope, the directory's entries for each institution include addresses, phone and fax numbers, hours, annual closings and listing of professional personnel. Also included are some email addresses of individual libraries along with direct links to institutional home pages.

Many readers will lack easy access to a major art library. To locate public, academic/research and other libraries, consult the following directory, which is available in print in many libraries large and small:

American Library Directory. New York: R.R. Bowker. Annual; 1923– .
The definitive directory of U.S. libraries. Arranged geographically by state, subdivided by city or town. Entries include full contact information, general and special collection details.

Using the Library

This section is intended for the researcher who might be unfamiliar with libraries and the research process, and for those readers whose major experience in libraries predates the modern age of computerized catalogs, electronic journals, databases, and the like. The latter group will soon find that much of their experience in the print-based library world of the past has been replaced by electronic alternatives. With a little practice, though, even the least experienced researcher can get "up to speed" with electronic resources, from library catalogs to specialized databases. To this end, we'll begin with an introduction to the two library classification systems used by most of the nation's libraries—Dewey and the Library of Congress—and review some tips for effective catalog searching.

Finding Books: Classification Systems

Almost all libraries, whether large or small, wisely arrange their books, journals and other materials, wherever possible, by subject. This system is particularly useful in "open stack" libraries (those in which users can retrieve their own materials), because it allows the researcher to browse shelves effectively; once they've located one title of interest, chances are there will be others nearby. This works to a point, but the complexity of the print world makes it necessary, often, for the serious researcher to dig a little further.

Why can't research be made simpler? Why can't *all* of the books that deal, for example, with 18th century English furniture sit together, in a single place? In the first place, all of the titles that deal *exclusively* with such a narrow topic do, or at least should, receive the same classification number, whether Dewey or Library of Congress (more about these later). But what about titles that survey English furniture of all periods? Or histories of European furniture, with significant sections on English furniture? The physical reality of the book dictates that it can occupy only one physical space. That's where the subject catalog comes in; while the book can be in only one physical location, any number of subjects can be assigned to a single work. In a nutshell, this is why a good understanding of library arrangement is essential — and ultimately, time-saving — for any researcher.

The Library of Congress Classification System — Many large libraries utilize an alpha-numeric system of materials classification developed by the Library of Congress (LC). In broadest terms, LC divides the entire universe of knowledge into the following categories:

A	General Works (e.g., encyclopedias)	
B–BJ	Philosophy, Psychology	
BL–BX	Religion	
C	Auxiliary Sciences of History	
D	History: General and Old World (Eastern Hemisphere)	
E-F	History: America (Western Hemisphere)	
G	Geography	
H	Social Sciences	
J	Political Science	
K	Law	
L	Education	
M	Music	
N	**Fine Arts**	
	Subclass N	Visual Arts
	Subclass NA	Architecture
	Subclass NB	Sculpture
	Subclass NC	Drawing, Design, Illustration
	Subclass ND	Painting
	Subclass NE	Prints and Printmaking
	Subclass NK	Decorative Arts
	Subclass NX	Arts in General (e.g., titles that treat visual arts in connection with other artforms, e.g., theatre, literature, music)
P	Linguistics, Language and Literature	
Q	Science	
R	Medicine	
S	Agriculture	
T	Technology	
U	Military Science	
V	Naval Science	
Z	Bibliography, Library Science	

(*Source:* Library of Congress Cataloging Policy & Support Office)

Dewey Decimal System Classification — The Dewey Decimal System is even more well-known than the Library of Congress scheme. Most of us had some experience with this one in our school libraries, and many libraries of all sizes—but especially smaller, public libraries—continue to utilize Dewey today. Unlike the Library of Congress system, Dewey's scheme is purely numerical.

000..........	Generalities, e.g., encyclopedias, bibliography etc.	
100..........	Philosophy and Psychology	
200..........	Religion	
300..........	Social Science	
400..........	Language	
500..........	Natural Science and Mathematics	
600..........	Technology (Applied Science)	
700	**The Arts**	
	710	Civic & landscape art
	720	Architecture
	730	Sculpture
	740	Drawings & decorative arts
	750	Paintings & painters
	760	Graphic arts (Printmaking & prints)
	770	Photography
	780	Music
	790	Recreational & performing arts
800..........	Literature & Rhetoric	
900..........	Geography & History	

Because we're focusing here, and throughout this book, on the fine and decorative arts, it is safe to assume that the great majority of books and journals of interest will be found among those assigned the classification "N" in libraries that use the Library of Congress System, and in the 700s for their Dewey-based counterparts.

While it is true that most books devoted to painting, prints, furniture design and other media will indeed be found here, it is important to note that materials germane to the study of certain media and object classes will be found elsewhere in the library's collection. For example, photography was treated from the outset by the Library of Congress as a branch of technology, rather than art. Most titles, therefore, will receive the Classification "TR. " Similarly, the "crafts" have historically been separated from the fine arts, and hence a great many titles devoted to the decorative arts are also assigned classifications in the T's. Works of art produced in so-called primitive communities (e.g., tribal African arts) have only within recent decades been classified with other works dealing with art. Certain older materials of interest will be found in anthropology.

National Catalogs: RLIN and WorldCat

Over the last few decades, the automation of many tasks and services—from cataloging to book check-out to the latest trend in email and chat reference service—has transformed the way libraries function. Even before the world was connected via the Internet, many of our nation's larger libraries were closely connected via several networks—networks that are now available to "end-users" (i.e., library patrons) in many libraries large and small. The two major players in this arena—the Research Libraries Group (RLG) and Online Computer Library Center (OCLC)—serve as "super-catalogs" that can pinpoint the location of individual items (books, journals, magazines, and multimedia productions) in thousands of libraries around the world.

The Research Libraries Group (RLG) and The Research Libraries Information Network (RLIN)

The Research Libraries Group (RLG) was founded in 1974 by the New York Public Library and three universities—Columbia, Harvard and Yale. In its earliest years, this small consortium of very large libraries benefited from the kind of division of labor that is best fostered in a networked environment. Long before the advent of the Internet, libraries affiliated with RLG were connected via proprietary terminals that allowed member institutions to share acquisitions and cataloging data. As increasing numbers of large research libraries joined RLG, the shared catalog of holdings—the Research Libraries Information Network (RLIN)—came to represent an important resource not only for libraries, but also for their users who gained an unprecedented ability to find out who owns what. Many libraries in the RLG network came to share not only cataloging and other data, but also extended their collections to other members through a large interlibrary loan network.

RLIN has grown to over 135 million individual bibliographic records describing a total of over 45 million titles. RLIN includes records describing the collective holdings of more than 150 academic, museum and research libraries. Now available on the Internet and on-site at many libraries around the globe, RLIN's easy-to-use interface, Eureka, makes it easy to find who owns what among RLIN's many member institutions.

The Online Computer Library Center (OCLC) and WorldCat

The Online Computer Library Center, or OCLC, was founded in 1967 as the Ohio College Library Center; in its earliest days, OCLC was, as its name implies, a consortium of libraries in the state of Ohio—libraries that utilized the then-fledgling technology of computer networking to develop a system for sharing resources, cataloging data and other library functions. By 1981, OCLC changed its name to reflect its ubiquitous presence in libraries far afield from its native Ohio; today, "OCLC serves more than 50,540 libraries of all types in the U.S. and 84 countries and territories around the world."[1]

OCLC's shared union catalog, *WorldCat*, affords the researcher access to the collective holdings of more than 9,000 member institutions. At the end of 2004, the number of individual items included in *WorldCat* exceeded 57 million, making it a major resource for research.

Today, many of the largest libraries offer access to both RLIN and OCLC *WorldCat*, and between the two, just about everything ever published anywhere in the world can be located with relative ease. Find out if your library provides access to one or both of these major national catalogs. They can make the task of locating even the most obscure books, journals and other library materials an easy one.

Indexes and Databases

In this section, the reader is presented with a description of several databases that can be used to research artists, designers, and individual works of fine or decorative art. Before going into specific products, we'll begin with a very brief overview of database searching techniques and terminology intended for the novice searcher.

Most of the databases that we'll discuss in this and later chapters have their roots in the old-fashioned world of print. That makes things easier for researchers whose main experience with libraries is similarly print-based (i.e., those whose experience predates the 1980s). With just a bit of experimenting, they find that they can move from print to electronic resources and gain an appreciation of the power of online database searching. In this section, we'll go step-by-step through the process of formulating and refining a database search statement and identify some of the basic terminology of database searching.

Basic Terminology

Most databases allow the user to search in two or more ways. Usually, the default method is the basic "keyword" search. Anyone who has used an Internet search engine, like Google, is familiar with this process. Presented with a simple box, the user enters words and retrieves citations, or actual full-text articles, that contain those terms. Very often, beginners in particular wonder what went wrong, as they sift through the tens, hundreds or even thousands of items that aren't at all relevant to what they're hoping to find. Why does this happen?

When we perform a keyword search, we retrieve a list of everything and anything that contains the sought-after term anywhere in the record. A database record, like the following taken from *ArtBibliographies Modern* (described later in this chapter), includes individual pieces of information referred to as "fields."

TI:	Title The New York pre-school
AU:	Author Vetrocq, Marcia E.
SO:	Source Art in America (U.S.A.), vol. 85, no. 6, June 1997, pp. 82–7, 8 illus. (6 color) bibliog
AB:	Abstract Considers the status of Dada in New York, with reference to the exhibition Making Mischief: Dada Invades New York at the Whitney Museum of American Art in New York (21 Nov. 1996–23 Feb. 1997). The author traces the development of New York Dada from Duchamp's self-imposed exile in the city from June 1915 and his patronage by Walter Conrad and Louise Arensberg, assesses the importance of Duchamp's Fountain (1917), and cites the comments of the exhibition's curator Francis Naumann, who asserts that humour forms the basis of Dada in New York. She discusses the limitations of this assertion, compares the art of Duchamp and Man Ray, with reference to their appropriation of ready-mades, and examines the differences between the manifestation of Dada in Europe and in the U.S.A.
PY:	Publication Year 1997
PT:	Publication Type Journal article
SA:	Subject/Artist Dada; Duchamp, Marcel; Patronage of Art; Man Ray; ready-mades
AN:	Accession Number 29:01384

***ArtBibliographies Modern* record. Note that each information element, or "field" (author, title, etc.), is searchable in this database of 19th and 20th century art information (courtesy Cambridge Scientific Abstracts/CSA).**

Title, personal author, journal name, abstract, etc., are all **fields** which, taken together, comprise the complete database **record**. As databases grow in size, the concept of restricting search terms to certain fields becomes increasingly important.

Database records that include abstracts, or descriptions of their contents, are very valuable because they provide the searcher with enough information to decide whether to take the extra steps required to locate the actual article described in the record. A well-constructed abstract should include the terms that an experienced searcher has entered in a search statement. How does one instruct the database to retrieve only those articles or other bibliographic entities that include desired terms only in specific fields? Usually, the **advanced search** (or equivalent) option is the key.

Most web-based index databases make searching within specific fields relatively straightforward. Often called **advanced search**, **guided search**, or something similar, the "field-specific" search option allows the user to limit search terms to those fields most relevant. Searching for bibliographic items that contain a term in the title or abstract will obviously reduce the number of "hits," and consequently eliminate a great many items that are not at all relevant to the research problem at hand.

Another feature of almost all databases is the option of constructing a **Boolean** search; you might even have done this already without knowing it because web-based database forms often have the Boolean search option built into the form, as is the case with *ArtBibliographies Modern* and most other web-based systems.

"And," "Or," "Not": Constructing a Boolean Search Statement

A Boolean search statement instructs the database to retrieve records that

- contain a combination of terms— the "**and**" connector
- include one or more of a series of related or even synonymous terms— the "**or**" connector
- exclude records that contain certain terms— the "not" connector (use this one sparingly— more on this below).

Consider research question: "How can I find articles (in newspapers and/or magazines and journals) on the current market for 19th century French painting?"

Before even beginning to search online, parse the question into main concepts. We're really searching for articles that include "Market **and** 19th century **and** French **and** painting."

So, presumably, if we set up our search to retrieve any item that contains all of these terms in the abstract, some of them should relate directly to our research problem. But what might we miss if we limit our search to these specific terms? We might miss articles with titles like "Nineteenth Century French painting: What's Hot and What's Not in the Gallery Scene."

Here's where the "or" connector comes in. We've already decided on our main concepts. Now, expand those concepts by adding synonymous terms like the following:

Market	19th	French	painting
Auction	nineteenth	France	
Gallery			
Sales			
Prices			

The synonymous terms (market, auction, gallery, sales, prices, for example) are linked by "or" to create a logical statement of the following type:

Market **or** auction **or** gallery **or** sales **or** prices
and
19th **or** nineteenth
and
French **or** France
and
Painting

So, you might be thinking, what about that "not" connector? Experienced researchers use "not" sparingly with content words. Why? Imagine that we really don't want anything that deals with the market for 19th century English painting. If we added to our search statement **Not** England or English, we would miss some relevant, and potentially important items, such as: "Auction News: The Market for 19th Century French and **English** Painting on the Rise."

Judging only by its title, this article appears to be germane to our research project, but is excluded because of the presence of the word **English** that we excluded with our use of the Boolean "**not**."

Do we ever use "not," then? Of course, but usually in order to exclude certain kinds of materials rather than content terms. For example, some databases include records describing a great many types of articles, including book reviews. We might use the "not" connector to exclude a type of document, such as book reviews, that will not be useful for our particular needs.

Full Text Database Search Tips

The ability to construct a database search strategy that is adequately focused is increasingly essential, as the databases we use become increasingly large in terms of sheer volume of materials indexed. We have just seen that "field" searching, rather than simple keyword searching, can greatly reduce the number of irrelevant hits retrieved in a database. In the very large, full-text databases that include many thousands of full-text sources (described later in this chapter), the likelihood of almost any term appearing in an article that has nothing to do with the subject being researched can be very high. The ability to hone the research statement is critical in these mega-databases.

Novice full-text database users are advised to consider each step in the following checklist to ensure that their search statement retrieves the most relevant materials.

- Select "Advanced Search" option, if available. This option usually provides an easy-to-use form with which even the least experienced searcher can construct a complex search query.
- Use the full power of "Boolean searching." Boolean searches are those in which terms are connected, using "and," "or," "not."
- Use "word truncation" where appropriate. Truncating a search term instructs the database to retrieve anything that begins with a root term. While it varies from source to source, the truncation symbol is usually an asterisk or question mark. (Check the database's online "help" function for the relevant truncation symbol). Examples of truncated search terms include:

  Old Master? = Old Master, Old Masters
  Impressionis? = Impressionism, Impressionist, Impressionistic, etc.
- Investigate the database's options for limiting by type of material. Selecting "feature article," for example, can eliminate thousands of irrelevant hits—things like book reviews, exhibitions, even advertisements.
- Perform an initial search to find out if the database employs a standard vocabulary of subject terms (sometimes called descriptors). For example, the researcher investigating the life and work of sculptor David Smith in the database *ProQuest* Research Library faces the dilemma of sifting through the thousands of David Smiths retrieved in a simple search—and most of them are not the sculptor! Changing the search statement to "sculptor David Smith" yields a manageable number of items, and the first item tells us that works discussing the sculptor can be found by searching "Smith David sculptor."

Fine and Decorative Arts Databases

Earlier in this chapter, the reader was cautioned not to expect a great deal of art information in electronic formats, relative to the published literature of other disciplines. While it is true that the periodicals—journals, magazines and newsletters—required by the art researcher are very often only available in paper, the researcher is actually very well-served by excellent electronic indexes to this important body of literature.

The periodical literature of art and art history has been the subject of serious indexing since the earliest decades of the 20th century. Compared with those of many other disciplines, art history's journals were among the earliest to be systematically indexed, and the most important of these indexing sources are now available, by subscription, on the Internet. In this section, the primary indexes to the literature of art and design are described.

Researchers who lack ready access to a large library with a strong art collection might have access to much more art information than they realize, given the number of very extensive "all-purpose" databases that are often made available in many libraries large and small. Many of the periodicals subject to indexing by the major art databases are included among those appearing in some of these general databases—notably, *ProQuest*, *Factiva*, *EBSCO*, and *LexisNexis*. Later in this chapter, these subscription databases—along with a few that are freely available on the web—are described in detail.

The Art Index. New York: H.W. Wilson, 1932– . Electronic versions: *Art Index Retrospective* (1929–1984) and *Art Abstracts/Art Full Text* (1984–present).

One of the earliest indexes to the literature of art, architecture, design and related disciplines—the *Art Index*—continues to be published in print form, but is also made available electronically by subscription. The electronic version of the *Art Index* appears in two parts, *Art Index Retrospective* and *Art Abstracts / Art Full Text;* the former covers the years 1929 through 1984, while the latter commences in 1984 and continues to the current year.

Both components index English-language periodicals, yearbooks and museum bulletins, as well as selected non–English language journals. One of this source's unique features is its indexing of reproductions. Even reproductions appearing in advertisements (e.g., gallery exhibition announcements) can be found in *Art Index*. The reproduction indexing feature is a great boon to the art researcher in need of information on exhibitions. In some instances—particularly when the subject of research is a relatively unknown artist—citation to a reproduction can provide great leads for further investigation. For example, an advertisement for an artist's exhibitions in the 1930s might identify his or her primary dealer; with this information, the researcher might track down the gallery's archival records, which in turn might provide references to provenance, bibliography and other pertinent information about a subject work.

The period 1984 to the present is covered by two versions of the same product, *Art Abstracts* and *Art Full Text*; the former includes only abstracts (quite in-depth descriptions of 50 to 300 words), while the latter includes the complete text of articles from as early as 1997. Contrary to its title, *Art Index Full Text* provides only a selection of full text journal titles. For most projects, *Art Index Retrospective* and *Art Abstracts/Art Full Text* represent excellent starting points for periodical literature on artists and works of art.

Note that *Art Index Retrospective* and *Art Abstracts/Art FullText* are most useful for researching artists who have had at least a modicum of critical attention. Information on obscure or emerging artists will more likely be found in the larger news databases described in the next section.

ARTBibliographies Modern. Cambridge Scientific Abstracts.

ARTbibliographies Modern (ABM) is an online database that provides extensive coverage of modern and contemporary art, design, and related fields. *ABM* is uniquely strong in its indexing of numerous publication formats, including journals, books, essays, exhibition catalogs, doctoral dissertations and exhibition reviews. Entries include complete bibliographic records, along with extensive abstracts. Coverage begins in 1974, but some entries date as early as the late 1960s. The indexing is relatively current, with updates added six times each year.

ARTbibliographies Modern is an excellent starting point for researching the fine or decorative arts. Its online thesaurus and browsable indexes are useful for researchers at all levels, from novice to expert. *ABM*'s lengthy, high quality abstracts (a sample record appears earlier in this chapter) provide enough information to assist the user in deciding whether or not to pursue tracking down the indexed article, catalog or other publication. While there is some duplication of coverage with *Art Index* and its electronic versions described above, a significant amount of unique material is included in *ABM*; the researcher of fine or decorative arts from the 19th century to the present is advised, therefore, to use both of these excellent resources if they are available.

Arts & Humanities Citation Index. Thompson ISI (The Thomson Corp.).

Arts & Humanities Citation Index (AHCI) is a powerful research tool that provides access to journal references (1975–present) in nearly 1,130 major arts and humanities titles. *AHCI*'s indexing provides access not only to journal articles, but to the works cited by the authors of indexed articles—making it a uniquely powerful tool for historical research.

Arts & Humanities Citation Index offers three search methods:

- General Search allows the user to search by topic, author, or group author. The General Search by Topic retrieves items that include the search terms in articles' titles, keywords or abstracts.
- Cited Author Search allows the searcher to retrieve references that cite the sought-after author.
- Advanced Search offers the ability to perform complex "field" searches using the full range of Boolean search capability. Searchable fields include Topic, Title, Author, Group Author, Source, and more.

Bibliographic Index. New York: H.W. Wilson, 1937–present.

Many very useful bibliographies appear in books, journals and other formats. Since its inception in 1937, H.W. Wilson's *Bibliographic Index* has been a standard reference tool for locating some of these very highly specialized reference tools. Each year, the editors of *Bibliographic Index* survey over 2,800 periodicals and 5,000 books for specialized bibliographies to include in the annual index. The database includes over 271,000 individual bibliographies as of 2004.

Published quarterly with annual cumulations, the *Bibliographic Index* is also available on the Web at many libraries.

Bibliography of the History of Art. Vandoeuvre-lès-Nancy, France: Centre National de la Recherche Scientifique, Institut de l'Information Scientifique et Technique; Santa Monica, Calif.: J. Paul Getty Trust, Getty Art History Information Program, 1991– .

The *Bibliography of the History of Art* (*BHA*) provides indexing and abstracts of articles in more than 4,300 journals and magazines, as well as art books, conference proceedings, doctoral dissertations, and exhibition catalogs. Its subject coverage includes art of Europe and the Americas (4th century to modern); painting, sculpture, drawings, and prints; decorative and applied arts; architecture and industrial design; and popular and folk art. Updated quarterly, *BHA* includes records from the two databases that preceded it: *Repertoire d'Art et d'Archeologie* (1973 through 1989) and the *Repertoire Internationale de la Literature de l'Art* (1975 through 1989). *BHA*'s focus is on American and European art and architecture, dating from late antiquity to the present. The Getty Research Institute and the Institut de l'Information Scientifique et Technique du Centre National de la Recherche Scientifique currently contribute records. *BHA*, one of the databases made available by the Research Libraries Group (RLG), can be found in most libraries with strong art, design and art history collections.

Bibliography of the History of Art provides extensive coverage of non–English language publications and because it includes references to chapters in books, should be considered an indispensable tool for the serious art researcher. Because it focuses on lengthier, substantive articles, however, many smaller news items, so often of interest to the art market researcher, are *not* included. *BHA*'s limited coverage, as compared to *Art Full Text* (see above), is evidenced by the fact that it includes citations to only 168 articles from the 1999 issues of the journal *ArtForum*, while Art Full Text offers 657 *ArtForum* references for the same year.

Searches in *BHA* may be limited by language, country of publication, date, and article type. Subjects, authors, and other fields are hyperlinked, affording the user the ability to select items related by simply clicking on the desired link.

FRANCIS. Vandoeuvre, France: Institut de l'Information Scientifique et Technique (INIST), 1984–present.

FRANCIS is a very large, multidisciplinary database comprising over 1.5 million records as of late 2004. The *Bibliography of the History of Art*, described earlier, is a *FRANCIS* component; so, in those libraries lacking *BHA* as a separate system, *FRANCIS* serves as a substitute. *FRANCIS* indexes not only journal articles but also conference papers, books, reports and doctoral dissertations. Subjects covered are art, archaeology, architecture, and general humanities and social sciences, with some management materials. The vast array of European language sources indexed by *FRANCIS* make it a most valuable resource for the advanced researcher of fine or decorative arts objects.

Humanities Index. New York: H.W. Wilson, 1974/75– .

The *Humanities Index*, a product of the H.W. Wilson Company (providers of *Art Full Text* and *Art Index Retrospective*, described earlier), offers easy access to approximately 550 English-language periodicals covering all of the humanities. It is updated monthly. The interdisciplinary nature of some kinds of research makes general citation indexes of this type indispensable for certain projects. For example, the researcher seeking information on a particular type of furniture might find valuable leads in history journals, in addition to the more obvious titles in the fine arts. Many college and public libraries provide access to the *Humanities Index* online and, like other Wilson products, the index continues to be published in print form as well.

JSTOR. New York: JSTOR, 1995– .

JSTOR, a large and growing collection of electronic journals in the humanities, social sciences and sciences, is available in many libraries across the nation. Many larger academic and research libraries provide access to the complete collection, while some others opt for a particular component. *JSTOR*'s business model is an interesting one that appears to be working for libraries as well as for the journals' publishers. With the advent of Internet-based information delivery, journal publishers feared the loss of revenue that might result from the ubiquitous presence of their titles online. These fears are allayed by *JSTOR* policy of providing access only to backfiles—that is, articles that are not current. When *JSTOR* negotiates with a publisher, in most cases a "moving wall" of coverage is established. If the agreed upon moving wall is four years, *JSTOR* provides access to the title, but it is four years behind current. This ensures that subscribers will continue to maintain subscriptions, thereby protecting the interests of journal publishers.

Some core titles of interest to art researchers have been added to *JSTOR*, and these offer an unprecedented opportunity for the serious scholar. The fine art titles currently available through *JSTOR* include: *American Art*, 1991–2003 (*Smithsonian Studies in American Art*, 1987–1990); *Art Bulletin*, 1919–2000 (*Bulletin of the College Art Association of America*, 1917–1918) (*Bulletin of the College Art Association*, 1913); *Art Journal*, 1960–2000; *College Art Journal*, 1941–1960; *Parnassus*, 1929–1941; *Burlington Magazine*, 1948-1999 (*Burlington Magazine for Connoisseurs*, 1903–1947); *Gesta*, 1963–1999; *Journal of the Society of Architectural Historians*, 1945–2001 (*Journal of the American Society of Architectural Historians*, 1941–1944); *Journal of the Warburg and Courtauld Institutes*, 1939-1999 (*Journal of the Warburg Institute*, 1937–1939); *October*, 1976–1999; *Winterthur Portfolio*, 1964–2001.

With *JSTOR*, researchers can perform complex searches of all of the art titles simultaneously, or limit their searches to one or more specific titles. Searching for an artist's name, subject matter, style, period, or any combination of these will retrieve scholarly articles of interest to researchers of fine and decorative art works from some of the most important titles in the field.

Periodicals Contents Index (*PCI*). Alexandria, Va.: Chadwyck-Healey, 1996– .

Most of the earliest, print-based subject indexes to periodical literature cover only those titles published in the 20th century to the present. For some disciplines, the advent of subject indexing is even more recent. *Periodicals Con-*

tents Index (*PCI*) fills a great void in subject access to journals by providing access to the contents of 4,547 periodicals in the humanities and social sciences. *Periodical Contents Index*'s coverage of some important journal titles goes back more than 200 years. As this book goes to press, *PCI* includes indexing to over 14.5 million articles, dating from the 18th century to the present day. Each year this unique indexing resource adds records for 300 to 500 journals comprising over one million articles. Its producers plan to include more than 5,000 journals ultimately, with the total number of individual articles exceeding 20 million.

Business, Economics and General Databases

The art market is, of course, covered in the various databases that index journals, magazines and books related to the fine and decorative arts. Increasingly, however, valuable information geared toward collectors and other art market participants is found in the popular and professional literature of business and economics.

The following databases will be found in libraries that serve the business community. Some public libraries offer one or more of these sources, but the greatest concentration will likely be found in academic libraries with advanced programs in business administration.

ABI/Inform

Available through the aggregate database *ProQuest*, *ABI/Inform* provides access to a great deal of full-text information related to topics in business, management, investment/finance, etc. Intended for the business professional, *ABI/Inform*'s coverage is limited to newspapers, newsletters and professional journals.

One very useful feature of *ABI/Inform* and other databases offered by *ProQuest* is the ability to set up a "Search Alert." Once a search is conducted in one or more of the *ProQuest* databases, the researcher can quickly and easily set up an "Alert," which will instruct *ProQuest* to send, via email, new citations that match the search profile. The user may request emails to be sent daily, weekly, monthly, or every three months for a period of up to one year.

Three components (searchable simultaneously) comprise the *ABI/Inform* system. These include:

- *ABI/Inform Dateline.* Covers 1985–present. Provides access to "hard-to-find local and regional business news coverage of large corporations, privately held companies, local start-ups, executive profiles, marketing, finance, and industry news. Provides access to business information not typically found in national news sources. Contains news and analysis, information on local markets, and more gathered from major business tabloids, magazines, daily newspapers, wire services, and city, state, and regional business publications." (Source: *ProQuest* website)
- *ABI/Inform Global.* Comprehensive database to the professional literature of business, finance and economics. Includes journals, company

profiles, and the *Wall Street Journal*; covers 1971–present. Includes a great deal of full-text journal content. Nearly 1800 international business periodicals indexed, including a great many that provide information to collectors, dealers and other art market researchers.

- *ABI/Inform Trade & Industry*. *ABI/Inform's Trade & Industry* provides indexing to and a good deal of full-text content from more than 750 periodicals and newsletters with a trade or industry focus. Covers 1971–present.

Searching all three *ABI/Inform* components simultaneously allows the researcher to obtain a broad range of publication types. The material indexed includes a great many smaller, regional publications, making it a very worthwhile database for locating information on lesser known and emerging artists internationally.

Business Periodicals Index. New York: H.W. Wilson, 1959– . (Full-text electronic version: *Wilson Business Full Text*.)

The H.W. Wilson Company is one of the nation's oldest, most highly regarded producers of indexes. The *Business Periodicals Index,* available in print format since 1958, is a basic business reference source providing indexing to over 800 publications in the areas of business management, finance and administration. The index is available in its electronic format, by subscription, either with full text content. (*Wilson Business Full* Text) or without. The latter represents the electronic equivalent of the early print-based volumes, while the former provides links to full text content from over 400 publications dating from 1995 to the present.

Some public and many academic libraries whose institutions offer degrees in business administration provide access to Wilson's *Business Full Text* or *Business Periodicals Index.* Either is a good source for business press articles related to the market for fine or decorative arts, coverage of the auction markets, and other related subjects.

EconLit. Nashville: American Economic Association, 1969– . (Print version: *Journal of Economic Literature*.)

Econlit is the preeminent database of scholarly economics information. It provides citations, some with abstracts, to academic economics literature found in over 300 international journals, books, doctoral dissertation and some conference proceedings. It is here that the advanced researcher will find lengthy articles detailing the market for various types of art, including some major historical studies. Focus is on scholarly material rather than newsstand business press.

Factiva. New York: Dow Jones, 1998– .

Factiva is an online archive of digital news sources (including Dow Jones and Reuters newswires). Among the nearly 9,000 full text titles included, *Factiva* provides easy access to many smaller, regional titles not found in other electronic information sources, as well as a vast array of non–English language titles. With its extensive coverage of major international newspapers, specialized newsletters and other economic planning sources, *Factiva* represents a good source for up-to-the-minute information on the economics of buying and selling art.

International Bibliography of the Social Sciences. London: The London School of Economics and Political Science.

A product of the British Library of Political and Economic Science of the London School of Economics, *International Bibliography of the Social Sciences (IBSS)* is a unique online reference tool that provides in-depth coverage of the social sciences, including economics and finance. The database provides access to approximately two million bibliographic references dating from 1951. Its historical depth, coupled with its broad scope of coverage, make *IBSS* a very important tool for the study of economic issues. In addition to its indexing of over 2,700 journals, current updates include records for some 7,000 book titles annually.

General Periodical Literature Databases

Some readers undoubtedly lack access to a library that offers access to any of the fine arts databases described in the previous section. The advent of Internet-based information delivery, however, has given rise to quite a few general, "all-purpose" databases that index many of the most important journals included in the more specialized fine and decorative arts sources, along with a great many magazines, newspapers and newsletters not included in the more academically-oriented tools. These general interest sources, which include *Readers' Guide to Periodical Literature, Wilson OMNI Full Text, EBSCO, ProQuest, LexisNexis* and others, can be especially useful for finding information on obscure artists.

American Periodicals Series Online 1740–1940.

Some of our most valuable digital research tools derive from microfilm or microfiche forebears; *ProQuest*'s *American Periodicals Series* (*APS*), a reference staple in most large libraries, is one such resource. The microfilm collection's more than 1,100 periodical titles spanning nearly 200 years (commencing in the year 1740) is now available in page-image format, searchable by keyword, title, abstract, author and other fields and combinations. Periodicals indexed include a broad range of special interest as well as general magazines, literary and professional journals, and many other important periodical titles.

EBSCO MasterFILE. Ipswich, Mass.: EBSCO Publishing.

EBSCO MasterFILE includes the full text of more than 750 periodicals covering a wide range of issues. In addition to its full-text offerings, *MasterFILE* provides indexing and abstracting for an additional 2,250 titles. Some of the full-text titles date from the mid–1980s, but the majority commence in the mid–1990s.

Find Articles.com. http://www.findarticles.com.

For the researcher lacking ready access to a library with significant database offerings, *Find Articles,* available free of charge on the web, provides indexing and full text articles dating as early as 1998 from more than 900 magazines. Some articles require payment of a fee, but most are available at no cost. Some art-related titles available through *Find Articles* include *Art in America*, *Art-Forum* and *Art Business News*. Note that the contents are not page images, but rather provide access to textual content only.

LexisNexis Academic Universe. [Dayton, Ohio?]: *LexisNexis*.

LexisNexis is one of the nation's oldest providers of digital information resources. Today, many academic and public libraries offer the user-friendly *LexisNexis Academic Universe*, which provides access to approximately 5,000 publications in the areas of news, financial, and legal information. Particularly useful for the collector is the full-text collection of academic law reviews, which provide a tremendous amount of information on issues related to provenance, fraud, art theft and a host of other legal topics. Daily updates to *LexisNexis*' news services make it an invaluable resource for the serious collector, dealer, or other art market stakeholder.

ProQuest Databases.

Many *ProQuest* users mistakenly confuse the name of the vendor (*ProQuest*) with a specific product. *ProQuest* actually makes a number of databases available to institutions on a subscription basis; one library's *ProQuest* offerings, therefore, often will differ from those of another. The following represent a few of the more important general databases made available via *ProQuest*. (*ABI/Inform*, described in the preceding section, is another database made available via *ProQuest*.)

- *ProQuest Research Library*. *ProQuest Research Library* is widely available in college, university, larger public and some other types of libraries. A truly multi-disciplinary resource, it provides various levels of access to well over 1,600 periodical titles. Coverage dates from the early 1970s through the present.

  ProQuest Research Library is made up of two basic components: its "core list" of approximately 800 periodicals, and 15 "subject-specific" modules intended to supplement the core list. While some periodicals provide indexing/abstracting only, many (over 1,700 titles) are available in full text—either as page images ("PDF" format), or in HTML format with images inserted. For our purposes, of course, the inclusion of images is all-important because we are, in most cases, using the database to research visual materials.
- *ProQuest Historical Newspapers and Other Periodicals*. Today, the digitization of large collections of historical material represents one of the most exciting trends in research and scholarship. In recent years, *ProQuest* has introduced a number of retrospective sources that have made historical research infinitely easier than ever before. Until the advent of digitized newspapers, researchers were faced with the arduous task of scanning annual printed indexes or citation databases to identify the dates, pages, and columns of potentially useful articles; once the citations to articles were located, the researcher then had to find, load, and read the corresponding microfilm reels. This highly labor-intensive process has at last been supplanted by the full-text, searchable version of many of our nation's leading newspapers and magazines.

  For the art researcher, there is one unfortunate reality in this realm of digitization. Many of the images of artworks are not included, but are rather blocked for obvious copyright restrictions. In some instances, the researcher might gain enough information from a description of the work to be able to track down an image in another source, whether in print or online. In others (e.g., those artists whose works lack unique titles), verification of the item under discussion might require consulting the microfilm or, if recent enough, the print issue of the newspaper. This single caveat notwithstanding, digitized newspapers and magazines represent a great boon for the modern research of fine or decorative arts.

Full-text searching for an artist's name in the following newspapers is often of particular value for researching an artist who is not very well known. Consider, for example, an artist who had a modicum of success in the 1940s. A search of the artist's name will retrieve not only articles and exhibition reviews, but will also pinpoint advertisements for exhibitions. Identifying the subject artist's gallery representation at a specific point in time can be a good lead to further information; for example, the researcher might pursue the galleries' archival records to identify information relating to sales, provenance, additional exhibitions or other aspects of the subject artist's work and life.

Currently, the following digital newspapers are available via *ProQuest*: *New York Times*, 1851–2002; *Wall Street Journal*, 1889–1988; *Washington Post*, 1877–1989; *Christian Science Monitor*, 1908–1992; *Los Angeles Times*, 1881–1985; *Chicago Tribune*, 1849–present

Readers' Guide to Periodical Literature. New York: H.W. Wilson, 1900– .

The *Readers' Guide to Periodical Literature* is undoubtedly one of the world's best-known indexes to journals and magazines. Available in print since the turn of the last century, the *Readers' Guide* is an essential source for the researcher seeking information in general news magazines, along with a selection of more specialized titles, including some relating to art and design. Virtually every school and public library of any size provides access to the *Readers' Guide*, and a number of electronic offshoots are increasingly available in libraries large and small.

Internet Searching Basics

While the reader has been cautioned about relying upon free-of-charge Internet resources for many fine and decorative arts research projects, there are some extremely valuable resources to be found there. A good number of these are described throughout this book, intermingled with printed sources.

In some instances, a newfound knowledge of database searching might provide real surprises as a researcher surfs the net. Beyond the obvious—directories, gallery and auction announcements, artists' biographies and the like — often some very obscure but valuable information is simply there for the taking. Where to look and how to evaluate what one finds remain the real challenges, as the number of websites indexed grows exponentially.

The gateway to the vast array of Internet resources is the search engine. Recall from our discussion of database searching techniques that large databases are most effective when search terms are limited to specific fields. The Internet is certainly the largest database at our disposal, and so some fine-tuning of our searches can make the experience much more fruitful. How can we hone our Internet search strategies? Let's consider how Google — the most popular of the search engines— allows us to tailor our search statement, thereby limiting the number of irrelevant results.

Like many of the databases we've discussed, the default search option in Google is the basic keyword search — that single box into which the user enters keywords he or she hopes will retrieve links to relevant web pages. Unless the terms are unique, these kinds of searches often deliver far too many results. Why does this happen? For the simple reason that Google is now searching not millions, but billions of web pages, hundreds of millions of images, and more. The likelihood of any single term appearing in a page completely irrelevant to our search is very high.

Google Features

We saw earlier that limiting our search terms to specific fields (notably, the title and abstract of a database record) in most commercial databases helps to limit the number of irrelevant items retrieved. A basic Google search can be similarly tailored by selecting the "Advance Search" option. An exploration of this and some other very powerful features of Google follow.

Advanced Search

Google's advanced search feature allows the searcher to construct a complex statement, including full Boolean functionality (see discussion of Boolean searching earlier in this chapter). The search term form provides the following options:

Find results >> with **all** of the words (the Boolean "and" connector)
with the **exact phrase**
with **at least one** of the words (the Boolean "or" connector)
without the words (the Boolean "not" connector)

Consider the following research question: "How can I find websites with information on the authentication of paintings by Martin Johnson Heade?"

We might construct the search query as follows:

With **all** of the words:	Martin Johnson Heade
With **at least one** of the words:	authentication attribution

Field Searching

Recall from our discussion of database searching techniques that limiting the occurrence of search terms to specific fields can limit the number of irrelevant results. In Google Advance Search, this functionality is offered, in a limited way. Searchers may limit the occurrence of terms to the following:

Anywhere in the page
In the title of the page
In the text of the page
In the URL of the page
In links to the page

One would expect that limiting the occurrence of search terms to "In the title of the page" would be the most effective way of eliminating irrelevant search results. But the "title" of a web page is not a "title" in the most commonly understood sense of the word. Rather, the title is simply a tag that may or may not include all of the most descriptive search terms. The page's "header" represents what most people would refer to as the title. Web page developers are increasingly savvy in their use and placement of terminology, but some very good information can be overlooked when terms are limited to the title field.

Additional options available on the advanced search form include limiting by language, file format (e.g., Microsoft Powerpoint), and date.

Google Images

If the researcher is armed with the proper search terms—an artist's name, a chair's style or period—Google makes it easy to pinpoint images of works of art. Frequently, even emerging artists with few credits to their name have images of their works on the Internet. To find images, simply select the "Images" option above the basic keyword search box. As this book goes to press, Google boasts access to 880 million images—many of them works of art.

Google Groups

Email based discussion groups (Usenet) have been around since the late 1970s, and so represent a rich and diverse source of information for the advanced researcher. Google Groups contains the world's largest archive of

Usenet postings—dating all the way back to 1981. Searching this vast archive of email-based information allows the researcher to locate a great deal of information, but the novice researcher should be careful; the groups are, for the most part, completely open, and so the quality of information found will run the gamut from very sound to downright ridiculous. Judgment is certainly the most important tool required of the researcher using this portion of the Google menu.

Google Answers

Google Answers is an innovative, fee-based service that has received mixed reviews in the research community. Interested users may post a question, and set the price they're willing to pay for an answer. Answers are archived, and searchable, free of charge, by the public. The researchers who answer the questions are independent contractors who have been tested and screened by Google.

As a researcher, I occasionally search the Google Answers archive before embarking on a project. On a few occasions, I have been surprised to find some lengthy, in-depth answers to some very complex questions. Sometimes the answers only partially satisfy the research question at hand, but often they identify some sources that might not have been considered.

Further Reading about Database and Internet Searching

Calishain, Tara, and Rael Dornfest. *Google Hacks*, 2nd edition. Sebastopol, Calif.: O'Reilly, 2004. 479p.

For the serious Internet searcher, this easy-to-read manual explains all of the advanced features of the Google search engine.

Search Engine Watch. http://searchenginewatch.com/

Search Engine Watch (*SEW*) is a free-of-charge website that provides in-depth information on all aspects of search engines, including many tips for the advanced researcher. In addition to its website, *SEW* offers a free, email *Search Engine Report* that provides the latest news on the rapid developments in search engine technology.

Expert Opinion

Traditional library research often represents just one facet of the overall research strategy. Very often, input from one or more experts—including dealers, authentication boards and committees, appraisers, and museum or university-affiliated scholars—is absolutely necessary.

As long as there has been a market for works of art, there has been incentive for individuals to dupe the public with fakes and forgeries. Over the years, art historians and other experts have uncovered a great many outright forgeries and have identified countless additional "misattributions." As the market for works of art has grown, and is characterized by skyrocketing prices for major works, the role of the expert is increasingly important. In this section, we'll discuss experts: how to find them, how to approach them, and how to assess the validity of their opinions.

Unfortunately, there is no directory or database of experts on various artists, schools, or styles. One rather out-of-date but still useful and extremely informative article on the subject of experts, with a good list of recognized authorities on various artists, styles and periods, is Grace Glueck's "The Great Experts," *Art News*, vol. 91 (September 1992), pp. 90–101.

Often, the compiler of a catalogue raisonné is considered the expert on any given artist's oeuvre. (Catalogues raisonnés—chronologically arranged inventories of all known works by particular artists— are discussed in much greater detail in the next chapter.) Catalogue raisonné authors are often academics or museum curators, but sometimes art dealers are considered the ultimate experts on an artist's oeuvre. Surprisingly little is written on the often crucial role that dealers play in art scholarship. But "precisely because members of the art trade have a strong practical motivation to find out about the art they are buying and selling, they are the ones who often provide the bedrock of scholarship that enables collectors, academic and the public to understand an artist or a style."[2]

One way to identify potential expert assistance on a particular artist is to use a general Internet search, like Google. Try using terms like "authentication," "committee," "expert," or "raisonné" along with the artist's name. A recent attempt to identify a potential source for authentication of a Picabia drawing took just seconds; "Picabia" and "committee" led right to the official site of "Archives Picabia: the Official Site of the Picabia Committee." There, explicit guidelines for requesting authentication were posted.

Ethics and Expert Opinion

While the network of recognized experts in the art world is an unofficial one, most valid practitioners presumably belong to one or more professional or scholarly associations, part of whose raison d'être includes the construction of standards and guidelines for professional practice. Most reputable associations have a clearly defined "Code of Ethics" that outlines procedures to be followed in a variety of settings. In the field of art and artifacts, issues surrounding the art historian's responsibility to discourage the illegal traffic in works of art, for example, is clearly defined in the association's

Code of Ethics for Art Historians and Guidelines for the Professional Practice of Art History.[3] Similarly, potential conflicts of interest in the establishment of fees for services are identified. Of particular importance is the following provision vis-à-vis the establishment of a fee for the art historian's authentication of a work of art (source: College Art Association's *Code of Ethics for Art Historians and Guidelines for the Professional Practice of Art History*):

> **IV. Conflict of Interest**
>
> It is extremely important that an art historian be aware of the potential for conflicts of interest when scholarship and market interests become entangled. In cases where an art historian is asked to render professional judgments on works, it is imperative that reasonable disclosure of an art historian's relationship to a seller, art dealer, auction house, etc., be made. Reasonable disclosure shall be determined in the context of a particular professional judgment, as that degree of disclosure necessary to avoid both actual conflict of interest or impropriety based on self interest or the appearance of bias based on self (financial) interest.
>
> A. To avoid conflict of interest situations, CAA recommends that art historians set fees for attribution and connoisseurship at a fixed fee reasonable for the services provided rather than at a percentage of the sale price of the work of art. This latter practice was, and is, widespread and has led to the damaging of the reputations of art historians who depended upon large fees for a livelihood. Art historians, when consulted on such matters as scholarly attribution, can avoid the appearance of self-interest by establishing in advance, fees which bear no relation to the monetary value of any work of art in question and which do not otherwise relate to the financial complications of any research investigation, opinion or statement by the art historian. It is unethical for an art historian to engage in attributions and/or the publishing or exhibiting of works of art if the art historian or his or her university or other employer has a vested financial interest in selling, brokering, or seeking tax deductions regarding such works, without full disclosure on the part of the art historian of his/her personal financial involvement (other than normal salary and curatorial remunerations) in the said dealings.

Before retaining any professional—whether an art historian, appraiser, or lawyer, for that matter—investigate the accepted or professionally mandated principles surrounding fees and other ethical matters. Again, most professions have codified the acceptable practices in these arenas. Some of those that relate to appraisers follow.

Appraisers: How to Find Them

There are three major professional associations of appraisers, and each maintains a website with a directory of member appraisers. The three associations are

American Society of Appraisers
555 Herndon Pkwy, Suite 125
Herndon, VA 20170
http://www.appraisers.org

Appraisers Association of America
386 Park Avenue South, Suite 2000
New York, NY 10016
http://www.appraisersassoc.org

International Society of Appraisers
1131 SW 7th St.
Suite 105
Renton, WA 98055
http://www.isa-appraisers.org

Appraisers and Ethics

Just as the art historians' professional society (College Art Association) has identified potential ethical concerns for its members' conduct, so have all three major appraisal associations identified practices that are considered unethical.

Consider the following scenario: You've hired an appraiser to provide a fair market valuation of two paintings. The final report seems quite professional, and you're actually surprised with the high values assigned to the two works. The same appraiser contacts you, a few weeks later, and offers to buy the paintings. What is wrong with this picture? Surprisingly, there are cases in which appraisers' clients have agreed to sell works to the appraisers who assigned their values! That's very comparable to a buyer in a major upscale department store assigning the values to the items they purchase. This offer should never even be made by an ethical appraiser, and certainly no client should ever agree to it. In fact, the very offer casts doubt on the validity of the appraisal itself, and should be reported to the appraiser's professional association.

What an Appraisal Should Provide

A well prepared appraisal is much more than a description of an object and its value. It should also provide information on the methodology employed in assigning the appraised value, comparable works that were sold and used as benchmarks, and a number of additional elements. The following document, reprinted with permission of the Appraisers Association of America, represents a very thorough overview of what a client should expect in a well-prepared, professional appraisal.

Appraisers Association of America
ELEMENTS REQUIRED FOR A CORRECTLY PREPARED APPRAISAL

1. NAME AND ADDRESS OF CLIENT
2. NAME, CONTACT INFORMATION AND QUALIFICATIONS OF THE APPRAISER
   Statement of professional qualifications—curriculum vitae
   Statement of personal physical on-site inspection by the appraiser (or disclosure of other methods/circumstances)
   Statement that appraisal is prepared in accordance with USPAP including date of USPAP followed
   Statement of disinterest on the part of the appraiser (no financial interest)
   Statement of fee structure (basis for charge; that it is not contingent upon the value of the objects appraised)
   Clear division of appraisal when one or more than one appraiser is involved, who did what and inclusion of all CV's
3. PURPOSE OF THE APPRAISAL
   Insurance
   Donation
   Estate
   Equitable Distribution
   Inventory
   Damage/Loss
   Other ________________________
4. VALUATION METHOD USED & DEFINED
   Market Data Comparison Approach
   Cost Approach
   Income Approach
5. TYPE OF VALUATION USED & DEFINED
   Replacement Value
   Fair Market Value
   Market Value
   Marketable Cash Value
6. MARKETPLACE IN WHICH VALUATION IS APPLIED
7. RELEVANT DATES
   Date of on-site inspection
   Effective date of the appraisal
   Date appraisal report issued
8. DESCRIPTION OF APPRAISED OBJECTS
   Item
   Country/region of origin
   Medium
   Date(s)/period of creation
   Markings (e.g. signatures, maker's marks, manufacturer's marks, inscriptions)
   Full detailed description (including all observable physical characteristics)

Dimensions (measurements)
Condition (A representation as to condition must always be included, whether in a per object, per group or general statement.)
Firm statement of value — no estimates (exception may occur in Professional Opinion of Value statements)

9. GENERAL FORMAT AND STATEMENTS
Statement in belief of authenticity (only that the objects appraised correspond to the descriptions provided in the appraisal)
Statement of assumptions and limiting conditions
Statement of the number of pages in the appraisal
Pagination indicated on each page (e.g., '1/50' or 'page 1 of 50')
Statement of the number of photographs. (Generally the numbers correspond to the item numbers; if under separate cover, reference the page the photo is located on in your description (e.g. 'Photo page 1/50').

10. FOR APPRAISALS RELATING TO IRS USAGE ESTATE (E) OR DONATION (D)
Statement that appraiser has not been disqualified by the IRS (E and D)
Appraiser's Tax ID# (E and D)
Statement of the appraiser's qualifications specific to the item(s) appraised (D)
Statement of how the objects were acquired (D)
Completion of IRS form 8283 (D — separate from report)

11. ADDITIONAL DESCRIPTION (IF APPLICABLE)
Name of artist/craftsperson
Name of historical style/school of work
Title of work
Provenance
Catalogue raisonné number or other reference
Frame information
Exhibition history
Publication history
Dimensions (weights, e.g. troy oz.)

12. SUPPORT FOR VALUATION CONCLUSIONS (IF APPLICABLE)
Comparables (fully presented and annotated as appropriate)
Biography of the artist/craftsperson/school
Related analysis and discussion of the object/artist/school, etc.
State of the market discussion/market analysis
Material provided by consultants (identified)

Further Reading about Expert Advice

Spencer, Ronald D., ed. *The Expert Versus the Object: Judging Fakes and False Attributions in the Visual Arts.* New York: Oxford University Press, 2004. 241p.
Contents: Authenticating the attribution of art: connoisseurship and the law in the judging of forgeries, copies, and false attributions; Rembrandt and a

brief history of connoisseurship; On forgeries; Issues of authenticity in the auction house; Catalogue Raisonné; Role of the catalogue raisonné in the art market; "The authentic will win out"; Attributing Old Master drawings; Signature identification: from pen stroke to brush stroke; International Foundation for Art Research; Museums and authenticity issues; Examining the techniques and materials of paintings; Preservation and authenticity in contemporary art; The art expert, the law, and real life; Risk of legal liability for attributions of visual art; Authentication in court: factors considered and standards proposed; Legal decision in New York gives experts protection for their opinions on authenticity; Establishing authenticity in French law.

Conclusion

Researching individual works of art is a bit like detective work, but if approached systematically, the process can be very rewarding. Always begin with as much information as possible about the actual object, or type of artwork, to be researched and be creative in your approach. In the following chapters, subject and medium-specific sources will be identified and described. First we'll look at those sources that are useful for researching the actual work; then we'll move on to those that provide market data for selected objects.

THREE

Researching Works of Art: Basic Methods and Resources

The process of researching a work of art usually begins with a careful analysis of the subject work with the goal of answering some key questions, including:

- Who is the artist?
- What is the work's medium?
- When was it made, and where?
- Has the work appeared in any exhibitions, and if it has, when and where?
- Is the work illustrated or discussed in any books, magazines, journals or other publications about the artist, the period or the style?

The answer to each of these questions will serve as a starting point for further research, and will also affect the value of the work under consideration.

To assist in the identification and further study of artworks, the modern researcher has access to an ever-increasing wealth of information sources, in both print and electronic formats. In this chapter, basic research tools—including artists' catalogues raisonnés, monographs, exhibition catalogs, and more—will be defined, and the reader will be guided in their use.

It is beyond the scope of this chapter to even attempt to identify all of the sources available for researching an artist or an artwork; such an endeavor would comprise a work of many volumes. While many of the primary research tools are identified throughout, this chapter places some emphasis on the *process* of identifying sources that are germane to the study of the artwork at hand. Note that our focus here is on art research methods and sources. The tools and processes involved in researching market information on fine and decorative art objects is covered in great detail in chapters six and seven.

General Fine Art Bibliographies

Technically speaking, a bibliography is simply a list of published or unpublished works, including books, journals, individual articles within journals, and other documents. But a simple list is often of little use to the researcher; rather, it is the description, or annotation, that adds value to any bibliography. Works of this type are described in this section.

Beyond the traditional bibliography, the contemporary art researcher has access to a vast array of resources, in the form of online library catalogs and the library networks RLIN and OCLC *WorldCat* (described in detail in the preceding chapter). To locate libraries with significant holdings in the fine arts, consult the *International Directory of Art Libraries,* developed and maintained by the International Federation of Library Associations and Institutions (IFLA), Section of Art Libraries; the directory is described in greater detail in the preceding chapter's section on library research.

The researcher of art and art history has access to a great many annotated bibliographies that range in scope from the general to the very highly focused. The most important of the general bibliographies are identified here. To find additional bibliographies of this type in libraries that utilize the Library of Congress cataloging system, conduct a search using the subject heading "Art—Bibliography."

Arntzen, Etta, and Robert Rainwater. *Guide to the Literature of Art History.* Chicago: American Library Association, 1980. 616p. (Update: Marmor, Max, and Alex Ross. *Guide to the Literature of Art History 2.* Chicago: American Library Association, 2005. 899p.)

Arntzen and Rainwater's *Guide...* is a comprehensive bibliography of sources for the study of art, design, architecture and related fields. Reference works, fully annotated, are followed by classified sections treating the various "Particular arts" (architecture, sculpture, etc.), subdivided where appropriate by continent or country.

Marmor and Ross' 2005 update uses the general classification scheme employed by Arntzen and Rainwater. Additional chapters include "Patronage and Collecting" and "Cultural Heritage."

Bell, Doris L. *Contemporary Art Trends 1960–1980: A Guide to Sources.* Metuchen, N.J.: Scarecrow Press, 1981. 171p.

Classified topical bibliographic essays on contemporary trends, including arte povera, earthworks, environments and happenings, mail art, video and others precede country surveys.

Bibliographic Index. New York: H.W. Wilson, 1937– .

Described in detail in chapter two, this often overlooked index represents an important tool for finding very specialized bibliographies in books, journals and other published materials. It is published quarterly, with an annual cumulative volume, and it is available on the Web at many libraries.

Blazek, Ron, and Elizabeth Aversa. *The Humanities: A Selective Guide to Information Sources.* 5th ed. Englewood, Colo.: Libraries Unlimited, 2000. 603p.

Most libraries with significant humanities collections use Blazek and Aversa as a standard reference source. The visual arts sources, like those of the other humanities disciplines, are selected for their high quality, and include very extensive, detailed annotations.

Chamberlain, Mary. *Guide to Art Reference Books.* Chicago: American Library Association, 1959. 418p.

Predecessor to Arntzen and Rainwater's *Guide to the Literature of Art History* (above). Good source for historical research and especially strong in non-English language material.

Ehresmann, Donald L. *Fine Arts: A Bibliographic Guide to Basic Reference Works, Histories and Handbooks.* 3rd ed. Littleton, Colo.: Libraries Unlimited, 1990. 373p.

Annotated guide to over 2,000 fine arts reference works. Author/title and subject indexes.

Freitag, Wolfgang M., ed. *Art Books: A Basic Bibliography of Monographs on Artists.* 2nd ed. New York: Garland, 1997. 542p. (Series: *Garland Reference Library of the Humanities,* 1264.)

A-Z list of books devoted to individual artists. Useful for its indication <CR> of which work is considered the definitive catalogue, or catalogue raisonné, of the subject artist.

Jones, Lois Swan. *Art Information: Research Methods and Resources.* 3rd ed. Dubuque, Iowa: Kendall/Hunt, 1990. 373p.

Very well organized, comprehensive research guide for art, architecture, and design. Offers the user a good deal of guidance in the research process, in addition to well-annotated sources.

Bibliography—Geographical Focus

The following titles represent the major published bibliographies of fine and decorative arts limited to specific geographic areas. Medium-specific (i.e., painting, sculpture) bibliographies will be found later in this chapter, along with other medium-specific reference sources.

Africa

Biebuyck, Daniel P. *The Arts of Central Africa: An Annotated Bibliography.* Boston: G.K. Hall, 1987. 300p. (Series: *Reference Publication in Art History.*)

Classified bibliography with brief annotations. Partial contents: General ethnographies; General studies of African art; General studies on Zairian art; Northwestern Zaire; Northeastern Zaire; West Central Zaire; East Central Zaire; Southwestern Zaire; Lunda-Cokwe Complex; Southeastern Zaire; South Central Zaire. Author, ethnic group and subject indexes.

Burt, Eugene C. *An Annotated Bibliography of the Visual Arts of East Africa.* Bloomington: Indiana University Press, 1980. 371p. (Series: *Traditional Arts of Africa.*)
Brief but informative annotations to over 2000 published works on East African art and aesthetics. Partial contents: East Africa: General; Kenya; Tanzania; Maskonde Group; Uganda. Culture, author and subject indexes.

Latin America

Berlo, Janet Catherine. *The Art of Pre-Hispanic Mesoamerica: An Annotated Bibliography.* Boston: G.K. Hall, 1985. 272p.
Following a brief but informative historiographic essay, this well-annotated bibliography includes references to more than 1500 sources, including monographs, exhibition catalogs, periodical literature, conference and symposia reports and more.

Findlay, James A. *Modern Latin American Art: A Bibliography.* Westport, Conn.: Greenwood Press, 1983. 301p. (Series: *Art Reference Collection.*)
Bibliographic survey of thousands of 19th and 20th century books, exhibition catalogs, and other published works on modern Latin American art. Arranged by broad geographic area — Latin America, Caribbean, Central America — and further subdivided by country. Subarranged by subject, e.g., Argentina — General — Dictionaries, etc.

See also: *Latin American Modern and Contemporary Art: Online Bibliography* (below).

Handbook of Latin American Art = Manual de Arte Latinoamericano. Joyce Waddell Bailey, general editor. Santa Barbara, Calif.: ABC-Clio, 1984.
Classified, briefly annotated entries to books, articles, anthologies, and exhibition catalogs published over the past century. Volume I: General references and art of the nineteenth & twentieth centuries; Volume II: Art of the colonial period.

Latin American Modern and Contemporary Art: Online Bibliography. New York: Museum of Modern Art. Edited and maintained by Taína B. Caragol, bibliographer, Latin American specialist, the Museum of Modern Art, New York. http://momaapps.moma.org/shtmlpgs/lab/Home.html
This very easy-to-navigate online bibliography provides access to the Latin American, Caribbean, and U.S. Latino holdings of MOMA's extensive collection. "In many ways, this bibliography is meant to be an update of James A. Findlay's *Modern Latin American Art: A Bibliography,* published by Greenwood Press in 1983. Findlay was Bibliographer of Latin American Art at MoMA from 1979 to 1982 and his important book drew heavily, though not exclusively, from the MoMA Library collection [Overview section of website]."

North America

Davis, Lenwood G. *Black Artists in the United States: An Annotated Bibliography of Books, Articles, and Dissertations on Black Artists, 1779–1979*. Westport, Conn.: Greenwood Press, 1980. 138p.

Extensive bibliography of writings on the lives and work of black artists, most citations provide substantial annotations. Particularly useful for its inclusion of early periodical articles appearing in journals that are not indexed elsewhere. Includes a list of works by black artists at the National Archives.

Frye, Daniel J. *African American Visual Artists: An Annotated Bibliography of Education Resource Materials*. Lanham, Md.: Scarecrow Press, 2001. 378p. (Series: *Global Art Resource Guides* 1.)

More than just a bibliography, this reference work provides a good directory of sources, including museums and galleries, book publishers and stores, collections, historical and research centers, journals and more. Partial contents: African American art: a contextual survey; Annotated bibliography: General; Surveys; Children's books; Artists; Artist groups and movements.

Karpel, Bernard, ed. *Arts in America: A Bibliography*. Washington, D.C.: Published for the Archives of American Art by the Smithsonian Institution, 1979. 4 vols.

See description, page 117.

Sokol, David M. *American Architecture and Art: A Guide to Information Sources*. Detroit: Gale, [1976]. 341p. (*American Studies Information Guide Series*, vol. 2.)

Provides brief annotations to a wide array of information sources relating to American fine and decorative arts. Partial contents: General reference sources; General histories, aesthetics, and taste; American painting; Period surveys of American painting; Individual painters; American sculpture; Individual sculptors; American decorative arts. Author, title and subject indexes.

Oceania

Hanson, Louise, and F. Allan Hanson. *The Art of Oceania: A Bibliography*. Boston: G.K. Hall, 1984. 539p. (Series: *Reference Publication in Art History*.)

International, multilingual bibliography of monographs, catalogs, theses, dissertations, and periodical literature. "Annotations are provided in cases where titles give incomplete or unclear information about works and their contents [preface]." Partial contents: Cross-region; Polynesia; Micronesia; Melanesia; Australia. Sales catalog section arranged by auction house, subdivided by date. Identifies lot numbers for Oceanic art lots. Personal name, title and subject indexes.

Sources for the Identification of Artists

The process of identifying the artist responsible for a particular work of art can run the gamut from very straightforward to virtually impossible. A work with a clear signature and date represents the former (unless, of course, it is a fake), while the unsigned genre painting, for example, might be taken to represent the latter. Depending upon the type of work under consideration, there are many levels of attribution in between, and very often only an expert on the artist, style or school will be able to provide a definitive opinion on authorship. For a discussion of the role of experts in the art market, see chapter two.

Works with Signatures, Monograms or Other Markings

A number of reference works are available to assist the researcher who is trying to verify the appearance of an artist's signature or monogram. Monographs frequently (and biographies sometimes) will include signature or monogram facsimiles and might even go into some detail as to the appearance of different types of marks used by the artist at various points in her or his career. Later in this chapter, we'll review at length the value of the catalogue raisonné in the process of researching an artist's oeuvre; for the purposes of identifying artists and researching signatures and marks, it should be noted here that these invaluable resources often provide a wealth of information.

The illustration on the next page, from John Castagno's *Latin American Artists' Signatures and Monograms: Colonial Era to 1996* (Lanham, Md.: Scarecrow Press, 1997), illustrates the value of signature identification tools. An expanded bibliography of specialized signature reference sources follows.

Note in the illustration that, in addition to the signature samples for Latin American artist Roberto Montenegro, Castagno's directory provides some valuable leads for further investigation of this relatively obscure artist, including exhibitions, one publication, and three dealers. Users of reference tools like this, however, are cautioned that forgers, capable of making convincing copies, can be equally adept at copying their subject artists' signatures!

For a brief but very informative discussion of signature identification in the art world by a noted graphologist, see Patricia Siegel, "Signature Identification: From Pen Stroke to Brush Stroke," in *The Expert versus the Object: Judging Fakes and False Attributions in the Visual Arts* (New York: Oxford University Press, 2004, pp. 89–94).

Signature and Monogram Sources

Online

In addition to the various print signature reference sources, several Internet sites— some free, and some fee-based — provide access to signature facsimiles.

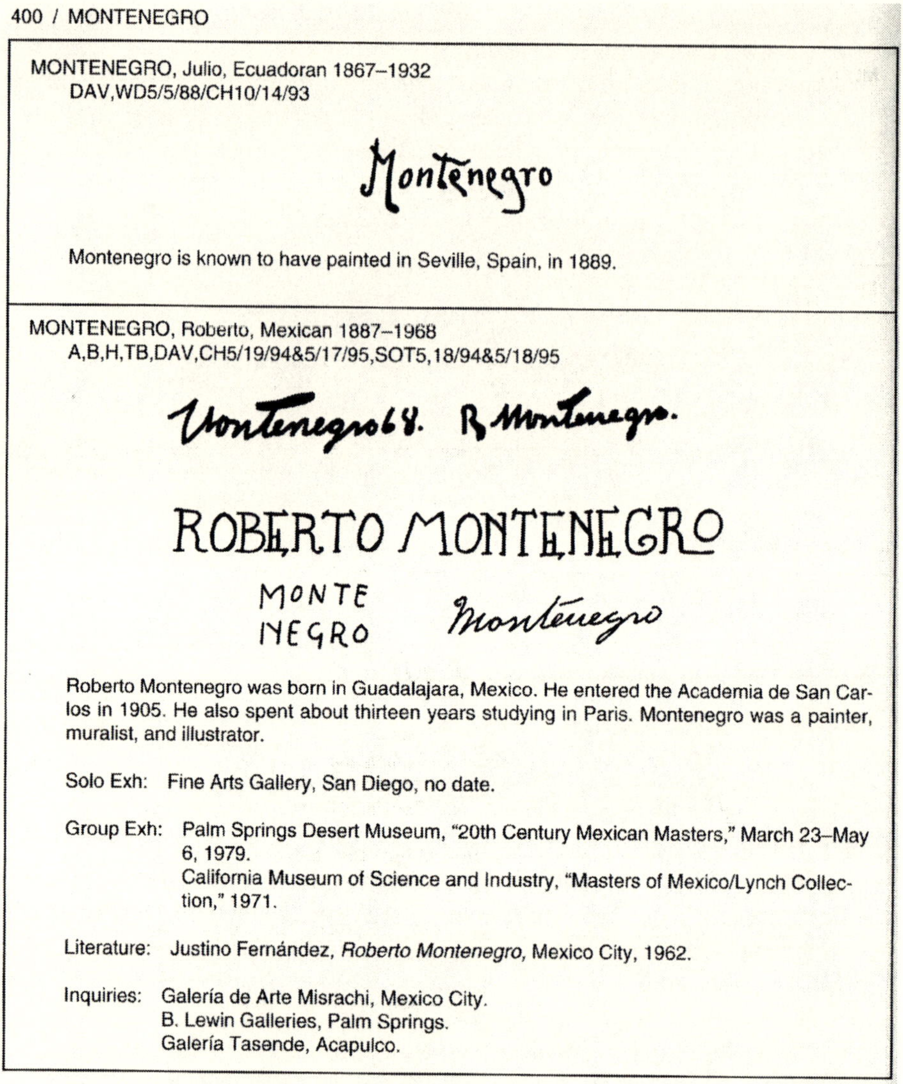
400 / MONTENEGRO

MONTENEGRO, Julio, Ecuadoran 1867–1932
DAV,WD5/5/88/CH10/14/93

Montenegro is known to have painted in Seville, Spain, in 1889.

MONTENEGRO, Roberto, Mexican 1887–1968
A,B,H,TB,DAV,CH5/19/94&5/17/95,SOT5,18/94&5/18/95

Roberto Montenegro was born in Guadalajara, Mexico. He entered the Academia de San Carlos in 1905. He also spent about thirteen years studying in Paris. Montenegro was a painter, muralist, and illustrator.

Solo Exh: Fine Arts Gallery, San Diego, no date.

Group Exh: Palm Springs Desert Museum, "20th Century Mexican Masters," March 23–May 6, 1979.
California Museum of Science and Industry, "Masters of Mexico/Lynch Collection," 1971.

Literature: Justino Fernández, *Roberto Montenegro,* Mexico City, 1962.

Inquiries: Galería de Arte Misrachi, Mexico City.
B. Lewin Galleries, Palm Springs.
Galería Tasende, Acapulco.

Entry for Latin American artist Roberto Montenegro, from John Castagno's *Latin American Artists' Signatures and Monograms: Colonial Era to 1996* (Lanham, Md.: Scarecrow Press, 1997).

artprice.com. http://*artprice*.com.

artprice.com provides access (for a relatively modest fee) to an inventory of approximately 36,000 signature examples. (Because it is most useful for its market information, *artprice*.com is described in great detail in chapter six.) The signatures included in *artprice*.com are derived from two sources: Frank Van Wilder's *Signatures & Monograms of 19th & 20th Century Artists*, and Caplan and Creps' *Encyclopedia of Artists' Signatures, Monograms and Symbols*.

Note that both of these sources are available in print and held in the collections of many larger libraries with good fine arts collections.

ArtArchiv.net. http://artarchiv.net.

Free Internet site includes an index to hundreds of artists' signatures and monograms.

Signatures and Monograms in Reference Works

In addition to those works that are composed entirely of signature and monogram facsimiles, some general biographical dictionaries supplement their entries with signature samples against which the researcher can check the signature on a given work. Included among this group of reference works are the following two sources.

Benezit, E. (Emmanuel). *Dictionnaire Critique et Documentaire des Peintres, Sculpteurs, Dessinateurs et Graveurs de Tous les Temps et de Tous les Pays, par un Groupe d'Ecrivains Specialistes Français et Etrangers.* Nouvelle ed., entierement ref. sous la direction de Jacques Busse. Paris: Grund, 1999. 14 vols.

Provides examples of artists' signatures and monograms for some entries. This standard biography reference source, usually called simply "Benezit," is described in greater detail later in this chapter.

Kindlers Malerei Lexikon: 1000 Malersignaturen, 1200 Garbige Reproductionen, 3000 Schwarzweisse Reproductionen in Sechs Banden. [Edited by Germain Bazin (et al.). Zurich: Kindler Verlag, 1964–71.

Critical and biographical dictionary of European artists. Many entries include signature or monogram example, list of public collections, bibliography. Very heavily illustrated with many good color reproductions.

Occasionally, sources that are devoted to a single artist's work will provide information on the subject artist's signature, monogram or other marks. Catalogues raisonnés in particular (described at length below), because they usually define their methodologies very clearly, often include signature facsimiles of their subject artist. Because a signature frequently changes over time, many catalogues raisonnés include a number of examples representing different periods of their subject artists' lives and careers.

Bibliography of Signature and Monogram Sources

Caplan, H. H. *The Classified Directory of Artists' Signatures, Symbols & Monograms.* H. H. Caplan; in association with Gale Research Company. Detroit: Gale Research, 1976. 738p.

Provides birth and death dates, place of birth, types of work, media, and signature/monogram examples. International in scope, 16th century to the present.

_____. *The Classified Directory of Artists' Signatures, Symbols & Monograms: American Artists with New U.K. Additions.* Enlarged and rev. ed. London: P. Grahame, 1987. 564p.

Enlarged, updated version of previous entry.

Castagno, John. *American Artists: Signatures and Monograms, 1800–1989.* Metuchen, N.J.: Scarecrow Press, 1990. 826p.

Provides signature examples for 5,100 artists, dating from 1800 to 1990. The volume serves also as an index to entries in major biographical dictionaries, encyclopedias, specialized reference works and periodicals. Volume 2, in press, is slated for publication at the end of 2005. It will include additional artists, as well as new material (e.g., additional signatures) for many artists included in the 1990 volume.

_____. *Artists as Illustrators: An International Directory with Signatures and Monograms, 1800–Present.* Metuchen, N.J.: Scarecrow Press, 1989, 625p.

Provides basic information and serves as an index to biographical reference sources; 14,000 entries include country or countries active, birth/death dates. Only a portion of the entries includes signature example.

_____. *Artists' Monograms and Indiscernible Signatures: An International Directory, 1800–1991.* Metuchen, N.J.: Scarecrow Press, 1991. 538p.

Signature examples for 3,700 artists (5,200 signatures). Section on illegible signatures most useful. Volume 2, slated for publication in late 2005, will include additional artists and new information on artists in the 1991 edition.

_____. *European Artists: Signatures and Monograms, 1800–1990, Including Selected Artists from Other Parts of the World.* Metuchen, N.J.: Scarecrow Press, 1990. 895p.

Includes signatures, biographical data, bibliographic and auction sales references for more than 4,800 artists. Includes some Australian, Japanese and South African artists. Volume 2, in press, is slated for publication at the end of 2005. It will include additional artists, and much updated information on artists included in the 1990 edition.

_____. *Latin American Artists' Signatures and Monograms: Colonial Era to 1996.* Lanham, Md.: Scarecrow Press, 1997. 673p.

Standard index to 1,100 artists includes 1,650 signatures. Provides references to auction sales catalogues, solo and group exhibitions, reviews, and other literature.

_____. *Old Masters: Signatures and Monograms, 1400— Born 1800.* Lanham, Md.: Scarecrow Press, 1996.

Includes 2,700 signature examples of 1,700 artists. Nationality, birth and death dates, along with references to auction catalogs that include images of the works cited.

Darmon, J. E. *Repertoire des Estampes Japonaises; les Artistes et Leurs Signatures, les Procédés, les Oeuvres et Leurs Prix dans les Ventes, Biographies et Bibliographies.* Paris: Editions Albert Morance, [1922]. 152p.

Biographical sketches include bibliographical references, signatures, and some 1920 sales prices.

Falk, Peter H. *Dictionary of Signatures & Monograms of American Artists: From the Colonial Period to the Mid 20th Century.* Madison, Conn.: Sound View Press; Land O'Lakes, Fla.: Distributed by Dealer's Choice Books, 1988. 556p.

Basic information on subject artist (name, dates, etc.), discipline/media. Entries record changes, inconsistencies (some have three or more examples). Shapes & symbols, index of "Undecipherable Monograms."

Jackson, Radway. *The Concise Dictionary of Artists' Signatures: Including Monograms and Symbols.* Introduction by Andrew Festing. New York: Alpine Fine Arts Collection, 1981, 1980. 224p.

Radway's *Concise Dictionary...* is a very handy guide to thousands of signatures, including a good proportion of lesser-known artists. The dictionary's "Visual Index" allows the user to pinpoint some of the more indiscernible of marks.

Lampe, Louis. *Signatures et Monogrammes des Peintres de Toutes les Écoles; Guide Monogrammiste Indispensable aux Amateurs de Peintures Anciennes.* Brussels: A. Castaigne, 1895–98. 3 v. in 1.

Names, dates, and signature examples of thousands of artists, all periods, schools.

Leblond, V. (Victor). *L'Art et les Artistes en Île-de-France au XVIe Siècle (Beauvais & Beauvaisis) d'après les minutes notariales; avec 7 phototypies et 80 marques, signatures et monogrammes.* Paris: E. Champion, 1921. 352p.

Primary documents relating to the fine and decorative arts. Includes signature and monogram examples of subject artists.

Pfisterer, Paul. *Signaturenlexikon = Dictionary of Signatures.* Berlin and New York: W. de Gruyter, 1999. 993p.

Perhaps the largest of the general signature directories, Pfisterer's includes examples of more than 16,000 artists' signatures and marks. Focus is on American and European artists of the 19th and 20th centuries.

Piron, Paul-L. *Signatures d'artistes Belges des XIXe et XXe Siècles = Handtekeningen van Belgische kunstenaars uit de XIXe en XXe eeuwen.* [Brussels]: Arts Antiques Auctions, [1989–1991] 2v.

Volume one includes over 4,000 artist's signature samples; volume two comprises thousands of additional signatures not included in the first volume.

Schwarz, Karl M. *Netsuke Subjects: A Study on the Netsuke Themes with Reference to Their Interpretation and Symbolism; Containing Photographs and Details on More than 400 Netsuke and 200 Signatures, 1000 keywords.* Vienna: Bohlau, 1992. 151p.

Guide for the serious netsuke collector and connoisseur. Partial contents: Carvers and signatures; Quality and genuineness; Identification of netsuke subjects; Collectors and collections; Prices and trends. Subject guide: Gods, saints, devils; Mythological beings and legends; Daily life; Animals and plants. List of carvers represented by signatures.

Self, James, and Nobuko Hirose. *Japanese Art Signatures: A Handbook and Practical Guide.* Floating World Editions. [s.l.]: Distributed by Weatherhill, 2003.

Includes thousands of names, facsimile signatures of Japanese artists and artisans.

Signatures et Monogrammes d'Artistes des XIXe et XXe Siècles.— Paris: Editions Van Wilder, 1998.

Over 8,500 signatures, 1,600 monograms. Entries include name, birth/death dates, signature sample.

Signatures and Seals on Painting and Calligraphy: The Signatures and Seals of Artists,

Connoisseurs, and Collectors on Painting and Calligraphy Since Tsin Dynasty. Compiled by the Joint Board of Directors of the National Palace Museum and the National Central Museum, Taichung, Taiwan, the Republic of China. Kowloon, Hong Kong: Cafa, 1964.

Vol. 1: Tsin to Yüan Dynasty (265–1368 A.D.); Vol. 2. Ming Dynasty (1368–1643 A.D.); Vol. 3. Ch'ing Dynasty (1644–1911 A.D.); Vol. 4. Brief Biographies.

Stewart, Basil. *The Dating of Japanese Prints, List of Ukyoye Artists, Reproductions of Artists' Signatures, Publishers' Seals, and Actors' Crests: From Subjects Portrayed in Japanese Colour-Prints; Appendices I, III and IV.* Geneva: Reda, [1973?]. 376p.

Reference work detailing artists' signatures, publishers' seals and actors' crests. Artist entries include name, dates (if known), qualifier, e.g., "follower of ...," signature and seal examples.

The Artist's Catalogue Raisonné

The *catalogue raisonné,* or "reasoned catalogue," is essentially a list of works believed to by created by its subject artist. The individual entries in artists' catalogues raisonnés are arranged in chronological order, and depending upon the artist's output, the catalogue may comprise anywhere from one to numerous volumes.[1] Some artists' catalogues raisonnés appear in the form of doctoral dissertations, and occasionally they are simply appendices (often lacking reproductions) to monographs on the subject artist's work.

The artist's catalogue raisonné might include works in all media (drawings, paintings, sculpture, etc.) by the subject artist, or it might be medium-specific. Individual entries in an artist's catalogue raisonné can be expected to include some or all of the following pieces of information about each work:

- Title
- Date
- Reproduction
- Dimensions
- Medium
- Information on signature or marks
- Exhibition history
- Provenance
- Bibliographical references
- Other pertinent information (e.g., for prints, number of artist's proofs, edition size, publisher, etc.)

Some early catalogues raisonnés are simple lists of works (see illustration on next page). Others are far more complex, and might include special sections, like inventories of works that are believed to be fakes or forgeries.

Inclusion of a work of art in a catalogue raisonné should *never* be taken as the final word on its authenticity. Catalogues published decades ago, in particular, should be used with caution. Works by artists long-deceased continue to be discovered; if their existence was unknown at the time of the catalogue's publication, such works will of course not be included in the subject artist's catalogue raisonné.

Occasionally, catalogues raisonnés are updated with supplementary volumes that incorporate changes like corrections, newly discovered information about works included in the original catalogue, and entries for works that have been discovered subsequent to publication of the catalogue raisonné. Occasionally, scholars propose additional entries, or challenge works attributed to an artist, in the form of articles or news items in magazines and journals. A thorough review of the major art periodical literature databases (see below) will retrieve such items in the journal literature.

Finding Catalogues Raisonnés

To find artists' catalogues raisonnés in libraries that utilize the Library of Congress classification system, conduct a subject search of the library's catalog using subject headings like "Whistler, James McNeill, 1834–1903 — Catalogs" or "Degas, Edgar, 1834–1917 — Catalogues Raisonnés."

Some catalogues raisonnés are not identified as such in their titles (see, for example, the Fantin-Latour illustration just shown) and some libraries' catalogs might not include the descriptive sub-heading "catalogues raisonnés." A very useful tool for identifying these elusive catalogs is Wolfgang Freitag's *Art Books: A Basic Bibliography of Monographs on Artists* (New York: Garland, 1985), where they are indicated by the notation <CR>.

Print researchers have access to a very useful source for identifying print catalogues raisonnés, published by the Print Council of America:

The Print Council Index to Oeuvre-Catalogues of Prints by European and American Artists. Compiled by Timothy A. Riggs under the sponsorship of the Print Council of America. Millwood, N.Y.: Krause, 1983. 834p.

Arranged by name of artist or publisher, provides publication information on oeuvre-catalogues, defined as "any listing of the artist's total output in prints, or some clearly defined section of that output." The more comprehensive online version is available (free of charge) at http://www.printcouncil.org.

Note that the *Print Council Index* does more than simply list catalogues and monographs. See, for example, the following entry; note particularly the indication of "doubtful and rejected prints."

ANNÉE 1883

PEINTURES

1099. — ***Portrait de Mme Fantin***. Toile. H. 1m. L. 0m80. Signé en haut, à gauche : Fantin 83. Salon de 1883, n° 909. Exposé à Bruxelles, en 1883, à la Royal Academy, à Londres, en 1884 ; à Copenhague, en 1888, puis à Stuttgart et enfin à Berlin, en 1896. Exposition Fantin, n° 53. A la Galerie nationale de Berlin.

Elle est assise, de trois quarts, à gauche, presque de face, sur le coin d'un canapé de velours rouge, vêtue d'une robe vert foncé, retenue par une broche près d'un petit col tuyauté. La tête est levée, le front dans la lumière, tandis que ses mains sont posées sur un livre ouvert sur ses genoux.

1100. — ***L'Étude***. Toile. H. 1m. L. 1m80. Exposé à la Royal Academy de Londres, en 1883, et à Paris, au Salon de 1884; à l'exposition de Bruxelles, en 1884. Exposition Fantin, n° 54. A M. Guillaume Charlier (Collection Henri Van Cutsem).

Une jeune femme, la robe recouverte d'un tablier de travail, est assise de profil, à droite, devant une toile neuve, fixée sur un chevalet, sur laquelle elle se prépare à peindre; elle tient sa palette de la main gauche et une brosse dans la main droite, posée sur les genoux croisés. En avant du chevalet, un meuble à peindre sur lequel est posé un petit vase de fleurs.

1101. — ***Portrait de Fantin***. Toile. H. 0m54. L. 0m44. Exposé au Salon triennal de Paris en 1883, n° 275; à Copenhague en 1888. Au Musée des Offices, à Florence.

Il est de trois quarts vers la gauche, la droite éclairée.

1102. — ***Baigneuses***. Toile. H. 0m27. L. 0m41. Même composition que la lithographie n° 37 du catalogue Hédiard.

Sur un massif de verdure sombre, s'enlèvent deux figures de jeunes femmes. Celle de droite, vue de face, s'essuie le sein avec le bout de la draperie sur laquelle elle est assise. A gauche, auprès d'elle, sa compagne est vue de dos, enveloppée de draperies à partir des hanches. Eclaircie et massif de verdure à droite.

1103. — ***Baigneuses***. Toile. H. 0m347. L. 0m362 ?. Même composition que la lithographie n° 38 du catalogue Hédiard.

Gersaint, Edmé François. *Catalogue Raisonné de Toutes les Pièces qui Forment l'Oeuvre de Rembrandt, Composé par Feu m. Gersaint, et mis au Jour avec les Augmentations Nécessaires, par les Sieurs Helle et Glomy....* (Paris: Chez Hochereau l'ainé, 1751). Entries: 342 prints by, 27 doubtful and rejected prints, 50 prints after. Pre-metric. Inscriptions. States. Described.

Catalogues Raisonnés in Progress

Researching a work in an existing catalogue raisonné is a relatively straightforward process. Decrying the fact that "art is now an international commodity," author and antiquarian book dealer Peter Kraus goes on to note that "accurate and unimpeachable catalogues raisonnés are the bedrock on which the confidence of the marketplace is based."[2] For just this reason dealers, collectors and other art market stakeholders have an interest in making sure that the works they own, or plan to sell, are accepted for inclusion in catalogues raisonnés that are "in the works" but not yet published. Unfortunately, there is no single source for this information — no one-stop, online inventory of catalogues in progress. So how can one determine if a catalogue raisonné is in the planning or production stage?

Catalogue raisonné authors and compilers seek information on individual works by contacting artists' dealers, associates and family members (in the case of contemporary or recently deceased artists); they may even seek out works through advertisements in art magazines and journals. The promise of inclusion in a forthcoming catalogue raisonné can have a profound effect on the salability of an artwork; collectors and dealers, therefore, should make every attempt to identify catalogues in progress by

- contacting dealers who handle, or who have handled, the subject artist
- contacting auction house department experts
- identifying foundations set up in the artist's name
- searching art magazines and periodicals
- searching the Internet, using keywords including "artist's name" and "catalogue raisonné"
- contacting experts on the artist, whether university-affiliated, museum-affiliated, or independent. Experts can be very forthcoming with information, and occasionally, the interested researcher might even stumble upon the person who is actually compiling the artist's catalogue raisonné.

Opposite: **Page from *Catalogue de l'Oeuvre Complet de Fantin-Latour: 1849–1904*, the catalogue raisonné of works by French painter Henri Fantin-Latour. This catalog, published in 1911, is a good starting point for developing a list of exhibitions in which Fantin-Latour's works were shown.**

General Fine Art Reference Sources

Dictionaries and encyclopedias are staples of the art history reference collection. The works described in this section include entries on artists, their works, methods and materials. This group of resources is by no means exhaustive, but rather represents a selection of the major works in each of three categories: dictionaries, encyclopedias, and manuals for collectors and connoisseurs of various media.

Dictionaries

Every field of study has its own terminology, and the art world is no exception. Art and art history, in fact, have engendered an enormous specialized vocabulary replete with specialized terms for various styles, periods, materials and media, and technical processes. Before going into specific print and electronic dictionaries of art terminology, the following few tools, which in a way represent indexes to groups of specialized dictionaries, are worthy of note.

Art and Architecture Thesaurus Online. Getty Foundation Research Institute. http://www.getty.edu/research/conducting_research/vocabularies/aat/.

The Getty Foundation's *Art and Architecture Thesaurus Online* is a structured vocabulary of art terms, intended for use by catalogers and indexers of art information. Because it is most useful for researchers of objects, a full description can be found in the next chapter.

Urdang, Laurence. *Fine and Applied Arts Terms Index*. Detroit, Mich.: Gale Research, 1983. 773p.

Faced with an enormous number of specialized indexes, researchers often find that identifying the one or two with good definitions of a specialized term can be most time consuming. Available in many libraries' fine art reference collections, *Fine and Applied Arts Terms Index* can make the process of locating definitions much less daunting, because it serves as an index to many of the best sources. Includes references to more than 45,000 fine and decorative arts terms.

Often illustrated, the following sources provide short definitions of styles, media, technical and related terminology. To locate additional sources of this type in libraries that utilize the Library of Congress Classification System, use the following subject headings:

Art — Dictionaries
Painting — Dictionaries

Hume, Helen D. *The Art Lover's Almanac: Serious Trivia for the Novice and the Connoisseur*. San Francisco: Jossey-Bass, 2003. 818p.

Definitions, odd or interesting facts, tips for collectors, interesting statistics on the art world.

Langmuir, Erika, and Norbert Lynton. *The Yale Dictionary of Art and Artists.* New Haven: Yale University Press, 2000. 753 p.

Some definitions of art-related terms, but primarily a source for biographical sketches of major artists, all periods.

Lucie-Smith, Edward. *Thames & Hudson Dictionary of Art Terms.* 2nd ed. New York: Thames & Hudson, 2003.

Well-illustrated, brief definitions. Particularly good for clear descriptions of media, technical terminology.

Mayer, Ralph. *The HarperCollins Dictionary of Art Terms and Techniques.* Revised and edited by Steven Sheehan. 2nd ed. New York: HarperPerennial, 1992. 474 p.

Ralph Mayer's *Dictionary of Art Terms and Techniques* is a classic reference source used by artists, conservators, and historians. Numerous editions since 1940 attest to Mayer's status as one of the very best dictionaries of artists' techniques and materials.

Murray, Peter, and Linda Murray. *The Penguin Dictionary of Art and Artists.* 7th ed. Harmondsworth and New York: Penguin, 1997. 579p.

Very useful, concise dictionary of major movements, schools, and styles, but primarily artist biography. Biographical entries include references to subject artists' works in major museums.

The Oxford Companion to Western Art. Edited by Hugh Brigstocke. Oxford and New York: Oxford University Press, 2001.

Brief biographies, short essays on styles and movements, some technical material.

Pierce, James Smith. *From Abacus to Zeus: A Handbook of Art History.* 7th ed. Upper Saddle River, N.J.: Pearson/Prentice Hall, 2004. 230p.

This widely used dictionary provides very clear definitions of art terms. Definitions are keyed to the illustrations contained in H.W. Janson's classic textbook *History of Art* (6th edition), Marilyn Stokstad's *Art History* (2nd edition), and *Gardner's Art through the Ages* (11th edition).

Encyclopedias and Textbooks

The following entries represent a selection of the major general encyclopedias and surveys of art and art history. To find additional works of this type in libraries that utilize the Library of Congress Classification System, perform a subject search using the subheading "Encyclopedias," e.g.:

Art — Encyclopedias
Art — History

Cambridge Introduction to the History of Art. Cambridge and New York: Cambridge University Press, 1981–1983. 8 vols.

Contents: Art of Greece and Rome; Middle Ages; Renaissance; Seventeenth century, Eighteenth century; Nineteenth century; Twentieth century; Looking at pictures.

Dictionary of Art. Edited by Jane Turner. New York: Grove's Dictionaries, 1996. 34 vols. Also available on the web.

Available in many libraries, the print edition of the *Dictionary of Art* is a good starting point for basic art research. It includes over 45,000 articles on the visual arts, including painting, sculpture, graphic arts, architecture, decorative arts and photography, from prehistory to the present day. Compiled over a period of 15 years, the *Dictionary of Art* represents the work of more than 6,800 scholars around the world, each writing on his or her own special field of study.

Many libraries provide the electronic version of the *Dictionary of Art.* While it lacks most of the illustrations found in the print edition, it is updated and hence includes new articles, updated bibliographies, and other material not found in the original print edition.

Encyclopedia of World Art. New York: McGraw-Hill, 1958. 15 vols. Supplementary Volumes: Volume XVI: *World Art in Our Time*, 1983. Volume XVII: *New Discoveries and Perspectives in the World of Art*, 1987.

While somewhat dated, still a staple in every fine arts reference collection. Very good biographies, surveys of periods and styles, overviews of various media (e.g., printmaking). Essays are signed, quite well illustrated, and usually include very good bibliographies for further research.

Gombrich, E.H. *The Story of Art.* 16th ed. London: Phaidon Press, 1995. 688p.

Latest edition of this standard art history textbook traces the development of painting and sculpture from ancient times through the 20th century.

Honour, Hugh. *The Visual Arts: A History.* 6th ed. New York: Abrams, 2002. 960p.

Standard art history textbook covers development on a global scale, ancient through contemporary.

Kleiner, Fred S., and Christin J. Mamiya. *Gardner's Art Through the Ages.* Belmont, Calif.: Thomson/Wadsworth, 2005. 2 vols. + CD ROM

Now in its 12th edition, *Gardner's* remains one of the most heavily used standard textbooks for introductory art history courses in colleges and universities.

Silver, Larry. *Art in History.* New York: Abbeville, 1993. 496p.

This survey textbook, covering Egyptian through the 20th century, is one of the more accessible and most appropriate for the novice art researcher.

Stokstad, Marilyn. *Art History.* Upper Saddle River, N.J.: Pearson/Prentice Hall, 2005. 2 vols. + CD ROM.

This massive survey text is one of the most popular among art history faculty in colleges and universities. From prehistory through post–World War II, this wide-winged global survey presents a very scholarly, but accessible overview of the visual arts, including those of Africa and Asia.

Encyclopedias and Surveys—Modern

The following represent a selection of major surveys of 19th and 20th century art. Similar works may be found by searching Library of Congress subject headings like "Art, Modern—19th Century"; "Art, Modern—20th Century"; "Minimal Art"; or "Postmodernism—United States."

The Age of Modernism: Art in the 20th Century. Berlin: Zeitgeist-Gesellschart e.V.; Ostfildern-Ruit [Germany]: G. Hatje, 1997. 672p.
Exhibition catalog surveys the art of the 20th century in a series of thematic chapters; very well illustrated, with essays by leading critics. Lengthy biographies of artists include references to major exhibitions, good bibliographies.

Archer, Michael. *Art Since 1960*. 2nd ed. New York: Thames & Hudson, 2002. 256p. (Series: *World of Art*.)
Traces the development of contemporary art, from Pop through media and performance.

Arnason, H. Harvard. *History of Modern Art: Painting, Sculpture, Architecture, Photography*. 4th ed. New York: Abrams, 1998. 856p.
Standard text traces the development of modern art from the 19th century through the mid–1990s.

Battcock, Gregory. *Minimal Art: A Critical Anthology*. Berkeley: University of California Press, 1995. 454p.
Battcock's collection of critical essays is considered a basic text in contemporary art. The articles, all by major scholars in the field, are reprinted from a variety of sources, including books and journals. Lots of illustrations make this a useful source for identification of comparable works.

Bihalji-Merin, Otto, and Nebojša-Bato Tomaševic, eds. *World Encyclopedia of Naïve Art: A Hundred Years of Naïve Art*. London: F. Muller, 1984. 735p.
Encyclopedic overview of naïve art and artists, with an emphasis on Western countries. Individual artists profiled, along with survey articles on individual countries.

Hunter, Sam. *Modern Art: Painting, Sculpture, Architecture*. 3rd rev. ed. New York: Abrams, 2000. 448p.
Traces the origin of modern art and architecture styles and trends, from 19th century precedents through the turn of the 21st century.

Kostelanetz, Richard. *A Dictionary of the Avant-Gardes*. New York: Schirmer Books, 2000. 708p.
Biographical sketches and articles on the 20th century avant-garde in film, visual art, music and popular culture.

Lucie-Smith, Edward. *Art Today*. London: Phaidon Press, 1995. 511p.
Encyclopedic survey of movements in post–1960s art, including modest sections on non–Western art and artists.

_____. *Movements in Art Since 1945*. London and New York: Thames & Hudson, 2001. 304p. (Series: *World of Art*.)
Concise, readable and well-illustrated survey of post–World War II movements. Partial contents: Abstract expressionism; European scene; Post-painterly abstraction; Pop, environments and happenings; Abstract sculpture, minimal art, conceptual art; Arte povera, post-minimalism and their heritage; Neo-Expressionist tendencies in the 1980s; America in the 1980s; Questioning the Western modernist canon from the "margins"; Issue-based art: African-American, Afro-Caribbean, feminist and gay art.

Rosenblum, Robert, and H.W. Janson. *19th Century Art. Painting*, Robert Rosenblum; *Sculpture*, H.W. Janson. Upper Saddle River, N.J.: Pearson/Prentice Hall, 2005. 544p.

Heavily revised edition of standard text on 19th century art surveys painting and sculpture from last quarter of the 18th century through 1900, with an emphasis on Western European art.

Sandler, Irving. *Art of the Postmodern Era: From the Late 1960s to the Early 1990s.* New York: IconEditions, 1996. 636p.

Encyclopedic survey treats in depth the art of the last three decades. Extensive bibliography, including selective works on individual artists.

Stangos, Niko, ed. *Concepts of Modern Art.* 3rd enl. and updated ed. New York: Thames and Hudson, 1994. 424p. (Series: *World of Art.*)

Collection of essays by prominent art historians on styles and movements in 20th century art, from Fauvism to Conceptual art and Postmodernism.

Vaughan, William. *Arts of the 19th Century.* New York: Abrams, 1989–1999. Vol. 1: 1780 to 1850; Vol. 2: 1850 to 1905.

Very beautifully illustrated survey of 19th century art, originally published in French.

Wheeler, Daniel. *Art Since Mid-Century: 1945 to the Present.* New York: Vendome, 1991. 344p.

Illustrated, scholarly survey of post–World War II art. Major trends in contemporary art (Pop, New Realism, Minimalism, etc.), and their representative artists are treated in considerable depth.

Encyclopedias and Surveys— Geographical Focus

African Countries

Africa: Art and Culture. Edited by Hans-Joachim Koloss. Munich and London: Prestel, 2002. 240p.

Excellent source for the identification of masks, figural sculpture and utilitarian objects. Essays on regional works authored by world-renowned experts. Partial contents: Ife; Benin; Afro-Portuguese ivories from ancient Owo; West Africa; Cameroon Grasslands; Congo; East Africa.

Africa: The Art of the Continent. Edited by Tom Phillips. Munich and New York: Prestel, 1995. 613p.

This massive survey text includes hundreds of excellent images of fine, decorative and utilitarian objects. Organized by area: Ancient Egypt and Nubia; Eastern Africa; Southern Africa; Central Africa; West Africa and the Guinea Coast; Sahel and Savanna; Northern Africa.

Gillon, Werner. *A Short History of African Art.* Harmondsworth, England: Penguin, 1986. 405p.

Partial contents: Ancient Nubians; Nok culture; Kingdoms of the Western Sudan; Art of the Sherbro, Bulom and Kissi; Kanem-Borno and the "Sao" culture; "Kororofa"— the Jukun and related peoples; Art of the Akan; Igbo-Ukwu, the Niger Delta and the Cross River; Yoruba and their neighbors; Benin — the art of the Edo City State; Art of the Southern Savanna; Eastern Africa; Arts of Southern Africa.

History of Art in Africa. Monica Blackmun Visonà ... [et al.]. New York: Abrams, [2000]. 544p.

Standard textbook intended for advanced courses in African art history surveys and contextualizes the works of all of the major art forms of Africa, from ancient through the African diaspora, including some contemporary artists' works.

Kings of Africa: Art and Authority in Central Africa, Collection Museum für Völkerkunde Berlin. Edited by Erna Beumers and Hans-Joachim Koloss. [Utrecht, Netherlands]: Foundation Kings of Africa, [1992?]. 327p.

Published in conjunction with an exhibition exploring imagery of power in Central African art (primarily sculpture), this catalog's high quality reproductions provide an excellent resource for the identification of various periods and styles.

Leiris, Michel, and Jacqueline Delange. *African Art*. New York: Golden Press, 1968. 453p. (Translation of *Afrique Noire, la Création Plastique*.)

This classic study of traditional (pre–Colonial) African arts, now somewhat dated, presents a good overview of two and three dimensional arts, textiles, environmental arts, and more.

Preston, George Nelson. *African Art Masterpieces*. Hugh Lauter Levin Associates, Inc.; Dist. by Macmillan, New York: 1991. 120p.

Analysis of 48 major works from public and private collections, including sculpture, decorative arts, textiles.

Willett, Frank. *African Art*. London: Thames & Hudson, 2002. 272p. (Series: *World of Art*.)

New edition of a standard primer, *African Art* provides an excellent introduction to the history, and historiography, of African art. Latest edition includes an overview of current research in textiles and costume, pottery, metalwork and other areas of art and craftsmanship.

Asian Countries

Clunas, Craig. *Art in China*. New York: Oxford University Press, 1997. 255p. (Series: *Oxford History of Art*.)

Surveys the visual arts in China, from Neolithic through the nineteenth century. Of particular interest to art market history: Art in the market-place: Song and Yuan Dynasties 9960–1368; Ming Dynasty (1368–1644) painting; printing; textiles and crafts; Amateur and professional problem in late Ming painting; Qing Dynasty (1644–1911); Prints and perspective; Shanghai in the 19th century; Republic of China; Art in the PRC; Art in China since the 1970s.

Hutt, Julia. *Understanding Far Eastern Art: A Complete Guide to the Arts of China, Japan and Korea: Ceramics, Sculpture, Painting, Prints, Lacquer, Textiles and Metalwork*. New York: Dutton, 1987. 208p.

Intended for the beginning researcher or student of Asian art forms, very accessible but informative. Partial contents: Painting; Prints and printed books; Ceramics; Metalwork; Sculpture and carvings; Lacquer.

Lee, Sherman. *A History of Far Eastern Art*. 5th ed. New York: Abrams, 1994. 576p.

Widely available in libraries, Lee's encyclopedic survey is a standard text for upper-level college art history courses on the subject. Treats in depth the visual arts of India, Indonesia, China, Korea and Japan from pre-history through the modern era.

Munroe, Alexandra. *Japanese Art After 1945: Scream Against the Sky*. New York: Abrams, in association with the Japan Foundation and InterCultura: 1994. 416p.

Published on the occasion of an exhibition organized by the Yokohama Museum of Art and shown there Feb. 4–Mar. 31, 1994, and at the Guggenheim Museum, New York, Sept. 12, 1994–Jan. 15, 1995. Surveys post–World War II Japanese art through a series of well-illustrated essays. Artists' statements, numerous primary documents and an extensive bibliography make this an essential reference source for the researcher of 20th century Japanese art.

Roberts, Laurance P. *A Dictionary of Japanese Artists: Paintings, Sculpture, Ceramics, Prints, Lacquer*. Tokyo and New York: Weatherhill, 1990. 299p.

Basic biographical data and index to scholarly literature and public collections.

Sullivan, Michael. *Art and Artists of Twentieth-Century China*. Berkeley: University of California Press, 1996. 354p.

Scholarly survey by expert in the field of Chinese art history. Partial contents: 1900–1937 — Impact of the West; 1937–1949 — war and civil war; 1949–1976 — art in the era of Mae Zedon; Other currents; After Mao— art enters a new era.

Tregear, Mary. *Chinese Art*. Rev. ed. New York: Thames and Hudson, 1997. 216p. (Series: *World of Art*.)

Like other titles in the *World of Art* series, Tregear's *Chinese Art* is highly informative, but quite accessible for the novice. Partial contents: Annotated chronology of Chinese historical periods, dynasties and reigns; Neolithic crafts; Hieratic art and the bronze age; Status and decoration; Nationalism and expression; Imprint of Buddhism; Internationalism and showmanship; Court and Chan Buddhist arts; Tradition and invention; Eclecticism and innovation; Individualism and eccentricity; Enquiry and dislocation.

Watson, William. *The Arts of China 900–1620*. New Haven: Yale University Press, 2000 286p. (Series: *Yale University Pelican History of Art*.)

Partial contents: Landscape painting under Northern Song 960–1126; Decorative style under Song; Decorative style under Song and Jin: the later phase; Painting under Southern Song 1127–1279; Sculpture; Landscape, plants and trees painted under Yuan 1279–1368; Painting under Ming 1368–1643; Decorative themes under Yuan and Ming.

Australia

Allen, Christopher. *Art in Australia: From Colonization to Postmodernism*. New York: Thames & Hudson, 1997. 224p. (Series: *World of Art*.)

Well-illustrated survey of Australian art and artists.

Heathcote, C.R. *A Quiet Revolution: the Rise of Australian Art, 1946–1968*. Melbourne, Vic.: The Text Pub., 1995. 267p.

From post–World War II to the present, traces the development of contemporary art in Australia. Chapter titled "An Artist's Lot: the Art Market Develops, 1956–64" details the cultivation of an audience for works of art by contemporary Australian artists and the development of Australia's gallery scene.

McCulloch, Alan. *The Encyclopedia of Australian Art*. 3rd ed. Honolulu: University of Hawaii Press, 1994. 879p.

Comprises largely illustrated biographical entries on individual artists, including education, appointments, collections, awards and gallery representation. Some essays on movements and stylistic trends.

Robb, Gwenda. *Concise Dictionary of Australian Artists.* Carlton, Vic.: Melbourne University Press, 1993. 288p.
Brief biographical entries on Australian artists of all periods; entries include indications of the subject artist's inclusion in public collections.

Smith, Bernard. *Place, Taste and Tradition: A Study of Australian Art Since 1788.* 2nd ed., rev. Melbourne and New York: Oxford University Press, 1979. 304p.
Surveys major movements in Australian art, from Colonial period through mid–20th century. Partial contents: Early Australian primitives; Impressionism; Modern movement; Surrealism and neo-surrealist developments; Contemporary art.

Canada

Belton, Robert James. *Sights of Resistance: Approaches to Canadian Visual Culture.* Calgary: University of Calgary Press, 2001. 398p. + CD ROM
Presents representative examples of Canadian visual art forms (17th century to the present), including paintings, sculpture, photography.

Burnett, David G. *Masterpieces of Canadian Art from the National Gallery of Canada.* Edmonton, AB, Canada: Hurtig, 1990. 230p.
Chronologically arranged survey of Canadian artists' works from the mid–18th through late 20th century.

France

Blunt, Anthony. *Art and Architecture in France, 1500–1700.* New Haven: Yale University Press, 1999. 319p. (Series: *Yale University Pelican History of Art.*)
Well-researched, scholarly survey of French art and architecture by a leading scholar in the field. Well illustrated, intended for the serious researcher or student of French art and culture.

Chastel, André. *French Art.* Paris; New York: Flammarion, 1994– . Vol. 1: *Prehistory to the Middle Ages*; Vol. 2: *The Renaissance, 1430–1620*; Vol. 3: *The Ancien Régime, 1620–1775.*
This English translation of the author's *Art Français* is a richly illustrated survey of the major works of French art and architecture.

Levey, Michael. *Painting and Sculpture in France, 1700–1789.* New Haven: Yale University Press, 1993. 318p. (Series: *Yale University Pelican History of Art.*)
Surveys French painting and sculpture through analysis of works by major and some lesser known artists of the 18th century.

Germany

Adam, Peter. *The Arts of the Third Reich.* London: Thames and Hudson, 1992. 332p.
Partial contents: The Nordic myth: National Socialist ideology; The "Great German Art Exhibitions"; Exhibition of "Degenerate Art"; Sculpture. Extensively illustrated, b/w and color plates.

Behr, Shulamith. *Expressionism.* Cambridge, England: Cambridge University Press, 1999. 80p. (Series: *Movements in Modern Art.*)

This brief survey of German Expressionism is intended as an introduction to the movement for the layman. Emphasis on the plastic arts, but decorative arts and architecture covered minimally. Partial contents: Expressionism: its origins, meaning and historiography; Nature, culture and modernity: Dresden; Utopianism and abstraction: Munich; Modernity and its conflicts: Berlin; War, revolution and counter revolution.

Crockett, Dennis. *German Post-Expressionism: The Art of the Great Disorder, 1918–1924*. University Park: Pennsylvania State University Press, 1999. 215p.

Partial contents: State of art in Germany, 1918–1924; Post-Expressionism in Germany ...the artists ... the critics. Appendix: Artists included in Hartlaub's Neue Sachlichkeit exhibitions of 1925–26.

Droste, Magdalena. *Bauhaus, 1919–1933*. Cologne: B. Taschen, 1990. 256p.

Concise, readable account of the origin and development of the Bauhaus. Partial contents: On the origins of the Bauhaus; Art and technology — a new unity [explores the various decorative arts workshops]; Dessau Bauhaus— Institute of Design. Includes brief biographical sketches of key figures.

Elger, Dietmar. *Expressionism: A Revolution in German Art*. Cologne and New York: B. Taschen, 1998. 255p.

Brief surveys precede overviews of key figures in the movement. Partial contents: Brücke Group of artists; Northern German Expressionism; Blaue Reiter; Rhenish Expressionism; Subject of the city; Expressionism in Vienna.

German Art in the 20th Century: Painting and Sculpture 1905–1985. Edited by Christos M. Joachimides, Norman Rosenthal, and Wieland Schmied. London: Royal Academy of Arts; Munich: Prestel, 1985. 518p.

This beautifully illustrated exhibition catalog offers an overview of major movements in German art of the 20th century. Essays by top scholars in the field are supplemented by lengthy biographies of artists featured in the exhibition.

Gillen, Eckhart, ed. *German Art from Beckmann to Richter: Images of a Divided Country*. Cologne: DuMont Buchverlag. 546p.

Scholarly survey of 20th century German art (painting, sculpture, photography, video and performance works) from the early work of Max Beckmann through the 1990s.

Michalski, Sergiusz. *New Objectivity: Painting, Graphic Art and Photography in Weimar Germany 1919–1933*. Cologne and Los Angeles: B. Taschen, 2003. 220p.

Explores the return to representation in the plastic arts of post–Expressionist Germany. Detailed biographical sketches of major and lesser-known artists of the period include many references to exhibitions and commissions.

Great Britain

Buckman, David. *Dictionary of Artists in Britain Since 1945*. Bristol: Art Dictionaries, 1998. 1344p.

Brief biographical entries on "painters, sculptors, draughtsmen, teachers, video film, installation and performance artists born in the United Kingdom" [intro].

Graham-Dixon, Andrew. *A History of British Art*. Berkeley: University of California Press, 1999. 256p.

First published in conjunction with a BBC Television series, very basic and readable history of British art suitable for the non-specialist.

Handbook of Modern British Painting and Printmaking, 1900–1990. 2nd ed. Edited by Alan Windsor. Aldershot, Eng., and Brookfield, Vt.: Ashgate, 1998. 321p.

Dictionary consisting primarily of short biographical essays surveys 20th century major and lesser-known British artists.

Johnson, Jane, and A. Greutzner. *The Dictionary of British Artists, 1880–1940.* Suffolk, Eng.: Antique Collectors' Club, 1976. 576p. (Series: *Dictionary of British Art*, vol. 5.)

Approximately 41,000 artists, including painters, decorative artists, costume designers. Very brief biographical entries include some exhibition histories and professional affiliations; major subject matter and media noted in some instances.

Spalding, Frances. *20th Century Painters and Sculptors.* Suffolk, Eng.: Antique Collectors' Club, 1990. 482p. (Series: *Dictionary of British Art*, vol. 6.)

Approximately 7,000 artists included. Some b/w illustrations, a few good quality color plates. Entries include name, birth/death dates, etc., birthplace, education, some information on exhibitions.

The Thames and Hudson Encyclopedia of British Art. London: Thames and Hudson, 1985. 320p.

Brief entries on artists, schools and styles, techniques, patronage and other aspects of British art from Anglo-Saxon period through contemporary.

Ireland

Snoddy, Theo. *Dictionary of Irish Artists: 20th Century.* 2nd ed. Dublin: Merlin, 2002. 768p.

Lengthy biographical essays on Irish artists, designers, illustrators, and others active in the visual arts. Entries include highly selective bibliography, references to public collections, and notes on signatures and monograms.

Italy

History of Italian Art. Cambridge, Eng.: Polity Press; Cambridge, Mass.: Blackwell, 1994. 2 vols.

Comprehensive survey of the arts in Italy. Partial contents: Vol. 1: The Italian artist and his roles; Italian art and the art of antiquity; Dispersal and conservation of art-historical property; Public reception of art. Volume 2: Periodization of the history of Italian art; Iconography of Italian art 1100–1400; History of art and the forms of religious life; Renaissance and pseudo-Renaissance; Toward the modern manner.

Wittkower, Rudolf. *Art and Architecture in Italy, 1600–1750.* 6th ed. New Haven: Yale University Press, 1999. 3 vols. (Series: *Yale University Pelican History of Art.*)

Provides a general overview of Italian art and architecture of the Baroque period. Used in a great many upper-level and graduate courses on the subject, Wittkower is most appropriate for the more advanced art history researcher.

Latin America and the Caribbean

Barnitz, Jacqueline. *Twentieth-Century Art of Latin America.* Austin: University of Texas Press, 2001. 400p.

Commencing with a very brief overview of 19th century trends, this textbook traces the evolution of modernism in the early part of the 20th century through contemporary 1980s movements, including neofiguration, pop, political art and more.

Congdon, Kristin G., and Kara Kelley Hallmark. *Artists from Latin American Cultures: A Biographical Dictionary*. Westport, Conn.: Greenwood Press, 2002. 314p.

Lengthy biographical essays on more than 75 important Latin American artists. Major works are interpreted, and each entry has a "Places to See" section with public collections and the titles of works to be found there. Good highly selective bibliographies for further research.

Cruz Díaz, Ursulina. *Diccionario Biográfico de las Artes Plásticas*. Havana: Editorial Pueblo y Educación, 1999. 412p.

Brief biographical sketches of Cuban and Latin American artists. Most entries include signature example; no reproductions.

Encyclopedia of Latin American & Caribbean Art. Edited by Jane Turner. London: Macmillan; New York: Grove's Dictionaries, 2002. 782p. (Series: *Grove Library of World Art*; *Grove Encyclopedias of the Arts of the Americas*.)

One of several "spin off" publications of the 34-volume *Grove Dictionary of Art*, includes many updated and substantially revised versions of the original *Dictionary of Art*'s essays, along with additional biographical entries on contemporary artists and updated bibliographies throughout.

Gerón, Cándido. *Enciclopedia de las Artes Plásticas Dominicas: 1844–2000*. [Dominican Republic?]: Editora Corripio, 2000. 737p.

Hundreds of color reproductions of individual works precede biographical sketches of major and minor artists who currently work or who have been active in the Dominican Republic.

Latin American and Caribbean Art: MoMA at El Museo. Edited by Miriam Basilio, et al. New York: El Museo del Barrio and the Museum of Modern Art, 2004. 184p.

Works by major and lesser-known artists of Latin America and the Caribbean, drawn from the collection of MoMA (N.Y.), and a fascinating account of the history of MoMA's extensive collection of Latin American artists' works.

Latin American Art in the Twentieth Century. Edited by Edward J. Sullivan. London: Phaidon, 2000. 352p. (Originally published: 1996.)

Edward Sullivan, preeminent historian of Latin American art, coordinated and edited this volume of country studies by experts in the field. Contents: Mexico; Central America; Cuba; Dominican Republic; Puerto Rico; Venezuela; Colombia; Ecuador; Peru; Brazil; Bolivia; Paraguay; Uruguay; Argentina; Chile; Chicano Art.

Tovar de Teresa, Guillermo. *Repertory of Artists in Mexico: Plastic and Decorative Arts*. [Mexico]: Grupo Financiero Bancomer, 1995–1997. 3 vols. (Translation of *Repertorio de Artistas en México*.)

Approximately 600 artists (including architects) are profiled. Each essay well-illustrated with color plates, bibliography. Colonial through 20th century artists included.

Shipp, Steve. *Latin American and Caribbean Artists of the Modern Era: A Biographical Dictionary of More Than 12,700 Persons*. Jefferson, N.C.: McFarland, 2003. 864p.

Entries include basic biography, bibliographical references, exhibitions, and private and public collections. Appendices include Artists listed by country; Chronology of exhibitions; Museums (directory); Galleries (directory); Bibliography.

Poland

Sokol, Stanley S. *The Artists of Poland: A Biographical Dictionary From the 14th Century to the Present.* Jefferson, N.C.: McFarland, 2000. 263p.

Brief biographical entries include references to other published works.

Portugal

Tannock, Michael. *Portuguese 20th Century Artists: A Biographical Dictionary.* Chichester, Eng.: Phillimore, 1978. 188p.

Basic biographical details on over 2,000 artists active between 1900 and 1974. Entries include names and dates, media, exhibition history and awards.

Russia and the Soviet Union

Milner, John. *A Dictionary of Russian and Soviet Artists, 1420–1970.* Woodbridge, Suffolk: Antique Collectors' Club, 1993. 483p.

Presents biographical entries ranging in length from a few sentences to several pages, depending upon the stature of the subject artist. Artists known for work in other fields (e.g., film, theatre design, etc.) included. Most entries include selected bibliography for further research, as well as an indication of public collections.

South Africa

Ogilvie, Grania. *The Dictionary of South African Painters and Sculptors, Including Namibia.* Johannesburg, South Africa: Everard Read, 1988. 799p.

Detailed biographical information on "over 1,800 artists who were born, lived in, or are presently living in South Africa or Namibia [Introduction]." Entries include education, profile (memberships in art societies, teaching positions, other positions in art-related fields, etc.), exhibitions, awards, representation, public commissions, publications by and about the subject artist.

Spain

Bonet, Juan Manuel. *Diccionario de las Vanguardias en España, 1907–1936.* Madrid: Alianza Editorial, 1995. 654p.

Dictionary of movements in literature, the visual and interrelated arts. Includes a great many biographical entries, many cross references.

Spanish Artists from the Fourth to the Twentieth Century: A Critical Dictionary: Frick Art Reference Library. New York: G.K. Hall, 1993–96. 4 vols.

The Frick Art Reference Library's authority file of Spanish artists includes nearly 90,000 names. This published version of the authority file serves as a master index to additional sources of information on the subject artist. Many of the basic biographical sources listed in this chapter, and a great many additional, more specialized sources are included among the references.

United States

Dawdy, Doris Ostrander. *Artists of the American West: A Biographical Dictionary.* Chicago: Sage Books, [1974]-1985. 3 vols.

Biographical dictionary of artists born before 1900 and active in the Western United States. Entries include birth and death dates, locations of activity, and references to additional biographical sources.

Encyclopedia of American Folk Art. Edited by Gerard C. Wertkin; Lee Kogan, associate editor; in association with the American Folk Art Museum. New York: Routledge, 2004. 612p.

Well-indexed encyclopedic overview of artists, object types and media employed by American folk artists. Entries by experts in the field include good bibliographies for further reading.

Grauer, Paula L. *Dictionary of Texas Artists, 1800–1945.* College Station: Texas A&M University, 1999. 240p.

Short biographical sketches on major and lesser-known artists of Texas. Includes a number of indexes to artists who have exhibited in regional exhibitions, e.g., Annual Houston Artists Exhibition Index, state fairs and the like.

Groce, George C. (George Cuthbert), and David H. Wallace. *The New York Historical Society's Dictionary of Artists in America, 1564–1860.* New Haven: Yale University Press; London: Oxford University Press, 1957. 759p.

Standard reference source for early American artists' biography. Entries include all or some of the following elements: name; dates and places of birth and death; media and subject matter; chronology of residences and exhibitions; pupils, locations and reproductions of representative works.

Heller, Jules, and Nancy G. Heller, eds. *North American Women Artists of the Twentieth Century: A Biographical Dictionary.* New York: Garland, 1995. 612p.

Biographical essays on major and lesser-known women artists. Entries include very selective bibliographies of primary and secondary source materials.

Kort, Carol, and Liz Sonneborn. *A to Z of American Women in the Visual Arts.* New York: Facts on File, 2002. 258p.

Substantial essays on painters, sculptors, photographers and other art professionals. Entries include selective bibliography.

Kovinick, Phil. *An Encyclopedia of Women Artists of the American West.* Austin: University of Texas Press, 1998. 405p.

Biographical encyclopedia of painters, graphic artists and sculptors who had gained some acclaim as "depictors of Western subjects by 1980 [Preface]." Entries range from one-half to several pages, offering references to exhibitions, books, catalogs and some archival sources.

Otfinoski, Steven. *African Americans in the Visual Arts.* New York: Facts on File, 2003. 262p.

Signed essays on artists, illustrators and writers include highly selective bibliography for further research.

Reno, Dawn E. *Contemporary Native American Artists.* Brooklyn, N.Y.: Alliance Publishing, 1995. 230p.

Brief entries include location, media and related arts professions, education, awards, gallery representation and inclusion in public collections.

Rosenak, Chuck. *Museum of American Folk Art Encyclopedia of Twentieth-Century Americana Folk Art and Artists.* New York: Abbeville Press, 1990. 416p.

Biographical entries on artists includes some or all of the following elements: General background; Artistic background; Subject and sources, Materials and techniques; Artistic recognition.

_____, and Jan Rosenak. *Contemporary American Folk Art: A Collector's Guide.* New York: Abbeville, 1996. 320p.

Offers some practical tips for the beginning collector, followed by regional overviews of folk artists and museum and gallery guides. Brief biographical entries on individual artists include information on where to see, and where to buy works by the subject artist.

Sellen, Betty-Carol, with Cynthia J. Johanson. *Self Taught, Outsider, and Folk Art: A Guide to American Artists, Locations and Resources.* Jefferson, N.C.: McFarland, 2000. 326p.

Overview of sources for the study of outsider art. Contents: Galleries; Fairs and festivals; Auctions; Art centers; Museums, libraries, archives; Exhibitions; Organizations; Publications; Educational opportunities; Artists. Updates and supplements the author's *20th Century American Folk, Self-Taught, and Outsider Art* (New York: Neal-Schuman, 1993.)

Sharylen, Maria. *Artists of the Pacific Northwest: A Biographical Dictionary, 1600–1970.* Jefferson, N.C.: McFarland, 1993. 252p.

Brief entries on artists who have "actively worked within the geographical boundaries of Oregon, Washington, Idaho, British Columbia and Alaska prior to 1970 [Introduction]." Some exhibitions, public collections, association memberships indicated.

Who Was Who in American Art, 1564–1975: 400 Years of Artists in America. Edited by Peter Hastings Falk. 3 vols. Madison, Conn.: Sound View Press, 1999. 3,724p.

Biographical dictionary. Each entry includes some or all of the following elements: name, birth and death dates; profession; education (colleges, art schools); exhibitions; works in public collections; additional comments; some signature and monogram samples.

Collectors' Manuals and Conservation Handbooks

Some of the standard manuals, intended for the serious collector and connoisseur, go into considerable detail about their subject media; similarly, most provide good quality images that are indispensable for conveying information about visual arts media and methods. The following entries represent some of the better guides for serious collectors of art. General guides of interest to collectors of all media, periods and styles are identified first. More specialized handbooks, arranged by media, follow.

Conservation Concerns: a Guide for Collectors and Curators. Edited by Konstanze

Bachmann. New York: Cooper-Hewitt National Museum of Design; Washington, D.C.: Smithsonian Institution Press, 1992. 149p.

Collection of essays by leaders in the field of collection management, assessment and conservation. In addition to basics of good storage practices and emergency planning, essays include material on the conservation of various media including works on paper, photographs, textiles, paintings, furniture and artifacts.

David, Carl. *Collecting and Care of Fine Art.* New York: Crown, 1981. 148p.

This short primer includes some good basic information (for the beginning collector). Topics include provenance, signatures, restoration, fakes and experts, insurance, appraisals, tax issues and more.

Fine Art Collector's Guide to Securing, Preserving and Conserving Works of Art, Including Tax Planning. Edited by Axel von Saldern. [New York?]: Nordstern Insurance Company of America, 1996. 106p.

Practical guidance for the fine art collector. Partial contents: Securing private art collections; Care of paintings; Framing & hanging; Works on paper & photographs; Books; Wooden sculptures; Furniture; Metals; Ceramics & glass; Ivories; Carpets & textiles; Packing & shipping; Legal aspects of owning art.

Frank, Jeanne. *Discovering Art: A User's Guide to the World of Collecting.* New York: Thunder's Mouth Press, 1997.

Basic primer on collecting art for the novice collector. Discusses the basics of auction, commercial gallery and other sales venues. Offers practical advice on provenance, authentication and fakes, care and framing.

Samuels, Peggy. *Everyone's Guide to Buying Art.* Englewood Cliffs, N.J.: Prentice-Hall, 1984. 268p.

Offers practical information on art acquisition, including everything from selecting to tax implications of art collection. Partial contents: How to buy winners in art; Whether to specialize; Categories of condition; Theory of appraisal; Auctions; Reporting dealers' sales.

See also *The Winterthur Guide to Caring for Your Collection*, p. 119.

Specialized Reference Sources (Medium-Specific)

This section includes references to published works that can assist in the identification of works of art. Most are very widely held in libraries,[3] and all deal with a single medium (e.g., painting, sculpture).

PAINTING: BIBLIOGRAPHY

Clement, Russell T. *Les Fauves: A Sourcebook.* Westport, Conn.: Greenwood Press, 1994. 683p.

Extensive bibliography on Fauvism precedes individuals artists' entries: Raoul Dufy; Georges Roualt; Maurice de Vlaminck; André Derain; Kees van Dongen; Albert Marquet; Emile-Othon Friesz; Charles Camoin; Henri Manguin; Jean Puy; Louis Valtat. Artist entries include biographical sketch, chronology, and bibliography including archival materials, books, articles, audiovisual materials, individual and group exhibitions.

_____, and Annick Houze. *Neo-Impressionist Painters: A Sourcebook on Georges Seurat, Camille Pissarro, Paul Signac, Theo Van Rysselberghe, Henri Edmond Cross, Charles Angrand, Maximilien Luce, and Albert Dubois-Pillet.* Westport, Conn.: Greenwood Press, 1999. 396p.

Each subject artist entry provides a short biographical sketch, chronology and bibliography including references to: Archival materials; Books; Articles; Individual exhibitions; Group exhibitions.

Cutul, Ann-Marie. *Twentieth-Century European Painting: A Guide to Information Sources.* Detroit: Gale Research, 1980. 520p.

Classified, annotated bibliography and research guide for the serious scholar and collector. Includes major reference works, exhibition catalogs, writings by and about subject artists.

Fredeman, William E. *Pre-Raphaelitism: A Bibliocritical Study.* Cambridge: Harvard University Press, 1965. 327p.

Scholarly, annotated bibliography of works on major and minor Pre-Raphaelite artists. Includes overview of public collections, individual artists' exhibitions, artists' illustrations in books and periodicals, sales information and sources for researching provenance.

Keaveney, Sydney Starr. *American Painting: A Guide to Information Sources.* Detroit: Gale Research, 1974. 260p.

Annotated bibliography of sources for the study of American painting. Partial contents: General reference sources; General histories and surveys; Early painting in America; Nineteenth century American painting; Modern painting: the twentieth century; Individual artists; Early writings on American art.

Lucus, Samuel Thomas. *Bibliography of Water Colour Painting and Painters.* London: White Lion, 1976. 132p.

Classified, annotated bibliography of writings on watercolor painting, pre–1700 through the 20th century. Section on "Societies and groups" provides references to published histories of British and American watercolor painting societies.

Sullivan, Mark White. *The Hudson River School: An Annotated Bibliography.* Metuchen, N.J.: Scarecrow Press, 1991. 225p.

Annotated bibliography includes references to books, exhibition catalogs, journal articles. General works precede section on individual artists including: Albert Bierstadt; Frederic E. Church; Thomas Cole; Jasper Cropsey; Thomas Doughty; Asher B. Durand; Sanford R. Gifford; Martin J. Heade; George Inness; John F. Kensett; Fitz Hugh Lane; Homer D. Martin; Thomas Moran; Worthington Whittredge; Alexander H. Wyant. Author-Subject indexes.

Weisberg, Yvonne M.L., and Gabriel P. Weisberg. *The Realist Debate: A Bibliography of French Realist Painting, 1830–1885.* New York: Garland, 1984. 213p. (Series: *Garland Reference Library of the Humanities*, vol. 473.)

Annotated bibliography of books, catalogues, articles, dissertations and reviews, arranged by material type. Author and subject indexes.

Wind, Barry. *Genre in the Age of the Baroque: A Resource Guide.* New York: Garland, 1991. 178p.

Highly selective, annotated bibliography of writings on the Baroque. Formats include books, exhibition catalogs, and journal articles. Geographic coverage includes Italy, Spain, France and the Low Countries. Author and subject indexes.

PAINTING: COLLECTORS' MANUALS

Carr, Dawson W. *Looking at Paintings: A Guide to Technical Terms.* Malibu, Calif.: J. Paul Getty Museum in association with British Museum Press, 1992. 84p.

Described as a "guide for the museum visitor who wishes to know more about the materials and techniques of paintings," this short primer is an excellent, nicely illustrated guide for the beginning researcher.

Keck, Caroline K. *A Handbook on the Care of Paintings: For Historical Agencies and Small Museums.* [Nashville, Tenn.]: American Association for State and Local History, 1965.132p.

Basic primer on collection maintenance techniques for the curator and collector. Contents: Anatomy of paintings: pastel, watercolor, gouache; Anatomy of paintings: Oil on fabric and solid supports; Laboratory examination and treatment; Conservation priorities and procedures.

_____. *How to Take Care of Your Paintings: The Art Owner's Guide to Preservation and Restoration.* New York: Scribner's, 1978. 96p.

Contents: Structural composition of a canvas painting; Small troubles and what to do about them; Cleaning a painting on your own; Varnishing and other finishing touches; Familiar misfortunes and how to prevent some of them; Serious trouble and important first aid; How a painting can change without any apparent cause; What happens when a painting is restored.

PAINTING: SELECTED COUNTRY STUDIES

The following sources include survey texts, exhibition and museum catalogs. They have been selected for their usefulness in identifying styles, periods, and individual artists' painted works.

Asian Countries

Akiyama, Terukaz. *Japanese Painting.* Geneva: Skira; New York: Rizzoli, 1977. 216p. (Series: *Treasures of Asia.*)

Survey text on Japanese painting from pre–Buddhist era through the 19th century.

Barnart, Richard M. *Along the Border of Heaven: Sung and Yüan Paintings from the C.C. Wang Family Collection.* New York: Metropolitan Museum of Art, 1983.

Richly illustrated catalog of a major collection of paintings dating from the 10th century.

_____. *Painters of the Great Ming: The Imperial Court and the Zhe School.* Dallas, Texas: Dallas Museum of Art, 1993. 360p.

Scholarly catalog surveys the development of Ming painting. Partial contents: Foundation of Ming painting; Visions of grandeur: The life and art of Dai Jin; Great masters of the Ming Court and the Zhe School.

Cahill, James. *Chinese Painting*. New York: Rizzoli; [Geneva]:Skira, 1977. 211p. (Series: *Treasures of Asia*.)

Chronological survey of Chinese painting by a noted scholar and curator. Covers Chinese painting from the 2nd through 18th centuries.

Cho, Cha-yong. *Traditional Korean Painting: A Lost Art Rediscovered*. [Translated by John Bester.] Tokyo and New York: Kodansha International, 1990. 176p.

Superb color plates precede scholarly essays on primarily 19th and 20th century Korean painted works.

Fong, Wen. *Beyond Representation: Chinese Painting and Calligraphy, 8th—14th Century*. New York: Metropolitan Museum of Art; New Haven: Yale University Press, 1992. 549p. (Series: *Princeton Monographs in Art and Archaeology*, 48.)

Partial contents: Of the human world: Narrative representation; Of nature and art: Monumental landscape; Art of the scholar-officials; Sung Imperial art; Introspection and lyricism: Southern Sung painting; Some Buddhist and Taoist themes; Yüan Renaissance; Revival and synthesis: Yüan literati painting.

Japanese Modern Art: Painting from 1910 to 1970. Edited by Irmtraud Schaarscmidt-Richter. Zurich and New York: Edition Stemmle, 2000. 207p.

Published in conjunction with an exhibition at the Japan Foundation (New York). Traces the evolution of painting in Japan during the first three-quarters of the 20th century. Partial contents: Growth of modern Japanese painting; Burgeoning of abstraction in Japanese art after 1910; Japanese Surrealism in the late 1930s: The "space of formless matter" and the "space of macroscopic creatures;" Japanese art in the 1950s and 1960s.

Sirén, Osvald. *Chinese Painting: Leading Masters and Principles*. New York: Ronald Press, 1956– . 7 vols.

Classic study of Chinese painting from its earliest history through the Late Ming period. Includes two volumes of plates.

Australia and New Zealand

Australian Painters of the Twentieth Century. Selected and edited by Lou Klepac. Sydney: Beagle Press, 2000. 252p.

Presents the work of a representative selection of 19 painters, with an emphasis on artists active during the century's middle years. Good quality color reproductions.

Docking, Gil. *Two Hundred Years of New Zealand Painting*. Wellington: A.H. & A.W. Reed, [1971]. 212p.

Encyclopedic survey of two centuries of New Zealand painting, commencing with the earliest commissioned artists included among the first settlers. Well illustrated with good quality tipped-in color plates.

Dunn, Michael. *Contemporary Painting in New Zealand*. Australia, N.S.W.: Craftsman House, 1996. 235p.

Profiles the work of 48 painters, with a focus on works created during the first half of the 1990s.

_____. *New Zealand Painting: A Concise History*. Auckland, N.Z.: Auckland University Press, 2003. 218p.

Brief introductory chapters on colonial and Victorian landscape precede more in-depth analyses of primarily 20th century movements and styles.

Johnson, Vivien. *Aboriginal Artists of the Western Frontier: A Biographical Dictionary*. Roseville East, N.S.W.: Craftsman House, 1994. 137p.

Brief overview precedes individual biographical sketches of Aboriginal artists. Appendices include "Guide to artists by community" and "Artists' dreamings—Yuendumu."

McCulloch, Susan. *Contemporary Aboriginal Art: A Guide to the Rebirth of an Ancient Culture*. Honolulu: University of Hawaii, 1999. 240p.

Geographically arranged survey of contemporary Aboriginal art, very well illustrated. Partial contents: Introduction to contemporary Aboriginal art; Central and Western Desert; the Kimberley; Arnhem Land; Urban and new forms of art; Buyer's guide.

Smith, Bernard. *Australian Painting, 1788–2000*. 4th ed. South Melbourne, Vic.: Oxford University Press, 2001. 630p.

Encyclopedic history of Australian art, from 1788 through 2000, with an emphasis on the 20th century.

Terry, Martin. *Maritime Paintings of Early Australia, 1788–1900*. Carlton South, Vic.: Melbourne University Press, 1998. 111p.

Australia has produced a great many painters of maritime subjects, and this is one of the most comprehensive surveys of this often overlooked genre. Organized thematically (shipwrecks, emigration, etc.), very well illustrated, with a good bibliography of further research.

Canada

Duval, Paul. *Canadian Impressionism*. Toronto: McClelland & Stewart, 1990. 166p.

Primarily a compilation of bio-critical essays on major and lesser-known Canadian Impressionists.

Harper, J. Russell. *Painting in Canada: A History*. 2nd ed. Toronto: University of Toronto Press, 1977. 463p.

Historical survey of three centuries of Canadian painting. Partial contents: French colony, 1665–1759; English colonial period 1759–1867; New Dominion 1867–1910; Nationalism and internationalism after 1910.

Lowrey, Carol, curator. *Visions of Light and Air: Canadian Impressionism, 1885–1920*. New York: Americas Society Art Gallery, 1995. 152p.

Presents a fascinating account of the introduction and reception of the Impressionist tradition in Canada. Each of the major Canadian Impressionists is represented by at least one good quality color reproduction, a well-chosen bibliography and a brief biographical sketch.

Reid, Dennis R. *A Concise History of Canadian Painting*. Toronto: Oxford University Press, 1973. 319p.

Standard historical survey of painting in Canada from the 17th century through the 1960s. Substantive, illustrated chapters on Canada's most important painters.

France

Conisbee, Philip. *Painting in Eighteenth-Century France.* Ithaca, N.Y.: Cornell University Press, 1981. 223p.

Contents: The artist's world; Religious painting; History painting; Portraiture; Minor genres; Landscape.

Eitner, Lorenz. *French Paintings of the Nineteenth Century; Part I: Before Impressionism.* Washington, D.C.: National Gallery of Art, 2000.

Like other volumes of the National Gallery's Systematic Catalog, provides very detailed analysis of works, including extensive notes on condition, attribution, and provenance. Included are a number of anonymous 19th century genre and portrait painters.

Leymarie, Jean. *French Painting: The Nineteenth Century.* [Geneva]: Skira, [1962]. 229p.

Surveys the evolution of French painting from David and Ingres through the Impressionists. Beautifully illustrated with tipped-in plates. Contents: Classical nostalgia; Romantic exaltation; Rise of landscape painting; Battle of realism; Impressionist revolution.

The New Painting, Impressionism, 1874–1886: An Exhibition Organized by the Fine Arts Museums of San Francisco with the National Gallery of Art, Washington. Directed and coordinated by Charles S. Moffett. San Francisco: The Museums, [1986]. 507p.

Exhibition catalog with excellent reproductions, reprints of primary material and supporting documents, organized around the original eight exhibitions of Impressionist painting.

Paintings in the Musée d'Orsay. Edited by Serge Lemoine. [translation of *Peinture au Musée d'Orsay.*] New York: Abrams, 2004. 767p.

This exquisitely produced inventory groups this collection of French paintings chronologically, with each period explored in-depth by one of a series of experts in the field.

Rathbone, Eliza E., and George T.M. Shackelford. *Impressionist Still Life.* [Washington, D.C.]: Phillips Collection in Association with Harry N. Abrams, 2001. 240p.

Each work included in this major exhibition catalog is accompanied by a substantial essay. Includes works by all of the major and a few of the less well-known French Impressionist painters.

Tinterow, Gary, and Henri Loyrette. *Origins of Impressionism.* New York: Metropolitan Museum of Art, 1994. 486p.

Exhibition catalog published on the occasion of an exhibition at the Metropolitan Museum. Introductory essays survey various themes represented in the salons commencing in 1859. Catalog entries, fully documented, are arranged by artists' names.

Wine, Humphrey. *The Seventeenth Century French Paintings.* London: National Gallery; Dist. by Yale University Press, 2001. 438p.

This extensive catalog of the National Gallery's collection includes a chapter on the collection's assembly, with extensive technical and attribution notes on each work.

Germany and Austria

Austrian Painting 1945–1995: The Essl Collection. Munich and New York: Prestel, 1996. 296p.

This major collection of Austrian paintings includes major as well as lesser-known Austrian artists of the postwar period. All works illustrated in color; includes artist biographies and chronologies.

Finke, Ulrich. *German Painting from Romanticism to Expressionism*. London: Thames and Hudson, 1974. 256p.

Chronological overview of German painting organized around brief biographical entries on major and lesser-known artists. Contents: Romanticism; Late Romantic painting 1830–50; From realism to Impressionism; Transition to the twentieth century.

Roh, Franz. *German Painting in the 20th Century*. Greenwich, Conn.: New York Graphic Society, 1968. 259p.

Short surveys of major trends and movements in German art, including German Impressionism; Divisionism; Expressionism; Blaue Reiter; Dadaism; Surrealism; Abstraction.

Stärk, Beate. *Contemporary Painting in Germany*. Roseville East, N.S.W.: Craftsman House; G+B Arts International, 1994. 253p.

Well-illustrated overview of contemporary German painting in the form of lengthy biographical sketches on major artists. For each artist, provides basic biographical details, selective exhibition record, collections, and selected bibliography.

Vaughan, William. *German Romantic Painting*. 2nd ed. New Haven and London: Yale University Press, 1994. 260p.

Well-illustrated survey, intended "to provide an introduction to a subject that is little studied in the English speaking world. [Preface.]" Partial contents: Painter's Germany, 1800–50; Classicism and Expressionism; Philipp Otto Runge; Caspar David Friedrich; Naturalism and the naïve; Nazarenes; Legends and fairy-tales; Art and propaganda.

Vergo, Peter. *Twentieth-Century German Painting: The Thyssen-Bornemisza Collection*. London: Sotheby's, 1992. 386p.

Catalogue raisonné of an important collection. Numerous works by major artists are illustrated and fully documented. Excellent source for the identification of major German artists' works.

United Kingdom

Cherry, Deborah. *Painting Women: Victorian Women Artists*. London and New York: Routledge, 1993. 275p.

In-depth social history of women painters in Victorian England, by a noted historian and curator.

Child, Dennis. *Painters in the Northern Counties of England and Wales*. 2nd ed. Leeds: Dennis Child, 2002. 335p.

Excellent starting point for research, particularly for lesser-known artists of England and Wales. Entries include basic biographical facts, subjects and media, an indication of the artist's sales activity, and pointers to additional sources of information, including exhibition sources, dictionaries and other reference tools.

Crookshank, Anne. *Painters of Ireland, 1660–1920.* 2nd ed. London: Barrie & Jenkins, 1979. 303p.

Chronologically arranged survey of portrait, landscape, genre and decorative painting styles and movements from the 17th through early 20th centuries.

Hardie, William R. *Scottish Painting, 1837 to the Present.* 2nd ed. London: Studio Vista, 1990. 223p.

Overview of Scottish painters' work from early Victorian period through the 20th century. Extensive references to books and periodicals for further research.

Holsby, Julian, and Paul Harris. *The Dictionary of Scottish Painters 1600–1960.* Edinburgh: Canongate, 1990. 236p.

Very brief biographies of major and lesser-known Scottish painters. Some entries include example of artist's signature or monogram.

Macmillan, Duncan. *Painting in Scotland: The Golden Age.* Oxford: Phaidon, 1986. 206p.

Published in conjunction with a large exhibition at the University of Edinburgh and the Tate Gallery, London, this scholarly, well-illustrated catalog provides a good overview of portraiture and landscape painting from the late 18th through 19th centuries.

Mallalieu, Huon. *The Dictionary of Watercolour Artists Up to 1920.* 3rd ed. Woodbridge: Antique Collectors' Club, 2002. 2 vols.

Basic biography of major and lesser-known British watercolor artists. Entries include description of the artist's watercolor oeuvre, institutional collections, and bibliographical references. Some very obscure artists included.

McKonkey, Kenneth. *British Impressionism.* New York: Abrams, 1989. 160p.

In this survey of the Impressionist tradition in Britain, the author investigates major and lesser-known English artists' contact with works by the French Impressionists and their reception in the British art world of the 19th and early 20th centuries.

National Gallery of Art (U.S.). *British Paintings of the Sixteenth Through Nineteenth Centuries.* Washington, D.C.: National Gallery; [New York]: Cambridge University Press, 1992. 407p.

Arranged in alphabetical order by name of artist, this inventory of the National Gallery's illustrious collection serves as an excellent resource for the identification of artists' styles. Each work is fully documented, with technical notes (condition) as well as provenance.

National Gallery of Ireland. *Irish Paintings in the National Gallery of Ireland.* Volume 1 [of 3]. Dublin: National Gallery of Ireland, 2001– .

This survey of paintings by Irish artists includes multiple works by some of Ireland's best-known painters. In all it lists 222 works, with full documentation, artist biography, etc., making this a good source for the study of Irish painting.

Prettejohn, Elizabeth. *The Art of the Pre-Raphaelites.* Princeton, N.J.: Princeton University Press, 2000. 304p.

Historical overview of the landscape and narrative paintings of the Pre-Raphaelite artists, including technique, working methods and short biographical entries on named artists.

Redgrave, Richard, and Samuel Redgrave. *A Century of British Painters.* Ithaca, N.Y.: Cornell University Press, 1981. 612p. (Series: *Landmarks in Art History.*) Reprint; originally published 1947.

Stewart, Brian, and Mervyn Cutten. *The Dictionary of Portrait Painters in Britain up to 1920.* Woodbridge, Suffolk: Antique Collectors' Club, 1997. 502p.

Brief biographical essays include bibliographical references, collections, and in some cases, references to engravers who produced copies of the subject artist's work.

Tickner, Lisa. *Modern Life & Modern Subjects: British Art in the Early Twentieth Century.* New Haven, Conn.: Yale University Press, 2000. 336p.

Traces the modernist movement in British painting from the 1914 exhibition of contemporary works at the Whitechapel Art Gallery. Provides analyses of major works by Walter Sickert, Augustus John, Wyndham Lewis, Vanessa Bell and David Bomberg.

Waterhouse, Ellis Kirkham. *The Dictionary of British 18th Century Painters in Oils and Crayons.* Woodbridge: Antique Collectors' Club, 1981. 443p.

Biographical sketches include details on major and lesser-known artists, subjects, media, and indications of engraved versions of the paintings along with bibliographic references.

_____. *Painting in Britain, 1530 to 1790.* 5th ed. New Haven, Conn.: Yale University Press, 1994. 394p.

When Time Began to Rant and Rage: Figurative Painting from Twentieth-Century Ireland. Edited by James Christen Steward. London: Merrell Holberton, 1998. 288p.

This scholarly exhibition catalog includes several introductory essays that trace the evolution of Irish painting from the early 19th through late 20th centuries.

Wilton, Andrew. *Five Centuries of British Painting: From Holbein to Hodgkin.* London: Thames & Hudson, 2001. 256p. (Series: *World of Art.*)

Brief survey of British painting, from Renaissance portraiture of the 16th century through late 20th century styles.

Wood, Christopher. *Victorian Painters.* 3rd ed. Woodbridge, Suffolk: Antique Collectors' Club, 1995. 2 vols. (Series: *Dictionary of British Art*, Vol. 4.)

Biographical dictionary of major and lesser-known Victorian painters. Entries include bibliographical references, indications of society memberships.

Latin America

Pintura Latinoamericana: Proyecto Cultural, los Colegios y el Arte: Breve Panorama de la Modernidad Figurativa en la Primera Mitad del Siglo XX. Buenos Aires, Argentina: Banco Velox, 1999. 493p.

Presents one or more examples of major and lesser known artists of Latin American countries. Good quality reproductions make this an excellent resource for the identification of artists. Includes short biographical essay on each artist.

Low Countries

Leymarie, Jean. *Dutch Painting.* [Geneva and New York]: Skira, [1956].
Historical survey of major 17th century Dutch painters, illustrated with very good quality plates.

Looking at Seventeenth-Century Dutch Art: Realism Reconsidered. Cambridge and New York: Cambridge University Press, 1997. 274p.
Series of essays on Dutch art and art historiography by leading experts in the field.

Maere, J. de, and M. Wabbes. *Illustrated Dictionary of 17th Century Flemish Painters.* Brussels: Renaissance du Livre, 1994. 3 vols.
Brief biographies of artists, including lesser-known genre painters of the 17th century. Entries include biographical basics, bibliography, institutional collections, and in some cases, signature or monogram examples.

National Gallery (Great Britain). *The Dutch School, 1600–1900.* 2nd ed. rev. and expanded by Christopher Brown. London: National Gallery, 1991. 2 vols.
Provides extensive documentation, including provenance, technical conservation notes, and bibliographical references for Dutch paintings in the collection of the National Gallery.

Slive, Seymour. *Dutch Painting 1600–1800.* New Haven, Conn.: Yale University Press, 1995. 378p.
In-depth analyses of major artists' lives and works, as well as chapters devoted to various genres: landscape, marine, still life, etc.

Spicer-Durham, Joaneath Ann. *Masters of Light: Dutch Painters in Utrecht During the Golden Age.* Baltimore: Walters Art Gallery; [San Francisco]: Fine Arts Museums of San Francisco; New Haven : Distributed by Yale University Press, 1997. 480p.
Essays on 17th century painting in Utrecht precede beautifully illustrated entries for each work in this major exhibition. For each work, full description, provenance and bibliographic references for further research; for many works, related source material identified.

Spain

Lassaigne, Jacques. *Spanish Painting.* [Geneva and New York]: Skira, [1952]. 2 vols.
Like other national surveys published by Skira, offers a readable but scholarly account of painting in Spain. Vol. 1: From the Catalan Frescos to El Greco; Vol. 2: From Velazquez to Picasso.

Post, Chandler Rathfon. *A History of Spanish Painting.* Cambridge, Mass.: Harvard University Press, 1930–1966. 14 vols. in 20.
Classic multi-volume survey text traces the development of painting in Spain from medieval period through Renaissance in Castille. Includes extensive bibliographies.

Switzerland

Deuchler, Frorens. *Swiss Painting: From the Middle Ages to the Dawn of the Twentieth Century.* Geneva: Skira; New York: Rizzoli, 1976. 197p.
Partial contents: Swiss art or art in Switzerland? The beginnings of painting;

Late Gothic and Renaissance art; From the baroque era to the age of Enlightenment; Sense of a common heritage from the late eighteenth to the early twentieth century.

United States

Gerdts, William H. *American Impressionism.* Seattle: Henry Art Gallery, University of Washington, 1980. 179p.

History of American Impressionism, beautifully illustrated with many examples by artists including Childe Hassam, John Twachtman, Edmund Tarbell, William Merritt Chase and others.

_____. *Art Across America: Two Centuries of Regional Painting, 1710–1920.* New York: Abbeville Press, 1990. 3 vols.

Richly illustrated survey of regional painting trends in the United States by a major historian of American art. Lengthy essays, arranged by region and subdivided by state, present a chronological survey of major and lesser-known painters and their works.

Henkes, Robert. *Themes in American Painting: A Reference Work to Common Styles and Genres.* Jefferson, N.C.: McFarland, 1993. 260p.

Unlike the typical chronologically-arranged survey, this unique reference work includes survey chapters on various subjects (e.g., the city, wars, etc.) and genres (e.g., still life), each with a well-selected bibliography of books for further investigation.

Lucie-Smith, Edward. *American Realism.* New York: Abrams, 1994. 240p.

Particularly appropriate for the beginning researcher of fine art, provides clearly written survey chapters on various aspects of American realism (primarily painting) from the American Revolution through 20th century.

Museum of Fine Arts, Boston. *American Painting.* Elliot Bostwick Davis, et al. Boston: MFA; New York: Distributed Art Publishers/D.A.P., 2003. 222p. (Series: *MFA Highlights.*)

With the MFA's superlative collection as its basis for discussion, this guide explores themes and styles in American painting from the Colonial era through mid–20th century. Illustrated paintings are supplemented by brief artist biographical sketches.

_____. *American Paintings in the Museum of Fine Arts, Boston: An Illustrated Summary Catalogue.* By Carol Troyen, et al. Boston: Museum of Fine Arts, 1997 360p.

Summary catalog provides an A-Z, illustrated inventory of major and lesser-known American painters' works in the collection of the MFA.

National Gallery of Art. *American Paintings: An Illustrated Catalogue.* Washington, D.C.: National Gallery of Art, 1992. 545p.

Summary catalog of the National Gallery's American painting collection. Small but adequate photographic reproductions include full documentation, provenance, etc. Includes works from Colonial era through mid–20th century.

Prown, Jules David, and Barbara Rose. *American Painting: From the Colonial Period to the Present.* Geneva: Skira; New York: Rizzoli, 1977. 276p.

Oversize survey, revised edition of two-volume study published in 1969. Traces the development of American painting from beginning through 1970s.

Weinberg, H. Barbara, Doreen Bolger and David Park Curry. *American Impressionism and Realism: The Painting of Modern Life, 1885–1915.* New York: Metropolitan Museum of Art, 1994. 384p.
Meticulously researched, well-illustrated exhibition catalog includes a significant amount of source material. Major and lesser-known Impressionists' works included.

SCULPTURE: BIBLIOGRAPHY

Ekdahl, Janis. *American Sculpture: A Guide to Information Sources.* Detroit: Gale, 1977. 260p. (Series: *Art and Architecture Information Guide Series*, vol. 5.)
Somewhat dated but still useful guide to a wide variety of sources for the study of American sculpture. Partial contents: General research tools; Surveys of American sculpture; Folk, primitive and naïve carving; First school of American sculpture; American sculpture in the late nineteenth and early twentieth centuries; Surveys of twentieth-century American sculpture; American sculpture since 1960; Individual sculptors. Author, title and subject indexes.

Wilk, Sarah Blake. *Fifteenth-Century Central Italian Sculpture: An Annotated Bibliography.* Boston: G.K. Hall, 1986. 401p.
Extensive bibliography of primary and secondary sources on 15th century Italian sculpture. Includes writings on individual artists, special topics (e.g., patronage, museum collection, etc.), other reference works.

SCULPTURE: COLLECTORS' MANUALS

Bassett, Jane, and Peggy Fogelman. *Looking at European Sculpture: A Guide to Technical Terms.* Los Angeles: J. Paul Getty Museum in association with the Victoria & Albert Museum, 1997. 103p.
A-Z list of largely technical terminology.

Finn, David. *How to Look at Sculpture.* New York: Abrams, 1989. 144p.
Basic primer on the aesthetics of sculptural works. Partial contents: Different kind of reality; What makes a sculpture great?; Exquisite details; Naked beauty; Material truth and beyond; Living with sculpture.

SCULPTURE: ENCYCLOPEDIAS AND SURVEYS

American Sculpture in the Metropolitan Museum of Art. Edited by Thayer Tolles. New York: The Metropolitan Museum of Art, 1999–2001. 2 vols.
Arranged chronologically by sculptor's birth date, each entry includes a substantial biographical essay, image and documentation on subject work.

Bazin, Germain. *A Concise History of World Sculpture.* Newton Abbot, UK: David & Charles, 1981. 317p.
Basic text on development of sculpture, from prehistoric through the mid–20th century.

Berman, Harold. *Bronzes: Sculptors & Founders, 1800–1930.* Chicago: Abage, 1971–1981. 4 vols.
An essential tool for research in bronze sculpture. Each work fully documented.

Additional reference material: Criteria for evaluation of bronzes; Founders' seals; Identifying characteristics of bronzes and white metals; What is meant by signed, listed, dated and numbers; Characteristics and identification of patinas; Care, cleaning and polishing.

British Sculptors of the Twentieth Century. Edited by Alan Windsor. Aldershot, Eng. and Burlington, Vt.: Ashgate, 2003. 199p.

Brief biographical entries on major and minor sculptors; some bibliographical references, indications of gallery representation and public collections.

Conner, Janis C. *Rediscoveries in American Sculpture: Studio Works, 1893–1939*. Austin: University of Texas Press, 1989. 208p.

Presents an illustrated overview of 20 major and lesser known sculptors' work.

Encyclopedia of Sculpture. Edited by Antonia Boström. New York: Fitzroy Dearborn, 2004. 3 vols.

Truly global survey of individual sculptors and works, as well as overviews of individual countries, periods and styles. Individual sculptor entries include biography, chronologically-arranged list of major works with their current location, and well-chosen, brief biographies for further research.

Gunnis, Rupert. *Dictionary of British Sculptors, 1660–1851*. New revised ed. London: Murrays Book Sales, 1968. 515p.

Standard reference source for basic biographical information. Some entries include description of selected statues, busts, reliefs, monuments and other sculptural works.

Hammacher, Abraham Marie. *Evolution of Modern Sculpture: Tradition and Innovation*. New York: Abrams, [1969]. 383p.

Survey textbook focusing on 19th and 20th century Western sculpture. A brief chapter on Renaissance sculpture precedes in-depth analyses of various contemporary movements (cubism, constructivism, etc.) illustrated with examples by major and some lesser-known artists.

Hibbard, Howard. *Masterpieces of Western Sculpture from Medieval to Modern*. New York: Harper & Row, 1977. 239p.

Provides a brief history of Western sculpture through quite good, color reproductions of major works from the Middle Ages to the 20th century.

Ivory: An International History and Illustrated Survey. New York: Abrams, 1987. 352p.

International history traces the development of ivory sculpture from ancient times through contemporary. Includes excellent glossary of terms, tips for collectors, basics of care and repair.

Lami, Stanislas. *Dictionnaire des Sculpteurs de l'École Française au Dix-Neuvième Siècle*. Paris: E. Champion, 1914–21. 4 vols. (Reprint: Nendeln, Liechtenstein: Kraus, 1970.)

Standard reference source for biography of major and lesser-known French sculptors. Many entries include references to other sources of biography.

MacKay, James A. *The Dictionary of Western Sculptors in Bronze*. [Woodbridge, Eng.]: Antique Collectors' Club, 1977. 414p.

Provides brief biographical entries with details on various castings, methods of production. Some introductory material of interest to collectors, including patination, signatures and stamps, comments on market values.

Maresca, Frank, and Roger Ricco. *American Vernacular: New Discoveries in Folk, Self-Taught, and Outsider Sculpture*. Boston: Little, Brown, 2002. 303p.

Copious illustrations of works from major public and private collections, this beautiful monograph presents an overview of some unique sculptural works.

Optiz, Glenn B. *Dictionary of American Sculptors: 18th Century to the Present, Illustrated With Over 200 Photographs*. Poughkeepsie, N.Y.: Apollo, 1984.

Basic biographical entries on over 5,000 American sculptors, including some living at date of publication. Entries include birth/death dates, educational background, selected exhibitions, contact addresses of [then] living artists.

Pyke, E.J. *A Biographical Dictionary of Wax Modellers*. Oxford: Clarendon, 1973. 216p.

The definitive reference source on wax modelers of the 18th through 20th centuries. Technical material on wax analysis, inventories of private and public collections, and an A-Z dictionary of artist biographies. Biographical entries include description of technique, list of extant works, details of principal references (including pre–1939 sales records), and bibliographical references.

Rheims, Maurice. *19th Century Sculpture*. New York: Abrams, 1977. 430p. (Translation of the author's *Sculpture au XIX Siècle*.)

One of the very best pictorial surveys of 19th century sculpture — including public works, religious works, portraits, funerary art, and more. Major artists are treated in depth, but many relatively obscure works are included as well.

Rubinstein, Charlotte Streifer. *American Women Sculptors: A History of Women Working in Three Dimensions*. Boston: G.K. Hall, 1990. 638p.

Encyclopedic survey of the lives and contributions of women sculptors in America. Partial contents: Three-dimensional art of the early native Americans; Patience Wright: founding mother of American sculpture; Pioneering American women sculptors, 1800–1875; Gilded Age: 1876–1905; Fauns and fountains — the traditional women sculptors, 1905–1929; Women in the avant-garde, 1905–1929; New Deal; Triumph of abstractions, 1940–1959; High tech and hard edge, the 1960s; The 1980s and beyond.

Sculpture: An Illustrated Catalogue. Washington, D.C.: National Gallery of Art, 1994. 283p.

Illustrated inventory of a major collection, individual artists' works illustrated and fully cataloged.

Sculpture: From Antiquity to the Present Day: From the Eighth Century BC to the Twentieth Century. Edited by Georges Duby and Jean-Luc Daval. Cologne and London: Taschen, 2002.

Survey of Western sculpture originally published in four volumes. Greek and Roman; Late antiquity to the Middle Ages (Romanesque and Gothic); Renaissance, Mannerism, Baroque and Rococo; Modern (19th and 20th centuries).

Watson-Jones, Virginia. *Contemporary American Women Sculptors*. Phoenix, Ariz.: Oryx, 1986. 665p.

Provides biographical details on living [at date of publication] women sculptors. Entries include some or all of the following elements: Education and training; Selected individual and group exhibitions; Selected public collections; Selected private collections; Selected awards; Media; Related professions; Teaching positions; Selected bibliography.

Wittkower, Rudolf. *Sculpture: Processes and Principles.* New York: Harper and Row, 1977. 288p.

Basic textbook on the history of Western sculpture from Antiquity through the mid–20th century.

Drawings and Prints: Bibliography

Abrams, Leslie E. *The History and Practice of Japanese Printmaking: A Selectively Annotated Bibliography of English Language Materials.* Westport, Conn.: Greenwood Press, 1984. 197p.

Annotated bibliography of writings on individual periods (Primitive, Edo, modern), subjects, techniques, and the influence of Eastern art on Western, and vice-versa.

Bridson, Gavin, and Geoffrey Wakeman. *Printmaking & Picture Printing: A Bibliographical Guide to Artistic & Industrial Techniques in Britain 1750–1900.* Oxford: Plough Press; Williamsburg [Va.]: Bookpress, 1984. 250p.

Classified bibliography of writings on technical processes related to printing and printmaking. Section introductions employ a minimum of jargon to describe relatively complex processes in a very clear manner.

Doumato, Lamia. *American Drawing: A Guide to Information Sources.* Detroit: Gale Research, 1979. 246p.

Annotated bibliography. Partial contents: General reference sources; Histories, surveys and general works; Technical handbooks; Nineteenth century; Twentieth century; Individual artists; Periodicals and museum bulletins; Important library Collections; Museums with important collections.

Green, William. *Japanese Woodblock Prints: A Bibliography of Writings from 1822–1992, Entirely or Partly in English Text.* Leiden: Ukiyo-e Books, 1993. 291p.

Classified bibliography of writing on Japanese prints. Includes works on Subjects depicted in prints; Types of prints; Print artists; Dating seals, signatures, and symbols; Care, conservation and repair; Collecting and connoisseurship.

Karpinski, Caroline. *Italian Printmaking, Fifteenth and Sixteenth Centuries: An Annotated Bibliography.* Boston: G.K. Hall, 1987. 305p.

Classified bibliography by an expert in the field. Includes references to works devoted to printmaking in Italy, including the work of German, French and other nations working in Italy.

Ludman, Joan, and Lauris Mason. *Fine Print References: A Selected Bibliography of Print-Related Literature.* Millwood, N.Y.: Kraus International, 1982. 227p.

While lacking annotations, this classified bibliography is extremely useful. Partial contents: Collecting and connoisseurship; History of printmaking; Medium and technique; Museum collections; Private collections; Topical prints: works grouped by subject matter.

_____, and Harriet P. Krauss, compilers. *Old Master Print References: A Selected Bibliography.* White Plains, N.Y.: Kraus, 1986. 279p.

References to more than 3,000 citations, including exhibition catalogs, articles, museum, dealer and other catalogs. While entries lack annotations, still a highly useful tool for researching Old Masters.

Drawings and Prints: Collectors' Manuals

Dolloff, Francis W., and Roy L. Perkinson. *How to Care for Works of Art on Paper.* 4th ed. Boston: Museum of Fine Arts, 1985. 48p.

Basic primer on paper conservation for collectors. Partial contents: History of papermaking; Enemies of paper; Matting and framing; Note on restoration; Materials and services.

Donson, Theodore B. *Prints and the Print Market: A Handbook for Collectors and Connoisseurs.* New York: Thomas Y. Crowell, 1977. 493p.

This comprehensive overview of prints and the print markets includes an excellent chapter on "Spurious print: Fakes, Forgeries and Falsified Proofs." One of the appendices, "Bibliography: A Comprehensive and Definitive Catalogue of Publications on Prints by Familiar Artists and Related Matters," is a good (but not exhaustive) listing of individual printmakers' oeuvre catalogues.

Ellis, Margaret Holben. *The Care of Prints and Drawings.* Nashville, Tenn.: American Association for State and Local History Press, 1987. 253p.

Manual for the professional conservator, includes some information of interest to serious collectors. Contents: Parchment and paper: supports for prints and drawings; Media of prints and drawings; Matting, hinging and framing; Storage and environment; Basic conservation procedures.

Kosek, Joanna M. *Conservation Mounting of Prints and Drawings: A Manual Based on Current Practice at the British Museum.* London: Archetype Publication, 2004. 185p.

Practical manual provides guidance for mounting works on paper. Some scientific information, overview of materials, mounting for display purposes, housing for storage, stamping, studio organization and tools & equipment for conservation lab.

Gascoigne, Bamber. *How to Identify Prints: A Complete Guide to Manual and Mechanical Processes from Woodcut to Ink Jet.* [New York]: Thomas and Hudson, 1991. 208p.

Very clearly written, well-illustrated introduction to various printmaking methods, from traditional to contemporary.

Ivins, William Mills. *How Prints Look: Photographs with a Commentary.* Boston: Beacon Press, 1958, 1943. 164p.

This very well illustrated guide to printmaking processes used detailed photographs of prints to explain the various graphic processes. Includes some very clear examples of fakes and facsimile prints.

Zigrosser, Carl, and Christa M. Gaehde. *A Guide to the Collecting and Care of Original Prints.* Sponsored by the Print Council of America. New York: Crown, [1965]. 120p.

This excellent guide to print collecting and connoisseurship includes a good discussion of original prints, glossary of printmaking terms, and tips for the care and conservation of prints.

Drawings and Prints: Indexes

International Index of Multiples from Duchamp to the Present. Edited by Daniel Buchholz and Gregorio Magnani. Tokyo: Spiral/Wacoal Art Center and Cologne: W. König, 1993. 223p.

Drawings and Prints: Encyclopedias and Surveys

Bartsch, Adam von. *The Illustrated Bartsch.* New York: Abaris Books, 1978- . (Translation of *Peintre Graveur, 1922–1988.*)

The Illustrated Bartsch, based upon Adam von Bartsch's 19th century catalog of prints of Western European countries, is an essential tool for print research. The print version is available in some academic and museum libraries, but recently, ARTstor has made this important resource available in hundreds of additional libraries. ARTstor is a digital image archive consisting of a number of collections, including *The Illustrated Bartsch.* The online version is preferable to the print edition because it is keyword searchable, allowing the user to retrieve images of prints by name of printmaker, iconography, country, etc.

British Sporting and Animal Prints, 1658–1874: A Catalogue Compiled by Dudley Snelgrove. London: Tate Gallery for the Yale Center for British Art, 1981. 257p.

Records prints which span 200 years up to the mid–19th century and provide an extensive pictorial survey of the principal subjects: hunting, shooting, racing, riding and coaching. Chronological table of artists, list of engravers, list of publishers. Catalog entries arranged by artist's name, subdivided by subject matter, list of prints with dimensions, media, publication details and other descriptive elements.

Bury, Michael. *The Print in Italy, 1550–1620.* London: British Museum, 2001. 248p.

Published in conjunction with an exhibition at the British Museum, this beautiful catalog examines the growth of the commercial printmaking industry in Italy from the mid–16th through early 17th centuries.

Carey, Frances, and Antony Griffiths. *The Print in Germany 1880–1933: The Age of Expressionism, Prints from the Department of Prints and Drawings in the British Museum.* London: British Museum, 1984. 272p.

Presents a scholarly survey of printmaking in Germany. Biographical entries on individual artists. Most entries include good bibliographies and a discussion of selected works from the British Museum collection.

Castleman, Riva. *Prints of the Twentieth Century: A History.* New York: Museum of Modern Art, 1976. 216p.

Scholarly history of major 20th century movements, including Expressionism, Cubism, Dada and Surrealism, post–WWII movements, through Pop and Conceptual art.

Eichenberg, Fritz. *The Art of the Print: Art, Masterpieces, History, Techniques.* New York: Abrams, [1976]. 611p.

Encyclopedic history of the print, with very well-illustrated sections on relief, intaglio, lithographic, and silkscreen printmaking processes. Partial contents: Parchment and paper; Supports for prints and drawings; Media of prints and drawings; Matting, hinging, and framing; Storage and environment; Basic conservation procedures.

Goldman, Paul. *Sporting Life: An Anthology of British Sporting Prints.* London: British Museum, 1983. 126p.

Exhibition catalog presents a good selection of sporting prints arranged by subject matter (e.g., horse-racing, hunting). Heavily illustrated, a good tool for identification of prints.

Hults, Linda C. *The Print in the Western World: An Introductory History.* Madison: University of Wisconsin Press, 1996. 948p.

Basic survey textbook on the evolution of printmaking in the Western world. Chronological and geographical arrangement, from pre–Dürer (14th century) through late 20th century. Includes discussion of reproductive prints and their role in disseminating knowledge of Western painting. Excellent "Selected Bibliography of Print Reference Catalogs" arranged by geographic area, including multinational, American, British, French, German, Italian, Netherlandish.

MacKenzie, Ian. *British Prints: Dictionary and Price Guide.* Rev. ed. Woodbridge, Suffolk: Antique Collectors' Club, 1998. 368p.

Provides very brief biographical entries on artists, description of prints, auction price range, bibliographical references, including catalogue raisonné. Includes references to printmakers' reproductions of other artists' works, designated by the term "after."

Melot, Michel. *The Impressionist Print.* New Haven, Conn.: Yale University Press, 1997. 296p. (Translation of *Estampe Impressioniste.*)

Scholarly survey of the painter-printmakers Degas, Cassatt, Renoir, Pissarro, Manet and Whistler. Relates the great interest in printmaking of the period to social and political events, while commenting on the role of the 19th century art market.

Prints. (Essays by Michel Melot, Antony Griffiths and Richard S. Field.) New York: Rizzoli, 1981. 278p.

Surveys the evolution of the print from the earliest woodcut through the contemporary edition. Partial contents: Definition, function and language of the print; Product and work of art; Art of the bourgeoisie; Industrialized pictures and their effect on the print; Art and hand of the printmaker; Contemporary trends.

Siltzer, Frank. *The Story of British Sporting Prints.* 2nd ed., rev. and enl. London: Peter Loveday Prints, 1979. 412p.

Overview of sporting prints, includes biographical essays on major artists along with chronologically arranged catalog of works, including name of engraver, date, dimensions and other descriptive cataloging.

Photography: Periodical Literature Databases

Use the following online databases to identify articles, news items, exhibitions and book reviews on photography-related topics. They're available at many larger public, academic and museum libraries.

Abstracts / Art Full Text (see description, pages 32–33).
ArtBibliographies Modern (see description, page 33).
Design and Applied Arts Index (see description, pg. 118)

Photography: Periodicals

The following journals are among the most important in the field of photography and its history. All are widely held in U.S. libraries. To find additional journals devoted to photography, in libraries that use the Library of Congress Classification System, conduct a subject search using headings like "Photography — Periodicals"; and "Photography, Artistic — Periodicals."

Afterimage. Rochester, N.Y.: 1972– . Bimonthly. ISSN: 0300–7472.
Newsletter format, includes some lengthy feature articles on contemporary as well as historical and vintage photography. Excellent reviews and calendar of forthcoming events, book reviews.

Art on Paper. New York: Fanning Pub., 1998– . Bimonthly. ISSN: 1521–7922.
Excellent source for the researcher of both prints, works on paper, artists' books and photography.

History of Photography. London: Taylor & Francis, 1977– . Quarterly. 0308–7298.
One of the most highly-regarded of the scholarly, peer-reviewed journals devoted to the history of photography and related subjects. Excellent in-depth critical reviews of new books in the field.

Image. Rochester, N.Y.: George Eastman House. 1952– . Frequency varies. ISSN: 0536–5465.
Lengthy articles on topics of interest to photographer and historians of photography. Some issues devoted to specific themes and photographers.

PSA Journal. Oklahoma City, Okla.: 1998– . Monthly. ISSN: 0096–5812.
News of interest to photographers, includes a good deal of reporting on gallery and museum exhibitions.

Photography: Bibliography

To find additional bibliographies in libraries that utilize the Library of Congress Classification System, perform a subject search using headings like "Photography — Bibliography"; "Photography — History — Bibliography"; "Photography — United States— Bibliography."

Barger, M. Susan. *Bibliography of Photographic Processes in Use Before 1880: Their Materials, Processing, and Conservation*. Rochester, N.Y.: Graphic Arts Research Center, Rochester Institute of Technology, 1980. 149p.
Annotated bibliography of technical processes, conservation, etc. of 19th century photography. Entries include author, title, journal information (volume, pages, etc.), keywords, and abstracts. Index by process and material.

Boni, Albert. *Photographic Literature: An International Bibliographic Guide to General and Specialized Literature on Photographic Processes, Techniques, Theory,*

Chemistry, Physics, Apparatus, Materials & Applications, Industry, History, Biography, Aesthetics. Associate editors: Hubbard Ballou, et al. New York: 1962. 335p.

Important overview of the historical literature on photography, covering works published between 1727 and 1960. From the "camera obscura" through the late 1950s, this is an essential bibliography of published works on photography.

_____. *Photographic Literature, 1960–1970: An International Bibliographic Guide to General & Specialized Literature on Photographic Processes, Techniques, Theory, Chemistry, Physics, Apparatus, Materials & Applications, Industry, History, Biography, Aesthetics, etc.* Hastings-on-Hudson, N.Y.: Morgan & Morgan, 1972. 535p.

Subject index to books and periodical articles, with particular emphasis on technical processes. Updates previous entry.

Gernsheim, Helmut. *Incunabula of British Photographic Literature: A Bibliography of British Photographic Literature, 1839–75, and British Books Illustrated with Original Photographs.* London and Berkeley: Scholar Press in association with Derby Lonsdale College of Higher Education, 1984. 159p.

Annotated inventory of albums and published books, compiled by a major scholar of the history of photography.

Johnson, William. *Nineteenth-Century Photography: An Annotated Bibliography, 1839–1879.* Boston: G.K. Hall, 1990. 962p.

Subject access to nearly 21,000 books and periodical titles published between 1839 and 1879. Covers both technical and critical and theoretical works. Extensive coverage of the publications on the history of photography in individual countries.

Kreisel, Martha. *American Women Photographers: A Selected and Annotated Bibliography.* Westport, Conn.: Greenwood Press, 1999. 350p.

Bibliography of works, including books and periodical literature, devoted to the lives and works of women photographers. Major published works are very well annotated and provide an indication of where a particular work has been reproduced.

Lambrechts, Eric, and Luc Salu. *Photography and Literature: An International Bibliography of Monographs.* London and New York: Mansell, 1992. 296 p.

This interesting bibliography provides information on some 3,900 titles, including "books, exhibition catalogues, dissertations, and special issues of magazines. [Scope note]." Included are books with photographers mentioned by name, books containing photographic works by writers, anthologies of writings on photography by a single author, books that deal with the relationship between photography and writing, and a number of other categories.

New York Public Library. Research Libraries. *Photographica: A Subject Catalog of Books on Photography: Includes Books, Pamphlets, and Selected Periodical Articles on Still Photography and Allied Topics.* Boston: G.K. Hall, 1984. 380p.

Photo-reproduction of the New York Public Library card catalog provides subject access to this rich historical collection of reference materials. Note that the library's most recent decades' acquisitions can be searched online: www.nypl.org (select "CATNYP," the catalog of the Research Libraries of NYPL).

Roosens, Laurent, and Luc Salu. *History of Photography: A Bibliography of Books.* London and New York: Mansell, 1989– .

Subject guide to more than 11,000 books on the history of photography, arranged by subject and subdivided, in most cases, chronologically. (One noteworthy exception is the subject heading "Criticism," under which works are arranged alphabetically by author.)

Photography: Collectors' Manuals

To find additional works in libraries that utilize the Library of Congress Classification System, perform a subject search using the heading "Photographs— Collectors and Collecting."

Badger, Gerry. *Collecting Photography.* London: M. Beazley, 2003. 199p.
Good introduction to collecting photography, suitable for the beginning collector. Offers a good deal of practical advice on building a collection, buying and selling, and displaying photographic works. Includes a very good glossary of technical terminology as well as brief biographies of "Key Photographers," including price ranges for their works.

Baldwin, Gordon. *Looking at Photographs: A Guide to Technical Terms.* Malibu, Calif.: J. Paul Getty Museum in association with British Museum Press, 1991. 88p.
Useful for the novice photography researcher, includes very clearly written entries on various photographic processes.

Bennett, Stuart. *How to Buy Photographs.* Oxford: Phaidon / Christie's, 1987. 159p. (Series: *Christie's Collectors Guides.*)
The market for photography has changed considerably since 1987, but this brief guide for collectors of photography is still quite useful. Partial contents: Rarity, taste and technique in photography collecting; Areas of specialization; Modern photography; Buying and selling; Collecting pitfalls: some cautionary tales; Looking after photographs.

Howarth-Loomes, B. E. C. *Victorian Photography: An Introduction for Collectors and Connoisseurs.* New York: St. Martin's Press, 1974. 99p.
Contents: Invention of photography; Daguerrotype; Calotype; Wet plate period; Stereoscopic photography; Cartes-de-visite; Dry plate; Photographic collections; Selected reading list.

Mace, O. Henry. *Collector's Guide to Early Photographs.* 2nd ed. Iola, Wis.: Krause, 1999. 214p.
General overview of vintage photograph collecting for beginning to serious collectors. Includes information on photographic processes and their identification, restoration and conservation, and prices.

The Photograph Collector's Resource Directory. 3rd ed. New York: Photographic Arts Center, 1989. 267p.
Partial contents: Collecting — where to buy photographic art; Looking — museums & other not-for-profits; Reading — books, newsletters & magazines; Caring — conservation, restoration, appraisal.

Witkin, Lee D., and Barbara London. *The Photograph Collector's Guide.* Boston: New York Graphic Society, 1979. 438p.
Excellent source for the serious photography collector. Partial contents: Col-

lector's glossary; Care and restoration of photographs; Selected photographers: a collector's compendium (includes lengthy biography, bibliography, major collections, and signature or other identifying marks).

Photography: Encyclopedias and Surveys

To find additional works of this type in libraries that utilize the Library of Congress Classification System, perform a subject search using headings like "Photography — Encyclopedias"; "Photography — History"; "Photography, Artistic — History."

Browne, Turner. *Macmillan Biographical Encyclopedia of Photographic Artists & Innovators.* London: Collier Macmillan, 1983. 722p.

Biographical dictionary of photographers and related professionals (historians of photography, critics, etc.) includes publications, collections. Dealer representation and contact information now obviously dated.

Darrah, William Culp. *Cartes de Visite in Nineteenth Century Photography.* Gettysburg, Pa: W.C. Darrah, 1981. 221p.

Traces the development and overwhelming popularity of the carte de visite, including an overview of most common subject matter — including portraiture, celebrity portraiture, native peoples of the world, etc. A subject guide to carte de visite, and in-depth information on documentation and interpretation make this an essential tool for the collector of cartes de visite.

Daval, Jean Luc. *Photography, History of an Art.* New York: Skira/Rizzoli, 1982. (Translation of *Histoire d'un Art, la Photographie.*) 269p.

Explores all aspects of photography, from its invention to its relationship with other branches of the visual arts.

The Focal Encyclopedia of Photography. Edited by Leislie Stroebel and Richard Zakia. Boston: Focal Press, 1993. 914p.

Includes some biographical entries (major photographers), but most useful for its coverage of technical material. All articles signed, by experts in the field.

Gernsheim, Helmut. *The Origins of Photography.* London: Thames and Hudson, 1982. 280p.

Revised and expanded edition of this survey by an important historian of photography, originally published in 1955. Surveys the development of photography from earliest techniques.

_____. *The Rise of Photography: 1850–1880, the Age of Collodion.* New York: Thames and Hudson, 1988. 285p.

Good reproductions of vintage photographs by pioneers in the field illustrate the history of the development of photography in the mid–19th century.

McDarrah, Gloria S., Fred W. McDarrah, and Timothy S. McDarrah. *The Photography Encyclopedia.* New York: Schirmer Books, 1999. 689p.

Encyclopedia of biography and technical terms and processes. Includes also listings of: galleries, magazines, manufacturers, museums, Pulitzer Prize winners.

Nadeau, Luis. *Encyclopedia of Printing, Photographic and Photomechanical Processes: A Comprehensive Reference to Reproduction Technologies, Containing Invaluable*

Information on Over 1500 Processes. Fredericton, N.B.: Atelier Luis Nadeau, 1989. 2 vols.

Overview of reproductive technologies, defines approximately 1,500 processes. English and German terms.

Newhall, Beaumont. *The History of Photography: From 1839 to the Present*. Rev. and enl. 5th ed. New York: Museum of Modern Art; Boston: Distributed by Bulfinch Press / Little Brown, 1994. 319p.

Widely available in libraries, this edition of Newhall's history of photography represents an extensive update of the previous editions. Surveys the development of technology along with an overview of major photographers, styles and periods.

On the Art of Fixing a Shadow: One Hundred and Fifty Years of Photography. Washington, D.C.: National Gallery of Art; Chicago: Art Institute of Chicago, 1989. 510p.

Very well-illustrated exhibition catalog traces the development of photography through the late 1980s. Essays by scholars precede hundreds of very good plates, making this an excellent tool for identification of major and lesser-known photographers' works.

Orvell, Miles. *American Photography*. Oxford and New York: Oxford University Press, 2003. 256p. (Series: *Oxford History of Art*.)

Scholarly but very readable history of photography, from the mid–19th century through the late 1990s. Major trends, including photojournalism, treated quite in-depth.

Rosenblum, Naomi. *A History of Women Photographers*. 2nd ed., updated and expanded. New York: Abbeville, 2000. 400p.

Historical survey of women's contribution to the science and art of photography from its earliest years through the 1990s. Survey chapters, arranged chronologically, discuss the emergence of the professional photographer; portraiture; "amateur" photography; photography between the wars; photography as an art form, and contemporary feminist perspectives.

_____. *A World History of Photography*. 3rd ed. New York: Abbeville, 1997. 695p.

Standard textbook on the development and history of photography. Includes chapters devoted to landscape and architecture, early precedents to photojournalism, art photography, the origins of color photography, and a very concise overview of technical history.

Photography: Biographical Sources

To find additional sources of this type in libraries that utilize the Library of Congress Classification System, perform a subject search using headings like "Photographers—Biography"; "Photographers—United States—Biography"; "African American Photographers."

American Photographers: An Illustrated Who's Who Among Leading Contemporary Americans. Edited by Lee Krantz. New York: Facts on File, 1989. 352p.

Brief biographical sketches, including information on subjects, education, awards, and contact information. Dated, but still useful for many photographers.

Auer, Michele. *Encyclopédie Internationale des Photographes de 1839 à Nos Jours = Photographers Encyclopaedia International, 1839 to the Present.* Hermance, Switzerland: Camera Obscura, 1985. 2 vols.

A-Z biographical dictionary offers brief entries on over 1,600 photographers and peripheral artisans (e.g., inventors, reporters, etc.) of the 19th and 20th centuries. Entries include birth and death dates, chronology, bibliography of published works, exhibition history and in many cases, an example of the photographer's signature or monogram.

Contemporary Photographers. Edited by Martin Marix Evans. New York: St. James Press, 1995. 1,234p.

The St. James Press biographical series are among the very best. Now in its third edition, this work provides for each photographer a substantial biographical essay with information on education as well as contact information. Additionally, each has a list of exhibitions, galleries and museums, bibliography of works (by and about), and a critical essay.

Edwards, Gary. *International Guide to Nineteenth-Century Photographers and Their Works: Based on Catalogues of Auction Houses and Dealers.* Boston: G.K. Hall, 1988. 591p.

An excellent finding aid to photographs sold at auction. Each entry includes basic biographical data, along with processes, formats, typical subjects, location of studio, and references to auction and dealer catalogs. Particularly useful for researching lesser-known photographers.

Mautz, Carl. *Biographies of Western Photographers: A Reference Guide to Photographers Working in the 19th Century American West.* Nevada City, Calif.: Carl Maytz Publishing, 1997. 601p.

Arranged by state, subdivided by alphabetical listing of photographers' names. Entries range from very short to one or two paragraphs. Of interest to collectors, includes sections on "Photographers' imprints and information on antique photographs," and "Dating early photographs by format and mount information."

McEuen, Melissa A. *Seeing America: Women Photographers Between the Wars.* Lexington: University Press of Kentucky, 2000. 360p.

Documents the contribution of women photographers, with particular reference to Doris Ulmann, Dorothea Lange, Marion Post, Margaret Bourke-White and Berenice Abbott.

Moutoussamy-Ashe, Jeanne. *Viewfinders: Black Women Photographers.* New York: Writers & Readers, 1993. 201p.

Surveys the lives and work of photography by black women from the mid–19th century through the mid–1980s. Bio-bibliography provides brief entries on each photographer, including dates of activity, source material, studio locations, and other pertinent facts.

Palmquist, Peter E., and Thomas R. Kailbourn. *Pioneer Photographers of the Far West: A Biographical Dictionary, 1840–1865.* Stanford, Calif.: Stanford University Press, 2000. 679p.

In-depth biographical essays on major and lesser-known photographers of the

Western U.S. Includes indications of inclusion in public collections, select bibliographies.

Willis-Thomas, Deborah. *Black Photographers, 1840–1940: An Illustrated Bio-Bibliography*. New York: Garland, 1985. 141p.

An excellent glossary of photographic processes precedes chapters devoted to the subject photographers: Daguerreans, 1840–1859; Daguerreans and photographers, 1860–1899; Photographers, 1900–1919; Photographers, 1920–1940. Well illustrated with reproductions from several major collections.

_____. *An Illustrated Bio-Bibliography of Black Photographers, 1940–1988*. New York: Garland, 1989. 483p.

Continuation of, and modeled on, previous entry.

Biographical Sources

The literature of art history has given rise to a great number of biographical works. Indeed, Giorgio Vasari (1511–1574), often cited as the first Western art historian, is best known for his *Le vite de piu eccellenti architetti, pittori, et scultori italiani, da Cimabue in sino a' tempi nostri* (commonly referred to in the English-speaking world as *Lives of the Artists*), a series of short, chronologically-arranged biographies of the artists of Italy. Today, the art researcher has literally thousands of biographical reference tools at his or her disposal. In this section, the major tools are identified and described, and tips for locating biographical material for established, as well as relatively obscure artists, are offered.

Indexes to Biography

Two good print indexes are the following:

Havlice, Patricia Pate. *Index to Artistic Biography*. Metuchen, N.J.: Scarecrow Press, 1973. 2 vols. 1,362p. (Supplements: 1981; 2002.)

Index to 64 major biographical reference works. Entries include names, dates, nationality, and media, references to biographical sources.

Mallett, Daniel Trowbridge. *Mallett's Index of Artists, International-Biographical; Including Painters, Sculptors, Illustrators, Engravers and Etchers of the Past and the Present*. New York: P. Smith, 1948 [1935].

Index to biographical and bibliographical information, earlier equivalent to Havlice's *Index to Artistic Biography* (see previous entry).

Many libraries provide access to indexes and increasingly, to full-text, computerized sources of biographical reference materials. In addition to these, some quite good, free-of-charge sources can be located on the Internet. One of the most valuable of the latter is the Getty Research Institute's *Union List of Artists' Names* (*ULAN*), discussed below along with two other online tools. *ULAN* stands out as a very powerful index to some of the major biographical tools described later.

Biography and Genealogy Master Index. Detroit: Gale Research, 1980– . Electronic Version: Farmington Hills, Mich.: Gale, 2001–).

One of the most valuable sources for researching artists' biographies, or any biography, is the *Biography and Genealogy Master Index* (*BGMI*). Once available only in hard-copy (annual) and cumulated each five years, this wonderful source is now on the Web, and is made available in many larger libraries.

BGMI offers indexing to hundreds of biographical tools, including *Who's Who*, biographical dictionaries, subject encyclopedias, and even indexes to other sources of information. At present, more than 13.6 million biographical sketches are indexed, and according to information posted on the company's website, approximately 600,000 sketches are added each year. New citations are drawn from approximately 100–150 volumes and editions of 60–90 major biographical dictionaries, including new specialized titles, and new editions of previously indexed works.

Because it serves as a master index to literally hundreds of biographical sources, *BGMI,* if available, should be considered the first-stop for artist biography research. Its very comprehensive coverage of art's many specialized titles allows the user to pinpoint works that contain biographies of even some of the most obscure artists of all periods.

Biography Reference Bank. New York: H.W. Wilson.

Biography Reference Bank is an online biographical database with information on approximately a half-million persons, dating from Antiquity to the present day. It provides instant access to more than 100 H.W. Wilson reference volumes, including *Current Biography* (described below), *World Artists,* and others. Additionally, *Biography Reference Bank* provides millions of magazine and journal citations as well as book review excerpts from the company's *Book Review Digest Plus.* Particularly valuable for researching contemporary artists.

Union List of Artists' Names. Getty Foundation Research Institute. http://www.getty.edu/research/conducting_research/vocabularies/ulan/.

The *Union List of Artists' Names* is one of several "vocabulary" projects[4] supported by the Getty Research Institute. Like any "controlled vocabulary," the goal of *ULAN* is to provide a standard inventory of language—in this case, artists' names—for uniformity in cataloging and documentation. The novice researcher might be surprised to learn that an artist might have multiple name variants. The 17th century Dutch master commonly referred to as "Rembrandt," for example, might be referred to as "Rembrandt van Rijn," "Rembrandt van Rhyn," "Rembrandt Hermansz van Rijn," or one of several other variants in the international art historical literature. For the cataloger, *ULAN* serves to systematize this variation. Because the name forms are derived from biographical sources, *ULAN* is a tremendously powerful index to these important research tools.

ULAN comprises more than 250,000 entries on artists dating from Antiquity to the present. Entries on major artists, like Rembrandt, will lead the user to many major published sources, including some of the biographical dictionaries described in this section. *ULAN* can be even more useful for lesser-known artists. The entry for contemporary artist Idelle Weber (born 1932), for example, leads the researcher to three sources, including the 1978 edition of *Who's Who in American Art.*

While the vast majority of sources indexed will be found only in libraries, *ULAN* serves as a free, online index to these sources.

Artist Biography—Reference Sources

The following works are encyclopedic in scope, providing biographical information on artists of various countries, periods and styles. Included are the most well-known sources. To find additional biographical resources of this type in libraries that utilize the Library of Congress Classification System, conduct a subject search using the heading "Artists— Biography — Dictionaries."

Benezit, E. *Dictionnaire Critique et Documentaire des Peintres, Sculpteurs, Dessinateurs, et Graveurs ... de Tous les Temps et de Tous les Pays par un Groupe d'Écrivains Specialists Français et Étrangers.* Paris: Gründ, 1999.

This French-language biographical dictionary is a standard art reference tool. It provides birth/death dates, place of birth, geographical area of activity, subject matter and media, museum collections, bibliography, some public sales information, and occasionally, a signature facsimile. The latest (1999) edition provides very good coverage of contemporary and recently deceased artists.

Bryan, Michael. *Bryan's Dictionary of Painters and Engravers.* Under the supervision of George C. Williamson ... with numerous illustrations. New ed., rev. and enl. London: G. Bell, 1926–34. 5 vols.

First published in 1816, considered a standard source of artist biography. Many signed entries, including some long biographies of major artists. Some entries include marks, monograms, signatures.

Current Biography. Bronx, N.Y.: H.W. Wilson, 1940– .

Lengthy (often 2–3 page) essays on living persons in all fields, including the fine arts. Includes references for further research. Published monthly (except December) with annual cumulations.

International Dictionary of Art and Artists. Edited by James Vinson. Chicago: St. James Press, 1990. 2 vols.

Encyclopedic overview of major European and American artists and artworks. Individual entries include some or all of the following elements: biographical details; major and "other" collections; publications by subject artist; publications about subject artist; lengthy bio-critical essay.

Marks, Claude. *World Artists, 1950–1980: An H.W. Wilson Biographical Dictionary.* New York: H.W. Wilson, 1984. 912p.

_____. *World Artists. 1980–1990.* New York: H.W. Wilson, 1991. 413p.

Lengthy essays on major contemporary artists include exhibition histories, public collections, and bibliography.

Museum of Modern Art. *The Museum of Modern Art Artists Files.* Alexandria, Va.: Chadwyck-Healey, 1986. 5,699 microfiche.

This massive collection of primary source documents includes exhibition announcements, magazine and newspaper clippings, reviews and other ephemeral materials amassed by the Museum of Modern Art. More than 20,000 artists (painters, sculptors, performance artists, graphic designers, etc.) represented.

The New York Public Library Artists File. Alexandria, Va.: Chadwyck-Healey, 1987–89. 11,300 microfiches + Index (10 microfiche).

The New York Public Library's clippings file offers more than 1.5 million items on more than 80,000 artists, including painters, sculptors, architects, furniture and other decorative arts designers. Included are newspaper and magazine clippings, press releases, auction and gallery exhibition catalogs, and other ephemeral material. Particularly valuable for researching relatively obscure artists.

Artist Biography—Specialized

Over the past few decades, a number of highly specialized dictionaries of artist biography have been published. Many of these focus on specific subjects, while others concentrate on narrowly focused styles or periods. The following titles represent a selection of the most important artist biographical reference works. Note that medium-specific biographical reference works (i.e., biographical dictionaries of painters, photographers, etc.) will be found later in this chapter along with other medium-specific reference tools. Sources with a geographical focus (e.g., biographical dictionaries of American artists) are included among the "Encyclopedias and Surveys" section, pages 68–77 of this chapter.

Brewington, Dorothy E. R. *Dictionary of Marine Artists.* Salem, Mass.: Peabody Museum of Salem; Mystic, Conn.: Mystic Seaport Museum, 1982. 431p.

Brief biographical entries include references to pieces in public collections, society affiliations, some monograms.

Folk Artists Biographical Index. Edited by George H. Meyer; George H. Meyer, Jr. and Katherine P. White, associate editors; foreword by Robert Bishop. Detroit: Gale Research, 1987. 496p.

A-Z index of artist biography includes references to over 200 published sources. Approximately 9,000 artists included. Basic biographical data (birth/death dates, locations, etc.), type of work, and biographical sources for further information.

Gaunt, William. *Marine Painting: An Historical Survey.* London: Secker & Warburg, 1975. 264 p.

Historical survey of marine painters and painting, from ancient through mid–20th century. Some color, primarily black-and-white illustrations. Brief biographical entries on major and lesser-known subject artists. Partial contents: From ancient times to the sixteenth century; Seventeenth century—

north and south; Eighteenth century—Britain, France and Italy; Romantic impulse; Turner, Constable and their contemporaries; Nineteenth century developments in Britain and America; Naïve painters of the sea; Marine painting in the Impressionist age; Far East.

Jackson, Christine E. *Dictionary of Bird Artists of the World.* Woodbridge, Suffolk: Antique Collectors' Club, 1999. 550p.

Encyclopedic international survey of bird artists. Each entry includes name, dates, country of origin or adoption, biography, location of work in museums and galleries, some sales, and very well-chosen bibliography for further research.

St. James Guide to Black Artists. Edited by Thomas Riggs. Detroit: St. James Press, 1997. 625p.

Biographical dictionary includes references to "African, African diasporan, modern and postmodern" Black artists (preface). Entries include basic biographical data, along with all or some of the following elements: Exhibitions (individual and selected groups), publications (by, and about), artist's statement.

ARTIST BIOGRAPHY—CONTEMPORARY

Contemporary Artists. London: St. James Press 2002. 2 vols.

Excellent source for researching the lives and careers of contemporary artists, including nationality, birth dates, education, family, awards, mailing addresses, websites, and agent or dealer. Entries also include good listings of solo exhibitions, selected group exhibitions, individual and public collections, publications (by and about), artist's statement, and biographical essay.

Lucie-Smith, Edward. *Lives of the Great 20th-Century Artists.* New York: Thames and Hudson, 1999. 352p.

Well-illustrated essays on major artists of the 20th century.

Who's Who in American Art. Washington, D.C.: American Federation of Arts, Vol. 1 (1936–37)– . See also *Who Was Who in American Art* for biographical information on deceased artists of the United States, Canada and Mexico.

Latest edition, covering the years 2001–2, includes brief profiles on 11,100 visual artists in the United Sates, Canada and Mexico. Entries include some or all of the following information, among other points: birth date, location, education and training, works in public collections, commissions, exhibitions, publications. Inclusion of dealer(s) and mailing address make this an indispensable tool for the collector or researcher of contemporary artists.

Indexes to Reproductions

One of the factors that can affect the value of a work of art is its publication record. Numerous sources are available to assist in locating reproductions of particular works. First, consult the artist's catalogue raisonné and retrospective exhibition catalogs. The catalogue raisonné often includes a list of sources in which the subject work has been reproduced.

Sources devoted to the subject artist's work represent just one potential publication type. Journals, newspapers, surveys and reference works might also include reproductions, and pinpointing these can be a daunting task. To find reproductions of works that appear in multi-artist volumes (i.e., monographs or reference works that include images of multiple artists' works) the following sources can be indispensable.

Havlice, Patricia Pate. *World Painting Index.* Metuchen, N.J.: Scarecrow Press, 1977. 2 vols. Supplements: *First Supplement, 1973–1980.* Metuchen, N.J.: Scarecrow Press, 1982; *Second Supplement, 1980–1989.* Lanham, Md.: Scarecrow Press, 1995; *Third Supplement, 1990–1999.* Lanham, Md.: Scarecrow Press, 2003.

Patricia Pate Havlice's *World Painting Index* and its supplements index the image contents of thousands of books. Arranged alphabetically by artist's name, reproductions in color are identified as such. Contents: Bibliography; Paintings by unknown artists (arranged by title); Painters and their works; Titles of works and their painters.

Monro, Isabel Stevenson. *Index to Reproductions of American Paintings; A Guide to Pictures Occurring in More than Eight Hundred Books.* New York: H.W. Wilson, 1948. 731p. *First Supplement*: 1964.

Basic artist — title guide to published reproductions. Some very broad subject headings (e.g., various genre paintings) included.

_____. *Index to Reproductions of European Paintings: A Guide to Pictures in More Than Three Hundred Books.* New York: H.W. Wilson, 1956. 668p.

Dated but still useful guide to finding reproductions in multi-artist works and catalogs.

Smith, Lyn Wall, and Nancy Dustin Wall Moure. *Index to Reproductions of American Paintings Appearing in Over 400 Books Mostly Published Since 1960.* Metuchen, N.J.: Scarecrow Press, 1977. 931p.

Index to reproductions of American paintings by artist; index to reproductions of American paintings by subject. Indicates color illustrations.

Monographs and Exhibition Catalogs

Monographs and exhibition catalogs are two of the primary sources of information on any artist's life and work. Technically speaking, any single book is referred to as a "monograph." In the art world, the monograph refers to a stand-alone volume devoted to the work of a single artist.

Exhibition catalogs, once simple lists of works in an exhibition (lacking illustrations, in many cases) have evolved over the past few decades. Today, the exhibition catalog is more of a scholarly tome; while in most cases contemporary exhibition catalogs continue the function of listing the works included in the exhibition they accompany, more often than not they also include essays, additional works not included in the exhibition, chronology of the artist's career, lengthy bibliographies and additional supporting materials. Finding the catalogs to an artist's major exhibitions can provide many leads for further research.

In libraries that utilize the Library of Congress system, artists' monographs can be located by using the subject headings (for example) "Heade, Martin Johnson, 1819–1904" and "Heade, Martin Johnson, 1819–1904 — Criticism and interpretation." Exhibition catalogs will be found by searching (for example) "Heade, Martin Johnson, 1819–1904 — Exhibitions."

Some very useful tools are available to assist the researcher who is attempting to develop a bibliography of monographs and exhibition catalogs. These include:

Freitag, Wolfgang M. *Art Books: A Basic Bibliography of Monographs on Artists*. 2nd ed. New York: Garland, 1997. See complete description, page 52.

International Federation of Library Associations. Section of Art Libraries. *International Directory of Art Libraries*. http://artlibrary.vassar.edu/ifla-idal/.

This easy-to-use web-based directory provides access to major libraries' online catalogs and websites. Individual entries include complete contact information, collection details, key personnel, and links to websites.

The Worldwide Bibliography of Art Exhibition Catalogues, 1963–1987. Millwood, N.Y.: Kraus International; Ithaca, N.Y.: Worldwide Books, 1992. 3v.

Worldwide Books is a major vendor of exhibition catalogs and other art books. This classified bibliography can be used to identify basic information about exhibitions and assist the user in tracking down desired titles.

Worldwide Books Database. http://www.worldwide.com.

Worldwide books maintains a database of its offerings, and has very wisely made the decision to retain items even as they go "out-of-print." The database currently includes records for over 37,000 exhibition catalogs, over 11,000 major trade and university press books, and other items of interest to the art researcher.

Exhibition Indexes

The sources used to locate information about exhibitions and their accompanying catalogs are not usually very useful for identifying individual works; to do this, the researcher must consult specialized indexes to the exhibition histories of individual museums. To find out when and where a specific work has been exhibited, the following sources are indispensable.

Before investing a great deal of time searching through museum exhibition indexes, be sure to thoroughly review the subject artist's catalogue raisonné and exhibition catalogs. Very often, these contain very exhaustive listings of exhibitions in which the artist's work has been featured.

Canada

McMann, Evelyn de R. (Evelyn de Rostaing). *Royal Canadian Academy of Arts/ Académie Royale des Arts du Canada Exhibitions and Members, 1880–1979.* Toronto and Buffalo: University of Toronto Press, 1981. 448p.

Surveys exhibitions and members of the Royal Canadian Academy. Approximately 3,000 artists, 25,560 works included in 92 annual and 12 special exhibitions. Primarily Canadian, few American, British, Continental European artists included. Entries include name, dates, birthplace, status in Academy, address, media, dates of and works included in exhibitions. Some lenders' names included.

France

Catalogues of the Paris Salon 1673 to 1881. Compiled by H.W. Janson. New York: Garland, 1977. 60 vols.

Facsimile reprint edition of the catalogues of the Paris Salons.

Modern Art in Paris: Two Hundred Catalogues of the Major Exhibitions Reproduced in Facsimile. New York: Garland, 1981–82. 47 vols.

Facsimile reproductions of exhibition catalogues, including World's Fairs, Salons of the "Indépendants" and the "Refusés" and numerous other important exhibitions and exhibition series.

Sanchez, Pierre. *Les Salons de Dijon, 1771–1950: Catalogue des Exposants et Liste de Leurs Œuvres.* Dijon: Echelle de Jacob, 2002. 505p.

List of exhibitions precedes artist entries. Entries include name, dates, birth/death places, short biography, memberships, address, catalog number, exhibition place code, medium if known. Some additional information on selected works.

Latin America

Sanurjo, Annick. *Contemporary Latin American Artists: Exhibitions at the Organization of American States, 1941–1964.* Lanham, Md.: Scarecrow: 1997. 506p.

_____. *Contemporary Latin American Artists: Exhibitions at the Organization of American States, 1965–1985.* Lanham, Md.: Scarecrow: 1993. 720p.

Chronological arrangement of all catalogs emanating from OAS exhibitions. Many catalogs include important biographical details— particularly useful for researching the more obscure artists and their works. Some one-person, but primarily group exhibitions included. Index of artists makes it easy to identify relevant exhibition catalogs.

United Kingdom

Graves, Algernon. *The British Institution, 1806–1867: A Complete Dictionary of Contributors and Their Work from the Foundation of the Institution.* London: G. Bell, and A. Graves, 1908. 617p.

Dictionary of Royal Academy Exhibiting artists with emphasis on paintings, some sculpture, engravings, miniatures. Entries include artist's name, address, date, catalog number, title, dimensions, price realized, if sold.

_____. *A Century of Loan Exhibitions, 1813–1912.* London: A. Graves, 1913–15. 5 vols.
Finding aid to exhibitions in London area. Alphabetical (by artist's name) arrangement. Indications of ownership make this a useful source for the provenance researcher.

_____. *A Dictionary of Artists Who Have Exhibited Works in the Principal London Exhibitions of Oil Paintings From 1760–1880.* Compiled by Algernon Graves. London: G. Bell, 1884. 3rd ed. London : H. Graves, 1901. Facsimile reprint, Bath: Kingsmead Reprints, 1969.
Index to artists (including many lesser known British artists) who contributed works to exhibitions including: Society of Artists, Free Society of Artists, Royal Academy, British Institution, Society of British Artists, Royal Water-colour Society, Royal Institute, Grosvenor Gallery, and New Gallery.

_____. *The Royal Academy of Arts: A Complete Dictionary of Contributors and Their Work from its Foundation in 1769 to 1904.* London: Graves, 1905–6. Reprint: Wakefield, Yorkshire, England: S.R. Publishers; Bath, England: Kingsmead Reprints, 1970. 8 vols.
Arranged alphabetically by artist's name, provides descriptive details on paintings exhibited at the Royal Academy.

Morris, Edward. *The Liverpool Academy and other Exhibitions of Contemporary Art in Liverpool, 1774–1867: A History and Index of Artists and Works Exhibited.* Liverpool: Liverpool University Press, 1998.
Includes index by artists' name, sales records (1845–1865) including purchasers' names, list of Academy's prize winners.

Norwich Society of Artists 1805–1833: A Dictionary of Contributors and Their Work. Compiled by Miklos Rajnai for the Paul Mellon Center for Studies in British Art. Norfolk, England: Norfolk Museum Service, 1976.
Exhibition records of the society's artists, including some illustrations of catalogs and policy statements. Entries include medium, title, and in some instances, lender information. Some poetry and biblical references included (from original catalogs).

125 Years of Exhibitions at the Fine Art Society PLC, 1876–2001. London: The Society, [2001]. 57p.
Inventory of exhibitions, arranged by year. Indexed by artist, and by contributors of (catalog) notes, prefaces, etc.

Royal Academy Exhibitors, 1905–1970: A Dictionary of Artists and Their Work in the Summer Exhibitions of the Royal Academy of Arts. Wakefield: EP, [1973]–1982. 6 vols.
A-Z listing of artists, including major media, year of Royal Academy exhibition, and title of works exhibited. Most works exhibited were by living artists, with the exception of those Summer Exhibition works that immediately followed an artist's death.

Royal Academy Exhibitors, 1971–1989: A Dictionary of Artists and Their Work in the Summer Exhibitions of the Royal Academy of Arts. Edited by Charles Baile de Laperriere. Wiltshire, England: Hilmarton Manor Press, 1989. 546p.
Updates item described in previous entry.

The Royal Glasgow Institute of the Fine Arts 1861–1989: A Dictionary of Exhibitors at the Annual Exhibitions of the Royal Glasgow Institute of the Fine Arts. Compiled by Roger Billcliffe. Glasgow: Woodend Press, 1990–1992. 4 vols.

Exhibition history of approximately 10,000 artists— primarily painters, some engravers, sculptors and architects. Entries alphabetical by artist's name, include discipline, address, date, catalog number, price as listed in catalog.

Royal Hibernian Academy of Arts: Index of Exhibitors and Their Works, 1826–1979. Compiled by Ann M. Stewart; with a summary history of the R.H.A. by C. de Courcy. Dublin: Manton, 1985–1987. 3 vols.

Three-volume dictionary arranged by artist's name. Residence, date of exhibition, and title of work included, along with some "asking" prices.

The Royal Scottish Academy Exhibitors, 1826–1990: A Dictionary of Artists and Their Work in the Annual Exhibitions of the Royal Scottish Academy. Edited by Charles Baile de Laperriere; compiled by Meta Viles and Joanna Soden Calne. Wiltshire, Eng.: Hilmarton Manor Press, 1991. 4 vols.

Basic exhibition history index includes artist's name, birth/death dates, exhibition year, catalog number, discipline, addresses, lender's name.

Royal Society of Painters in Water-Colours. *The Royal Watercolour Society: The First Fifty Years, 1805–1855.* Woodbridge: Antique Collectors' Club, 1992. 299p.

Index to exhibitors includes names, exhibition, catalog number, title, price, buyer's name, years of active membership in the society.

Society of Women Artists Exhibitors, 1855–1996: A Dictionary of Artists and Their Works in the Annual Exhibitions of the Society of Women Artists. Edited by Charles Baile de Laperriere. Calne, Wiltshire: Hilmarton Manor Press, 1996. 4 vols.

Index to annual exhibitions, includes brief history of the society, chronological list of patrons. Artist index includes addresses, where known. Each work includes catalog number, title (with medium, where known) and prices (rounded to nearest pound sterling).

Stewart, Ann M. *Irish Art Loan Exhibitions, 1765–1927.* Dublin: Manton, 1990–1995. 3 vols.

Exhibition index for native artists of Ireland. Includes shows in Dublin, Cork, Belfast, etc. Entries include artist's name, medium, place and title of exhibition, exhibition date, catalog number, size, price and, in some instances, lender's name.

United States

The Annual & Biennial Exhibition Record of the Whitney Museum of American Art, 1918–1989. Edited by Peter Hastings Falk. Madison, Conn.: Sound View Press, 1991. 468p.

Since 1932, the Whitney Annual and Biennial Exhibitions have had a tremendous impact upon the contemporary art scene. This reference work provides an artist index to each exhibition, and a comprehensive bibliography of published exhibition catalogs.

The Annual Exhibition Record of the Art Institute of Chicago, 1888–1950: Incorporating Three Annual Exhibition Series, Annual Exhibition of American Paintings & Sculpture, 1888–1950, Annual Exhibition of Works by Artists of Chicago & Vicinity,

1897–1950, Annual Exhibition of Watercolors by American Artists, 1888–1950 (Including the International Exhibition of Water Colors, 1921–1943). Madison, Conn.: Sound View Press, 1990. 1,117p.

Contents: Statistical chart of the exhibitions; Medals and prizes awarded; Index of juries by year; Alphabetical index to the jurors; Index by artist; Index by owner; Index by places and last names.

The Annual Exhibition Record of the National Academy of Design, 1901–1950: Incorporating the Annual Exhibitions, 1901–1950 and the Winter Exhibitions, 1906–1932. Edited by Peter Hastings Falk. Madison, Conn.: Sound View Press, 1990. 622p.

Partial contents: Analytic chart of the annual and winter exhibitions; Medals and prizes awarded in the annual exhibitions; Index of juries by year; Alphabetical index to the jurors; Index by artist; Index by owner; Index by places and last names.

The Annual Exhibition Record of the Pennsylvania Academy of the Fine Arts: 1807–1870. [Being a Reprint with Revisions of the 1955 Edition of Anna Wells Rutledge's Cumulative Record of Exhibition Catalogues, Incorporating The Society of Artists, 1810–1814 and The Artist's Fund Society, 1835–1845]. Madison, Conn.: Sound View Press, 1988–1989. 3 vols.

Indexes by artist, owner, and subject entries in the Annual Exhibitions of the Pennsylvania Academy of the Fine Arts.

Archives of American Art. *Collection of Exhibition Catalogs.* Boston: G. K. Hall, 1979. 851p.

Excellent resource for locating artists' one-person exhibitions.

The Biennial Exhibition Record of the Corcoran Gallery of Art, 1907–1967. Edited by Peter H. Falk. Madison, Conn.: Sound View Press, 1991. 335p.

Index by name, with works listed in chronological order. Titles, catalog number and exhibition date for each work. Includes indexes of jurors and owners.

Boston Art Club: Exhibition Record, 1873–1909. Compiled and edited by Janice H. Chadbourne, Karl Gabosh, and Charles O. Vogel. Madison, Conn.: Sound View Press, 1991. 479p.

Artist index, includes titles, media, addresses, and asking prices for works offered for sale.

Detroit Institute of Arts. Research Library and Archives. *Detroit Institute of Arts Exhibition Catalogues.* http://www.dalnet.lib.mi.us/dia/catalogues.php.

Digitized versions of the exhibition catalogues produced by the Detroit Museum of Art (1886–1919) and the Detroit Institute of Arts (1919–). "The exhibition catalogues listed correspond with special exhibitions, including selections from the museum's collection, collections lent by other institutions or individuals for temporary display at the DMA or the DIA, as well as a combination of both. Each exhibition catalogue has been digitized and made available as .PDF files."[5]

Halteman, Ellen. *Nineteenth-Century San Francisco Art Exhibition Catalogues: A Descriptive Checklist and Index.* Davis: Library Associates, University Library, University of California, Davis, 1981. 180p.

Primarily San Francisco artists. Entries for catalogs include all wording from title page, list types of items exhibited (decorative arts, furnishings, etc.).

Entries for artists include names, dates, catalog numbers, title, some purchaser information. Reproductions of exhibition catalog covers.

Marlor, Clark S. *A History of the Brooklyn Art Association with an Index of Exhibitions.* New York: J. F. Carr, [1970]. 421p.

Local history of the Brooklyn Art Association, including exhibitions, ownership records, and prices of art works, where applicable. Chapter one offers historical data on paintings from the 1860s. Index of exhibitions, index of organizations. Exhibition index includes: Artist, nationality, additional information (e.g., "active in New York"), some artists' addresses and biographical details, catalogue number, price, medium. Focus on watercolor, illustrations and sketches, some etchings and miniatures, porcelain paintings.

_____. *The Salons of America, 1922–1936.* Madison, Conn.: Sound View Press, 1991. 242p.

Artist index to annual index of short-lived group that broke away from the *Society of Independent Artists.* Entries include artists' addresses, year of exhibition and titles of works.

_____. *The Society of Independent Artists: The Exhibition Record 1917–1944.* Park Ridge, N.J.: Noyes Press, 1984. 600p.

Index by artist's name to the society's annual exhibitions. Artists' addresses, titles of works included, along with locations and dates of exhibitions. List of purchases includes artist's name, title and price paid for work.

Moure, Nancy Dustin Wall. *Artists' Clubs and Exhibitions in Los Angeles Before 1930.* Los Angeles: Dustin, 1975. ca. 150p. (Series: *Publications in Southern California Art,* no. 2.)

Extensive inventory of artists' clubs in L.A., alphabetical and dated list of exhibitions by title. Artist entries include names, dates, addresses, exhibition dates, item number in exhibition, title, some prices, description of work.

National Academy of Design Exhibition Record, 1826–1860. New York: Printed for the Historical Society, 1943. 2 vols.

Index to annual exhibitions of the National Academy. Index includes names of owners, subjects of landscapes and portraits, biblical scenes and characters, literary works illustrated, genre titles. Generic titles (e.g., "landscape") not included in index.

Naylor, Maria. *The National Academy of Design Exhibition Record, 1861–1900.* New York: Kennedy Galleries, 1973. 2 vols.

Artist index to annual exhibition, includes artists' addresses and prices for works offered for sale.

Perkins, Robert F., and William J. Gavin, III. *The Boston Atheneum Art Exhibition Art Index, 1827–1874.* Boston: Library of the Boston Atheneum, 1980. 325p.

Records approximately 1,500 artists' works exhibited between 1827–1874. Artist index includes name, nationality, city, dates, addresses, years of occupancy (if known), catalog number, title. In some cases, owner's name is recorded; if no name, artist is assumed owner. Owner index includes name, name of artist, title, year exhibited, occasionally notes medium or type (e.g., sculpture).

Record of the Carnegie Institute's International Exhibitions, 1896–1996. Edited by Peter Hastings Falk. Madison, Conn.: Sound View Press, 1998. 378p.

Artist index to works included in Carnegie's "serial exhibition" (annual until

1950, triennial thereafter) from 1896 to 1996. Includes rejected entries for the years 1896 through 1931, when Carnegie staff stopped the practice of recording rejections.

Smithsonian American Art Museum Research Database: Pre–1877 Art Exhibition Catalogue Index. http://siris-artexhibition.si.edu.

Free online index to artists of all nationalities who exhibited in North America prior to 1877. Over 135,000 records. The catalogue indexes information from thousands of exhibition catalogs, broadsides, newspaper articles and gallery notices. Excluded are exhibitions adequately covered elsewhere, including those held at the American Academy of Fine Arts & American Art Union, Boston Athenaeum, Brooklyn Art Association, National Academy of Design, Pennsylvania Academy of Fine Arts, and the Combined Art Organizations of San Francisco.

Wilson, Raymond L. *Index of American Print Exhibitions, 1882–1940.* Metuchen, N.J.: Scarecrow Press, 1988. 906p.

Indexing to individual artists' prints included in exhibitions at the New York Etching Club, Chicago Society of Etchers, California Society of Etchers, Printmakers Society of California, Brooklyn Society of Etchers, Fine Prints of the Year, Fifty Prints of the Year, Panama-Pacific International Exposition, Victoria & Albert Museum, and New York World's Fair.

_____. *Index of American Watercolor Exhibitions, 1900–1945.* Metuchen, N.J.: Scarecrow Press, 1994. 776p.

Artist/title indexing to works featured in juried exhibitions. Includes works exhibited: American Watercolor Society; Brooklyn Museum; Art Institute of Chicago; San Francisco Art Association; Oakland Art Gallery; California Water Color Society.

Yarnall, James L., and William H. Gerdts. *The National Museum of American Art's Index to American Art Exhibition Catalogues: From the Beginning Through the 1876 Centennial Year.* Boston: G. K. Hall, 1986. 6 vols.

Various indexes to American exhibition catalogs, including title index by location, individual artist's name index, unidentified artists and owners.

FOUR

Decorative Arts Research: Basic Methods and Resources

In decades past, the so-called decorative arts were relegated to a kind of second-class status in the art world and in academia. While sales of fine furniture, glass, porcelain and other "antiques" have dominated the auction market since its earliest days, it was not until the 1980s that the term "decorative arts" came to be used consistently to describe such sales in the auction world.[1] Serious decorative arts scholarship is similarly slow to develop; few colleges of universities have offered courses, much less awarded degrees, until recent decades.[2]

Today, the decorative arts researcher has access to a wealth of published resources, including books, reference works, periodicals, and doctoral dissertations. Recall from the previous chapter that the process of researching art works (prints, paintings, etc.), while often extremely challenging, can also be very straightforward because, in many instances, we know the name of the work's creator. Knowing the artist, we can proceed to search for books, magazine articles, exhibition reviews and the like. By contrast, researching the decorative arts (furniture, ceramics, glass, etc.) can be daunting, because decorative art works are rarely signed, although many bear an identifying mark, monogram or symbol that can be used to determine the origin of the subject piece.

In this chapter, we'll explore a good selection of the most important reference tools for decorative arts research. As in the preceding chapter, the section on each major type of resource (dictionaries, encyclopedias, etc.) begins with some tips (e.g., Library of Congress subject headings) for locating additional, similar sources of information.

General Decorative Arts Bibliographies

Bibliographies are essential research tools for the serious decorative arts researcher. The indexes to periodical literature identified in the preceding chapter yield a considerable amount of decorative arts information, but chapters in books, exhibition brochures, and trade catalogs represent some of the basic sources for in-depth research in this area.

In addition to the general and specialized bibliographies described here, readers are advised to also consult the *Bibliographic Index*, an index to bibliographies in books, magazines, and journals, described in the preceding chapter (page 52). Additionally, some of the fine arts bibliographies include significant amounts of material on the decorative arts. See, particularly, Arntzen and Rainwater's *Guide to the Literature of Art History* (Chicago: American Library Association, 1980), p. 51, and its recently published successor, Max Marmor and Alex Ross's *Guide to the Literature of Art History II.*

To find additional works of this type in libraries that utilize the Library of Congress Classification System, conduct a subject search using headings like "Decorative arts— Bibliography" and "Antiques— Bibliography."

Creswell, K. A. C. (Keppel Archibald Cameron), Sir. *A Bibliography of the Architecture, Arts, and Crafts of Islam to 1st Jan. 1960.* [Cairo]: American University at Cairo Press; London: Distributed by Oxford University Press, 1961. 1,330 columns. Supplements: First: January 1960 to January 1972. [Cairo]: American University in Cairo Press; Second: January 1972 to December 1980. [Cairo]: American University in Cairo Press, 1984.

Extensive bibliography, with supplements, provides access to thousands of references to Islamic art, architecture, and the decorative arts. Writings on "Arts and Crafts" are classified by type. Partial contents: Arms and armour; Astrolabes, etc.; Bookbinding; Calligraphy and epigraphy; Ceramics; Glass and rock crystal; Ivory; Jade; Lacquer; Metal; Mosaics; Ornament.

Ehresmann, Donald L. *Applied and Decorative Arts: A Bibliographic Guide.* 2nd ed. Englewood, Colo.: Libraries Unlimited, 1993. 629p.

This is probably the most important and comprehensive of the English language decorative arts bibliographies. Classified and fully annotated, with an excellent subject index. Major areas covered include: General sources; Ornament; Folk art; Arms and armor; Ceramics; Clocks, watches, automata and scientific instruments; Costume; Enamels; Furniture; Glass; Ivory; Jewelry; Lacquer; Leather and bookbinding; Medals and seals; Metalwork; Musical instruments; Textiles; Toys and dolls; Wallpaper.

Franklin, Linda Campbell. *Antiques and Collectibles: A Bibliography of Works in English, 16th century to 1976.* Metuchen, N.J.: Scarecrow Press, 1978. 1,091p.

Classified bibliography of more than 10,000 English language titles. Included are the holdings (as of 1976) of the Library of Congress, New York Public

Library, Winterthur Library, and the British Museum, among many others. Partial contents: Antiques, collectibles and interior design; Ceramics: pottery and porcelain; Glass; Silver and gold; Metalwork and metals; Textiles and textile arts. Subject and author indexes.

Specialized Bibliographies

American Folk Art: A Guide to Sources. Edited by Simon J. Bronner. New York: Garland, 1984. 313p.

Classified bibliography of books, periodical articles and exhibition catalogs devoted to folk art in the United States.

Arts in America: A Bibliography. Edited by Bernard Karpel. Washington, D.C.: Published for the Archives of American Art by the Smithsonian Institution Press, 1979. 4 vols.

Extensive bibliography of the arts in America, includes references to approximately 25,000 works. Focus on architecture, the visual and decorative arts, art of Native Americans, and the performing arts. Reference works, books, exhibition and trade catalogs, journals and journal article citations included.

Decorative Arts and Household Furnishings in America, 1650–1920: An Annotated Bibliography. Edited by Kenneth L. Ames and Gerald W.R. Ward. Winterthur, Del.: Henry Francis du Pont Winterthur Museum; Charlottesville: Distributed by the University Press of Virginia, 1989. 392p.

Classified bibliography of reference works, books, and periodical literature on the decorative arts in America. Contents: References and surveys; Architecture; Furniture; Metals; Ceramics and glass; Textiles; Timepieces; Household activities and systems; Artisans and culture.

De Winter, Patrick M. *European Decorative Arts, 1400–1600: An Annotated Bibliography.* Boston: G.K. Hall, 1988. 543p.

Very well-organized guide to the literature. Each major object section (e.g., "Pewter, Tin, Lead and Latten") includes works on "multi-country of origin; Single country of origin" subdivided by type of work (e.g., "surveys and histories," "permanent collections," "exhibition catalogs," etc.). An indispensable tool for serious research.

Kempton, Richard. *Art Nouveau: An Annotated Bibliography.* Los Angeles: Hennessey & Ingalls, 1977. 303p. (Series: *Art & Architecture Bibliographies* 4.)

Extensive bibliography of books and periodical articles treating general subject of Art Nouveau, including individual decorative art forms (furniture, glass, etc.), as well as individual designers and country-specific works. Serves as a very good bibliography to some of the major periodicals on Art Nouveau.

Sokol, David M. *American Decorative Arts and Old World Influences: A Guide to Information Sources.* Detroit: Gale Research, [1980]. 294p.

Classified, annotated bibliography of reference works, books and specialized periodical literature on the decorative arts.

Decorative Arts Periodical Indexes

In chapter two, the major indexes to the literature of art and its history were described in some detail. While they do focus on art and architecture, these primary indexes—*Art Index,*[3] *ArtBibliographies Modern,* and *Bibliography of the History of Art (BHA)*— also include references to a substantial amount of decorative arts information. Note also that numerous very general databases, also described in detail in chapter two, are widely available and offer a tremendous amount of decorative arts information, including magazine, journal, newsletter and newspaper articles on a wide array of topics. Finally, the following indexes deal more exclusively with the decorative arts literature.

Bibliothèque Forney. *Catalogue d'Articles de Périodiques, Arts Decoratifs et Beaux-Arts, Bibliothèque Forney, Paris.* Boston: G.K. Hall, 1972. 4 vols.

Provides citations to periodical literature on the decorative arts. Hundreds of titles, many of them non-English language, are analyzed. Particularly useful for the historian of decorative arts.

Design and Applied Arts Index. Burwash, England: Design Documentation, 1988– . Also available on CD-ROM, web.

Design and Applied Arts Index (*DAAI*) is the major index to the journal literature on industrial design, crafts, typography and related topics. While it is intended primarily for the designer and craftsperson, it also provides a great many valuable citations to the decorative arts literature for the collector and connoisseur. In addition to subject/author/title indexing of feature articles, news items and other journal literature, *DAAI* on the Web includes the supplementary databases *International Directory of Design and Craft Courses*; *Design and Craft Organisations*; *Design and Craft Archives*; and *Design and Craft Journals.*

General Collectors' Manuals

This section comprises reference works that are geared toward the practical issues faced by collectors; the individual works included here are relevant to collectors in more than one specific area (e.g., a work that addresses ceramics, glass and metalwork will be found here). More highly specific collectors' manuals, such as those related to furniture collecting, are found in their respective sections, below.

Bly, John, ed. *Is It Genuine? How to Collect Antiques with Confidence.* London: Miller's, 2002. 224p.

Experts present concrete advice on how to discern various types of fakes and copies. Included are examples of furniture, pottery, porcelain, glass, silver and other areas of design and decorative arts.

Chervenka, Mark. *Antique Trader Guide to Fakes & Reproductions.* 3rd ed. Iola, Wis.: Krause, 2003. 368p.

In a market that is now flooded with some good quality fakes and reproductions, determining authenticity can be a daunting task. This very useful guide presents photographic comparisons of fakes and originals. Includes everything from pottery and porcelain to glass, as well as a great many collectible objects.

Mayer, Barbara. *Contemporary American Craft: A Collector's Guide.* Salt Lake City: Peregrine Smith, 1988. 248p.

Dated, but still useful guide for the beginning collector of crafts. Individual media surveys include: Ceramics; Fiber; Glass; Jewelry and metalwork; Art furniture and other forms in wood.

Seton, Alistair. *Collecting Japanese Antiques.* Boston: Tuttle, 2004. 303p.

See description, page 217.

The Winterthur Guide to Caring for Your Collection. Gregory J. Landrey ... [et al.]. Winterthur, Del.: Henry Francis du Pont Winterthur Museum; Hanover [N.H.]: Distributed by University Press of New England, 2000. 154p.

Contents: General care; Science and your collection; Books, manuscripts and ephemera; Organic materials; Ceramics and glass; Textiles; Photographs; Metals.

General Dictionaries, Encyclopedias, and Surveys

Decorative arts researchers have no shortage of dictionaries, glossaries and encyclopedias at their disposal. Some of the large, general reference works described in the preceding chapter provide substantial essays on the various decorative arts. Notably, Grove's *Dictionary of Art* [page 66], includes many authoritative entries on decorative arts objects of all periods and geographic locations.

Dictionaries

Given the vast number of objects that comprise the decorative arts, it is no surprise that the field has an extensive vocabulary of its own. Until recent decades, the lack of standardized vocabulary made the task of classifying decorative arts objects exceedingly difficult. The Getty Foundation's *Art and Architecture Thesaurus* (*AAT*), a very extensive online thesaurus for art, architecture, and the decorative arts, was developed as a tool for catalogers of objects and related information, but for the object *researcher*, it serves as an extremely powerful index to many standard reference sources.

Because it serves as a good index to dictionaries, encyclopedias and other reference works, we begin this section with an exploration of the *Art and Architecture Thesaurus*, and proceed to review some of the primary print and electronic dictionaries that can be indispensable for the researcher of decorative arts objects.

Art & Architecture Thesaurus Online. Getty Foundation Research Institute. http://www.getty.edu/research/conducting_research/vocabularies/aat/.

Librarians, indexers, museum registrars and others who are charged with describing objects and information have long been aware of the need for standardized terminology in their work. Consider the case of books. A library with a large collection of books about films would not be serving its users well if each cataloger applied her or his preferred terminology to each title. The result would be a catalog in which some film books are assigned the subject "film," while others might be classified as "cinema," and still others might be classified "motion pictures." The use of standardized vocabularies imposes some order upon the natural variability of language, and provides guidance to the cataloger or indexer and, ultimately, to the catalog user, or researcher.

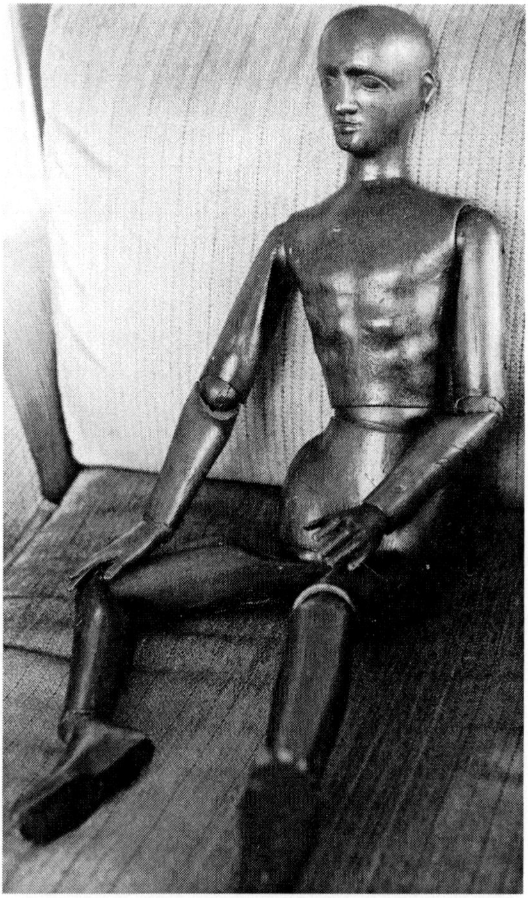

19th century artist's mannequin, or "lay figure" (photograph by Marc Posnock).

Because the terms that comprise standardized vocabularies are sometimes derived from standard reference sources, some offer an additional benefit to the researcher. Such is the case with the *Art & Architecture Thesaurus*, a product of the Getty Foundation's Research Institute. The following example demonstrates the usefulness of the *AAT* in the research process.

The author was asked to research what appeared to be an artist's mannequin or model (see photograph)—a very nicely

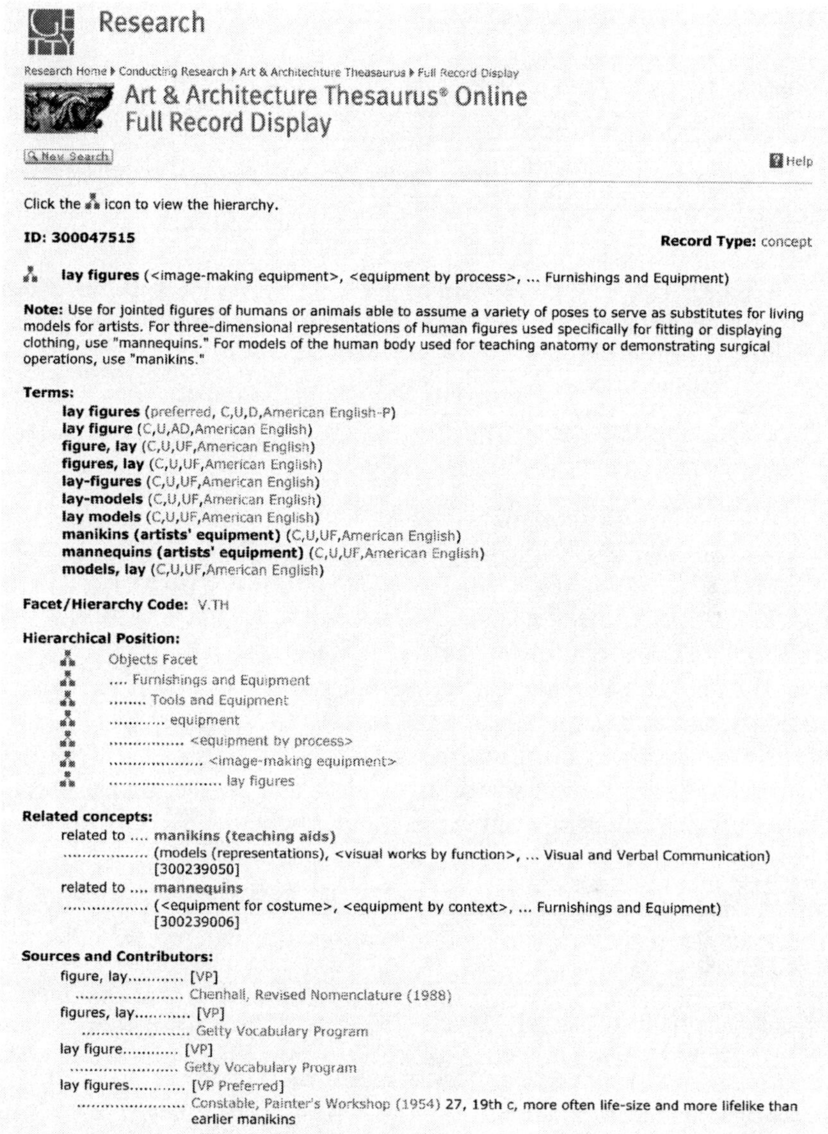

Research

Research Home ▸ Conducting Research ▸ Art & Architechture Theasaurus ▸ Full Record Display

Art & Architecture Thesaurus® Online
Full Record Display

New Search | Help

Click the icon to view the hierarchy.

ID: 300047515 **Record Type:** concept

lay figures (<image-making equipment>, <equipment by process>, ... Furnishings and Equipment)

Note: Use for jointed figures of humans or animals able to assume a variety of poses to serve as substitutes for living models for artists. For three-dimensional representations of human figures used specifically for fitting or displaying clothing, use "mannequins." For models of the human body used for teaching anatomy or demonstrating surgical operations, use "manikins."

Terms:
- **lay figures** (preferred, C,U,D,American English-P)
- **lay figure** (C,U,AD,American English)
- **figure, lay** (C,U,UF,American English)
- **figures, lay** (C,U,UF,American English)
- **lay-figures** (C,U,UF,American English)
- **lay-models** (C,U,UF,American English)
- **lay models** (C,U,UF,American English)
- **manikins (artists' equipment)** (C,U,UF,American English)
- **mannequins (artists' equipment)** (C,U,UF,American English)
- **models, lay** (C,U,UF,American English)

Facet/Hierarchy Code: V.TH

Hierarchical Position:

Objects Facet
.... Furnishings and Equipment
.... Tools and Equipment
.... equipment
.... <equipment by process>
.... <image-making equipment>
.... lay figures

Related concepts:

related to .... **manikins (teaching aids)**
.... (models (representations), <visual works by function>, ... Visual and Verbal Communication) [300239050]
related to .... **mannequins**
.... (<equipment for costume>, <equipment by context>, ... Furnishings and Equipment) [300239006]

Sources and Contributors:

figure, lay............ [VP]
.... Chenhall, Revised Nomenclature (1988)
figures, lay............ [VP]
.... Getty Vocabulary Program
lay figure............ [VP]
.... Getty Vocabulary Program
lay figures............ [VP Preferred]
.... Constable, Painter's Workshop (1954) 27, 19th c, more often life-size and more lifelike than earlier manikins

Entry for term "lay figure" from the Getty Research Institute's *Art & Architecture Thesaurus* (*AAT*). (Courtesy of the Getty Vocabulary Program and the Art & Architecture Thesaurus®.

carved, mahogany mannequin in quite good condition. It has been in the collection of its current owner since the early 1940s, and most likely dates from the latter half of the 19th century.

Preliminary research for information on artists' mannequins yielded no results, prompting the researcher to go back to basics and attempt to find synonymous terms for the subject work. An *AAT* search for the term "mannequin" yielded the record shown on page 121, and most importantly, it identified the proper descriptive term for our subject piece. It is not called a mannequin, but a "lay figure."

Because its terminology comes from a great many highly respected reference sources and databases, the *AAT* not only discloses correct or accepted terminology, but it also indicates which tools provided terms. Because its sources are included, the *AAT* serves as an index to specialized reference tools, including many of the dictionaries, handbooks and encyclopedias described throughout this and the preceding chapters. The sources indicated for "lay figure," for example, include several of the standard works described below. Note that the presence of an illustration is even indicated. Our *AAT* search informs us in a matter of seconds which terms should be used for research, and also provides a good list of titles with which to commence the research project.

Another very useful index to specialized dictionaries, Laurence Urdang's *Fine and Applied Arts Terms Index* (Detroit: Gale Research Co., 1983) was described in the previous chapter. Like the Getty *AAT*, it can be used to identify which reference work or works include an entry on the sought-after object type, medium, process, etc.

The following represent just a sampling of the most important general dictionaries of decorative arts terminology. To find additional works of this type in libraries that utilize the Library of Congress Classification System, conduct a subject search using the headings "Decorative Arts—Dictionaries"; "Antiques—Dictionaries"; and "Decoration and Ornament—Dictionaries."

Barber, Edwin Atlee, Luke Vincent Lockwood, and Hollis French. *The Ceramic, Furniture, and Silver Collectors' Glossary*. New York: Da Capo Press, 1976. (Reprint of *The Ceramic Collectors' Glossary*, *The Furniture Collectors' Glossary*, and *A Silver Collectors' Glossary and a List of Early American Silversmiths and Their Marks*, published 1914, 1913, and 1917, respectively, by the Walpole Society.)

Well-illustrated glossaries with very concise, relatively jargon-free definitions. The Silversmiths' list includes markings for most entries.

Bernasconi, John R. *The Collectors' Glossary of Antiques and Fine Arts. With Over 100 Illus., Including Reproductions from the Books of Chippendale, Sheraton and Hepplewhite*. [Rev. ed.] London: Estates Gazette, [1963]. 587p.

Widely held in libraries, this illustrated glossary is an excellent source for the serious collector or researcher.

Bingham, Don, and Joan Bingham. *Tuttle Dictionary of Antiques & Collectibles Terms*. Rutland, Vt.: C.E. Tuttle, 1992. 243p.

Very brief definitions of terms and styles, some short biographical entries on major artists and designers.

Fleming, John, and Hugh Honour. *The Penguin Dictionary of Decorative Arts*. New ed. London: Viking, 1989. 935p.

Illustrated (some color), encyclopedic dictionary of terms, styles, some biography. Includes section on ceramic marks, hallmarks on silver, marks on silver and pewter.

Hiesinger, Kathryn B., and George H. Marcus. *Antiquespeak: A Guide to the Styles, Techniques, and Materials of the Decorative Arts, from the Renaissance to Art Deco.* New York: Abbeville Press, 1997. 215 p.

Very readable discussions of European and American styles (e.g., Baroque, art deco), materials, object types, specialized areas of collecting, and technical processes. The essays on styles (e.g., regence) include the following sections: "Who" identifies principal artists, designers, etc.; "When" identifies time period; "Where" provides geographical information, and "What" defines the origins, nature and implications of the style.

Materials & Techniques in the Decorative Arts: An Illustrated Dictionary. Edited by Lucy Trench. Chicago: University of Chicago Press, 2000. 572p.

Lengthy, illustrated essays on materials and processes involved in the decorative arts.

The Oxford Companion to the Decorative Arts. Edited by Harold Osborne. Oxford [Oxfordshire] and New York: Oxford University Press, 1985. 865p.

Encyclopedic dictionary of decorative arts, international in scope. Entries range from short (a few sentences) to very lengthy (e.g., the entry on "China" is 56p.)

Savage, George. *Dictionary of Antiques.* New York: Praeger, [1970]. 534p.

Excellent source for biography of major designers, lengthy descriptions of decorative arts firms, and technical aspects of the decorative arts. Includes an index of marks and monograms, and a very good bibliography of sources for additional reading.

Terraroli, Valerio. *Skira Dictionary of Modern Decorative Arts.* Milan, Italy: Distributed by Rizzoli International, 2001. 223p.

Brief essays, some illustrated. Includes some biographical material. Coverage begins with first London World Fair (1851) "up to the definitive trend of the market and production toward industrial design after the Second World War and especially since the early 1950s." (Introduction, p.6).

Encyclopedias and Surveys

General

The Bullfinch Illustrated Encyclopedia of Antiques. Consulting editors Paul Atterbury and Lars Tharp. Boston: Little, Brown, 1994. 332p.

Partial contents: Pottery and porcelain; Glass; Silver; Furniture; Clocks and watches; Oriental wares. Well-illustrated, each major section includes an overview along with relevant reference materials (e.g., "hallmarks" in the chapter on silver; "Chronology of cabinetmakers and designers" in furniture chapter).

The Connoisseur's Complete Period Guides to the Houses, Decoration, Furnishing and Chattels of the Classic Periods. Edited by Ralph Edwards and L.G.G. Ramsey. London: The Connoisseur, 1968. 1,536p.

Scholarly, encyclopedic reference work. Contents (Major Sections): Tudor period 1500–1603; Stuart period 1603–1714; Early Georgian period 1714–1760;

Late Georgian period 1760–1810; Regency period 1810–1830; Early Victorian period 1830–1860. Each major section includes signed, authoritative articles on various relevant topics including furniture, architecture, textiles, etc.

Davidson, Paul. *Antique Collector's Directory of Period Detail: How to Identify the Key Characteristics, Shapes and Forms of Period Styles.* Hauppauge, N.Y.: Barron's Educational Series, 2000. 224p.

Easy-to-use guide to identifying characteristics of decorative arts objects from the Baroque through 20th century modernism, by a major expert in the field. Well-indexed and illustrated, this title is an excellent source for the collector of furniture, ceramics, glass, and other decorative arts categories.

Digital Library for the Decorative Arts and Material Culture. Madison: University of Wisconsin. http://decorativearts.library.wisc.edu.

This magnificent subject guide to decorative arts includes a good number of very high quality original texts and images, including works in the Chipstone Foundation Collection (furniture and ceramics). The very well-organized list of links for further research includes an annotated listing of major decorative arts digital imaging projects.

Evaluating Your Collection: The 14 Points of Connoisseurship. Compiled by Dwight P. Lanmon. Winterthur, Del.: Henry Francis du Pont Winterthur Museum; Hanover, N.H.: Distributed by University Press of New England, 1999. 123p.

Very readable, nicely illustrated primer on the basics of connoisseurship.

The Illustrated History of Antiques: The Essential Reference for All Antique Lovers and Collectors. General editor, Huon Mallalieu. Philadelphia: Running Press, 1991. 640p.

Very well illustrated overview of decorative arts and some collectible objects. Many entries include lists of designers and craftsmen, with dates, locations, marks, excellent bibliographies.

Knowles, Eric. *Miller's 100 Years of the Decorative Arts: Victoriana, Arts & Crafts, Art Nouveau & Art Deco.* London: Miller's, 1998. 254p.

Popular, well-illustrated overview. Partial contents: Furniture; Glass; Ceramics; Sculpture; Silver and Metalwork; Jewelry and precious objects; Prints and posters; Rugs and textiles.

Miller, Judith, and Martin Miller. *Miller's Understanding Antiques: New Edition.* London: Mitchell Beazley, 1997. 280p.

Offers practical advice for collectors in 13 major areas, including vital information on determining authenticity.

Miller's Antiques Encyclopedia. General editor, Judith Miller. Rev. ed. London: Mitchell Beazley, 2003. 560p.

Extensive overview of decorative arts, each section includes major designers, craftsmen, factories, etc. Some marks, signatures, and tips for collectors of various media and object types included. Contents: Furniture; Ceramics; Silver; Jewellery; Glass; Rugs & carpets; Textiles; Clocks & watches; Arts and Crafts & Art Nouveau; Art Deco; Dolls & teddy bears; Toys & games; Postwar design; Oriental works of art.

Prisant, Carol. *Antiques Roadshow Primer: The Introductory Guide to Antiques and Collectibles from the Most-Watched Show on PBS.* New York: Workman, 1999. 366p.

Provides a great deal of valuable information for the collector of a variety of objects. Partial contents: Furniture; Silver; Porcelain, pottery and glass; Paintings; Jewelry; Clocks and watches; Metalwork; Rugs, quilts and samplers; Toys, dolls and collectibles; Books and manuscripts.

Ramsey, L. G. G. *The Complete Encyclopedia of Antiques.* Compiled by the *Connoisseur.* New York: Hawthorn Books, 1962. 1472p.

Each major section includes a good glossary of terms. Contents: Arms and armour; Barometers, clocks and watches; Books and book bindings; Carpets and rugs; Coins and medals; Furniture; Glass; Jewellery; Metalwork; Mirrors; Needlework and embroidery; Painting; Pottery and porcelain; Prints and drawings; Scientific instruments; Sculpture and carving; Silver.

The Random House Collector's Encyclopedia, Victoriana to Art Deco. New York: Random House, 1974. 302p.

Surveys decorative arts and antiques from 1851, the year of the Great Exhibition, through 1939, the start of World War II. Well illustrated and very useful for identifying individual designers' styles.

Specialized

This section includes encyclopedias that focus on a particular style or period (e.g., art deco), or on country or continent of origin. Encyclopedias of individual media and object types are offered later in this chapter, under their respective object headings (e.g., furniture, porcelain, etc.)

Anscombe, Isabelle. *Arts & Crafts Style.* New York: Rizzoli, 1991. 232p.

Traces the development of Arts & Crafts style in furniture, interior and garden design from its inception in the mid–19th through the 20th century. Examples of carpets, silver, ceramics, furniture and other objects.

Avery, Derek. *Art Deco.* London: Chaucer Press, 2004. 160p.

Traces the origins and development of art deco sculpture, ceramics, furniture, glassware and other decorative arts objects. Well-illustrated, indexed.

Byars, Mel. *The Design Encyclopedia.* New York: Wiley, 1994. 612p.

Largely biographical, some entries on styles, factories, etc. Very good bibliographies, many obscure designers included.

Catley, Bryan. *Art Deco and Other Figures.* 2nd ed. Woodbridge, Eng.: Antique Collectors' Club. 2003. 398p.

Extensive inventory of figures arranged alphabetically by artist's name. Excellent source for identification of figures and statuettes. Each work identified with dimensions provided. Special sections include: Lamps; Bookends; Animal, bird and fish figures; Car mascots; Clocks. Brief biographies of artists.

Encyclopedia of Art Deco. Edited by Alistair Duncan. New York: Knickerbocker Press, 1998. 192p.

Illustrated encyclopedia of Art Deco decorative arts. Contents: Architecture; Sculpture; Furniture and interior decoration; Lighting; Paintings, graphics and bookbinding; Glass; Ceramics; Metalwork; Jewelry and accessories; Textiles. Each chapter includes an overview and brief biographies of major artists and designers.

Fehrman, Cherie, and Kenneth Fehrman. *Postwar Interior Design, 1945–1960*. New York: Van Nostrand Reinhold, 1987. 198p.

Good overview of works by major designers, including: Charles Eames; Eero Saarinen; George Nelson; Harry Bertoia; Florence Knoll; Gilbert Rohde; Isamu Noguchi; Arne Jacobsen; Borge Mogensen; Hans J. Wegner; Russel Wright.

Garner, Philippe. *The Contemporary Decorative Arts from 1940 to the Present Day*. London: Park Lane, 1990. 224p.

Surveys postwar design. Partial contents: Silver & metalwork; Ceramics; Jewellery; Glass; Textiles; Fashion.

Grow, Lawrence, and Dina von Zweck. *American Victorian: A Style and Source Book*. New York: Harper & Row, 1984. 223p.

This very heavily illustrated survey of Victorian decoration and ornament is a good starting point for beginning research on the period. Through photographs, line drawings and facsimile reproduction of advertisements, it presents a basic overview of decorative hardware, furniture, wall coverings and other domestic details.

Haslam, Malcolm. *Marks and Monograms of the Modern Movement, 1875–1930: A Guide to the Marks of Artists, Designers, Retailers, and Manufacturers, from the Period of the Aesthetic Movement to Art Deco and Style Moderne*. New York: Scribner, 1977. 192p.

Major sections arranged by type or work: Ceramics; Glass; Metalwork and jewelry; Graphics; Furniture and textiles. Object-type sections subdivided geographically: British; American; French, etc.

Hiesinger, Kathryn B., and George H. Marcus. *Landmarks of Twentieth-Century Design: An Illustrated Handbook*. New York: Abbeville Press, 1993. 431p.

Very well-illustrated discussion of modern design. Includes lengthy biographies of major designers. Contents: Toward industrialization, 1895–1910; Movements for change, 1910–1920; Styles of modernism, 1920–1930; Machine age, 1930–1940; Austerity, 1940–1950; Good design, 1950–1960; Alternatives, 1960–1970; Responsible design, 1970–1980; Postmodernism and pluralism since 1980.

Inspiring Reform: Boston's Arts and Crafts Movement. Marilee Boyd Meyer, consulting curator; essays by David Acton, et al. Wellesley, Mass.: Davis Museum and Cultural Center, Wellesley College; New York: Distributed by Abrams, 1997. 247p.

Lavishly illustrated, scholarly history of the Boston Arts and Crafts movement. Essays by experts cover diverse media including furniture, pottery, metal, textiles, book design and photography. Individual designers' biographies comprise lengthy appendix.

Kovel, Ralph, and Terry Kovel. *Kovels' American Antiques: 1750 to 1900*. New York: Random House Reference, 2004. 384p.

Basic reference source includes a vast amount of information for the serious collector of American furniture, pottery, porcelain, silver and more.

Phipps, Frances. *The Collector's Complete Dictionary of American Antiques*. Garden City, NY: Doubleday, 1974. 640p.

Well illustrated dictionary of terms related to decorative arts. Contents: Historic periods and styles; Rooms—their placement and use; Crafts, trade and useful professions; Weights and measures; Terms used by joiners and cabinetmakers; Woods and their preferred uses; Paints, dyes, finishes, varnishes; Cleaning, polishing and repairing; Metals—antique formulae and uses; Pottery, porcelain and minerals; Glass.

Pile, John F. *Dictionary of 20th-Century Design*. New York: Da Capo Press, 1994. 312p.

Short essays on trends and styles in the decorative arts; brief biographies of major and lesser-known artists and designers.

Sembach, Klaus-Jürgen. *Art Nouveau: Utopia, Reconciling the Irreconcilable*. London: Taschen, 2000. 240p.

Scholarly analysis of the emergence of the Art Nouveau movement and the social and political forces that affected the style's development. Partial contents: Movement—the modern style's first steps; Unrest-uprisings in the provinces: Brussels; Nancy; Barcelona; Munich; Weimar; Darmstadt; Glasgow; Helsinki; Chicago; Vienna—the modern style arrives.

Todd, Pamela. *The Arts & Crafts Companion*. New York and Boston: Bulfinch Press, 2004. 320p.

Contents: Makers of the movement; Architecture; Architectural interiors; Furniture; Textiles & wallpaper; Stained glass & lighting; Pottery & ceramics; Metalwork & jewelry; Printed word; Gardens.

Marks, Hallmarks and Signatures

Reference sources that identify marks and signatures are extremely important to the decorative arts researcher. The following tools include works that provide marks and signatures for more than one of the decorative arts, e.g., silver and furniture. Guides devoted to a single form are included in the relevant subject-specific sections (e.g., porcelain) that follow.

Chervenka, Mark. *Antique Trader Guide to Fake & Forged Marks*. Iola, Wis.: Krause, 2002. 304p.

As the market for decorative arts objects has grown, so has the world of fakes and forgeries. This handy reference source provides a categorized pictorial guide to fake marks, side-by-side with the originals. Included are identifying marks of glass, porcelain, china and other decorative arts objects.

Macdonald-Taylor, Margaret. *A Dictionary of Marks*. Rev. ed. [i.e., 4th ed.], revised by Lucilla Watson. London: Barrie & Jenkins, 1992, 1989. 332p.

Partial contents: British metalwork; British silver—London; British silversmiths; British silver; Marks on English gold plate; Irish silver—Dublin; Marks on Irish gold plate; Irish silversmiths—Dublin; British pewterers' marks; American silversmiths' marks; American pewterers' marks; English furniture marks; French furniture marks; Tapestry marks; Ceramics: European marks; Japanese date marks; Chinese reign marks.

Furniture: Bibliographies

Semowich, Charles J. *American Furniture Craftsmen Working Prior to 1920: An Annotated Bibliography*. Westport, Conn.: Greenwood Press, 1984. 381p.

Extensive annotated bibliography of published works (books, periodicals, and trade publications) on American furniture craftsmen. Contents: Works about individual craftsmen; Works about groups of craftsmen; General works; Trade catalogs; American furniture periodicals; Manuscript collections; Craftsman-biographical index; Author-title, subject indexes.

Viaux, Jacqueline. *Bibliographie du Meuble (Mobilier Civil Fançais)*. Paris: Société des Amis de la Bibliothèque Forney, 1966. 589p. Supplement 1: *Supplément 1965–1985*. Paris: Agence Culturelle de Paris, 1988. 624p. Supplement 2: *Bibliographie du Meuble: Mobilier Civil Français: Second Supplement, 1985–1990 et Complements*. Paris: Bibliothèque Forney: Agence culturelle de Paris, 1998.

This extensive classified bibliography provides citations to periodical articles on French furniture dating from the medieval period through the 20th century. While perhaps not as widely available as the other titles selected here, Viaux's bibliography is selected for its comprehensive coverage of the subject.

Furniture: Collectors' Manuals

Jackson, Albert, and David Day. *Care & Repair of Furniture*. Newtown, Conn.: Taunton Press, 1994. 160p.

Practical "how to" book on the basics of furniture repair and conservation.

Jenkins, Emyl. *Emyl Jenkins' Reproduction Furniture: Antiques for the Next Generation*. New York: Crown, 1995. 204p.

Interesting history of the advent of antique reproduction in the U.S. Offers practical tips for the collector on identification and dating of reproduction furniture. The author, a well-known appraiser, offers pricing guidelines for good, fine, and exceptional examples of various types of reproduction furniture.

_____, with Joe E.A. Wilkinson. *Emyl Jenkins' Guide to Buying and Collecting Early American Furniture*. New York: Crown, 1991. 148p.

Part one comprises technical information for the collector, including advice on detecting fakes, various surface detailing (shrinkage, patina, finish), basic repair and restoration. A series of "case studies" offers guidance on such topics as "acceptable structural restoration," "acceptable replacement," etc.

Kaye, Myrna. *Fake, Fraud, or Genuine?: Identifying Authentic American Antique Furniture*. Boston: Little, Brown, 1987. 214p.

Expert advice on spotting fake furniture, for the serious collector or connoisseur.

Obbard, John. *Early American Furniture: A Practical Guide for Collectors*. Paducah, Ky.: Collector Books, 1999. 335p.

Good introduction to basics of early American furniture. Individual pieces organized by type (e.g., "Wing chairs and sofas"). Useful reference material, including: Understanding period and style; Evaluating quality; Antiques as an investment; Fakes and frauds.

Ormsbee, Thomas H. *Field Guide to Early American Furniture.* Boston: Little, Brown, 1951. 464p.

Dated, but still useful primer on the identification of early American furniture. Major sections arranged by furniture type, such as chairs and tables, and illustrated with clear, simple line drawings. Glossary of terms, essays on various periods and methods of detecting genuine pieces.

Taylor, V.J. *How To Be a Furniture Detective.* Iola, Wis.: Krause, 2004. 192p.

Suitable for the beginning collector, provides basic information on identifying fakes, identifying various styles, etc. Good clear line drawings illustrate periods and styles.

Furniture: Dictionaries

Dictionary of Furniture. Edited by Charles Boyce. 2nd ed. New York: Facts on File, 2001. 378p.

Encyclopedia of styles and forms, materials, craftsmen and designers. Some Asian but primarily Western design. Illustrated with clear line drawings. Includes practical advice for the beginning collector. "Places to Visit" chapter identifies and describes some important public collections for further research.

Gloag, John. *A Complete Dictionary of Furniture.* Revised and expanded by Clive Edwards. Woodstock, N.Y.: Overlook Press, 1991. 828p.

Illustrated dictionary of terms, periods and styles. Partial contents: Description of furniture; Design of furniture; Dictionary of names and terms; Furniture makers in Britain and America; Books and periodicals on furniture and design.

Furniture: Encyclopedias and Surveys

Aronson, Joseph. *The Encyclopedia of Furniture.* 3d ed. New York: Crown, [1965]. 484p.

Illustrated encyclopedia of terms and styles. Useful for clear descriptions and illustrations of individual objects types, designers, etc.

Ash, Douglas, et al. *World Furniture: An Illustrated History.* London: Hamlyn, 1969. 320p.

Very well-illustrated, encyclopedic survey of furniture, from ancient Egyptian through mid–20th century. Western countries, from Renaissance through 20th century, treated in great detail. Glossary of terms and bibliography.

Blakemore, Robbie G. *History of Interior Design and Furniture: From Ancient Egypt to Nineteenth-Century Europe.* New York: Van Nostrand Reinhold, 1997. 392p.

Contents: Egypt, c. 3200–341 B.C.; Greece, 500–30 B.C.; Rome, 509 B.C.–A.D. 476; Middle ages, 1150–1550; Italian Renaissance, 1460–1600; French Renaissance, 1450–1600; English Renaissance, 1500–1660; Italian baroque, 1600–1700; French baroque, 1600–1715; English baroque, 1660–1702; French rococo,

1700–1760; Early Georgian, England, 1715–1760; Early French neoclassic, 1760–1789; Early English neoclassic, 1770–1810; Late French neoclassic, 1789–1820; Late English neoclassic, 1810–1830; Nineteenth century French revival styles, 1815–1870; Nineteenth century English revival styles, 1830–1901.

Boger, Louise Ade. *The Complete Guide to Furniture Styles.* Enl. ed. New York: Scribner's, 1969. 500p.

Excellent encyclopedic source for the identification of (primarily Western) furniture styles.

Boidi Sassone, Adriana. *Furniture: From Rococo to Art Deco.* Cologne: Evergreen, 2000. 814p.

Comprehensive history of styles, arranged by century and subdivided by country, focus on Western Europe.

Classical Furniture. Editing director, Jordi Vigue. New York: Whitney, 1998. 208p.

Excellent source for the identification of classical and neoclassical styles, from the Renaissance to the 20th century. Glossary of terms.

Crochet, Treena. *Designer's Guide to Furniture Styles.* 2nd ed. Upper Saddle River, N.J.: Prentice Hall, [2003], 2004. 345p.

Textbook style work, good for identification of styles, periods and countries of origin. Ancient world through 20th century.

Edwards, Clive. *Encyclopedia of Furniture Materials, Trades, and Techniques.* Brookfield, Vt.: Ashgate, 2000. 254p.

Encyclopedia of processes, materials, forms and styles of furniture, with an emphasis on technical aspects of production. Historical focus, but some 20th century materials and styles are adequately covered.

Fiell, Charlotte, and Peter Fiell. *Modern Furniture Classics Since 1945.* London: Thames and Hudson, 1991. 192p.

Decade-by-decade survey of major innovations in contemporary furniture design. Partial contents: 1945 to 1950 Reconstruction and rationalism; 1950 to 1960 Ascendancy of organic design; 1960 to 1970 Pop culture and anti-design; 1970 to 1980 Conformist, reformist or contesting; 1980 to the present day, Eclectic years.

______. *1000 Chairs.* Cologne and New York: Taschen, 1997. 768p.

If you think you have a 20th century classic, this easy-to-use guide will assist in identifying the style and, if you're lucky, the actual piece. Chronological arrangement, includes 19th and 20th century chairs. Primarily residential, but some contemporary office and institutional pieces included.

Forrest, Tim. *The Bulfinch Anatomy of Antique Furniture: An Illustrated Guide to Identifying Period, Detail, and Design.* Paul Atterbury, consulting editor. Boston: Little, Brown, 1996. 160p.

Aptly described as an "anatomy" of furniture, major styles are deconstructed and fully illustrated with photographs and good quality line drawings. Arranged by furniture type (e.g., chairs and stools, upholstered furniture, etc.); serves as an excellent guide for the serious collector.

Furniture Design = Möbel Design. Edited by Paco Asensio. New York: TeNeues, 2002. 400p.

Arranged by furniture type, well illustrated survey of the latest in contemporary furniture design.

Greenberg, Cara. *Mid-Century Modern: Furniture of the 1950s.* 1st rev. ed. New York: Harmony Books, 1995. 176p.

Well-illustrated overview of classic 1950s furniture.

Linley, David. *Classical Furniture.* New York: Abrams, 1993. 192 p.

Contents: Classical idea; Golden age of Classicism; Pattern of perfection; Directory of furniture; Arrangement and display. A richly illustrated study, the directory is particularly useful for the identification of styles.

Mang, Karl. *The History of Modern Furniture.* Translation by John William Gabriel of *Geschichte des Modernen Mobels.* New York: Abrams, 1979. 185p.

Scholarly but very readable history of the evolution of contemporary furniture styles. Covers major developments from the 19th century through post World War II. Partial contents: Anonymous furniture in the nineteenth century—harbingers of the Machine Aesthetic; Theories of William Morris and the challenge of industry; From de Stijl to the International Style; Scandinavian furniture—from anonymity to world renown; Furniture design after World War II.

Morley, John. *The History of Furniture: Twenty-Five Centuries of Style and Design in the Western Tradition.* Boston: Little, Brown, 1999. 352p.

Contents: Antiquity; Disintegration of classicism 300–1450; "Pointed" styles—Islamic and Gothic; Renaissance revival of antiquity—classicism and anti-classicism; Baroque contrasts; Battle of styles: English classicism, rococo and "gŏut Grec"; Modified rococo and the new neo-classicism; Grotesque and "archaeological" classicism; Eclectic revivalism; Frugality and functionalism; Wilder shores of style: China, Japan, India, Egypt, Africa; Latter-day polarities.

_____. *Regency Design, 1790–1840: Gardens, Buildings, Interiors, Furniture.* New York: Abrams, 1993. 473p.

Regency style furniture is inextricably related to interior design trends of the period. Both are very well covered here. Line drawings, original designs, and interiors depicted in early 19th century works of art, along with photographic reproductions of pieces from public and private collections make this an excellent source for the identification of stylistic variations in Regency furniture.

Ostergard, Derek E., ed. *Bent Wood and Metal Furniture: 1850–1946.* Washington, D.C.: University of Washington Press in association with the American Federation of Arts, 1987. 366p.

Traces the development of bent wood and metal furniture from the pre-industrial age through mid–20th century. Many reproductions, original advertisements, designers' drawings and other source material make this an excellent source for bent wood and metal furniture identification and dating.

Riccardi-Cubitt, Monique. *The Art of the Cabinet; Including a Chronological Guide to Styles.* London: Thames and Hudson, 1992. 224p.

Scholarly study, illustrated with many examples of magnificent cabinetry. Particularly useful for its "Illustrated Chronological Guide to Styles" which traces the development of the cabinet visually from 1400 through 1900, and biographical sketches of major cabinetmakers, craftsmen and designers.

Sotheby's Concise Encyclopedia of Furniture. General Editor Christopher Payne. New York: Harper & Row; Toronto: Fitzhenry & Whiteside, 1989. 208p.

Authoritative, signed articles on Western furniture styles. Contents: Early furniture; Renaissance; Baroque; Rococ revival; Eclecticism; Craft and design; Machine age; Modern times; Bibliography; Guide to recognizing and dating furniture.

Stimpson, Miriam F. *Modern Furniture Classics*. New York: Whitney Library of Design, 1987. 207p.

Classic examples of furniture dating from the 18th century through the 1980s. Each piece is illustrated and fully described. Brief designer biographies and other details included.

Synge, Lanto. *Mallett Millennium: Fine Antique Furniture and Works of Art*. London: Mallet, in association with Antique Collectors' Club, 1999. 360p.

Richly illustrated history of prestigious British antique gallery active since the 19th century. Comprises primarily furniture offerings, but also includes sections on sculpture, clocks, textiles, and glass.

Victoria and Albert Museum. *Western Furniture: 1350 to the Present Day in the Victoria and Albert Museum*. Edited by Christopher Wilk. New York: Cross River Press, 1996. 231p.

History of the Victoria and Albert collection. Chronologically-arranged discussion of primarily Western European pieces traces the evolution of furniture design from the 14th through late 20th centuries.

White, Antony, and Bruce Robertson. *Furniture & Furnishings: A Visual Guide*. New York: Design Press, 1990. 109p.

Visually-oriented guide to furniture styles, arranged by furniture type (beds, chairs, etc.). Sections on "Construction and Parts," and "Decoration and Finish" similarly arranged. Very good basic reference tool for the beginning collector.

Furniture: Country Studies

Australia

Fahy, Kevin. *Nineteenth Century Australian Furniture*. Sydney: David Ell Press, 1985. 624p.

Encyclopedic survey of colonial furniture of Australia. Introductory essays on the furniture of each Australian colony precede pictorial survey of the furniture, arranged by type. Partial contents: New South Wales; Queensland; South Australia; Tasmania; Victoria; Western Australia; Styles and sources; Labels, stamps, stencils and inscriptions; Directory of cabinet, chair and furniture makers.

Canada

Fleming, John A. *The Painted Furniture of French Canada, 1700–1840*. Camden East, Ont.: Camden House, 1994. 179p.

Explores the various styles, materials, and methods of construction of French Canadian painted furniture.

Pain, Howard. *The Heritage of Country Furniture: A Study in the Survival of Formal and Vernacular Styles from the United States, Britain and Europe found in Upper Canada, 1780–1900.* New York: Van Nostrand Reinhold, 1978. 548p.
Encyclopedic overview of Canadian furniture and domestic tools and implements. Each section focuses on influence of particular national traditions, arranged by furniture type. Partial contents: Style influences in the furniture of upper Canada; Anglo-American tradition; Germanic tradition; Polish tradition; French Canadian tradition.

Palardy, Jean. *The Early Furniture of French Canada.* Translated from the French by Eric McLean. 2nd rev. ed. Toronto: Macmillan of Canada; New York: St. Martin's Press, 1965. 413p.
Copious illustrations of pieces in public and private collections illustrate the structure, design and decoration of primarily 18th and 19th century French Canadian furniture.

Wright, Virginia. *Modern Furniture in Canada, 1920 to 1970.* Toronto and Buffalo: University of Toronto Press, 1997. 208p.
Surveys the evolution of modern furniture design in Canada, from the earliest European-inspired commercial pieces through the 1970s. Well-illustrated and indexed, good source for identification.

Caribbean

Nije-Statius van Eps, Georgette E. *Furniture from Curacao, Aruba, and Bonaire: Three Centuries of Dutch Caribbean Craftsmanship.* Translation from the Dutch by Wendy Leivesley Thompson. Zutphen, the Netherlands: Walburg Pers, 1995. 175 p.
Well-illustrated study of Dutch Caribbean furniture design. Very brief introduction to pre-Columbian period precedes chronologically-arranged sections on the furniture of Curaçao, Aruba and Bonaire.

China

Berliner, Nancy, et al. *Beyond the Screen: Chinese Furniture of the 16th and 17th Centuries.* Boston: Museum of Fine Arts, 1996. 158p.
Scholarly exhibition catalog on evolution and history of Chinese furniture.

Clunas, Craig. *Chinese Furniture.* London: Bamboo, 1988. 119p.
Pieces in the collection of the Victoria and Albert Museum serve to illustrate this very readable overview of Chinese furniture.

Ellsworth, Robert Hatfield. *Chinese Furniture: Hardwood Examples of the Ming and Early Ching Dynasties.* New Fairfield, Conn.: The Author, [1998?]. 299p.
Composed largely of illustrations arranged by type of furniture (tables, stands, etc.). Excellent source for identification. Scholarly treatment for the serious collector.

Handler, Sarah. *Austere Luminosity of Chinese Classical Furniture.* Berkeley: University of California Press, 2001. 417p.
Scholarly history of Chinese furniture, arranged by type. Partial contents: Revolution and discovery; Chairs; Beds; Tables; Cabinets and screens; Stands.

Shixiang, Wang. *Connoisseurship of Chinese Furniture: Ming and Early Qing Dynasties.* Translation of *Ming shi cia chü yen chiu.* Chicago: Art Media Resources; Hong Kong: Joint Publishing (H.K.), 1990. 2 vols.

Translation of classic study of classic Chinese furniture styles. Partial contents: Ming and early Qing furniture; Types and forms of furniture; Construction and joinery; Decoration; Materials; Problems of dating and alterations.

France

Bouzin, Claude. *Meuble et Artisanat: XIIIe-XVIIIe Siècle.* Paris: Amateur, 2003. 207p.

Scholarly study of materials, methods and styles. Appendix includes biographies of major cabinet makers.

Claret Rubira, Jose. *Encyclopedia of French Period Furniture Designs.* Translation of *Muebles de Estilo Frances.* New York: Sterling, 1983. 416p.

Very well-illustrated selection of French period designs, presented in chronological order. Line drawings clearly depict examples of Romanesque, Gothic, Renaissance, Louis XIV, Regency Louis XV and XVI. Excellent source for period identification.

Duncan, Alastair. *Art Deco Furniture: The French Designers.* New York: Thames and Hudson, 1992, 1984. 192p.

Well-illustrated introduction to French Art Deco includes substantial biographies of major designers.

French Cabinetmakers of the Eighteenth Century. Foreword by Pierre Verlet. Translation of *Ebenistes du XVIIIe Siècle Français.* [Paris]: Hachette; [New York: French & European, 1965]. 341p. (Series: *Collection Connaissance des Arts "Grands Artisans d'Autrefois.*)

Standard history of 18th century French furniture in the form of chronologically arranged biographical essays of prominent cabinetmakers. Many entries include monogram or signature sample.

Hinckley, F. Lewis. *A Directory of Antique French Furniture, 1735–1800; Over 300 Illustrations of Provincial, Parisian, and other European Antique Furniture.* New York: Crown, [1967]. 214p.

This source comprises largely illustrations, and is therefore very useful for identifying various types of furniture. Partial contents: Designers and craftsmen of Paris and other metropolitan furniture centers of France; Register of master cabinet makers of provinces other than Île de France; Vocabulary of French terms applied to 18th-century furniture.

_____. *Le Meuble Français et Europeen du Moyen Age à Nos Jours.* Paris: Editions de l'Amateur, 1991. 591p.

Excellent source for identifying various styles and periods of French furniture, from Gothic and Renaissance through Art Nouveau and Art Deco.

Kjellberg, Pierre. *Le Mobilier Français du XVIIIe Siècle: Dictionnaire des Ébénistes et des Menuisiers.* New ed. Paris: Editions de l'Amateur, 2002. 927p.

Beautifully illustrated, A-Z dictionary of 18th century French furniture craftsmen. Entries include birth/death dates, stamps and monograms, French, American, British and other museums' holdings.

Ledoux-Lebard, Denise. *Les Ébénistes du XIXe Siècle, 1795–1889: Leurs Œuvres et Leurs Marques.* Paris: Éditions de l'Amateur, 1989. 700p.

Scholarly survey of 19th century French cabinetmakers and their identifying marks.

Pradère, Alexandre. *French Furniture Makers: The Art of the Ébéniste from Louis XIV to the Revolution.* Translation by Perran Wood of *Les Ébénistes français: de Louis XIV à la Revolution.* Malibu, Calif.: J. Paul Getty Museum, 1989. 442p.

A-Z encyclopedia of important French furniture makers; individual entries illustrated, often in color, followed by: Glossary of woods; Glossary of French terms; List of identified Ébénistes of the 17th and 18th centuries; Bibliography.

Thirion, Jacques. *Le Mobilier du Moyen Age et de la Renaissance en France.* Dijon: Éditions Faton, 1998. 279p.

Beautifully illustrated overview of the evolution of furniture styles from the middle ages through the Renaissance. Types of furniture, decoration, and iconographic analysis of figural ornamentation.

Verlet, Pierre. *French Furniture and Interior Decoration of the 18th Century.* Translated from the French by George Savage. London: Barrie & Rockliffe, 1967. 292p.

The evolution of 18th century furniture designs is surveyed in a social historical context. Interiors and their furnishings depicted by artists of the period supplement good photographic reproductions of pieces in major public and private collections.

Viaux, Jacqueline. *French Furniture.* Translation of *Le Meuble en France.* New York: Putnam, [1964]. 200p.

Contents: Technical introduction; Middle ages; Renaissance; Louis XIII; Louis XIV; Regency and Louis XV; Louis XVI; Directory and Empire; Restoration; Second Empire; Third and Fourth Republics.

Great Britain

Bowett, Adam. *English Furniture: 1660–1714: From Charles II to Queen Anne.* Woodbridge, Eng.: Antique Collectors' Club, 2002. 323p.

Beautifully illustrated, scholarly history of furniture styles of the 17th and early 18th centuries. Pieces from major museum collections illustrate the evolution of various furniture forms, as well as technical aspects of furniture production, including lacquer, japanning and other surface treatments.

Chinnery, Victor. *Oak Furniture: The British Tradition: A History of Early Furniture in the British Isles and New England.* Woodbridge, Suffolk [England]: Antique Collectors' Club, 1986, 1979. 618p.

In-depth analysis of the early furniture trades includes a good deal of primary source material of interest to the furniture historian. Copious reproductions, and the "Pictorial Furniture Index" (arranged by type of furniture) make this an excellent tool for the identification of style and dating.

Collard, Frances. *Regency Furniture.* Woodbridge, Suffolk, England: Antique Collectors' Club, 1985. 346p.

Beautifully illustrated survey of Regency furniture styles. Appendix, "Prominent Regency craftsmen and designers," provides brief biography of major figures. Partial contents: Henry Holland, French taste and Neoclassicism; Thomas Sheraton and the pattern books of the early Regency; Thomas Hope and Greek Revival; French influence in the later Regency; Historic revivals; Exotics and rustics; Upholstery; Techniques and materials.

Dictionary of English Furniture Makers, 1660–1840. Edited by Geoffrey Beard and Christopher Gilbert; assistant editors, Brian Austen, Arthur Bond, Angela Evans. [Leeds]: Furniture History Society: W.S. Maney, 1986. 1,046 p.

This biographical dictionary includes information culled from a great variety of primary sources, including trade and post office directories, newspapers, trade cards, sales catalogues, personal and corporate records. Identifies designers, finishers, tradesmen, auctioneers and others active in the furniture industry.

Gilbert, Christopher. *English Vernacular Furniture 1750–1900.* New Haven, Conn.: Published for the Paul Mellon Centre for Studies in British Art by Yale University Press, 1991. 294p.

Scholarly study of vernacular, or "common" furniture of the period. In addition to domestic furnishings, institutional pieces and settings (e.g., schools, lunatic asylums, etc.) are treated in depth.

_____. *Pictorial Dictionary of Marked London Furniture, 1700–1840.* [London]: Furniture History Society; [Leeds]: W.S. Maney & Son, 1996.

For the serious collector of British furniture, serves as an excellent identification source. Includes information on over 300 British furniture makers, including reference source material on their marks and labels.

Knell, David. *English Country Furniture: The Vernacular Tradition, 1500–1900.* 2nd ed. Woodbridge, Eng.: Antique Collectors' Club, 2000. 415p.

Very well-illustrated, scholarly study. Arranged by furniture type (tables, seating, etc.), represents an excellent source for identification of furniture of the period.

Macquoid, Percy, and Ralph Edwards. *The Dictionary of English Furniture: From the Middle Ages to the Late Georgian Period.* 2nd ed. Barra Books, 1983, 1954. 3 vols.

In-depth analysis of English furniture includes long survey articles on the development of furniture types (bureaus, chairs, etc.), as well as miscellaneous works of decorative art. Some biographical essays on major figures.

Parissien, Steven. *Regency Style.* London: Phaidon Press, 1992. 240p.

Overview of Regency style, including architecture, architectural details, gardens, "joinery and plasterwork," and furniture.

Pictorial Dictionary of British 18th Century Furniture Design: The Printed Sources. Compiled by Elizabeth White. Woodbridge, Suffolk, Eng.: Antique Collectors Club, 1990. 503p.

Classified, heavily illustrated guide to 18th century British furniture. Images are culled from 18th century (primarily British) books on furniture and design. Short biographies of furniture designers precede the classified section on furniture types.

Pictorial Dictionary of British 19th Century Furniture Design: An Antique Collectors' Club Research Project. Woodbridge, Eng.: Antique Collectors' Club, 1977. 583p.

Like the preceding entry, this richly illustrated work includes substantive biographies on major furniture designers, along with copious examples of their work as seen in 19th century publications.

Strange, Thomas Arthur. *English Furniture, Decoration, Woodwork & Allied Arts: During the Last Half of the Seventeenth Century, the Whole of the Eighteenth Century and the Earlier Part of the Nineteenth Century: A Guide to Collectors.* London: Studio Editions, 1986. 368p.

From bedposts to writing tables, 47 architects, designers and authors' works chart the evolution of English furniture and allied arts. In most cases, works are illustrated by clear line drawings from original sources.

India

Jaffer, Amin. *Furniture from British India and Ceylon: A Catalogue of the Collections in the Victoria and Albert Museum and the Peabody Essex Museum.* Salem, Mass: Peabody Essex Museum, 2001. 416p.

Brief social history of early British India precedes the descriptive catalog of pieces arranged by region.

Ireland

Kinmouth, Claudia. *Irish Country Furniture, 1700–1950.* New Haven, Conn.: Yale University Press, 1993. 249p.

Scholarly, well-illustrated study of Irish vernacular architecture and furniture. Major portion devoted to analysis of specific forms (beds, dressers, etc.).

Italy

Cera, Maurizio. *Il Mobile dell'Ottocento: 1815–1915.* Vicenza: Neri Pozza, 1997. 166p.

Illustrated survey of 19th century Italian furniture styles, arranged by type (chairs, tables, etc.).

Colle, Enrico. *Italian Empire Furniture: Furnishings and Interior Design from 1800 to 1843.* New York: Rizzoli, 2001. 438p.

Lavishly illustrated, scholarly history of Italian Empire. Partial contents: Evolution of the various "manners" of furnishing in Empire Style; Kingdoms of Naples and Sicily; Rome; Grand Duchy of Tuscany; Duchy of Lucca; Kingdom of Lombardy and the Veneto; Papal Legations and the Ducies of Modena and Parma; Kingdom of Sardinia.

Fioratti, Helen Costantino. *Il Mobile Italiano: Dall'Antichità allo Stile Impero.* Florence: Giunti, 2004. 331p.

Beautifully-illustrated monograph traces the evolution of Italian furniture styles. Includes many good quality color reproductions, along with clear line drawings of early, medieval, Renaissance, Baroque, Rococo, and Neoclassical pieces.

Japan

Clarke, Rosy. *Japanese Antique Furniture: A Guide to Evaluating and Restoring.* New York: Weatherhill, 1983. 150p.

Useful guide intended for professional appraisers, conservators, and other specialists. Partial contents: Identification; Evaluation; Restoration; Care and maintenance.

Koizumi, Kazuko. *Traditional Japanese Furniture.* Tokyo and New York: Kodansha International, 1986.

This well-illustrated overview of Japanese furniture is an excellent source for identifying and dating various styles, ancient through modern.

Korea

Wright, Edward Reynolds, and Man Sill Pai. *Traditional Korean Furniture.* 2nd ed. Tokyo and New York: Kodansha International, 2000. 192p.

In-depth survey includes hundreds of good quality color plates; excellent source for identification.

Russia

Chenevière, Antoine. *Russian Furniture: The Golden Age, 1780–1840.* Woodbridge: Antique Collectors' Club, 2001. 320p.

Meticulously researched overview of Russian furniture; hundreds of major pieces illustrated and fully documented. Appendix includes biographical sketches of architects, cabinet-makers, carvers and designers active during the subject period.

Spain

Burr, Grace Hardendorff. *Hispanic Furniture, from the Fifteenth Through the Eighteenth Century.* 2nd ed., rev. and enl. New York: Archive Press, 1964. 231p.

Surveys Hispanic furniture of the 15th through 18th centuries. Partial contents: Spanish Gothic furniture; Renaissance; Seventeenth century; Eighteenth century; Colonial furniture; Hispanic Society Collection.

Claret Rubira, José. *Encyclopedia of Spanish Period Furniture Designs.* Translation of *Meubles de estilo español.* New York: Sterling, 1984. 352p.

Line drawings illustrate Spanish furniture styles dating from the 14th through 19th centuries.

Sweden

Groth, Hakan. *Neoclassicism in the North: Swedish Furniture and Interiors, 1770–1850;* With a Catalog of Furniture Types and Styles and Notes on the architects, artists, and craftsmen. New York: Rizzoli, 1990. 224p.

Richly illustrated survey of the Swedish interior; "Catalogue of furniture types and styles" presents representative examples of various furnishings, arranged by type.

United States

American Furniture. [Milwaukee, Wis.]: Chipstone Foundation; Hanover, N.H.: Distributed by University Press of New England. Annual, 1993– .

"Interdisciplinary journal dedicated to advancing knowledge of furniture made or used in the Americas from the seventeenth century to the present." (Editorial Statement, p. vii, 1999 edition). Each annual issue contains several lengthy, well-illustrated scholarly studies of American furniture history.

Bartolucci, Marisa, and Cathy Lang Ho. *American Contemporary Furniture.* New York: Universe, 2000. 208p.

Survey of major contemporary furniture designers by leading journalists in the design field.

Clark, Michael E., and Jill Thomas-Clark. *The Stickley Brothers: The Quest for an American Voice.* Salt Lake City: Gibbs Smith, 2002. 176p.

Contents: Introduction : the voice and the players; A timeline of the Stickley brothers; The first twenty-five years; Gustav and Albert's contributions; Charles, Leopold and John George's contributions; An epilogue : the end of the quest; Stickley brothers furniture shop marks.

Evans, Nancy Goyne. *American Windsor Furniture: Specialized Forms.* New York: Hudson Hills Press, in association with the Henry Francis du Pont Winterthur Museum, 1997. 256p.

Partial contents: Writing-arm chair; Rocking chair; Special purpose seating; Settees and benches; Children's furniture; Miniature furniture or toys; Stools; Stands and tables; Wheels and reels.

Greene, Jeffrey P. *American Furniture of the 18th Century.* Newtown, Conn.: Taunton Press, 1996. 311p.

Partial contents: Origins and evolution of American furniture styles; Methods and materials of the 18th century cabinetmaker; Examples of style and structure: William & Mary, Queen Anne, Chippendale, Federal. Very good line drawings expose the structure of classic American pieces of the 18th century.

Hurst, Ronald L., and Jonathan Prown. *Southern Furniture, 1680–1830: The Colonial Williamsburg Collection.* Williamsburg, Va.: Colonial Williamsburg Foundation in association with Harry N. Abrams, 1997. 639p.

Scholarly history and analysis of previously under-researched Southern furniture styles and periods. Each piece is very well-illustrated, and documented with notes on construction, condition, materials, dimensions, provenance.

Kassay, John. *The Book of American Windsor Furniture: Styles and Technologies.* Amherst: University of Massachusetts Press, 1998. 195p.

Well-illustrated history of popular 18th century style, arranged by furniture type, e.g., low-back chairs, fan-back chairs, etc.

Ketchum, William C. *American Cabinetmakers: Marked American Furniture, 1640–1940.* New York: Crown, 1995. 404p.

Standard reference source for identification of marks by American furniture craftsmen.

Kirk, John T. *American Furniture: Understanding Styles, Construction, and Quality.* New York: Abrams, [2000]. 234p.

Practical advice for the serious collector and connoisseur. Partial contents: Seventeenth century, William and Mary style, Queen Anne style; Rococo period and Chippendale style; Two phases of the federal period; Modern practices.

Miller, Edgar George. *The Standard Book of American Antique Furniture.* New York: Greystone Press, [1950]. 856p.

Hundreds of adequate quality black and white reproductions make this an essential source for the beginning researcher of American antique furniture. Each illustrated work includes a good description, from which the novice might cull descriptive terminology for further research.

Naeve, Milo M. *Identifying American Furniture: A Pictorial Guide to Styles and Terms, Colonial to Contemporary.* 3rd ed., rev. and expanded. Walnut Creek, Calif.: AltaMira Press, 1998. 108p.

For the beginning collector, an excellent source for identification. Coverage spans medieval English-inspired styles through late 20th century.

Nutting, Wallace. *Furniture Treasury (Mostly of American Origin): All Periods of American Furniture with Some Foreign Examples in America, Also American Hardware and Household Utensils.* New York: Macmillan, [1928–1933]. 3v. in 2.

Thousands of illustrated entries, very useful for identification of American furniture through early part of the 20th century.

Petraglia, Patricia. *Sotheby's Guide to American Furniture.* New York: Simon and Schuster, 1995. 300p.

Professional level, but very readable. Each of the main chapters describes a particular period or style (e.g., Federal, Empire, etc.), and offers concrete advice for the collector and connoisseur, including: Look for (good example); Look for (outstanding example); Conservation issues; Cabinetmakers/firms important to style; Where public can see best examples; Department expert wish list; Miscellaneous.

Richards, Nancy E., and Nancy Goyne Evans. *New England Furniture at Winterthur: Queen Anne and Chippendale Periods.* Winterthur, Del.: Winterthur Museum ; [s.l.] : Distributed by University Press of New England, 1997. 514p.

Scholarly catalog arranged by furniture type: seating, bedsteads, tables, etc. Each work fully documented, with notes on construction, condition, dimensions, materials, provenance, inscriptions and marks.

Rieman, Timothy D., and Jean M. Burks. *The Complete Book of Shaker Furniture.* New York: Abrams, 1993. 400 p.

Beautifully illustrated study of Shaker furnishings. Primary sections arranged geographically, by name of bishopric. Includes glossaries of Shaker and technical terminology.

_____. *Encyclopedia of Shaker Furniture.* Atglen, Pa.: Schiffer, 2003. 576p.

Updated and expanded edition of previous reference. Arranged geographically (by bishopric), this encyclopedia is an excellent source for the study of regional variations on Shaker furniture styles.

Sack, Albert. *The New Fine Points of Furniture: Early American, Good, Better, Best, Superior, Masterpiece.* New York: Crown, 1993. 320p.

Major American furniture dealer Albert Sack juxtaposes "good," "better," "best" examples of major styles and periods of American furniture. Good photograph reproductions, and easy-to-read text create a primer for the would-be connoisseur of fine American furniture.

Santore, Charles. *The Windsor Style in America: The Definitive Pictorial Study of the History and Regional Characteristics of the Most Popular Furniture Form of Eighteenth-Century America, 1730–1840*. Philadelphia: Courage Books, 1997. 294p.

Comprising two volumes, this work is possibly the most extensive published inventory of Windsor furniture. Excellent source for the identification of regional examples.

Siegel, Jeanne. *How to Speak Furniture with an Antique American accent: An Extensive American Furniture Vocabulary*. Wilmette, Ill.: Paper Bird, 1987. 200p.

Handy, pocket-sized glossary of specialized terminology relating to American furniture styles. Coverage includes: Chippendale; Empire; Hepplewhite; Puritan; Queen Anne; Sheraton; Victorian; William and Mary.

Swedberg, Robert W., and Harriett Swedberg. *American Oak Furniture: Styles and Prices, Book III*. 2nd ed. Radnor, Pa.: Wallace-Homestead Book, 1991. 162p.

Practical advice for the collector of American oak furniture.

Pottery, Ceramics and Porcelain: Bibliographies

Campbell, James Edward. *Pottery and Ceramics: A Guide to Information Sources*. Detroit: Gale Research, 1978. 241p.

Contents: Reference works; General histories, dictionaries and encyclopedias; Ancient and pre-Columbian ceramics; Eastern ceramics; Western ceramics, Greece to the Middle Ages; Western ceramics, Middle Ages to the twentieth century; Ceramics of the United States, Canada and Mexico; Contemporary world ceramics; Ceramic collections; Ceramic marks; Technical works on ceramic materials and processes; Ceramic periodicals; Ceramic organizations and societies; Museum collections in the U.S.

Weidner, Ruth Irwin. *American Ceramics Before 1930: A Bibliography*. Westport, Conn.: Greenwood Press, 1982. 279p.

Subject-indexed bibliography of books and pamphlets, conference proceedings, book chapters, catalogs (exhibition, collections and sales), theses and dissertations, federal, state and municipal publications, trade materials and periodical articles.

Pottery, Ceramics and Porcelain: Collectors' Manuals

Williams, Nigel. *Porcelain Repair and Restoration*. 2nd ed., updated by Loretta Hogan and Myrtle Bruce-Mitford. Philadelphia: University of Pennsylvania Press, 2002. 160p.

Partial contents: Documentation and examination; Dismantling and cleaning; Reconstruction; Replacing missing parts; Colour mixing; Spraying and painting.

Pottery, Ceramics and Porcelain: Dictionaries

Cohen, David Harris, and Catherine Hess. *Looking at European Ceramics: A Guide to Technical Terms*. Malibu, Calif.: J. Paul Getty Museum in association with the British Museum Press, 1993. 91p.

Like other titles in the Getty Museum's *Looking at...* series, this brief primer on ceramics is very well illustrated (of ten in color) and offers clear but substantive definitions of technical and stylistic terms.

Savage, George, and Harold Newman. *An Illustrated Dictionary of Ceramics: Defining 3,054 Terms Relating to Wares, Materials, Processes, Styles, Patterns, and Shapes from Antiquity to the Present Day*. London: Thames & Hudson, 1985. 319p.

A-Z illustrated dictionary of terms, styles, etc. "Principle European factories and their marks" provides very brief sketch of factory and proprietor(s), products, styles and personalities, and identifying marks.

Pottery, Ceramics and Porcelain: Encyclopedias and Surveys

Cameron, Elisabeth. *Encyclopedia of Pottery and Porcelain: 1800–1960*. New York: Facts on File, 1986. 366p.

Biographical dictionary of pottery and porcelain designers and manufacturers. Most references include a highly selective bibliography for further research. Includes some marks and monograms.

Ceramics of the World: From 4000 B.C. to the Present. Lorenzo Carusso and Sandro Bortone, general editors. New York: Abrams, 1992. 399p.

Contents: The Near East, Egypt and the Mediterranean; Greek vases; Kilns of ancient Rome; Ceramics of the Islamic world; European majolica; European porcelain; North American ceramics; Chinese ceramics; Korean ceramics; Japanese ceramics.

Chaffers, William. *Marks & Monograms on European and Oriental Pottery and Porcelain*. Edited by Frederick Lichfield. 14th rev. ed. Los Angeles: Borden, [1946]. 1,095p.

Much more than a directory of marks and monograms, this standard reference tool serves as a comprehensive survey of pottery and porcelain, including works produced in Asian countries. Special features include historical price figures, taken from auction sales catalogs, through 1931.

Cox, Warren Earle. *The Book of Pottery and Porcelain*. 2 vol. New York: L. Lee and Shepard, distributed by Crown, [1944]. 1,158p.

Standard global history of pottery and porcelain, from ancient times through mid–20th century. Includes 3,000 illustrations, copious illustrations of marks and monograms.

Kingery, W.D. *Ceramic Masterpieces: Art, Structure, and Technology*. New York: Free Press; London: Collier Macmillan, 1986. 339p.

Ancient through 20th century. Egyptian, Asian, Islamic and Western masterpieces analyzed. Partial contents: History of ceramics, ceramic science, ceramic technology; Technical information on shaping and firing, glazes and decoration, etc.

Lane, Peter. *Contemporary Studio Porcelain.* 2nd ed. London: A & C Black; Philadelphia: University of Pennsylvania, 2003. 256p.

Survey of contemporary functional and sculptural porcelain, with an emphasis on techniques and materials.

McCready, Karen. *Art Deco and Modernist Ceramics.* Introduction by Garth Clark. New York: Thames and Hudson, 1995. 192p.

Reference work includes hundreds of color reproductions, along with an "A-Z of Ceramists, Designers and Factories." Excellent tool to identify works of 20th century pottery or porcelain.

Morley-Fletcher, Hugo, and Roger McIlroy. *Christie's Pictorial History of European Pottery.* Englewood Cliffs, N.J.: Prentice-Hall, 1984. 319p.

Geographically-organized survey of European pottery production. Partial contents: Spain and Portugal; Italy pre–1600; Italy post–1600; Northern Europe; France; Netherlands; England: Delft; England: Pottery. Includes auction prices dating from the 1960s through the 1980s.

Sentence, Bryan. *Ceramics: A World Guide to Traditional Techniques.* London and New York: Thames & Hudson, 2004. 216p.

Heavily illustrated essays on everything from "Forming techniques" (e.g., slab building) to firing methods and glazing techniques.

Pottery, Ceramics and Porcelain: Country Studies

Asia

Alphen, J. van (Jan). *Korea: Keramiek.* Antwerp and Leiden: Rijksmuseum voor Volkenkunde, [1993]. 149p.

Scholarly history of the development of Korean ceramics. Partial contents: Ceramics in Korea. History of influences and religious spheres; Korean potters' techniques and terminology; Pre-Koryŏ ceramics; Celadons of the Koryŏ Kingdom; Punch'ŏng stoneware; White porcelain of Chosŏn Dynasty; Influence of Korean ceramics on Japan.

Blumenfield, Robert H. *Blanc de Chine: The Great Porcelain of Dehua.* Berkeley: Ten Speed Press, 2002. 240p.

Partial contents: Brief history of blanc de Chine; Styles and forms of blanc de Chine; Crafting of blanc de Chine; Dehua manufacturers and their styles; Decorative sources; Dating blanc de Chine; Domestic and foreign markets for blanc de Chine; Development of porcelain manufacture in Europe; Non-blanc de Chine white wares.

Carswell, John. *Blue & White: Chinese Porcelain Around the World.* Chicago: Art Media Resources, 2000. 208p.

Traces the origin of blue and white porcelain in the Yuan dynasty. Many good color images make this a likely source for identification and stylistic analysis.

Howard, David Sanctuary. *The Choice of the Private Trader: The Private Market in Chinese Export Porcelain Illustrated from the Hodroff Collection.* London: Zwemmer, 1994. 298p.

Partial contents: Plates and dishes; Dinner service: other pieces; Tea and coffee set; Other drinking vessels; Utensils; Jars, vases and garnitures; Figures, birds, animals and fish.

Impey, O. R. (Oliver R.). *The Early Porcelain Kilns of Japan: Arita in the First Half of the Seventeenth Century.* Oxford: Clarendon Press; New York: Oxford University Press, 1996. 156p.

Traces the development of the porcelain industry in Japan (Arita) from the 17th century.

Litzenburg, Thomas V. *Chinese Export Porcelain in the Reeves Center Collection at Washington and Lee University.* London: Third Millennium, 2003. 288p.

Two hundred and eighty works (16th through 19th centuries) fully documented and beautifully illustrated.

Macintosh, Duncan. *Chinese Blue and White Porcelain.* 3rd ed. Woodbridge, Suffolk: Antique Collectors' Club, 1994. 236p.

Partial contents: Origins: the fourteenth century; Classical period: the 15th century; Late Ming wares: the 16th century; Later blue and white: the 18th and 19th centuries; Exports to Southeast Asia and Annamese wares; Blue and white and the West.

Walters, W. T. (William Thompson). *Oriental Ceramic Art: Illustrated by Examples from the Collection of W. T. Walters.* Text and notes by S. W. Bushell. New York: Crown, 1980. 429p.

Any serious study of porcelain must begin with China, where the medium was invented. This extensive history includes very in-depth chapters on Chinese porcelain, including a great deal of technical material. Korean and Japanese ceramic arts are covered minimally.

France

Dawson, Aileen. *A Catalogue of French Porcelain in the British Museum.* London: British Museum Press, 1994. 429p.

Scholarly treatment of the British Museum's collection serves as an excellent source for identification. Each work fully illustrated and documented, many with detail shots of marks and signatures.

Savage, George. *Seventeenth and Eighteenth Century French Porcelain.* London: Barrie & Rockliff, [1960]. 243p.

Partial contents: The earliest French porcelain; The Chantilly factory; Later soft porcelain factories; Vincennes-Sèvres; Hard porcelain in France; Factories of Alsace and Lorraine; Later Paris factories; Tuornai and St. Amand-les-Eaux; Forgeries; Marks, Date letters, Artists' marks.

Great Britain

Barrett, Franklin A. *Worcester Porcelain and Lund's Bristol.* London: Faber and Faber, 1966. 92p. 103 plates.

Contents: Lund's Bristol china works and the origins of china manufacture at Worcester; Worcester—the early productions; Worcester after the Chelsea migration; Black and other enamel printing; Underglaze blue decoration; Figures and kindred productions; Outside decoration; Later Worcester wares; Marks.

Battie, David. *David Battie's Guide to Understanding 19th & 20th Century British Porcelain: Including Fakes, Techniques and Prices.* Woodbridge [Eng.]: Antique collectors' Club, 1994. 320p.

The arrangement by object type (bowls, plaques, etc.), rather than by factory name, makes this work very useful for identifying manufacturer.

Bergesen, Victoria. *Encyclopaedia of British Art Pottery, 1870–1920.* London: Barrie & Jenkins, 1991. 304p.

Lengthy essays on pottery manufacturers; most include dates and area of practice, and a substantial number of references to other publications. In addition, many entries identify and describe the work of various artists, decorators and designers employed by the subject firms.

Cushion, John Patrick. *A Collector's History of British Porcelain.* Woodbridge, Suffolk: Antique Collectors' Club, 1992. 448p.

Encyclopedic overview of British porcelain factories and designers, from the mid–18th through the 20th centuries. Profile of each factory includes a good number of illustrations, brief history, and excellent bibliography for further research. Partial contents: British porcelain factories from the mid–late 18th century; British porcelain factories, late 18th—early 19th centuries; Victorian porcelain factories, c.1837—c.1900; 20th century industrial wares; brief overview of registration of design and forms.

Jewitt, Llewellyn Frederick William. *The Ceramic Art of Great Britain.* New ed., rev. Poole, Dorset: New Orchards Editions, 1985. 642p.

Published originally in 1877, this exhaustive history of British ceramics commences with the ancient and Romano-British periods, and proceeds with thorough analyses of the ceramic arts of Britain, arranged by geographic area.

Sandon, John. *The Dictionary of Worcester Porcelain.* Vol. 1, *1751–1851.* Woodbridge, Suffolk: Antique Collectors' Club, 1993. 384p.

Well-illustrated history of Worcester porcelain through its first hundred years. Appendices include "A Survey of Marks" and "Contemporary Accounts of Visits to the Bristol and Worcester Porcelain Manufactories."

Low Countries

Knowles, William Pitcairn. *Dutch Pottery and Porcelain.* London, Batsford, and New York: Scribner's, [1913]. 122p. 65 plates.

Somewhat dated, but still very useful survey of Dutch pottery and porcelain. Partial contents: Porcelain—the Hague, Arnheim, Amsterdam; Pottery—Harlem, Arnheim, Amsterdam, Utrecht, Rotterdam; Delft; The Guild of St. Luke; Masters and factors; Member of the Guild of St. Luke with their marks and monograms.

Russia and the Soviet Union

Lobanov-Rostovsky, Nina. *Revolutionary Ceramics: Soviet Porcelain 1917–1921.* London: Studio Vista, 1990. 160p.

Survey of porcelain production from the earliest years of the Soviet Union through 1930s Suprematist designs. Includes artist biographies, signatures and marks, initials, monograms, factory marks.

United States

Ceramics in America. Milwaukee, Wis.: Chipstone Foundation; Hanover, N.H.: Distributed by University Press of New England. 2001–[Annual].

Beautifully produced, annual collection of scholarly, interdisciplinary writings intended for the serious collector and scholar of American ceramics. Articles treat historical and technical topics in great depth; well-illustrated and indexed.

Henzke, Lucile. *Art Pottery of America.* Exton, Pa.: Schiffer, 1982. 368 p.

Illustrated encyclopedic history of art pottery manufacturers active in the United States in the 19th through mid–20th centuries. Entries (most 2–8 pages in length) include illustrations, lists of individual artists and their marks.

Pottery, Ceramics and Porcelain: Individual Firms

Belleek

Degenhardt, Richard K. *Belleek: The Complete Collector's Guide and Illustrated Reference.* 2nd ed. Radnor, Pa.: Wallace-Homestead Book, 1993. 244p.

History of Belleek, from earliest years through modern times; identification information including names, marks, etc. Reprint of the 1904 and 1928 catalogues.

Langham, Marion. *Belleek Irish Porcelain: An Illustrated Guide to Over Two Thousand Pieces.* London: Quiller, 1993. 192p.

Excellent source for identification. Includes marks, good color reproductions arranged by type (Parian statues and busts, center pieces, etc.).

Limoges

Du Tertre, Nancy. *The Art of the Limoges Box.* New York: Abrams, 2003. 144p.

Contents: Limoges boxes, antique and modern; Snuff and the origin of the snuffbox; Discovery of porcelain; Early snuffboxes and their makers; Trade secrets and industrial espionage; Snuffboxes in the nineteenth century; Modern Limoges box.

Meissen

Walcha, Otto. *Meissen Porcelain.* English translation of *Meissener Porzellan.* New York: Putnam, 1981. 516 p.

Very well-illustrated history of Meissen porcelain production includes numerous useful appendices, including: Chronology of the Meissen Porcelain Manufactory; Museums with significant collections; Chronological survey of Old Meissen; Chronological survey of form and decorations; Meissen marks.

Minton

Atterbury, Paul, and Maureen Batkin. *The Dictionary of Minton.* Historical introduction by Terence A. Lockett. Rev. ed. Woodbridge: Antique Collectors' Club, 1998. 370p.

Encyclopedic dictionary of Minton Wares; substantial section on individual artists,' designers' and decorators' biographies, marks and dating.

Jones, Joan. *Minton: The First Two Hundred Years of Design & Production.* Shrewsbury, Eng.: Swan Hill Press, 1993. 391p.

Partial contents: Early tablewares 1793–1836; Tablewares and useful wares of the Victorian era; Nineteenth century figures; Majolica; Tiles; Pâte-sur-Pâte; Minton's art pottery studio Kensington Gore; Art Nouveau; Art Deco; Commemorative, advertising and hotel ware. Appendices: Tableware pattern numbers, names, descriptions, introduction dates and composition of services; Figures; Ornamental wares and tiles; Picture tile series; Marks—printed, painted, relief molded and impressed; Year ciphers.

Rorstrand

Nystrom, Bengt. *Rorstrand Porcelain: Art Nouveau Masterpieces: The Robert Schreiber Collection.* New York: Abbeville Press, 1996. 190p.

Well illustrated history of Swedish porcelain. Directory of artists (1890–1915) includes marks.

Sèvres

Brunet, Marcelle, and Tamara Préaud. *Sèvres: Des Origines á nos Jours.* Fribourg: Office du Livre, 1978. 391p.

18th — 20th century marks and signatures, includes section on fakes.

Eriksen, Svend, and Geoffrey de Bellaigue. *Sèvres Porcelain: Vincennes and Sèvres, 1740–1800.* Danish text translated by R.J. Charleston. London and Boston: Faber and Faber, 1987. 379p.

Well illustrated, historical, chronologically arranged. Materials and techniques thoroughly described; directory of marks and forgeries.

Préaud, Tamara, et al. *The Sèvres Porcelain Manufactory: Alexandre Brongniart and the Triumph of Art and Industry, 1800–1847.* Edited by Derek E. Ostergard. New Haven, Conn.: Yale University Press for the Bard Graduate Center for Studies in the Decorative Arts, New York, 1997. 416p.

Scholarly exhibition catalog traces the development of Sevres porcelain in the 18th and early 19th centuries. Appendices include "Factory Marks" and glossary.

Spode-Copeland

Copeland, Robert. *Spode & Copeland Marks: And Other Relevant Intelligence.* London: Studio Vista, 1993. 173p.
History of Spode & Copeland, chronology, information on marks and dating, Patent Office registration marks, etc.

Pottery, Ceramics and Porcelain: Marks, Monograms and Signatures

For the decorative arts researcher, many published reference sources are available to assist in the identification of markings that might be found on a piece. Some of these are highly specialized, while others might cover the markings used by various foundries, factories or other manufacturers in a number of countries. The vast majority of reference works treat just one medium or object-type (e.g., porcelain, silver, etc.) The works chosen for inclusion here are arranged under object category, following a section devoted to those that record marks on a variety of decorative arts objects. Note that some of the entries in the preceding section also include information on marks. When this is the case, inclusion of marks is noted in the item's annotation.

Kovel, Ralph M., and Terry H. *Dictionary of Marks: Pottery and Porcelain.* New York: Crown, 1953. 278p.
Handy, A-Z arrangement of marks precedes sections broken down by graphical symbol or form, e.g., arrow, bird, crown, etc.

_____. *Kovels' New Dictionary of Marks: Pottery and Porcelain.* New York: Crown, 1995. 228p.
Guide to over 5,000 marks used to identify American, English and European porcelain. Includes information on factory or manufacturer, types of products, color and date ranges of marks.

Lage, Chad. *Pictorial Guide to Pottery & Porcelain Marks.* Paducah, Ky.: Collector Books, 2004. 413p.
Excellent reference source for identification of pottery & porcelain manufacturers. Good, clear (in most cases) photographic reproduction of marks, alongside examples of one or more pieces. Excellent indexing includes alphabetical (by maker or manufacturer's name), date, and "sight" index, which allows the user to identify likely manufacturers with only details of a mark (e.g., "eagle" marks).

Poche, Emanuel. *Porcelain Marks of the World.* Translated from the Czech by Joy Moss-Kohoutova. London and New York: Hamlyn, [1975]. 255p.
Concise, well-arranged handbook of porcelain marks arranged largely by subject matter (sun, water, flora, etc.). Index of manufacturers' names.

Thorn, C. Jordan. *Handbook of Old Pottery and Porcelain Marks.* New York: Tudor, [1947]. 176p.

Illustrated handbook of marks on Chinese, Japanese, European and American pottery and porcelain. Index of names and factories.

Dutch Marks

Justice, Jean. *Dictionary of Marks and Monograms of Delft Pottery.* London: H. Jenkins, [1930]. 171p.

Delft pottery marks, 16th through 18th centuries. Includes "Marks Undeciphered, Cyphers, Signs, etc.," Index of names.

Marks of Europe

Cushion, John Patrick. *Handbook of Pottery and Porcelain Marks.* 5th ed., rev. and expanded. London: Faber, 1996. 304p.

Marks and monograms organized by country, arrangement alphabetical by name of factory or artist. Each country section includes a brief review of major factories and centers, with maps indicating location of major production centers. Extensive index to artists and factories.

Danckert, Ludwig. *Directory of European Porcelain: Marks, Makers and Factories.* Translation by Rita Kipling of *Handbuch des Europaischen Porzellans.* Consultant editor: Pietro Raffo. London: N.A.G. Press, 1981. 688p.

Directory of factories, decorating studios, marks. Includes names of factory owners, artists and signatures, technical terms, etc. Coverage dates from the discovery of porcelain through the mid–20th century.

Lang, Gordon. *Miller's Pottery & Porcelain Marks.* London: Miller's, 1995. 399p.

Concise guide to initials, monograms, written name (signature), Staffordshire, Chinese and other pottery and porcelain identifying marks. Additional information on fakes and copies, various maps and bibliography.

Marks of Great Britain

Godden, Geoffrey A. *Encyclopaedia of British Pottery and Porcelain Marks.* London: Barrie & Jenkins, [1992]. 765p.

Exhaustive inventory of British pottery and porcelain marks, includes section on recent marks, index of monograms, index of signs and devices.

_____. *Godden's Guide to English Blue and White Porcelain.* Woodbridge: Antique Collectors' Club, 2004. 592p.

Very beautifully illustrated overview of English blue and white. Scholarly, in-depth treatment includes copious information on manufacturers' marks. Contents: On forming a collection; Blue and White, a general picture; Bow and Chelsea; Limehouse, Newcastle and Lund's-Bristol; Worcester prior to 1775; Vauxhall; Derby and Isleworth; Longton Hall, West Pan and Baddeley-Lttler; Lowestoft; Liverpool factories; Plymouth, Bristol and New Hall; Worcester 1775–1795; Caughley; Coalport; Some later factories; Some unattributed groups and problems; Fakes and reproductions.

_____. *New Handbook of British Pottery & Porcelain Marks.* 2nd ed., rev. and enl. London: Barrie & Jenkins, 1999. 254p.

Concise histories of pottery and porcelain firms. Contents: Pictorial glossary; Potters' initial marks; Registered designs 1839–1883; Registration numbers 1884–1999; Collectors' clubs, Societies and groups; Selected bibliography; Index.

Yates-Owen, Eric, and Robert Fournier. *British Studio Potters' Marks.* London: A & C Black, 1999. 660p.

Studio pottery refers to pieces which "were produced by an individual artist who was responsible for all steps in the design and execution."[4] This inventory provides good, clear reproductions of 4,750 marks of British studio potters and others who have worked in Great Britain. Birth and death dates, marks and monograms, and in many instances, mailing addresses for studios of contemporary ceramic artists are provided.

United States Marks

Barber, Edwin Atlee. *Marks of American Potters.* Ann Arbor, Mich.: Ars Ceramica, 1976. 174 p. [Reprint of 1904 ed. published by Patterson & White, Philadelphia].

Includes facsimile reproductions of approximately 1,000 marks. Geographical organization: Pennsylvania; New Jersey; New York; New England; Ohio; Southern states; Western states.

DeBolt, C. Gerald. *Debolt's Dictionary of American Pottery Marks: Whiteware and Porcelain.* Paducah, Ky.: Collector Books, 1994. 288p.

Good introduction to the identification of American pottery. This updated edition (original published in 1988) includes "A Partial Reprint of W. Percival Jervis's *1897 Marks Book.*"

Lehner, Lois. *Lehner's Encyclopedia of U.S. Marks on Pottery and Porcelain.* Paducah, Ky.: Collector Books, 1988. 634p.

Massive collection of more than 8,000 marks representing more than 1,900 companies.

Glass: Bibliographies

Bibliography of Glass (From the Earliest Records to 1940). Foreword by W. E. S. Turner. Edited by Viclet Dimbleby. Subject index prepared by Frank Newby. [London]: Dawsons of Pall Mall for the Society of Glass Technology, Sheffield, 1960. 544p.

Highly specialized bibliography of glass history, from earliest records to 1940. Entries include title in original language, English translation, and basic finding information (journal name, volume, etc.). Some patent information, abstracts.

A Bibliography of Stained Glass. Cambridge, [Cambridgeshire]: D.S. Brewer, 1982. 200p.

Classified bibliography of periodical literature, monographs and other works on stained glass.

Brady, Darlene A., and William Serban *Stained Glass, a Guide to Information Sources.* Detroit: Gale Research, 1980. 572p.

Annotated bibliography of more than 1,800 sources related to the study of stained glass. Formats include general reference sources, bibliographies, dissertations, theses, periodicals, library collections, archival materials and various additional resource directories.

The History and Art of Glass: Index of Periodical Articles 1956–1979. Compiled by Louise K. Bush and Paul N. Perrot; edited by Gail P. Bardham. Boston: G.K. Hall, 1982. 876p.

The History and Art of Glass: Index of Periodical Articles 1980–1982. Boston: G.K. Hall, 1984. 298p.

The Corning Museum maintains what is arguably one of the world's greatest collections of books, periodicals and other materials for the study of glass. These volumes, produced by the Corning Library, are a classified index to the contents of over 500 periodicals. Articles on individual collectible works of glass art are included under their countries of origin.

Note that the Corning Museum's *Journal of Glass Studies* produces an annual "Check List of Recently Published Articles and Books on Glass" which serves as an update. The library's online catalog is also available for browsing at http://www.cmog.org (select "Rakow Library," then "Online Catalog").

Glass: Dictionaries

Bray, Charles. *Dictionary of Glass: Materials and Techniques.* London: A & C Black; Philadelphia : University of Pennsylvania Press, 1995. 240p.

Dictionary of primarily technical terms related to glass and glassmaking.

Whitehouse, David. *Glass: Pocket Dictionary of Terms Commonly Used to Describe Glass and Glass-Making.* Corning: Corning Museum of Glass, 1983. 88p.

Illustrated guide to technical terminology. Includes small but good color illustrations (and some black and white) throughout.

Glass: Encyclopedias and Surveys

Barr, Sheldon. *Venetian Glass: Confections in Glass, 1855–1914.* New York: Abrams, 1998. 128p.

Traces development of Venetian glass in the 19th century. Popular treatment, well-illustrated.

Blair, Dorothy. *A History of Glass in Japan.* New York: Kodansha/USA, 1973. 479p.

Historical survey of pottery and glass from c. 10,000 b.c.e. through contemporary era.

Boggess, Bill, and Louise Boggess. *Reflections on American Brilliant Cut Glass: With Value Guide.* Atglen, Pa.: Schiffer, 1995. 256p.

Reference work for the identification of cut glass works. Very extensive and well-illustrated, includes a great deal of very useful reference material for the serious collector, including lists of museums, collectors' associations, tips on caring for and displaying glass, and a directory of signatures and marks.

Bohemian Glass: 1400–1989. Edited by Sylva Petroyà and Jean-Luc Olivié. New York: Abrams, 1990. 239p.

Published in conjunction with an exhibition, surveys the emergence and development of this important center of glassmaking. Emphasis on 19th and 20th century works.

Bossche, Willy Van den. *Antique Glass Bottles: Their History and Evolution (1500–1850): A Comprehensive, Illustrated Guide, with a World-Wide Bibliography of Glass Bottles*. Suffolk, UK and Wappingers Falls, N.Y.: Antique Collectors' Club, 2001. 439p.

Traces the history and evolution of utility glass bottles from c. 1500 b.c.e. through 1850. Intended for the serious collector, Bossche's monograph provides very well illustrated overviews of the glass bottles produced in Great Britain, Holland, Belgium, France, Italy, Spain, Portugal, Germany and the Scandinavian countries. Very extensive (35p.) bibliography of books and journal articles.

The Brilliance of Swedish Glass, 1918–1939: An Alliance of Art and Industry. Edited by Derek E. Ostergard and Nina Stritzler-Levine. New Haven, Conn.: Yale University Press, for the Bard Graduate Center for Studies in the Decorative Arts, 1996. 336p.

Partial contents: Swedish industrialization and the glassworks; Emergence of Swedish modern design, 1917–1939; Brief history of Swedish glass; Swedish glass between the World Wars; Modern Swedish glass in America, 1924–1939.

Chambers, Karen S., and Tina Oldknow. *Clearly Inspired: Contemporary Glass and Its Origins*. [Tampa, Fla.]: Tampa Museum of Art; San Francisco, Calif.: Pomegranate, 1999. 134p.

Exhibition catalog, illustrates evolution of contemporary glass art. Section on artists' biographies.

Charleston, R. J. (Robert Jesse). *Masterpieces of Glass: A World History from the Corning Museum of Glass*. Expanded ed. New York: Abrams, 1990. 256p.

Highlights of the Corning collection, represents an encyclopedic history of glass based upon major glass works, dating from the ancient world through the 20th century.

Dobbins, Norman, and Ruth Dobbins. *Etched Glass: Techniques & Designs*. Madison, Wis.: Hand Books Press, 1998. 144p.

This well-illustrated technical manual shows the processes involved in decorative glass etching. Included are examples of stencil and resist processes, surface etching, carving and shading.

Dorigato, Attilia. *Murano, Island of Glass*. Translation by Jeremy Scott of *Arte del Vetro a Murano*. San Giovanni Lupatoto (Vr) [Italy]: Arsenale, 2003. 396p.

Survey of glassmaking from the Middle Ages through the 20th century. Well-illustrated sections on various production methods through the ages.

Duncan, Alastair. *Orrefors Glass*. Woodbridge, Suffolk: Antique Collectors' Club, 1995. 231p.

Surveys the history of Orrefors, and illustrates selected works by individual designers, in chronological order of their joining the firm. Designers' and engravers' marks and signature information.

Eliens, Titus M. *Modern Glass in the Netherlands: 1880–1940.* Zwolle: Uitgeverij Waanders, [2002]. 163p.

Scholarly, well-illustrated overview of 19th — early 20th century Dutch art glass design.

Florence, Gene. *Florence's Glassware Pattern Identification Guide.* Paducah, Ky.: Collector Books, 1998. 176p.

Excellent source for the identification of glass works of the 1920s through 1960s. Entries are clearly illustrated, and provide details including manufacturer, date or date range, colors, etc. Indexed by manufacturer.

Glass Throughout Time: History and Technique of Glassmaking from the Ancient World to the Present. Edited by Rosa Barovier Mentasti, et al. Milan: Skira; New York: Distributed in North America and Latin America by Rizzoli International, 2003. 285p.

Encyclopedic survey of glass works, ancient through contemporary. Each work fully documented, with "typological comparisons" to other published works.

Heiremans, Marc. *Murano Glass: Themes and Variations = Thema und Variationen (1910–1970).* Translation by Claudia Fritzsche. Stuttgart: Arnoldsche, 2002. 223p.

Well-illustrated survey of Murano glass, includes section on "biographies of the manufactories," artists' biographies, and illustrated overview of labels and signatures.

_____. *20th Century Murano Glass: From Craft to Design = Murano-Glass im 20. Jahrhundert: Vom Kunsthandwerk zum Design.* Stuttgart : Arnoldsche, 1996. 231p.

Decade-by-decade survey of contemporary Murano glassworks, with directory of labels and signatures.

Hollingworth, Jane. *Collecting Decanters.* New York: Mayflower Books, 1980. 128p. (*Christie's International Collectors Series.*)

Suitable for the beginning collector, this short guide surveys the history of glass-making and the evolution of the decanter. Partial contents: Façon de Venise and the new metals; Art of enameling; Engraved and etched decanters; Brilliants of cut glass.

Klein, Dan. *Artists in Glass: Late Twentieth Century Masters in Glass.* London: Mitchell Beazley, 2001. 240p.

Richly illustrated compendium of 80 cutting-edge glass artists' works. Glossary of terms, signature samples.

Layton, Peter. *Glass Art.* London: A & C Black; Seattle: University of Washington Press, 1996. 216p.

Overview of history, current trends, and technical aspects of glass art and production.

Leier, Ray, Jan Peters, and Kevin Wallace. *Contemporary Glass: Color, Light & Form.* Madison, Wis.: Guild, 2001. 128p.

Illustrated survey of decorative and functional glass artists and their work.

Lynn, Martha Drexler. *American Studio Glass, 1960–1990: An Interpretive Study.* New York: Hudson Hills Press, 2004. 168p.

Scholarly, well-illustrated overview of the studio glass movement in the United

States. Includes excellent chapters on the evolution of the studio glass market, both retail and secondary (auction).

Madigan, Mary Jean Smith. *Steuben Glass: An American Tradition in Crystal.* Rev. and expanded. New York: Abrams, 2003. 384p.

Historical survey of Steuben glass and designers. Extensive catalog of works arranged by object type, excellent source for identification of pieces.

McConnell, Andy. *The Decanter: An Illustrated History of Glass from 1650.* Woodbridge, Suffolk: Antique Collectors' Club, 2004. 575p.

This encyclopedic history traces the evolution of the decanter from the earliest British examples through the 20th century. In-depth survey of technical processes illustrates the changes in glass decoration over the past five centuries. Of particular interest to the serious collector, includes information on attribution, collecting, reproductions and fakes.

Measell, James. *Imperial Glass Encyclopedia.* Marietta, Ohio: Glass Press, 1995–1999. 3 vols.

Encyclopedic overview of the output of the Imperial Glass Company attempts "to afford maximum photograph coverage to Imperial's products." Original catalog pages supplement color and black & white photographs of a great many Imperial glass objects. Most useful as an identification tool, but values, now dated, are provided.

Mehlman, Felice. *Phaidon Guide to Glass.* Oxford: Phaidon, 1982. 256p.

Basics of glass production, history and types for the collector. Well-illustrated selection of various types of glassworks, including utilitarian and decorative, lighting, etc. Brief section on collecting glass.

Mergl, Jan. *Loetz: Bohemian Glass 1880–1940.* Ostfildern, Germany: Hatje Cantz, 2003. 352p. + CD ROM.

Founded in the late 19th century, Loetz glass rose to distinction among the many Bohemian glass companies. Partial contents: Loetz glassworks, their significance and position in the international context; History of the firm, its production and sales; The period of Phäenomen decoration; Turn to art nouveau; Paris *Exposition Universelle* in 1900; Signatures and marks; Artist biographies. CD ROM includes a catalogue of Loetz "paper patterns" searchable by number and object.

Page, Jutta-Annette. *Beyond Venice: Glass in Venetian Style, 1500–1750.* Corning, N.Y.: Corning Museum of Glass, 2004. 339p.

Published in conjunction with exhibition *Beyond Venice*, held at the Corning Museum of Glass, May 20–Oct. 17, 2004, surveys the influence of Venice upon glassmaking in Austria, Spain, France, England and the Netherlands. Images of glass works in art (paintings, prints, etc.) supplement reproductions of works included in the exhibition.

Palmer, Arlene. *Glass in Early America: Selection from the Henry Francis du Pont Winterthur Museum.* Winterthur, Del.: Winterthur Museum, 1993. 425p.

Uses the Winterthur collection to survey the history of American glass, with particular reference to collecting and connoisseurship. Partial contents: Table glass associated with beverages; Table glass for serving of food; Accessories; Lighting devices; Bottles and flasks.

Phillips, Phoebe. *The Encyclopedia of Glass.* New York: Crown, 1981. 320p.

Encyclopedic overview of history and technical aspects of glass and glassmaking. Historical section consists of overviews of ancient and Roman glass, followed by individual country surveys.

Ricke, Helmut, and Eva Schmitt. *Italian Glass, Murano, Milan, 1930–1970: The Collection of the Steinberg Foundation.* Munich and New York: Prestel, 1997. 351p.

Richly illustrated overview of Murano glass production and works. Appendixes include lists of artists, manufacturers, and selected signatures.

Schwartz, Marvin D. *American Glass, from the Pages of Antiques.* Vol. 1: *Blown and Molded*; Vol. 2: *Pressed and Cut.* Princeton, N.J.: Pyne Press, 1974.

Collection of reprinted articles from *Antiques* magazine surveys all aspects of American glass, including regional styles and forms. Partial contents: Some major collections; Types and forms; European influences; Regions and glasshouses.

Sotheby's Concise Encyclopedia of Glass. Edited by David Battie and Simon Cottle. London: Conran Octopus, 1995. 208p.

Chronologically arranged survey of glass production and design, from pre-Roman through the 20th century. Overview of fakes and forgeries, tips for care and conservation, and glossary make this a most useful tool for the glass collector.

Spillman, Jane Shadel. *The American Cut Glass Industry: T.G. Hawkes and His Competitors.* Woodbridge, Suffolk: Antique Collectors' Club, in association with the Corning Museum of Glass, 1996. 320p.

This fascinating history of the cut glass industry identifies a great many primary source materials, including original catalog pages, company brochures, etc. Surveys glassworks produced by Hawkes, Egginton, Sinclaire, Steuben and other firms.

_____, and Suzanne K. Frantz. *Masterpieces of American Glass: The Corning Museum of Glass, the Toledo Museum of Art.* New York: Crown, 1990. 100p.

Partial contents: The beginning; 18th century factories; Independence achieved; Advent of mass production; Luxury glass: 1850–1900; Early 20th century glass; Mid-century modernism; Studio glassmaking; Glass artists.

Stern, E.M. *Roman, Byzantine, and Early Medieval Glass, 10 BCE— 700 BCE: Ernesto Wolf Collection.* Ostfildern, Germany: Hatje Cantz, 2001. 427p.

Scholarly catalog documenting a major collection of early glass works. Each item illustrated in color and fully cataloged.

Venetian Glass. Foreword by Nancy Olnick and Giorgio Spanu; Introduction by Holly Hotchner; essays by David Revere McFadden, Marino Barovier, Suzanne K. Frantz; photographs by Luca Vignelli. New York: American Craft Museum, 2000. 249p.

Exhibition catalog of contemporary Venetian glass works. Works fully documented, including bibliography and exhibition histories. Includes artist biographies and overview of workshops.

Venini Diaz de Santillana, Anna. *Venini: Catalogue Raisonné, 1921–1986.* Milan: Skira, 2000. 320p.

Historical precedents, and scholarly overview of the establishment and development of Venini glassworks. Catalogue raisonné arranged chronologically, serves as an excellent tool for identification.

Warmus, William. *Fire and Form: The Art of Contemporary Glass*. West Palm Beach, Fla.: Norton Museum of Art; Seattle, Wash.: Distributed by University of Washington Press, 2003. 128p.

Illustrated survey of major glassworks by contemporary artists.

Warren, Phelps. *Irish Glass: The Age of Exuberance*. New York: Scribner's, 1971. 155p.

Traces the development of glassmaking in Ireland from the mid–18th century. Major producers of "marked" glass described in detail with numerous reproductions include: B. Edwards Belfast, Cork Glass Co. Penrose Waterford, Waterloo Co. Cork, and others.

Whitehouse, David. Corning Museum of Glass. *The Corning Museum of Glass: A Decade of Glass Collecting, 1990–1999*. Corning, N.Y.: Corning Museum; New York: Distributed by Abrams, 2000. 128p.

Illustrated inventory of glass works, including fine examples of ancient and Islamic, European, American, Art Nouveau, and contemporary works.

Who's Who in Contemporary Glass Art. Munich: J. Waldrich Verlag, 1993– .

Provides a wealth of biographical information on international glass artists. In addition to biographical basics, entries include contact information, curriculum vitae, techniques employed, kinds of glass work, awards, commissions, exhibitions, collections and bibliography.

Wilson, Kenneth M. *American Glass, 1760–1930: The Toledo Museum of Art*. 2 vols. New York: Hudson Hills Press in association with the Toledo Museum of Art; [Lanham, Md.]: National Book Network [distributor], 1994. 879p.

Comprehensive survey of glassmaking in America, this work is an excellent source for the identification of styles, patterns and manufacturers. Coverage spans the period from the early 17th through mid–20th centuries. Libbey Glass Company trademarks directory.

Glass: Marks and Trademarks

Dictionary of Glass Marks. Heartland Discoveries. http://www.heartland-discoveries.com/dictionary.htm

Free web-based dictionary of manufacturers' marks on glass works. Organized around basic shapes (e.g., animals, arrows-crosses-lines, etc.), provides good clear images of marks.

Hartmann, Carolus. *Glasmarken Lexikon 1600–1945: Signaturen, Fabrik- und Handelsmarken: Europa und Nordamerika*. Stuttgart: Arnoldsche, 1997. 1,006p.

Contents: List of categories; Illustrations of marks; Biography of the artists and firms; various indexes and technical glossary.

Pullin, Anne Geffken. *Glass Signatures, Trademarks and Trade Names from the Seventeenth to the Twentieth Century*. Radnor, Pa.: Wallace-Homestead, 1986. 368p.

Contents: How to look at glass; Index of signatures, trademarks, and trade names; Glossary: translation of selected foreign words; Benchmark dates; technical and historical; Bibliography; Cross-reference index.

Victorian Glass Registration Lozenge Translator. http://1st.glassman.com/lozenge-translator.html

This translator, available on the web, can be used to decode the registration number on antique glass works registered in England between 1842 and 1883.

Metalwork: General Reference Sources

The following works include information on more than one metal (e.g., silver and pewter, etc.). Individual metals are treated separately, below.

Alcorn, Ellenor M. *English Silver in the Museum of Fine Arts, Boston: Catalogue.* Boston: Museum of Fine Arts; Distributed by Northeastern University Press, 1993– . Vol. 1: *Silver Before 1697*; Vol. 2: *1697—20th Century.*

Catalogue of the museum's holdings, each item fully documented. Includes, where appropriate, photographs of marks.

Fennimore, Donald L. *Metalwork in Early America: Copper and its Alloys from the Winterthur Collection.* Winterthur, Del.: Henry Francis du Pont Winterthur Museum, 1996. 472p.

Using pieces from the Winterthur Collection, this beautifully produced monograph surveys the development of utilitarian and decorative uses of metals in early American culture. Introductory material explores mining, manufacturing and marketing of copper and its alloys. The exhibition catalogue comprises over 300 items, fully cataloged, illustrated and interpreted.

_____. *Silver & Pewter.* Chanticleer Press ed. New York: Knopf, 1984. 478p. (Series: *The Knopf Collectors' Guides to American Antiques.*)

Illustrated guide for the serious collector. Each item includes description, marks and dimensions, maker, locality and date, comments, and hints for collectors. Partial contents: Simple way to identify silver, silver plate and pewter; Parts of representative objects; Good, better and best: silver and silver plate; Good, better and best: pewter; Caring for your collection; Illustrated guide to American makers and marks.

Gentle, Rupert. *Domestic Metalwork, 1640–1820.* Woodbridge, Suffolk: Antique Collectors Club, 1994. 461p.

Extensive study of primarily brass household implements and decorative arts objects. Introductory chapters survey the production methods and markets for brass during the 17th through early 19th centuries. Each of hundreds of pieces illustrated, many in color, and fully described and dated. Partial contents: Lighting [candelabra, chandeliers, etc.]; Kitchen [cooking-pots, hourglasses, etc]; Dining room [bowls, dishes, etc.]; Fireplace and smoking; Library; Bedroom; Door-knockers and locks; Accessories and ornaments; Domestic / hobbies; Coffin furniture. Appendix: Marks and signatures found on brass in Great Britain.

Kauffman, Henry J. *American Copper & Brass.* Morgantown, Pa.: Masthof Press, 1995. 288p. Reprint of 1968 ed. Camden, N.J.: T. Nelson.

In-depth survey of the early American copper and brass production industries, includes a great deal of primary source material. Well-researched and written, the introductory chapters provide technical information on brass and copper production and an overview of the related trades. Partial contents: Kettles; Pots and pans; Stills; Miscellaneous objects (e.g., mugs, measures); Andirons; Bells; Gun parts and cannon; Molds for casting objects of pewter; Miscellaneous objects of cast brass; Documented list of coppersmiths.

Metalwork: Encyclopedias and Surveys

Gold

Edgecombe, Richard. *The Art of the Gold Chaser in Eighteenth-Century London.* New York: Oxford University Press, 2000. 197p. 240 plates.

Chasing is a technique of modeling metal using only a hammer and punches. This lengthy monograph surveys the development of this popular technique in 18th–century London. Includes extensive biography of "chasers," including their preferred techniques and source materials, identifying marks, and reproductions.

Pewter

Cotterell, Howard Herschel. *National Types of Old Pewter.* Rev. and exp. ed. New York: Weathervane Books, 1972. 152p.

Surveys American and European pewter production, approximately 1600–1900. Partial contents: National types of old pewter; European continental pewter; Pewter of the Channel Islands; Identifying Dutch flagons; Church & town flagons of Holland; Identifying Dutch pewter; Pewter flagons of the former Austro-Hungarian Empire; Fine pewter of Austria-Hungary.

Hornsby, Peter. *Pewter of the Western World, 1600–1850.* Exton, Pa.: Schiffer, 1983. 381p.

Partial contents: History of the pewter industry; Decoration on pewter; Marks on pewter; Religious pewter; Institutional pewter; Medical pewter; Pewter for eating; Pewter for drinking.

Kauffman, Henry J. *The American Pewterer: His Techniques & His Products.* Mendham, N.J.: Astragal Press, 1994. 132p.

Basic overview of pewter and pewter objects, suitable for the beginning collector.

Montgomery, Charles F. *History of American Pewter.* Rev. and enlarged ed. New York: Dutton, 1978. 307p.

Scholarly, well-illustrated survey of pewter. Major chapters focus on object types, e.g.: Church pewter; Lighting; Drinking vessels; Pitchers; Plates, dishes and basins; Porringers; Spoons and ladles; Utensils for tea and coffee. Connoisseurship chapter provides practical information for the beginning collector. Some marks and monograms.

North, Anthony, and Andrew Spira. *Pewter at the Victoria and Albert Museum.* London: V&A, 1999. 192p.

Well-illustrated inventory of mostly European pewter works in the Victoria and Albert Collection. Partial contents: Medieval pewter; Guild pewter; Pewter for eating and drinking; Domestic pewter; Measures; Ecclesiastical pewter; Art nouveau and 20th-century pewter; Fakes.

Silver

El Arte de la Plateria Mexicana, 500 Años: Noviembre 1989-Febrero 1990. [Mexico]: Centro Cultural Arte Contemporaneo, [1989]. 595p.

Richly illustrated exhibition catalog with good hallmark reproductions.

Carpenter, Charles Hope. *Tiffany Silver.* Rev. ed. San Francisco: A. Wofsy Fine Arts, 1997. 260p.

Overview of Tiffany silverware, including hollow ware, flatware, presentation silver. Tiffany marks section arranged chronologically.

Elegant Plate: Three Centuries of Precious Metals in New York City. Edited by Deborah Dependahl Waters. New York: Museum of the City of New York. 2 vols., 2000. 621p.

Presents an in-depth history of silver production, trade and marketing in New York from the mid–18th century to the present. Catalog entries provide full descriptive cataloging of each work, including in many cases detail images of marks.

Glanville, Philippa. *Silver in England.* New York: Holmes & Meier; London: Unwin Hyman, 1987. 366p.

History of silver production including technique and trade development, design, and social aspects. "Antiquaries, collectors, fakers" presents a good overview of the history of silver collecting.

Hernmarck, Carl. *The Art of the European Silversmith, 1430–1830.* London and New York: Sotheby Parke Bernet, 1977. 2 vols.

Reference source on European silver production surveys all types of objects (bowls, cups, etc.). Entries include title, material (if other than silver — some gold included), place and year of manufacture, if known, collection, owner. Country surveys, styles (Gothic, Renaissance, etc.), secular silver, church silver, extensive bibliography.

Jadir, Saad. *Arab & Islamic Silver.* London: Stacey International, 1981. 216p.

Provides a brief overview of silverwork in the Islamic world, followed by chapters devoted to specific regions: North Africa and Spain; Arabian Peninsula; Levant, Mesopotamia, Persia, Turkey and Caucasia; Central and South-East Asia.

Johnston, Phillip M. *Catalogue of American Silver: The Cleveland Museum of Art.* Chardon, Ohio: Cleveland Museum of Art in cooperation with Indiana University Press, 1994. 180p.

Illustrated inventory of the museum's collection, includes very good photographic reproductions of hallmarks.

Krekel-Aalberse, Annelies. *Art Nouveau and Art Deco Silver.* New York: Abrams, 1989. 272p.

Country studies of Art Nouveau and Art Deco silver: Great Britain; France; Belgium; United States; Germany; the Netherlands; Austria; Scandinavia, Finland and Russia. Section on Silvermarks 1880–1940, makers' marks.

_____. *Silver 1880–1940: Art Nouveau, Art Deco.* Stuttgart: Arnoldsche, 2001. 144p.

Exhibition catalog of the Alfrons Leythe Collection. Partial contents: Design in silver; Modern silver up to 1918—flowers, lines, shapes; Individualism and functionalism between the two World Wars. Artists' marks.

Newman, Harold. *An Illustrated Dictionary of Silverware: 2,373 entries relating to British and North American Wares, Decorative Techniques and Styles, and Leading Designers and Makers, Principally from c.1500 to the Present.* New York: Thames and Hudson, 1987. 366p.

Illustrated dictionary of technical terms, object types, and biography and company histories.

A Personal Touch: The Seawolf Collection: Late 19th- and 20th-Century Silver. Rotterdam: Museum Boijmans Van Beuningen; NAi Publishers in association with Veena Duncker, VD Private Collections, Munich, 2003. 263p.

Catalogue for an exhibition of a private collection made up of four collections with different owners, all of which are advised by Veena Duncker. Fully documented works of English, American, and Continental European silver works.

Quimby, Ian M. G., with Dianne Johnson. *American Silver at Winterthur.* Winterthur, Del.: Henry Francis du Pont Winterthur Museum; [Charlottesville, Va.]: Distributed by the University Press of Virginia, 1995. 490p.

Excellent tool for the identification of American silverworks. Partial contents: Question of authorship; Style in American silver; Building a collection; Catalogue: New England; New York; Pennsylvania and the South.

Schroder, Timothy. *The Gilbert Collection of Gold and Silver.* Los Angeles: Los Angeles County Museum of Art, 1988. 688p.

Well-illustrated and documented, each work includes provenance, exhibition and publication records. Partial contents: British gold and silver; Continental European gold and silver; American silver; Indian silver; Goldsmiths' biographies.

_____. *The National Trust Book of English Domestic Silver, 1500–1800.* London: Viking in association with the National Trust, 1988. 338p.

Scholarly history of domestic silver production from early Tudor through the Victorian era. Biographical appendix includes "more prominent figures covered," some with examples of marks.

Sotheby's Concise Encyclopedia of Silver. Edited by Charles Truman. London: Conran Octopus, 1996. 208p.

Partial contents: Early silver; Medieval period; Renaissance and Mannerism; Baroque, Rococo and Neoclassicism; Nineteenth century; American silver; Arts & Crafts and Art Nouveau; Art deco; Post-War silver; Forgeries, fakes and concoctions; Hallmarks and standards.

Viennese Silver: Modern Design, 1780–1918. Edited for the Neue Galerie New York and the Kunsthistorisches Museum Vienna by Michael Huey. Ostfildern-Ruit, Germany: Hatje Cantz; New York: Distribution in the United States by D.A.P., 2003. 398p.

Beautifully illustrated, scholarly exhibition catalog explores 19th and 20th century Viennese silverware. Drawings, catalogue pages and other primary source materials illustrate lengthy essays on the evolution of silver design in Vienna.

Copper and Brass

Schiffer, Peter Berwind, Nancy Schiffer, and Herbert F. Schiffer. *The Brass Book: American, English and European, Fifteenth Century Through 1850*. Exton, Pa: Schiffer, 1978. 447p.

Decorative and utilitarian brass objects are surveyed in this well-illustrated historical overview. Included are fireplace accessories, candlesticks, tablewares, andirons and other objects. A great deal of reference material, including a section on the identification of fakes, makes this an important source for the collector or researcher.

Metalwork: Marks and Hallmarks

Marks on More Than One Metal

The following sources include marks or hallmarks found on more than one metal, e.g., silver and gold.

Beuque, Émile. *Dictionnaire des Poinçons Officiels Français et Étrangers, Anciens & Modernes de Leur Création (XIV Siècle) à Nos Jours*. Paris: Courtois, 1925–1928. 2 vols.

Standard source for the identification of gold and silver marks.

Bradbury, Frederick. *Bradbury's Book of Hallmarks: A Guide to Marks of Origin on English, Scottish and Irish Silver, Gold and Platinum and on Foreign Imported Silver and Gold Plate 1544 to 2001; Old Sheffield Plate Makers' Marks 1743–1860*. Millennium ed. Rev. ed. [Great Britain]: Frederick Bradbury, 1999. 112p.

Small handbook on silver hallmarks. Partial contents: Introduction to hallmarking; Tables of Assay Office marks on silver.

Citroen, K. A. *Dutch Goldsmiths' and Silversmiths' Marks and Names Prior to 1812: A Descriptive and Critical Repertory*. Leiden, Netherlands: Primavera Pers, 1993. 283p.

Partial contents: Maker's marks: Letter, figure, device; Silvermiths without recorded marks; Town marks; Date letters; Sources and works of reference.

Ridgway, Maurice H., and Philip T. Priestley. *The Compendium of Chester Gold & Silver Marks, 1570 to 1962: From the Chester Assay Office Registers*. Woodbridge, Suffolk, Eng.: Antique Collectors' Club, 2004. 520p.

Illustrated compendium of marks; each entry includes registration details, maker's address, illustration, company business address, and indication of maker's trade (jeweller, etc.).

Ris-Paquot, Oscar. *Dictionnaire des Poinçons, Symboles, Signes Figuratifs, Marques et Monogrammes des Orfèvres Français et Étrangers*. Paris: Librairie Renouard, H. Laurens, éditeur, 1890. 384p. Reprint: New York: Garland, 1978. (Series: *A Dealers' and Collectors' Bookshelf; 17: Metalwork.*)

Dictionary of marks on gold and silverwork, including jewelry.

Wyler, Seymour B. *The Book of Old Silver, English, American, Foreign: With All Available Hallmarks Including Sheffield Plate Marks*. New York: Crown, 1937. 447p.

MARKS ON SILVER

Bly, John. *Miller's Silver & Sheffield Plate Marks: Including a Guide to Makers & Styles.* London: Miller's, 1993. 192p.

Presents a concise overview of the hallmarking system for the novice collector, with facsimiles of major London and regional British marks.

Bohan, Peter J., and Philip Hammerslough. *Early Connecticut Silver, 1700–1840.* Middletown, Conn.: Wesleyan University Press, [1970]. 288p.

Partial contents: Connecticut silversmith; Tradition and innovation in Connecticut silver; Illustrations of hollowware and selected flatware; Biographical notes on the silversmiths; Index of marks. (Photographic reproductions of marks keyed to works in private and public collections).

Forbes, John. *Hallmark: A History of the London Assay Office.* London: Goldsmiths': Unicorn Press, 1999, 1998. 367p.

Appendix IV, "London Hallmarks for Silver."

Green, Robert Alan. *Marks of American Silversmiths.* Harrison, N.Y.: Green, 1977. 246p.

Excellent source for the identification of American silverworks. Partial contents: A primer for silver collectors; American silver trademarks; Notes on American silver trademarks and hallmarks (1655–1865); Marks of American silversmiths, jewelers, watchmakers, clockmakers and vendors.

Kane, Patricia E. *Colonial Massachusetts Silversmiths and Jewelers: A Biographical Dictionary Based on the Notes of Francis Hill Bigelow & John Marshall Phillips.* New Haven, Conn.: Yale University Art Gallery, 1998. 1241p.

Extensive biographical dictionary of silversmiths. Most entries include one or more photographic reproductions of silver marks.

Kovel, Ralph, and Terry Kovel. *Kovels' American Silver Marks.* New York: Crown, 1989. 421p.

Easy to use, comprehensive guide to American silver marks and monograms. Includes references to more than 10,000 silversmiths active from 1650 to the present. Extensive bibliography of books and articles on American silver.

MARKS ON PEWTER

Cotterell, Howard Herschel. *Old Pewter, Its Makers and Marks in England, Scotland, and Ireland; An Account of the Old Pewterer & His Craft.* Rutland, Vt.: C. E. Tuttle, [1963, 1975]. 432p.

The most extensive inventory of marks and monograms on European and American pewter to date. Partial contents: Alphabetical list of pewterers; Alphabetical list of initialed marks; Index to the devices.

Laughlin, Ledlie Irwin. *Pewter in America: Its Makers and Their Marks.* Barre, Mass.: Barre, 1969–71. 3 vols.

Well-illustrated reference source for identifying pewterers. Partial contents: The European background; Marks on pewter; Pewter-making in America; Household pewter; Ecclesiastical pewter; Pewterers of Massachusetts Bay; Rhode Island pewterers; Pewterers of the Connecticut Valley.

Thomas, John Carl. *Connecticut Pewter and Pewterers.* [Hartford]: Connecticut Historical Society, 1976. 194p.

Well-illustrated survey with good photographic reproductions of hallmarks, includes checklist of Connecticut pewterers.

Rugs and Carpets: Bibliographies

O'Bannon, George W. *Oriental Rugs: A Bibliography*. Metuchen, N.J.: Scarecrow Press, 1994. 744p.

Most extensive and up-to-date bibliography of books on Oriental rugs; general sources, as well as those with narrow geographic focus including: Anatolia/Turkey; Caucasus; Central Asia/Afghanistan; China/East Turkestan/Tibet; Eastern Europe; India; Other Middle East/North Africa/Iberia; Persia.

Rugs and Carpets: Indexes

Textile Museum, Arthur D. Jenkins Library. *Rug and Textile Arts: A Periodical Index, 1890–1982*. Boston: G. K. Hall, 1983. 472p.

Includes indexing of approximately 300 periodicals included among the holdings of the Jenkins Library. Author index; entries include author, title, article information (journal name, volume, etc.), subject area. Presence of illustrations noted.

Rugs and Carpets: Collectors' Manuals

Allane, Lee. *Chinese Rugs: A Buyer's Guide*. New York: Thames and Hudson, 1993. 144p.

Well-indexed, illustrated overview of Chinese rugs suitable for the beginning collector. Partial contents: Defining a Chinese rug; How Chinese rugs are made; Buying a Chinese rug; Cultural context; Designs; Old and antique rugs; Contemporary rugs.

_____. *Oriental Rugs: A Buyer's Guide*. London: Thames and Hudson, 1988. 136p.

Contents: What is an Oriental rug?; How Oriental rugs are made; Buying a rug; Designs; Rugs of the major producing countries; Major weaving groups; Minor weaving groups.

Rugs and Carpets: Dictionaries

Neff, Ivan C., and Carol V. Maggs. *Dictionary of Oriental Rugs: With a Monograph on Identification by Weave*. London: AD Donker, 1977. 237p.

For the serious scholar and collector, this dictionary provides references to geographical centers of production, rug types, and technical material related to weaving. Color reproductions make this a very good source for identification of various types of rugs and carpets.

Stone, Peter F. *The Oriental Rug Lexicon.* Seattle: University of Washington Press, 1997. 267p.

This A-Z dictionary of terms includes an overview of rug research, foreign terms and place-names, and brief (often illustrated) entries on technical processes, materials, design motifs, and other terms for the serious researcher of Oriental rugs.

Train, John. *Oriental Rug Symbols: Their Origins and Meanings From the Middle East to China.* London: Philip Wilson, 1997. 136p.

Handy illustrated primer identifies and describes symbols (animals, birds, flowers, etc.) used in Middle Eastern, Turkoman and Chinese carpet design.

Rugs and Carpets: Encyclopedias and Surveys

Carpet & Textile Art. Edited by Alan Marcuson. London: Hali, 1994. 247p. [The *Hali Annual*, no. 1].

See also individual issues of the periodical *Hali,* indexed in *Art Index* (print) and its electronic alternatives, *Art Index Retrospective* and *Art Abstracts/Art Full Text.*

Chaldecott, Nada. *Dhurries: History, Technique, Pattern, Identification.* [New York]: Thames and Hudson, 2003. 160p.

Survey of dhurry production, 1860 through 1949. Contents: Introduction [floor paintings, reed mats, history, materials and technique]; Striped dhurries; Pictorial dhurries; Floral dhurries; Medallion dhurries; Geometric dhurries; Prayer dhurries.

Davies, Peter. *Antique Kilims of Anatolia.* New York: W. W. Norton, 2000. 189p.

Scholarly overview of the history of kilim design and production; 73 stunning color plates make this an excellent reference work for the identification of kilim patterns and variations.

Day, Susan. *Art Deco and Modernist Carpets.* San Francisco: Chronicle Books, 2002. 224p.

Traces the development of the art deco carpet from the turn-of-the-century Wiener Werkstätte through mid-century British and American designs.

Denny, Walter B. *The Classical Tradition in Anatolian Carpets.* Washington, D.C.: The Textile Museum, 2002. 128p.

Richly illustrated exhibition catalog. Partial contents: Anatolian carpets and history; Technique and carpet design; Anatolia and its neighbors: history and artistic environment; Geometric designs in classical Anatolian carpets; Carpet designs from the world of silk textiles; The "design revolution," Ushak production, and its imitators; Carpet design and the Ottoman Court; Anatolian prayer rugs.

_____. *Sotheby's Guide to Oriental Carpets.* New York: Simon and Schuster, 1994. 203p.

Partial contents: Why collect Oriental carpets?; What is a carpet?; What are

Anatolian carpets?; What are Transcaucasian carpets?; What are Iranian carpets?; What are Turkmen carpets?; Where and how to purchase Oriental rugs and carpets; How to understand price, value, and the marketplace; How to display, maintain, and protect your Oriental carpets.

Eiland, Murray L., and Murray Eiland, III. *Oriental Carpets: A Complete Guide.* 4th ed. Boston: Little, Brown, 1998. 368p.

Encyclopedic study of Oriental carpets presents a good deal of technical information (construction methods and materials, dyes, etc.), followed by country-specific, or regional overviews of carpet design. Partial contents: Persia; Turkey; Central Asia; Caucasus; India & Pakistan; China; Eastern Turkestan; Tibet; North Africa; the Balkans.

Felton, Anton. *Jewish Carpets: A History and Guide.* Woodbridge, Suffolk: Antique Collectors' Club, 1997. 199p.

History of Jewish carpets from the first millennium b.c.e. through the late 20th century. Thorough analysis of symbolism and design, and a section on great examples in museums around the world.

Gantzhorn, Volkmar. *Oriental Carpets: Their Iconology and Iconography From Earliest Times to the 18th Century.* Translated by Charles Madsen. Cologne: Taschen, 1998. 532p.

Surveys the evolution of the knotted pile carpet from the 4th century b.c.e. through the modern era. Using art historical sources (primarily painting), illustrates the evolution of carpet designs. Many color illustrations make this an excellent source for identification of regional styles and variations.

Great Carpets of the World. Chapters by Valerie Berinstain, et al.; Introduction by Yves Mikaeloff; prefaces by Daniel Alcouffe and Marthe Bernus-Taylor. New York: Vendome Press, 1996. 377p.

Historical overview of rugs and carpets, geographical focus. Very well-illustrated, and useful as a source for the identification of styles and motifs.

Hull, Alastair, and Jose Luczyc-Wyhowska. *Kilim: The Complete Guide: History, Pattern, Technique, Identification.* London: Thames and Hudson, 1993. 352p.

This very beautifully illustrated study of the kilim is organized by region: North Africa; Anatolia; Persia and the Caucasus; Afghanistan and Central Asia. Additional information of interest to the collector and researcher includes technical production material, overview of motifs and symbolism, and notes on collecting and caring for kilims.

MacDonald, Brian W. *Tribal Rugs: Treasures of the Black Tent.* Woodbridge, Suffolk and [Wappingers' Falls, NY]: Antique Collectors' Club, 1997. 302 p.

Hundreds of very good quality color reproductions make this an excellent source for the identification of Near Eastern and Central Asian tribal rugs.

Milanesi, Enza. *The Bulfinch Guide to Carpets: How to Identify, Classify, and Evaluate Antique Oriental Carpets and Rugs.* Boston and New York: Little, Brown, 1993. 191p.

Concise overview of basics of rug and carpet structure and manufacture, decoration, styles, dating, etc.

_____. *The Carpet: An Illustrated Guide to the Rugs and Kilims of the World.* English translation by Rosanna M. Giammanco Frongia. London and New York: Tauris, 1999. 200p.

Nemati, Parviz. *The Splendour of Antique Rugs and Tapestries.* Woodbridge: Antique Collectors' Club: PDN Communications, 2001. 407p.

A most lavishly illustrated history of rugs and tapestries, each work included is exquisitely photographed and fully documented. Partial contents: History of rug making; Materials and techniques used in rug making; Persian rugs; Turkish rugs; Caucasian rugs; Turkmen rugs; Indian rugs; Chinese rugs; European rugs; Tapestries.

Opie, James. *Tribal Rugs: Nomadic and Village Weavings from the Near East.* Portland, Ore.: Tolstoy Press, 1992. 328p.

Encyclopedic survey of tribal rug design of the Middle East and Central Asia, arranged geographically or by name of tribe. Ancient through modern period works included. Excellent source for identification. Partial contents: Pazyryk rug; Ancient motifs in tribal rugs; Design origins—exploring a vast family of motifs. Tribal surveys: Lurs; Bakyityaris; Kurds; Quashqa'I Confederacy; Khamesh Confederacy; Afshars; Baluch & related tribes; Shah savan Confederacy; Anatolia; Caucasus; Turkomans.

Pickering, Brooke. *Moroccan Carpets.* London: Laurence King, 1998. 160p.

Well-illustrated overview of Moroccan carpets, very useful for the identification of regional designs and variations. Partial contents: Weaving traditions of Morocco; Plains of Marrakesh; High Atlas; Middle Atlas; Zemmour Confederation.

Rostov, Charles I. *Chinese Carpets.* New York: Abrams, 1983. 223p.

Surveys ancient through 20th century Chinese carpets, including overview of materials, construction, points of identification. Partial contents: History; Symbols & symbolism; Weaving methods & techniques; Materials; Identification & dating.

Rugs & Carpets of the World. Edited by Ian Bennett. London: Grange Books, 1996. 352p.

Well-illustrated, readable survey of the great rug producing areas of the world. Partial contents: Techniques and materials of Oriental carpet weaving; Oriental and African rugs and carpets; European rugs and carpets; North American rugs and carpets; Buying and maintenance of rugs and carpets.

Sherrill, Sarah B. *Carpets and Rugs of Europe and America.* New York: Abbeville Press, 1996. 463p.

Overview of the history of carpet and rug design and production in Europe and the U.S. Copious black & white and full color reproductions make this an excellent source for the identification of patterns and national styles. Survey chapters include: Spain & Portugal; France; Belgium; Great Britain; United States; Lesser-known rug traditions; 19th century to the present.

Sovereign Carpets: Unknown Masterpieces from European Collections. Edited by Edoardo Concaro and Alberto Levi. Milan: SKIRA, 1999. 253p.

Partial contents: Rugs of Anatolia; Persian carpet; Rugs of the Caucasus; Kilims; Rugs of the Turkmen and other peoples of Central Asia; Rugs of East Turkestan; Tibetan rugs; Chinese carpets; Carpets of Mughal India; Rugs of the Mediterranean countries.

Stone, Peter F. *Tribal & Village Rugs: The Definitive Guide to Design, Pattern and Motif.* New York: Thames & Hudson, 2004. 350p.

In-depth analyses of tribal rug patterns and motifs. Partial contents: Anatolian motifs; Motifs of the Baluch and neighboring tribes; Caucasian motifs; Kurdish motifs; Persian motifs; Turkmen motifs.

Walker, Daniel S. *Flowers Underfoot: Indian Carpets of the Mughal Era*. New York: Metropolitan Museum of Art; Distributed by Abrams, 1997. 199p.

Beautifully illustrated exhibition catalog offers in-depth analysis of Mughal era carpets: Persian style, flower style and later carpet types. Includes glossary of terms and very extensive bibliography.

FIVE

Provenance and Art Law Research

Throughout the preceding chapters, the issue of "provenance" has been touched upon, as it relates to artworks and decorative arts objects. British mystery novelist Michael Innes, in *From London Far*, defines the concept through his character Don Perez; for Perez, provenance research involves determining "who owned the picture last ... and who before that. The ideal is to trace it right back to the studio."[1] In a definite overstatement, Perez notes further that "there are very few works of art which have changed hands in what you would term an honest manner as often as in a dishonest one."[2]

The past decade's professional and popular media coverage of provenance issues has been fraught with disputes over rightful ownership, including many involving works of art looted during the Nazi era. Major museum professional organizations, including the American Association of Museums (AAM), the International Council of Museums (ICOM), and others, are actively pursuing provenance research issues and urging their member organizations to do the same. In this chapter, we'll review some of the work of these and other organizations, and discuss some of the tools that have been (or are being) developed to assist museums, collectors and other art market stakeholders to determine the chain of ownership of art works and artifacts.

Buyer Beware

The fact that a work of art is, or was, acquired from a reputable dealer, auction house or individual collector should provide the buyer with a degree of security—but only if it is accompanied by a documented provenance. But provenance documentation is not always available. Some works have been languishing in storage for decades, and even centuries, sometimes unknown to even their rightful owners.

In some cases, ownership disputes are played out in court, and the well-prepared collector—whether individual or institutional—who can document the steps undertaken to research the provenance of the contested work has a great advantage. Indeed, for a very valuable piece, the cost of retaining a professional to conduct provenance research might be a collector's wisest expenditure—especially if the research supports the collector's victory in court.

The potential impact that provenance can have on the market value of an artwork or object can indeed be great, as we've seen in some high profile auctions over the recent few decades. Prior inclusion in a celebrated collection can only enhance the value of a major painting, drawing, sculpture or other artwork. It remains to be seen, however, if the purely "associative value" of more common objects stands the test of time.

The modern provenance researcher has access to a large and growing number of resources that can assist in tracing the provenance of artworks. Some of these tools, including the Getty Research Institute's various databases, were developed for the serious provenance researcher. But just about everything discussed throughout this book—including exhibition catalogs, catalogues raisonnés, reference works, auction catalogs and databases—can provide some very important information for the researcher of provenance. In this chapter, we'll explore the primary sources of information for provenance research, and suggest some tips for conducting the kind of detective work that is necessary to establish the chain of ownership of works of art.

Provenance and Authentication

In the sometimes shady world of art dealings, issues of provenance and issues of authenticity can become intermingled. Unless a subject work is discovered buried in an attic or basement,[3] its appearance, seemingly "out of the blue," will certainly raise doubts among interested collectors, dealers, and other art market stakeholders. Remember that the wily forger, who has the skill to create a passable fake or forgery, will likely be equally adept at creating bogus documents—bills of sale, gallery labels, and the like. In fact, creating false documentation is much less challenging than creating paintings, drawings or other works of art!

Provenance Information in Published Works

Traditional art research tools, including the exhibition catalogs, monographs, catalogues raisonnés, and indexes discussed throughout the previous few chapters, are among the most straightforward tools for provenance research. Catalogues raisonnés in particular are usually a good starting point for tracing the record of ownership of a particular work of art. Most catalogues raisonnés include provenance details with each entry, when this information is available. In recent decades, however, it appears that collectors are increasingly reluctant to allow their ownership to be recorded; rather, many entries seem to list "private collection" in lieu of the collector's name.

Exhibition catalogs very often also provide a good deal of information on individual works' ownership. The indexes to exhibitions and the various fine and decorative art databases discussed in the preceding chapters are excellent starting points for the researcher seeking an exhibition history for a work of art. *Art Full Text*, and its predecessor, *Art Index Retrospective*, are particularly useful for this type of research, because their coverage dates from 1929 to the present; in addition to "content" coverage (i.e., indexing of articles, etc.), recall that these databases are unique in that they also index reproductions— including advertisements.

Archival Resources for Provenance Research

Before going into specific sources, including books, directories, databases and other tools for provenance research, one very important handbook on methodology is worth noting:

Yeide, Nancy H., Konstantin Akinsha, and Amy L. Walsh. *The AAM Guide to Provenance Research.* Washington, D.C.: American Association of Museums, 2001. 304p.

Although it focuses on provenance issues related to works looted during the Nazi era, the *AAM Guide* provides a wealth of information and resources of value to the general researcher of provenance. Several in-depth case studies demonstrate the processes involved in the successful resolution of provenance questions. Available from the AAM and in many libraries, the *AAM Guide to Provenance Research* is an essential tool for the serious provenance researcher.

The modern researcher has access to a tremendous wealth of resources, in the form of personal and institutional archives. For the provenance researcher, archival collections are often absolutely essential. Artists' own notes and letters, as well as dealer and gallery records, can be invaluable aids for the collector or provenance researcher.

The paper-based tools that predate the modern, electronic era were extremely cumbersome. Today, the researcher with access to a large academic or research library can use a variety of tools to quickly identify archival holdings that are potentially germane to the provenance research task. In fact, some of the better systems are freely available to the public; these tools are identified as such in the following bibliography.

Archival Resources. [Palo Alto], Calif.: Research Libraries Group.

In chapter two, the primary international inventories of libraries' holdings—OCLC's *WorldCat* and the Research Libraries Group's RLIN—were discussed in some detail. Both of these sources include references to their member libraries' archival collections. The Research Libraries Group has created a separate database of archival materials, with greatly enhanced access to finding aids to its members' archival collections.

RLG's *Archival Resources* provides an easy-to-use search interface to collection records that include archival finding aids. The database currently includes over 500,000 records (largely summary descriptions) of archives, manuscripts, and special collections and more than 5,000 collection guides (detailed lists describing the content of collections, often referred to as finding aids or inventories).

Archives USA. [Ann Arbor]: *ProQuest* Information and Learning Co.

Archives USA is a searchable database of approximately 5,500 archival repositories comprising well over 140,000 individual collections. It includes the complete contents of the Library of Congress's *National Catalog of Manuscript Collections* (NUCMUC) from 1959 onward, which in itself represents well over 90,000 collections.

Archival collections are searchable in a variety of ways, including: keyword; collection name; repository name; repository city; repository state; NIDS (National Inventory of Documentary Sources) fiche number; NUCMUC number; and collection dates.

Archives of American Art. *Archivos Virtuales: Papers of Latino and Latin American Artists.* http://artarchives.si.edu/guides/archivos/index.cfm

Searchable collection of the papers of Latino and Latin American artists held by the Archives of American Art. Some digitized images included.

Archives of American Art. *Guide to Commercial Art Gallery Records.* http://artarchives.si.edu/guides/artgall/artgalac.htm

A-Z list of gallery archives held by the Archives of American Art. Each entry is annotated, with an indication of the collection's size (linear feet), contents, and microfilm numbers.

For an excellent directory of dealer archives internationally, see the *AAM Guide to Provenance Research*, Appendix D: "Dealer Archives and Locations." It provides a brief description of various dealers, galleries and scholars' archives, along with the all-important repository name and location.

Archives of American Art. *Resources on Asian Pacific American Artists at the Archives of American Art.* http://artarchives.si.edu/guides/asianam/asianam.htm

A-Z list of archival materials, with descriptions of various collections. Includes references to personal papers, oral histories, etc.

OCLC *WorldCat* [Dublin, Ohio]: OCLC.

In chapter two, in our discussion of library catalogs, we saw that *WorldCat*, the online public access catalog developed by OCLC (Online Computer Library Center), includes references from literally thousands of libraries internationally. *WorldCat* provides access to well over 56 million items, including books, journals, videos, sound recordings, and archival materials. *WorldCat*'s easy-to-use interface allows even the novice researcher to quickly identify archival materials on artists, dealers, collectors, museums and other individuals or institutions germane to the study of provenance.

Smithsonian Institution Research Information System (SIRIS). http://www.siris.si.edu

The *Smithsonian Institution Research Information System* provides a number of very valuable research components, including: Smithsonian Libraries' catalog; Archival, Manuscript and Photographic Collections; Smithsonian American Art Museum Research Databases; Specialized Research Bibliographies; History of the Smithsonian. The following are of particular interest to provenance researchers:

- *Archival, Manuscript and Photographic Collections* catalog includes detailed descriptions of approximately 230,000 collections of personal papers, manuscripts, photographs, oral histories, sound recordings, films and organization records from nine repositories, including the Archives of American Art.
- *Art Inventories* catalog is a searchable database comprising two important Smithsonian inventories: the *Inventory of American Paintings Executed Before 1914*, and the *Inventory of American Sculpture.* Together, these inventories include detailed records on more than 335,000 works of art in public and private collections. Often, the record includes an indication of ownership, including in some instances the actual name and address of a private collector; institutional collections' addresses are, of course, freely available and hence indicated in the item record.

World Collectors Annuary. See description, page 200.

Yeide, Nancy H., and Konstantin Akinsha. "Dealer Archives and Locations." Appendix D in *The AAM Guide to Provenance Research*, (described above), pp. 214–242.

Identifies the repositories for the records of major dealers, galleries and scholars. Very useful addition to the provenance literature in that it supplements major print and online finding aids of major national repositories.

Object ID and Stolen Art

Recognizing the fact that the illicit trade in stolen art and antiquities represents one of the largest of international crimes, the Getty Art History Information Program convened a meeting with international governmental and nongovernmental agencies (including the International Council of Museums, UNESCO, Interpol and others) to address the issue. A series of meetings, surveys and other information-gathering methods were utilized, and it became clear that most participants agreed that part of the solution involved the development of a standard of documentation for identifying objects; the standard came to be known as "Object ID."

Object ID posits nine information categories for the description of artworks: Type of Object; Materials & Techniques; Measurements; Inscription and Markings; Distinguishing Features; Title; Subject; Date or Period; and Maker.

Some agencies, including the FBI and Interpol, are beginning to employ Object ID in their work. For more information on Object ID, consult the Object ID website at http://www.object-id.com. This official website of the Object ID program includes basic information about the development of the standard, along with a useful *Object ID Checklist* to assist in documenting art and artifacts.

Other works covering Object ID include

Thorns, Robin. Protecting Cultural Objects in the Global Information Society: *The Making of Object ID.* Los Angeles, Calif.: Getty Information Institute, 1997. http://www.object-id.com/final/index.html

Presents the Object ID Projects final report. Includes results of survey by members of the international art and museum communities, including: Cultural heritage organizations (museums, etc.), Law enforcement agencies; Customs agencies; Art trade; Appraisers; Insurance industry.

_____, and John Bold. *Documenting the Cultural Heritage.* Los Angeles: Getty Information Institute, 1998. 57p. http://www.object-id.com/heritage/index.html

Reports upon standards for documenting cultural heritage, including: Core Data Index to Historic Buildings and Monuments of the Architectural Heritage; International Core Standard for Archaeological Sites and Monuments; Object ID.

_____, and_____. *Protecting Cultural Objects Through International Documentation Standards: a Preliminary Survey.* Malibu, Calif.: Getty Art History Information Program, 1995. 51p. http://www.object-id.com/prelim/index.html

Reports on the early work of the Object ID and its questionnaire and survey findings.

_____, and_____, with Peter Dorrell and Henry Lie. *Introduction to Object ID: Guidelines for Making Records That Describe Art, Antiques and Antiquities.* Los Angeles, Calif.: Getty Information Institute, 1999. 61p. http://www.object-id.com/guide/guide_index.html

This short monograph introduces the concept of Object ID, its planning and implementation, including some good advice for photographic works. Partial contents: What is Object ID?; Why Object ID is needed; Making of Object ID; Describing art and antiquities using Object ID; Categories of information (see above); Additional recommended categories: Inventory number; Related written material; Place of origin/discovery; Cross reference to related objects; Date documented.

Tracking Stolen Works of Art

The possibility that a work of art has been stolen — whether by its current owner or at some earlier point in its travels— is certainly one of the collector's greatest fears. Sadly, researching lost or stolen artworks is a monumental task, since no single clearinghouse of lost and stolen works of art exists. Rather, the concerned "good faith" buyer or seller has at her disposal literally hundreds of databases to scan for notices of lost works of art.

A review of the legal literature reveals many sources that bemoan the lack of centralization in the reporting of stolen artworks and the lack of an internationally recognized standard of due diligence on the part of buyers and sellers.

> Some courts apply the due diligence standard to just the true owner, others apply it to both the true owner and the good-faith purchaser. In addition, a court may also consider the atmosphere of the art world at the time the artwork was discovered missing. Because of the uncertainty faced by good-faith purchasers, legitimate sellers and owners of stolen artworks, an internationally recognized standard of due diligence is needed.[4]

The author, Laura Marshall-Taylor, proceeds to note that

> there are literally hundreds of Websites dealing with stolen art and antiquities. This leaves true owners with no efficient way to look for their stolen artwork, and legitimate sellers and good-faith purchasers have no efficient way to discover if the work they want to purchase has been reported as stolen. The number of Websites dealing with stolen art, coupled with diverse rulings in the cases from the courts, leaves the parties involved with no clear understanding of how best to look for their stolen artwork, or how best to proceed in a case involving stolen artworks.[5]

The following represent some of the largest, and best known of the web-based stolen art databases. Most are free of charge, but the few that require a subscription are identified as such.

International Sources for Reporting Art Theft

Art Loss Register. http://www.artloss.com.

One of the earliest and best known and utilized registers of stolen art objects, the *Art Loss Register (ALR)*, was established by IFAR (International Foundation for Art Research) in 1976 under the name *Stolen Art Alert*. Users must register with *ALR*, and there is a fee for using most of the register's services.

In addition to the information contained in its database, the *Art Loss Register* provides information on stolen art and artifacts to the following publications, in its effort to increase chances of recovery: *The Art Newspaper*; *Art and Antiques*; *The IFAR Journal*; and *La Gazette de l'Hôtel Drouot*. These periodicals are described in much greater detail in Appendix A.

Art Theft / Most Wanted Art / Recovery Project. http://www.saztv.com.

This interesting site represents "a journalistic inquiry by Saz Productions, Inc. to acquire information for a television & new media production. In the process we hope to publicize lost art and offer assistance towards its recovery" (website's "update" page). The site's *Stolen Art Directory* is an extensive and very well-organized collection of links to a great many sites of research interest.

FBI Art Theft Program —*National Stolen Art File* (*NSAF*). http://www.fbi.gov/hq/cid/arttheft/arttheft.htm.

The *National Stolen Art File* is a database established and maintained by the FBI. It consists of records, including their images, of items that law enforcement agencies have reported as stolen. According to the FBI website, only law enforcement agencies may request searches of the *NSAF* database. A selection of items included in the *NSAF* database can be found on the Art Theft Program's website under the heading "Theft Notices and Recoveries."

FindStolenArt.com. http://www.findstolenart.com.

Find Stolen Art is an easy-to-navigate site that lists works of art, antiques and artifacts that have been stolen, and maintains an archive of recovered works.

Interpol. http://www.interpol.org.

The Interpol website includes an A-Z list of recent stolen works of fine art, decorative art and collectible objects. Rather cumbersome to use, because the searcher must know exactly how the work was handled (in the case of artworks, the title must be known), the Interpol list of recently stolen works is one that should be consulted by anyone who suspects theft of a work.

In addition to its online inventory of stolen works, Interpol has created a CD-ROM of stolen works.

> The CD-ROM is designed for police and customs services, museums, auction rooms, antique dealers, collectors and art lovers in general, and lists about 20,000 works of art and cultural property items such as paintings, sculptures and tapestries, with search possibilities based on different criteria: title of the work, name of the artist, description of the work or its dimensions and technique used. The CD-ROM is available in English, French and Spanish.[6]

Lost Art Internet Database. http://www.lostart.de.

The *Lost Art Internet Database* is a unique portal that offers a number of options. Maintained by the Koordinierungsstelle für Kulturgutverluste, Germany's central office for the documentation of lost cultural property, the database includes records and reports "about cultural objects taken from their owner(s) in connection with Nazi persecution or relocated as a result of the Second World War."[7]

Trace. http://www.trace.co.uk.

Trace, one of the companies associated with Invaluable.com (see description, page 195), is a British firm specializing in tracking and recovering stolen works of art. The firm maintains a central database that is checked against about 1,000 auction houses internationally. According to the Trace website, "over the past ten years ... [Trace] has assisted in the recovery of over 4,000 objects valued at more than £65 million."

Since 1989, Trace has published *Invaluable & Trace Magazine* (London: Catherine House), a journal that publicizes lost and stolen works of fine and decorative art.

Getty Provenance Indexes and Publications

Since 1974, the J. Paul Getty Museum has been actively involved in cataloging and making available a vast amount of information related to the provenance of artworks. The earliest projects included an inventory of Italian paintings in 19th century British auction catalogs and an index to paintings in American and British museums along with related information pertaining to the works' provenance. Renamed the Provenance Index in 1981, these projects became an independent department in 1983; as of 2004, the department's new name — the Project for the Study of Collection and Provenance — represents the breadth of the project's involvement in this critical area of art historical scholarship.

Currently, the following projects represent the department's main areas of involvement in provenance and collecting scholarship:

- Index to archival documents
- Index to auction sales catalogs
- Index to paintings in public collections
- Collectors' files, representing files on art collectors dating from the 16th through the 20th centuries.

Since its inception, the project has published the following works, which are available at many larger public, academic and museum libraries:

Documents for the History of Collecting Series

Italian Inventories

Collections of Paintings in Naples 1600–1780. (*Italian Inventories*, Vol. 1). Gérard Labrot, with Antonio Delfino. Edited by Carol Togneri and Anna Cera Sones. Munich and New York: K.G. Saur, 1992. 790p.

Documents 83 Neopolitan inventories including collections of artists, families and individuals.

Collezione dei Dipinti Colonna Inventari 1611–1795. (*Italian Inventories*, Vol. 2). Eduard A. Safarik, with Cinzia Pujia. Edited by Anna Cera Sones. Munich and New Providence [N.J.]: K.G. Saur, 1996. 1,058p.

Collezioni e Quadrerie nella Bologna del Seicento Inventari 1640–1707. (*Italian Inventories*, Vol. 3). Raffaella Morselli. Edited by Anna Cera Sones. Los Angeles: Getty Information Institute, 1998. 681p.

Seventy-seven unpublished collection inventories from the Archivio di Stato (Bologna). Approximately 6,000 works of art documented. Indexed by artist and subject.

Spanish Inventories

Collections of Paintings in Madrid 1601–1755. (*Spanish Inventories*, Vol. 1). Marcus B. Burke and Peter G. Cherry. Edited by Maria Gilbert. Los Angeles: Provenance Index of the Getty Information Institute, 1997. 2 vols. 1,693p.

Brief narrative description of inventories and valuations of Spanish collections (1601–1760s); Inventories arranged chronologically. Partial contents: Seventeenth-century Spanish taste; Golden age of collecting; Inventory process; Index of artists; Index of subjects; List of artist appraisers; List of Spanish inventories available at the Getty Provenance Index.

Netherlandish Inventories

Collections of Paintings in Haarlem 1572–1745. (*Netherlandish Inventories*, Vol. 1). Pieter Biesboer. Edited by Carol Togneri, Los Angeles: Getty Provenance Index, 2001. 691p.

Reference source for 3,536 inventories conducted between the years 1572–1745. Inventories include primarily paintings, some furniture, jewelry, maps, silver, books and other items. Organized chronologically. Entries include brief overview of the collection, bibliographical sources, lists of contents. Includes index of artists, objects.

French Inventories

Gordon, Alden, et al. *The Houses and Collections of the Marquis de Marigny* (*French Inventories*, Vol. 1). Edited by Carolyne Ayçaguer-Ron. Los Angeles: Provenance Index of the Getty Research Institute, 2003. 677p.

Inventories the estate of the Marquis, supplemented by various indexes: Index of art objects and household goods; Index of artists; Index of subjects; Index of proper names.

Indexes of Paintings in Auction Catalogues

Corpus of Paintings Sold in the Netherlands during the Nineteenth Century. 1: 1801–1805. Edited by Burton B. Fredericksen, with Ruud Priem and Julia I. Armstrong. Los Angeles: Provenance Index of the Getty Information Institute, 1998.

Like the other national sales catalog projects sponsored by the Getty Information Institute, this work records sales of paintings sold at auction, and provides some or all of the following elements for each transaction: date of sale, title, lot number, annotations, materials, dimensions, inscription, seller, price, present location and name of buyer. The project builds upon the card-file project of primarily Dutch and French sales conducted at the Rijksbureau voor Kunsthistorische Documentatie in the Hague.

The Index of Paintings Sold in the British Isles during the Nineteenth Century. Santa Barbara, Calif.: ABC-CLIO, 1988–1993.

See description, page 240. Included here for its value for the researcher of provenance.

Répertoire des Tableaux Vendus en France au XIXe Siècle. Vol. 1: *1801–1805.* Edited by Benjamin Peronnet and Burton B. Fredericksen, with Julia I. Armstrong, Sophie Hauser, and Armelle Jacquinot. Los Angeles: Provenance Index of the Getty Information Institute, 1998.

See complete entry, pages 242–243. Included here for its provenance details.

Verzeichnis der Verkauften Gemälde im Deutschsprachigen Raum vor 1800. [*Index of Paintings Sold in German-Speaking Countries Before 1800*]. Tilmann von Stockhausen and Thomas Ketelsen. Edited by Burton B. Fredericksen and Julia I. Armstrong, with the assistance of Michael Müller. Munich: K.G. Saur, 2002.

See description, page 240.

The Provenance Index Databases

Perhaps the most valuable of the Getty Provenance resources are the freely-available databases, including:

- *Database of Archival Documents*, which includes inventories from city, state, and national archives, and works of art from collections in France, Italy, the Netherlands and Spain.
- *Sales Catalogs Database*, which includes works sold at auction in Belgium, France, Germany, Great Britain, the Netherlands, and Scandinavia between the years 1650–1840.
- *Public Collections*, which includes description and provenance of paintings by artists born before 1900, including those held in American and British collections.

Art Law

Artists, dealers, auctioneers, collectors and other art market stakeholders have at their disposal a good number of sources to assist in researching the burgeoning field of art law. In addition to the reference books identified below, a great many libraries provide access to *LexisNexis*, the H.W. Wilson Company's *Legal Periodical Full Text*, and other databases of interest to the researcher of law. We'll begin this section with a very basic overview of the legal literature, and describe the most important databases that can be used to identify articles, law reviews, cases and the like.

Legal Databases

Like any other profession, law has engendered a distinct literature, with primary sources including city, state and local laws, international conventions and agreements, and the like. Secondary sources, including specialized legal newspapers, journals and academic law reviews provide commentary on legal matters. As the economy for art has skyrocketed over the past few decades, so have the numbers of individuals in art-peripheral fields, including law. Prior to the advent of user-friendly, Internet-based research databases, the vast array of legal research tools were available only to professional lawyers, law students, corporate researchers and the few others who might have been able to afford access to the very expensive databases to the literature of law. Today, some of the major art law databases and print reference tools are made available in many libraries.

Art Law Reference Sources

The following titles represent a selection of the most important reference sources for art law research. To find additional materials of this type, in libraries that utilize the Library of Congress Classification System, conduct a subject search using headings like "Law and art — United States" or "Artists — Legal status, laws, etc. — United States."

Darraby, Jessica L. *Art, Artifact & Architecture Law.* [Eagan, Minn.]: Thompson/West, 2002– . Annual. 2 vols.

Trading practices overview: Structure of art markets; Basic markets; Historical evolution of art trading; Dealers; Insurance; Provenance; Catalogue raisonné; Appraisals; Comparison of appraisal and authentication; Laws of auction.

DuBoff, Leonard D., and Christy O. King. *Art Law in a Nutshell.* 3rd ed. St. Paul, Minn.: West, 2000. 315p.

Summarizes key legal concepts in the visual arts, including the art market. Partial contents: Art — the Customs definition; Art as an investment; Art market; Investment factors and considerations; Methods of acquisition; Auctions; Authentication; Art experts; Warranties; Fine print and multiples legislation; Insurance; Tax problems; Collectors and dealers.

_____, Sherri Burr, and Michael D. Murray. *Art Law: Cases and Materials.* Buffalo, N.Y.: W.W. Hein, 2004. 666p.

Intended for the student of art and museum law; presents summaries of major legal cases along with secondary source material. Partial contents: Art reproductions and replicas; Preservation of art and cultural property; Artists' business relationships; Auctions; How auctions work; Auctioneer's role; Warranties.

_____, and Sally Holt Caplan. *The Deskbook of Art Law*. Dobbs Ferry, N.Y.: Oceana, 1993– . (Loose-leaf, frequent updates).

A standard reference source for arts lawyers, summarizes and explains legal concepts using various cases along with relevant secondary literature on the subject. Partial contents: Art — the Customs definition; International movement of art; Theft; Preservation of art; Protest art; Art as an investment; Authentication; Insurance; Auctions; Tax problems—collectors and dealers; Copyright.

Gerstenblith, Patty. *Art, Cultural Heritage, and the Law: Cases and Materials*. Durham, N.C.: Carolina Academic Press, 2004. 907p.

Summarizes legal concepts surrounding visual arts and cultural heritage issues. Partial contents: Art merchants— auction houses and dealers; Dealers' relationship to clients; Dealers' liability for implied warranty of title; Auction houses; Questions of quality and authenticity; Questions of title.

Lerner, Ralph E., and Judith Bresler. *Art Law: The Guide for Collectors, Investors, Dealers and Artists*. 2nd ed. New York: Practicing Law Institute, 1998. 2 vols.

Available in many large academic, research and law libraries, Lerner and Bresler's compendium is an indispensable tool for the serious art market researcher. This encyclopedic work uses landmark cases to illustrate the legalities surrounding everything from theft and forgery to artist-dealer relations. Partial contents: Private sales; Sales by dealers; Express and implied warranties; Statute of frauds; Title in works of art; Sales by collectors; Collector-dealer consignment; Theft, forgery, authenticity, and statutes of limitations; Auction house and the consignor; Prints and sculpture multiples; Commissioned works; Expert opinions and liabilities; Resale rights; Collection as investment property.

Lind, Robert C., Robert M. Jarvis, and Marilyn E. Phelan. *Art and Museum Law: Cases and Materials*. Durham, N.C.: Carolina Academic Press, 2002. 718p.

Partial contents: Art and artifacts as national or cultural property; Art and the investor; Authentications and appraisals; Stolen art; Fraudulent art; Art as a security.

Merryman, John Henry, and Albert E. Elsen. *Law, Ethics and the Visual Arts*. London and New York: Kluwer Law International, 2002. 4th edition. 1,342p.

Topical chapters summarize Supreme Court, state and other jurisdictions, along with secondary sources for explication of concepts. Partial contents: Acquisition of art — the art market; Commodification; Collecting art for pleasure and profit; Title problems; Collector and the artist; Counterfeit art; Theft and artnapping; Taxes, gifts to charity and appraisers.

Milrad, Aaron. *Artful Ownership: Art Law, Valuation, and Commerce in the United States, Canada and Mexico*. Washington, D.C.: American Society of Appraisers, 2000. 342p.

Intended for professional appraisers, lawyers and others involved in the international trade in art, but accessible to the non-lawyer. Partial contents: Title; Ownership; Limits on ownership; Role and responsibility of valuers; Auction and other marketplaces; Copyright; Insurance; Taxation; Cultural property legislation; Import and export.

SIX

Resources for Establishing the Value of Artworks

In the preceding chapters, we saw that researching the value of a work of art is a complex process that begins with a thorough analysis of the subject work. The artist's reputation and critical reception, rarity, quality and physical condition of the work, among other less obvious factors, all affect the value a work of art might be expected to attain if offered for sale. A large and growing number of tools, both print and electronic, provide the researcher with a great deal of information to assist in determining the value of artworks. In this chapter, we'll explore these resources in depth, along with what might seem some rather unconventional tools that are often overlooked by art market researchers.

In chapter one, we saw that there are two primary marketplaces for works of fine and decorative arts objects: the commercial gallery (retail market), and the auction (secondary market). The prices paid for works of art sold at auction are a matter of public record, and there is no simple formula for converting auction prices to retail, or gallery values. Because information on auction sales is publicly available and hence reliable and trustworthy, the vast majority of the sources described here reflect auction values. The very few sources that report gallery sales prices are included, but remember that the validity of the information recorded here is virtually impossible to verify.

The Auction Catalog

Printed auction catalogs are assembled and distributed to interested collectors and other subscribers a few weeks before the auction. Increasingly, catalog entries are also made available on the web, making it even easier for interested collectors to survey the offerings to be included in upcoming sales, and for sellers to gauge the market's performance before putting works up for sale. While the web-based catalog is a great boon to the collector, auction houses have little incentive to maintain a rich archive of past catalogs. Auction houses are, after all, in the business of selling art, not in maintaining an art sales library for interested collectors, scholars and other art researchers. While this situation differs from house to house, at present the printed catalog serves as the only stable, archived record of auction sales.

The larger auction houses hold thousands of sales annually, and these sales vary in their focus as well as in the level, or quality, of material offered for sale. Some sales are style- or period-specific (e.g., Impressionist paintings, contemporary art), while others offer a diverse range of objects. The individual estate sale, which might include decorative arts, fine arts and collectible objects from a single collection, represents a good example of the latter.

The larger auction houses have established calendars for their sales of certain categories of objects, allowing buyers and sellers to plan their activities in advance. For example, in May and November of each year, Christie's, Sotheby's and other major houses hold their auctions of highly important works of contemporary art, with schedules purposely staggered so that collectors can attend them all.

Depending upon the importance of the work of art being placed on the block, catalogs will provide a range of descriptive and sometimes even critical information on each work. Lower-level sales might include only brief descriptions of the lots offered for sale, with no accompanying reproductions. At the other end of the spectrum, a major work offered in an important sale will very often be accompanied by a catalog entry that is numerous pages in length. Individual artwork entries in auction catalogs can be expected to include some or all of the following elements:

- Reproduction (color or black and white); sometimes, details including signature if present
- Artist (if known) and dates of birth/death
- Descriptive Information (title, dimensions, medium)
- High and low estimates
- Provenance
- Bibliography of published references
- Exhibition history
- Critical essay (usually reserved for the most important offerings in a sale)

A multi-million dollar work of art often includes all of the above because, as discussed earlier, various factors (particularly provenance, publication and exhibition history) affect the value assigned to the work.

The Auction Price List

Art market researchers are usually most interested in the prices actually paid for works of art.[1] Once the auction is over, and the prices known and recorded, they are disseminated to catalog subscribers in the form of a price list, arranged simply by lot number. Today, most of the larger auction houses post their price lists on the web, but some continue to produce paper lists. Libraries, museums and other institutional subscribers usually affix the price list to the catalog, allowing the user to quickly locate the "price realized," or to easily determine those works that were unsold, or "bought-in." Some libraries, unfortunately, lack the staff required to complete this final step — a process that can be very time-consuming. In these cases, the researcher must consult one of the many "item-level" sources described below to determine the actual price paid for individual works.

Auction Catalogs and the Internet

Increasingly, auction houses are using the Internet to publicize information on forthcoming sales. Depending again upon the significance of the work under consideration, any or all of the data presented in print will be provided on the auction house's website. The larger auction houses make their offerings available on the web, while continuing to publish printed catalogs.

While electronic dissemination of auction information is a great boon to both the auctioneer and the collector, auction houses have little motivation to archive their catalogs after the sale has concluded. The resulting ephemeral nature of electronic auction information has some serious repercussions for the art market researcher. For the time being, however, most auction houses continue to disseminate their catalogs in print, and larger libraries provide access to historical runs of these all-important art market research tools.

Identifying Sales of Relevant Artworks at Auction

As noted in the preceding chapters, the first step in the process of determining the value of a particular work of art involves analysis of exactly what the piece is. This can be a simple project, as in the case of locating certain editioned prints,[2] or it can be extremely complex, involving the opinion of one or more experts on the particular artist, school or style of work. Once identified, however, the researcher can proceed in the search by finding auction houses that handle the same, or comparable, works of art. To assist in this process, numerous tools, described below, are indispensable.

Databases for Establishing Value

Many larger public and museum libraries maintain collections of auction sales catalogs. In order to use them effectively, the researcher usually needs to know which of the many sales include, or might include, items of interest. Various indexes— some in print, but many now in electronic format—can assist in this process.

Libraries that maintain good collections of auction house sales catalogs usually arrange them in one of two ways: by auction house name subdivided by date, or vice-versa, by date subdivided by auction house. Date and auction house name represent the two pieces of information absolutely required for the retrieval of catalogs in libraries' collections. We begin this section, therefore, with an introduction to *SCIPIO*, an often under-utilized but very powerful online database that provides instant access to these and other descriptive elements for each sales catalog.

SCIPIO (Sales Catalog Index Project Input Online). Research Libraries Group, Inc. *SCIPIO* can be best described as an online inventory of auction sales catalogs. A product of the Research Libraries Group, this important tool is updated on a daily basis by 21 large libraries. While *SCIPIO* serves as an inventory of these 21 libraries' holdings, the database can be used by researchers working in other libraries as well. As noted above, auction house name and date of sale are, in general, the two pieces of information a researcher must present in order to retrieve a specific catalog in a library with a catalog collection. With *SCIPIO*, the once daunting task of pinpointing sale dates and auction house names can be accomplished with ease.

It is important to note that *SCIPIO* does not serve as an index to each of the works that appears in the auction catalogs it indexes. That is, it will not disclose if a catalog contains an entry on a specific painting, drawing, piece of porcelain, or other work of fine or decorative art. For this level of specificity, myriad sources, described later in this and throughout the next chapter, must be consulted.

Each entry in the *SCIPIO* database includes numerous pieces of information about auction sales and their catalogs, including

- auction house name
- title information

- date of sale
- sale code
- place of sale
- collector or seller name(s)
- name(s) of individual auctioneer(s) if applicable
- subject heading(s) (optional)
- Lugt, Lancour, and other citation numbers
- notes pertinent to the sale as well as local notes
- unique ID number beginning with the code of the holding library.

Beyond the requisite auction house name and date of sale, the indexing provided by *SCIPIO* can be enormously helpful to the researcher. For example, a simple keyword search using the terms "garden statuary" yields 224 records,[3] each of which represents a sale catalog in which "garden statuary" is featured prominently. Note that a search of ubiquitous forms, styles or periods (e.g., "contemporary art" or "nineteenth century paintings") will yield far too many results to be usable, unless further limited by auction house name, date range, or other additional search criteria.

In addition to recent and even forthcoming sales, *SCIPIO* includes information on auctions dating as far back as the late 16th century—making it a very important tool for historical research. *SCIPIO*'s value as an historical art market research tool is explored in greater detail in chapter eight.

Because it does not index each item in a sale, *SCIPIO* is more useful for conducting research on decorative arts objects than it is for finding information on individual artists' works. The latter are very well-served by the item level indexes described below, while decorative arts information can be most elusive, for reasons explored in detail in the next chapter. For this reason, research on a piece of English Chippendale furniture or other object of its kind will likely require a considerable amount of catalog scanning. The researcher engaging in this type of search will quickly learn that the most relevant catalogs have the terms "English" and "furniture" in their titles, and that *SCIPIO* is indispensable for this type of broad term searching.

Library Catalogs with Significant Auction Catalog Holdings

Because it is so highly specialized, *SCIPIO* is not offered through most libraries—even the very large ones. In recent years, a few major contributors to *SCIPIO* have introduced a feature to their online catalogs that can be very useful to the researcher lacking full *SCIPIO* access: they have created a separate search capability for individual auction catalogs. The following libraries' online catalogs, freely available, can be used to identify individual sales catalogs for tens of thousands of auctions. By searching all six of these institutions' catalogs for a desired catalog or object category, users lacking access to *SCIPIO* can identify a great many useful sources.

Art Institute of Chicago. http://wwwartic.edu.

The Art Institute of Chicago's Ryerson and Burnham Libraries include an enormous number of auction catalogs,[4] and these are searchable via the libraries' online catalog. Search options include:

- auction house name/consignor
- title
- auction house/consignor and title
- words in the consignor (e.g., surname only)
- words in the title
- words in the notes
- date of sale
- sale code
- call number

The "words in the notes" feature is particularly useful, because the notes fields include references to some of the standard finding aids, e.g., "Lugt" numbers. Fritz Lugt's *Repertoire des Catalogues de Ventes Publiques...* is described in detail on page 235.

Cleveland Museum of Art Ingalls Library. http://library.clevelandart.org/cma.

The Cleveland Museum of Art's library maintains a collection of over 80,000 auction catalogs representing the major international and some of the important smaller, regional houses. The library's online catalog offers searchability by:

- keyword
- auction house name (exact)
- auction house keyword
- date of sale
- sale code

A number of other "sorting" options (e.g., sale date, descending) make this a particularly useful interface for the market researcher.

Frick Art Reference Library. http://www.frick.org.

Founded in 1920 by Helen Clay Frick, the Frick Art Reference Library maintains an extensive, historically rich, international collection of auction sales catalogs. The library's online catalog, FRESCO, allows the user to search the Frick's auction catalog offerings by auction house/auctioneer, title, subject or consignor, keyword, call number, sale code and date of sale.

Getty Research Institute Research Library Catalog. http://www.getty.edu/research/.

The Getty Research Institute maintains a very extensive collection of auction house catalogs, many of them annotated, historically significant titles. The online catalog of this important research center allow the user to limit searches to "auction catalogs only."

Metropolitan Museum of Art. http://library.metmuseum.org.

The Metropolitan Museum of Art's Watson Library maintains a very rich, historically significant collection of auction sales catalogs. Its holdings are now searchable on Watsonline, the library's online catalog. Search options include auction house, title, keyword, seller, date of sale and sale code.

Victoria & Albert Museum — National Art Library. http://www.vam.ac.uk/nal/.

The Victoria & Albert Museum's National Art Library maintains a strong collection of auction catalogs. The library's online catalog has a very intuitive interface that allows searchers to locate auction catalogs by title, owner name, auction house name, or sale date. Search results may be sorted in a variety of ways, including sale date (ascending or descending).

Auction Catalog Vendors

Sometimes, particularly when one or two specific catalogs will suffice for a research project, buying the needed volumes directly from a vendor can be the most time- and cost-efficient method of working. Several dealers maintain extensive inventories of auction catalog holdings. A few of the very best include

The Catalog Kid
http://www.catalogkid.com
Phone: 800.258.2056
Fax: 732.502.9156

The Catalog Kid specializes in post-auction catalog sales, and maintains an extensive inventory. In addition, the firm's offerings are browsable (by broad topic) and keyword searchable online. As such, the database represents yet another freely-available research tool. As this book goes to press, the Catalog Kid's website boasts over 200,000 catalogs in stock. Catalog Kid is very highly regarded among librarians, appraisers, auction houses and other auction catalog users.

Jeffrey Eger
http://www.dndgalleries.com/auction.html
Phone: 973–455–1843
Fax: 973–455–0186

Jeffrey Eger is an extremely knowledgeable dealer whose firm maintains an extensive collection of auction catalogs dating from 1800 to the present. Eger works closely with market researchers and vendors, and is often called upon to supply obscure titles to large research libraries, auction houses and other clients. From last year's contemporary sales to late 19th century estate auctions, Jeffrey Eger is likely to be able to supply the desired auction catalog. He also maintains an extensive collection of post-sale price realized lists.

Electronic Fine Arts Information Sources

The following represent the major electronic sources of valuation data for works of fine art. The majority are Internet-based, but some are available on CD-ROM. Larger research libraries will likely provide access to one or more of the major sources, but in certain cases, individual subscriptions are available.

Art Forum: Old Master Paintings. [CD ROM]. Alderney, Channel Islands: *artnet*, [199-]– .

A fully searchable photographic database of Old Master paintings that have passed through the major international auction houses. Continued by *I-On-Art* (see below).

Art Market Research

http://www.artmarketresearch.com
71 Oxford Gardens
London, England W10 5UJ

Art Market Research is an online econometric and charting tool intended for the serious collector and investor. Since its founding in 1985, *Art Market Research* has provided statistical data that is utilized by major auction houses, media and academic art market and economy scholars.

Art Sales Index

http://www.art-sales-index.com
Art Sales Index Ltd.
194 Thorpe Lea Road
Egham, Surrey, TW20 8Ha, United Kingdom

Founded in 1968 by Richard Hislop, *Art Sales Index* is a very well-established and trusted source of high quality art auction data. Its database is available by subscription, and offers the user an intuitive interface to more than 2.6 million auction entries, representing about 250,000 artists. Media covered are paintings, works on paper, sculpture, photographs, and prints. "Each year, *Art Sales Index* receives 3,000 auction catalogues from 500 auction houses and enters 150,000 entries into the database."[*Art Sales Index* website]. In order to be included, a work must sell for [the equivalent of] at least US $400. In addition to the usual description of lot and sales date, Art Sales Index can generate graphs and charts that can be very useful. Some samples are available on the firm's website (URL above).

The print version of *Art Sales Index* is included in many libraries' collections, and is described later, in the section on published art market information sources. See page 197.

artnet. http://www.*artnet*.com.

artnet is one of the largest and most powerful of the illustrated online auction information services. Like most of the other web-based tools described in this section, *artnet* offers some features without charge, but the art market research database is available only by subscription. *artnet* is indispensable to the professional art market researcher, but it is also very intuitive and user-friendly for the novice. Media covered are paintings, sculpture, prints, drawings and other works on paper, and photographs.

The following represent the most important of *artnet*'s free-of-charge components:

• **Artist Index** allows the searcher to identify the galleries that represent artists, or that have pieces by the sought-after artist on consignment. Many good images with descriptions, complete contact information, and occasionally, asking prices (the majority refer potential buyers and other researchers to contact the gallery for price, usually with a convenient email link).

• **Gallery Index** provides a convenient, A-Z listing of over 1,300 international galleries, with complete contact information and very often, a link to

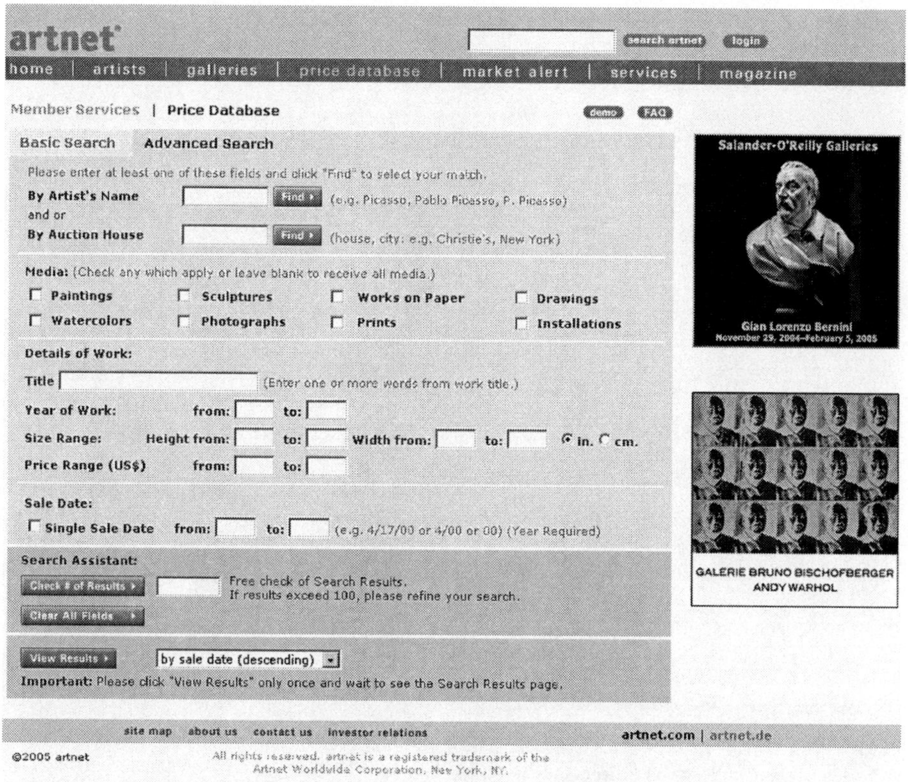

***artnet* Search Screen. Note the many options for searching, including media, date ranges, title and more (courtesy *artnet*).**

the gallery's inventory catalog. The "advanced search" mode is particularly valuable for the decorative arts researcher, and in fact represents a robust database of well-illustrated objets d'art.

• **Events Listings** includes daily, weekly and monthly auction and gallery happenings.

• **Galleries, Museum, Auction House** searchable directories.

• ***artnet Magazine*** provides feature articles, art market news, exhibition and book reviews, and much more — very high quality, not the normal "fluff" often found in free-of-charge online magazines.

Among *artnet*'s fee-based components is the *Fine Art Auction Database* (*FAAD*). In the not-so-distant past, generating a list of any artist's works sold at auction internationally was extremely time-consuming. With *FAAD*, *artnet*, one of the earliest providers of online auction data, has revolutionized the field.

artnet's *FAAD* provides very extensive and reliable coverage of the international auction world since the mid–1980s. Considering the fact that *FAAD*

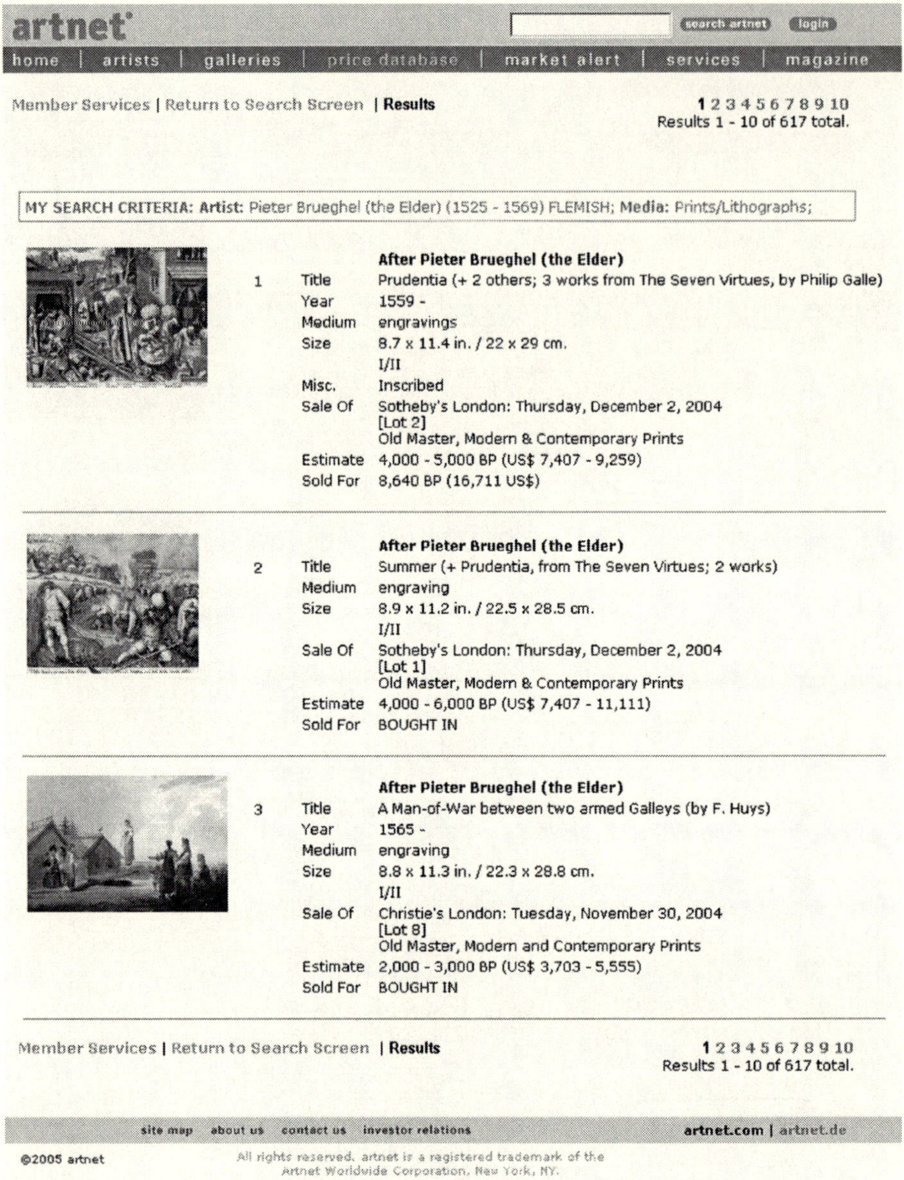

artnet

search artnet | login

home | artists | galleries | price database | market alert | services | magazine

Member Services | Return to Search Screen | **Results**

1 2 3 4 5 6 7 8 9 10
Results 1 - 10 of 617 total.

MY SEARCH CRITERIA: Artist: Pieter Brueghel (the Elder) (1525 - 1569) FLEMISH; **Media:** Prints/Lithographs;

After Pieter Brueghel (the Elder)

1

Title	Prudentia (+ 2 others; 3 works from The Seven Virtues, by Philip Galle)
Year	1559 -
Medium	engravings
Size	8.7 x 11.4 in. / 22 x 29 cm. I/II
Misc.	Inscribed
Sale Of	Sotheby's London: Thursday, December 2, 2004 [Lot 2] Old Master, Modern & Contemporary Prints
Estimate	4,000 - 5,000 BP (US$ 7,407 - 9,259)
Sold For	8,640 BP (16,711 US$)

After Pieter Brueghel (the Elder)

2

Title	Summer (+ Prudentia, from The Seven Virtues; 2 works)
Medium	engraving
Size	8.9 x 11.2 in. / 22.5 x 28.5 cm. I/II
Sale Of	Sotheby's London: Thursday, December 2, 2004 [Lot 1] Old Master, Modern & Contemporary Prints
Estimate	4,000 - 6,000 BP (US$ 7,407 - 11,111)
Sold For	BOUGHT IN

After Pieter Brueghel (the Elder)

3

Title	A Man-of-War between two armed Galleys (by F. Huys)
Year	1565 -
Medium	engraving
Size	8.8 x 11.3 in. / 22.3 x 28.8 cm. I/II
Sale Of	Christie's London: Tuesday, November 30, 2004 [Lot 8] Old Master, Modern and Contemporary Prints
Estimate	2,000 - 3,000 BP (US$ 3,703 - 5,555)
Sold For	BOUGHT IN

Member Services | Return to Search Screen | **Results**

1 2 3 4 5 6 7 8 9 10
Results 1 - 10 of 617 total.

site map about us contact us investor relations **artnet.com** | artnet.de

©2005 artnet

All rights reserved. artnet is a registered trademark of the Artnet Worldwide Corporation, New York, NY.

artnet **Search Results Screen (courtesy *artnet*).**

includes records from some 500 auction houses, and well over 2.5 million individual sales records, the cost of an *artnet* search is very reasonable. For the researcher who requires only occasional access to this type of information, *artnet*'s monthly subscription option is moderate. For the art world professional, various plans are available, including annual, unlimited access to *FAAD*.

FAAD provides "one-stop shopping" for the researcher who needs to generate a list of sales of works internationally. The search interface is very straightforward and intuitive (see illustration). The researcher begins by searching either an artist's name, or the name of an auction house. The search can be further delimited and refined using any of the following criteria:

- Auction house name
- Media categories (paintings, sculpture, etc.)
- Title words
- Year in which the work was executed
- Size range
- Price range
- Sale date, (or date range, e.g., from 2000 through 2004)

artnet's *FAAD* is an enormous inventory of sales records, and consequently, the ability to create highly focused searches is extremely important. Consider, for example, the researcher trying to identify sales of a certain type of work by Andy Warhol—arguably one of the most prolific artists of all time. The broadest search (by name only) yields 9,970 sales records. Imagine that the sought-after work is one of Warhol's iconic "flower" paintings. Limiting our search to "paintings" that have "flowers" in the title retrieves the 207 items we're looking for.

artprice.com. http://www.*artprice*.com.

Like other major vendors of art market information on the Internet, *artprice*.com offers the subscriber access to a variety of tools for researching the careers, and markets, of artists. Paintings, works on paper, prints, posters, sculpture, photography, and multimedia are covered. A few of the *artprice* components are available to the casual user at no cost; the more valuable tools are available by subscription. Various plans are available, ranging from short-term, for the infrequent researcher, to annual, unlimited use accounts for the serious collector or art market professional.

artprice provides the following tools and services:

- Detailed auction record. While lacking illustration, the data provided is extensive and provides a detailed citation to the sale's original auction catalog.
- Details of upcoming auction sales
- "Personal Research" feature. Recall from the discussion of auction catalogs that many entries provide a great deal of information about works of art, including provenance, exhibition record, publication history and more. None of the databases described in this section provide access to all of this data, and only the largest of libraries maintain extensive collections of catalogs. *artprice*.com's "Personal Research" delivers electronic images of actual catalog pages, including the catalogue cover, a reproduction of the catalogue flyleaf, the page of the catalogue on which the work appears, an enlarged reproduction of the work, the auction result, the sale terms, and other artists listed in this sale.

artprice.com maintains an archive comprised of more than several hundred thousand catalogs; for a reasonable fee, it supplies good jpeg images of catalog entries and supporting information by email, within two working days from receipt of order.

- Biography of the subject artist, including personal and professional data, selected exhibitions (solo and group), commissions, and selective bibliography.
- Signature samples. See chapter three (page 56), for a discussion of this and many additional signature reference tools.
- Artist index and statistics. Graphical analyses of individual artists' performance at auction.

ArtTactic. http://www.arttactic.com.

ArtTactic is a unique market research service that focuses on established and emerging contemporary artists. Founded by Anders Petterson, an art market analyst, ArtTactic differs from the other tools described in this section in that its artist reports include background and secondary information on artists and their careers, rather than simply providing a record of auction sales figures.

Recall from our discussion of value in chapter two that numerous factors contribute to the values assigned to works of art. These factors include provenance, exhibition records (including upcoming exhibitions), among others. ArtTactic's reports provide this kind of information for the serious collector. Record prices, private and museum collections, and forthcoming exhibitions can be particularly important to the collector in search of information on artists' careers. While coverage is limited to contemporary artists, ArtTactic's artist reports are easy-to-read, packed with valid information, and reasonably priced.

AskART. http://*AskART*.com.

AskART is a relatively inexpensive database (covering 1989–present) that provides the researcher with a great deal of information on American artists. Painting, drawing and sculpture are included. Certain of the system's components are available free, but for the art market researcher, the all-important auction record section is available only by subscription (daily and monthly rates available). As this book goes to press, *AskART* includes information on some 32,000 American artists, including some very difficult-to-find minor artists dating from as early as the 18th century.

AskART offers a great deal of information beyond auction sales results. The following sections of the *AskART* system are available free of charge on the web:

- Museums—a searchable directory
- Galleries and Dealers—searchable directory
- Auction House Directory
- Art Travel Directory
- Professional Associations Directory
- Art Glossary of Terms
- Art Available from Galleries

In the fee-based subscription service, the individual artists' search feature allows the subscriber to search a substantial number of auction records, many of which include a full-color reproduction of the subject work. The search interface is clear and intuitive, and allows the user to sort results by date, dimensions, lot number, and sale price. Similarly, searches can be limited by auction house, date-of-sale, title or title words, and media. The title word search can be particularly useful for the researcher seeking sales of works of some highly prolific artists (like Andy Warhol). Warhol produced a great many paintings titled *Flowers*, in various colors and dimensions. Limiting the search of Warhol sales to "flowers" retrieves only the *Flower* paintings, while excluding nearly one thousand irrelevant items featuring other Warhol subjects.[5]

Individual *AskART* records are clear, and usually include a good color reproduction. For Hudson River School artist Martin Johnson Heade, 129 auction records dating from 1989 are included, along with "artwork for sale" and "artwork wanted" postings, dealer and museum listings, a biography and listings of books and periodical articles on the artist.

Note that *AskART* provides only basic data on auction sales, like the other electronic sources described in this section and in the next chapter. The actual sales catalog often includes additional material, including provenance, exhibition history and bibliography.

In addition to its several directories, artist biographies and auction records, *AskART* generates graphical analyses of individual artists' works at auction. Graphical analyses include:

- Lots sold vs. unsold
- Lots (number) sold by year
- Average sale by medium
- Total $ sold by medium
- Number (of works) sold by medium

Use graphical information with caution, because one or two unusually high sales can skew the overall result, particularly for those artists whose works appear only infrequently at auction.

Australian Art Sales Digest

http://www.aasd.com.au/
John Furphy Pty. Ltd.
Australian Art Sales Digest/Carter's Price Guides
PO Box 8464
Armadale VIC 3143
Australia

Australian Art Sales Digest (*AASD*) is a web-based service that provides auction sales results and other information for over 130,000 works by artists who have either lived or work in Australia or New Zealand. Paintings, watercolors, other media and drawings, prints and graphics, ceramics, and sculpture are covered. Available by subscription at rates quite reasonable, *AASD* provides the following pieces of information for each of its subject artists:

- A listing of standard reference sources in which the artist is featured
- An *AASD* "Artist Profile," or brief biography
- Links to artist's website, where available
- List of galleries that stock work by, or represent the subject artist
- List of auction houses that have sold works by the subject artist
- Highest price and other statistics on sales
- Graphical presentation of prices and volume sold
- Price range of work sold by subject artist, by medium

Searching the "prices realized" at auction for individual artists is quite straightforward. The researcher simply enters the subject artist's last and first names, and is presented with a menu of options. For the researcher interested only in auction records that match specific criteria (e.g., only those works that actually sold), relevant criteria can be selected and applied.

For research involving the art of Australia or New Zealand, *Australian Art Sales Digest* is an invaluable source of current information. As this book goes to press, *AASD* has announced plans to extend its historical coverage by adding sales dating from the late 1970s through the present.

Gordon's Datastore

http://www.gordonsart.com
LTB Gordonsart, Inc.
13201 N. 35th Avenue, Suite B-20
Phoenix, AZ 85029
USA

Gordon's Art Reference is a very well-established publisher of high quality art market data products. Founded in 1978 by Martin Gordon, Gordon's Art Reference works are considered art market research staples, particularly in the fields of prints and photography. (Gordon's various printed publications are described later in this chapter, in their medium-specific categories.)

Datastore, the online gateway to several of Gordon's most valuable databases, allows the user to search each of the following products:

- *Gordon's Print Prices*, 1985—current. As this book goes to press, this portion of the Datastore includes some 650,000 print and poster auction records.
- *Lawrence's Dealer Print Prices* 1992—current. Over 250,000 records providing retail values reported by dealers.
- *Gordon's Photography Prices* 1970-present. Approximately 140,000 auction and dealer records for 19th, 20th, and 21st century photographs, as well as books and periodicals featuring original photographs.

Searching *Gordon's Datastore* is relatively straightforward. The user simply enters the name of the subject artist, and a spreadsheet appears, with individual lots arranged in alphabetical order by title of print or multiple. Records may be sorted by:

- Title / sale date lot
- Title / price
- Price / title
- Sale date / lot

The ability to sort results is especially important in a database of this scale that focuses on prints, particularly when the subject artist is very prolific. Search results for an artist like Picasso, for example, who produced a great many large editions, can result in very unwieldy result sets. *Datastore*'s ability to present search results by title, subdivided by date or price, can make the otherwise daunting task of identifying comparable sales much more manageable.

When an individual sale is selected, the pertinent data appears in a separate, easy-to-read window. Data elements include title, dimensions, edition number, some condition notes, date of sale and name of auction house, price realized, and reference number to catalogue raisonné.

Gordon's Datastore provides a good deal of reference material to facilitate research. Notably, the online "Bibliography" allows the user to identify key reference sources—catalogues raisonnés, monographs and other works—that are essential to proper identification of prints and multiples. Similarly, the searchable "Directory" provides easy access to auction houses, galleries, and contacts therein.

Use *Gordon's Datastore* to identify sales, and prices realized, for the following types of prints and multiples:

- Fine Art prints (e.g., Old Masters, contemporary)
- Decorative prints (historical, sporting, botanical, etc.)
- Posters
- Books (Illustrated, livres d'artiste, books and periodicals with original graphics)
- Ceramics by Picasso

For photographs, *Gordon's Datastore* is the definitive source for sales and prices on 19th, 20th and 21st century fine art and vintage photographs, as well as books and periodicals featuring original photographs.

Gordon's has announced that it will add *Davenport's Art Reference & Price Guide* to *Datastore*; *Davenport's*, which includes prices for over 250,000 artists, is particularly valuable for researching the sales of lesser-known artists.

I-On-art: Old Master Paintings at Auction. [CD ROM]. Alderney, Channel Islands: Global Art Systems, 2001.

I-On-art is a CD-ROM index of works of art by Old Masters that were sold at auction between 1990 and 2001. Individual entries are illustrated, and include a good deal of information included in the source catalogs, including provenance, exhibition history and bibliography.

Invaluable.Com

http://invaluable.com
Invaluable Ltd.
The Mews
1a Birkenhead Street
London WC1H 8BA United Kingdom

Founded in 1989, Invaluable.com is a British firm that offers a number of distinctive services to the art market research community. Invaluable.com maintains an extensive database including over 100,000 catalogs representing over 1,000 auction houses, and over 8 million "prices realized" for everything from fine art to collectible objects. The firm offers a number of subscription plans for users wishing access to this extensive database of art sales prices. For the serious collector, Invaluable's innovative auction alert service allows the user to set up a search profile; when a work of art or object appears in a forthcoming auction catalog, the system alerts the collector.

See page 176 for information on Invaluable.com's Trace Service for the recovery of stolen art and artifacts.

Leonard's Combined Price Index of Art Auctions [CD-ROM]. Newton, Mass.: Auctions Index, 1995.

Sadly, this very useful resource has not been updated, but for those seeking prices between the years 1980 and 1994, the CD-ROM version of *Leonard's* is an excellent tool. It includes the full contents of volumes 1–14 of the print title *Leonard's Annual Price Index of Art Auctions*, as well as volumes 1–3 of *Leonard's Annual Index of Prints, Posters and Photographs* (1991–1994). Provides hundreds of thousands of records for works of art.

Mayer's International Auction Records [CD-ROM]. Lausanne: Editions Acatos, 1998. *Mayer's International Auction Records* on CD-ROM includes the complete contents of 11 years' of the corresponding print edition. Searchable by artist, title, date, auction house, etc. The 2001 edition, unavailable for review, includes records spanning the years 1987–2000.

p4A.com
http://www.p4a.com
p4A.com offers a very easy-to-navigate system for auction house prices on works of fine and decorative arts. Coverage is somewhat limited compared with that of some of the other online systems described in this section, but users can identify a good selection of low- and middle-level material here, and all entries include good reproductions.

Several search options are available. Researchers may browse by object category (e.g., paintings), further limit by medium and support (e.g., oil on canvas) and place of origin. For more detailed searches, keyword searching is also available.

p4A.com can be very useful for research attempting to survey the market for a particular type of artwork or object. A search for "paintings" produced in England, with the keyword modifier "school" retrieved a good selection of unattributed, British School works of art, including miniatures, paintings on board, canvas, etc.

Published Guides to Art Market Information

Long before the advent of Internet-based information systems, art market professionals had access to many print sources to assist them in the identification of auction and, to a lesser extent, gallery sales information and prices. In fact, some of the providers of the databases described in the previous section have their roots in the traditional world of print, and some continue to produce print publications, often on an annual basis.

Several types of reference books offer art market data, and this section is arranged according to these categories. First, there are large, comprehensive auction sales record tools; arranged by artist's name, and sometimes subdivided by medium, these works provide "bare-bones" data on auction sales, including date of sale, auction house and location, physical description of the work, and price realized. In short, they represent the print predecessors of the larger online systems like *artnet* (but without the images). Because some predate the 20th century, these annual reference sources are particularly valuable to the researcher of art market history.

The second type of reference source is more highly focused concerning subject matter and media represented, or in geographic focus. For example, the researcher who seeks information on prints (lithographs, etchings, etc.) will find *Gordon's Print Price Annual* to be indispensable, even though prints are included in some of the more general sources comprising those in the first category. Those seeking price information on Latin American artists, similarly, will find *Leonard's Price Index of Latin American Art at Auction* most useful. This class of price guide is subdivided to reflect these two major divisions.

While it is assumed that most users of this book require relatively recent information on artworks, some might be interested in surveying the sources available for the study of art market history. These sources are identified and described in chapter eight.

Auction Season Reviews

Christie's Review of the Year. London: Christie's, 1996– . Continues *Christie's Review of the Season*. London: Hutchinson; New York: St. Martin's Press, 1972–1995. Annual.

Sotheby's Art at Auction. London and New York: Sotheby's, 1987– .

Christie's and Sotheby's annual reviews present beautifully illustrated overviews of major sales in both the fine and decorative arts, along with commentary on the state of the art market during their subject years.

General Auction Sales Indexes

ADEC—Annuaire Des Cotes International = International Art Price Annual. 1988–1997. See *Art Price Annual & Falk's Art Price Index* below.

American Art Analog. Compiled by Michael David Zellman. New York: Chelsea House, 1986. 3 vols. Vol. 1: 1688–1842; Vol. 2: 1842–1874; Vol. 3: 1874–1930.

This very useful resource provides biographies of hundreds of American artists, along with market data (graphs, sales figures) on each. Each artist's work is illustrated with a color example, making this an excellent source for tracking particularly less well-known, regional American artists.

Annual Art Sales Index. Weybridge, Eng.: Art Sales Index, 1976– . Annual. (Volumes for 1975/76—1977/78 titled *Annual Art Sales Index. Watercolours and Drawings* and *Annual Art Sales Index. Oil Paintings*. Continued by *Art Sales Index*, 1984– .)

One of the oldest auction sale price inventories. Chronological list of auction sales includes date, auctioneer (title, location). Entries include artist name, birth/death dates, nationality ("school," "style" also noted), price realized, date of auction, lot number in catalog, presence of catalog illustration noted. Price recorded is local currency of auction house. Highly reliable source; see also *Art Sales Index* (online), described on page 188. Latest, 2004 edition includes 166,400 entries records for 45,000 artists' auction sales internationally.

L'Annuel des Arts. [Paris]: Editions Armand Israel; Editions van Wilder, [1993]-2002. (Continues *Semestriel des Arts.*)

(Reviewed: 12th ed., 2001.) Auction records [Drouot] for approximately 800,000 objects sold at some 3,000 auctions worldwide. Basic details about individual works, signature/date information, dimensions, etc. Reports prices realized in currency of sale country, i.e., U.S. dollars, British pounds, French francs. International in scope; some Asian, but primarily European and American sales included.

Art and Auctions: International Art Dealers and Collectors Guide. Rotterdam: Van Kouteren, 1957–1969. (Continued by *International Art Market.*)

Records international auction prices, upcoming notable sales. Organized by country, further subdivided by date.

Art at Auction in America. Silver Spring, Md.: Krexpress, 1989– .

Scope: Some articles and commentary on art markets, market analysis. Coverage includes works of art, furniture and other decorative arts and collectible objects.

Art Price Index International. Produced in cooperation with the Institute for Art Research and Documentation. Annual, 1994–1997.

This index to basic auction information for works of art, covering 1992–1996, merged with *ADEC.*

Art-Price Annual. Munich: Kunst & Technik Verlag, 1969– .

English-language edition of Kunstpreisjahrbuch.

(2004 edition reviewed.) Sales records for paintings, miniatures, watercolors, pastels. Organized by place of sale, name of artist. Provides description of lots, signature/date information, auction house name, date of sale, price realized and catalog number.

Art Price Annual & Falk's Art Price Index. St. Romain au Mt. D'or, France: *artprice*.com, 2001– . Annual. (Continues *Art Price Annual International & Falk's Art Price Index; Art Price Index International*; and *Annuaire des Cotes International (ADEC).*

Print versions of *artprice*.com online auction database. Annual auction sales index. Includes records for tens of thousands of artists, 170,000 individual results, 5,200 auctions. Entries divided by medium, arranged by price realized. Includes records for paintings, decorative arts, sculpture, drawings, other works on paper, prints.

Art Price Index International. Madison, Conn.: Sound View Press, 1993– . Annual. Continues *Art Price Indicator International = International Annuaire des Cotes Moyennes.* Paris: ADEC: Ehrmann, 1987–2000.

Pocket-sized guide to the art market, includes records for paintings, drawings, miniatures, prints, posters, sculpture, photography. Provides data on significant auction results of an artist's work over the last three years.

Art Sales Index. Weybridge, Surrey, England: Art Sales Index, 1984– . See *Annual Art Sales Index*; above.

Bérard, Michèle. *Encyclopedia of Modern Art Auction Prices.* New York: Arco, 1971. 417p.

Coverage: 1960s, "all painters since the Impressionists, modern to 1970." Artists with at least one sale price over $2,000. Drawings, watercolors, gouaches, pastels, oils, collages. Organized by artist's name. Entries include name, dates, birthplace, "timeline biography." Sales records include media, dates, title, dimensions, catalog number and price realized.

La Cote des Dessins, Pastels, Gouaches, Aquarelles. Paris: Editions de l'Amateur, 1996– . Annual.

Drawings, pastels, watercolors, gouaches. Brief entries include title, date, medium, dimensions, price realized.

Davenport's Art Reference & Price Guide. Ventura, Calif.: Davenport's Art Reference, 1986– . Annual.

Provides basic biographical and pricing information for over 250,000 artists. *Davenport's* is particularly useful for researching obscure artists. In addition to auction sales references, this handy directory is keyed to major reference works, affording the user easy access to additional biographical material on the sought-after artist.

Hislop's Art Sales Index. Surrey, England : Art Sales Index, 2003– . See *Annual Art Sales Index*, above.

International Art Market. New York: Art in America. Monthly. Ceased publication with volume 23, no. 11 & 12 (Nov./Dec. 1983).

Scope and contents vary by issue. Many high-end sales reviewed, both decorative and fine arts. Provides auction prices, reports high-grossing sales ($20,000 and higher). Organized by collection and lot number. Typical entry includes name, title, signature/date information, dimensions, estimates and price realized. Numerous in-depth articles on art market issues.

International Auction Records [*Mayer*]. As of 1997, published by Acatos, Lausanne and Paris. 1964– . Annual.

(1997 edition reviewed). International auction sales prices for prints, drawings, watercolors, paintings, and sculpture. Edition reviewed records approximately 120,000 prices from 2,800 international sales. Entries include name, birth/death dates, lot number, indication of catalog illustration, some signature/date information, estimates, medium, dimension, and prices realized. Highly reliable data, but somewhat cumbersome to work with. (Individual entry refers user to sale number at the beginning of the volume.)

Kunstpreis Jahrbuch. 1978/79– .

(2004 edition reviewed.) Covers a great variety of media, including photography, decorative arts, textiles, as well as painting, sculpture, etc. Lists international auction houses by country. Partially illustrated. Sale listings arranged by artist's name, basic details of each lot along with price realized.

Leonard's Index of Art Auctions. West Newton, Mass: Auction Index, 1980–1998.

Covers sales at international auction houses, including a good selection of smaller, regional houses. Excellent source for sales data on lesser-known artists' works.

Miller's Pictures Price Guide. Annual. London: Miller's. 240p.

Provides sales information on over a thousand pictures, including oil, watercolor, pastels, gouaches and prints. This guide is particularly useful for researching lesser-known artists and lower-level genre pictures. In addition to the artists' A-Z listing, includes various useful directories including auctioneers, museums, galleries, specialists.

Novecento Italiano: Opera e Mercato di Pittori e Scultori, 1900–1945. Edited by Maurizio Agnellini. Novara, Italy: de Agostini. (Series: Biblioteca del Collezionismo d'Arte.) Annual.

Biographical dictionary of mid–20th century Italian artists, provides basic auction sales data.

World Collectors Annuary. Delft: Brouwer, [1950]– . 1946/49 to present.

Details on American and European auction houses. Entries include some or all of the following elements: artist, title, dimensions, media, price realized, bibliographic references, exhibition history. Unique in its inclusion of provenance information.

Medium- and Style-Specific Sources

Included here are published works that treat a single type or medium of artwork (e.g., paintings, prints) or period or style (e.g., Impressionism, Old Masters).

L'Argus des Ventes aux Enchères: Peinture Ancienne. Neuilly, France: Dorotheum. English language edition: *Valentine's Auction Sale Prices, Old Paintings.* 1996.

Over 2,000 reproductions included, with the focus on international sales. Entries include names, dates, description of work, auction sale information, prices realized in various currencies. Some market analysis.

Auction Prices of Impressionist and 20th Century Artists: 1970–1980. Edited by Richard Hislop. Weybridge, Surrey, England: Art Sales Index, 1981. 2 vols. 1,322 p.

Prices at auction for paintings, drawings and watercolors. Individual artists' records arranged by value (ascending).

Carl, William P. *Currier's Price Guide to American and European Prints at Auction.* 3rd edition. Prices edited by William P. Carl and William T. Currier. Stoneham, Mass.: Currier, 1994. 254p.

Provides prices ranges (not prices realized for specific works) for over 2,600 American and European artists. Partial contents: Pricing your print; Factors which determine value; Caution — reproduction prints; Artists in dealer catalogs; Print dealers.

La Cote des Peintres. Paris: Editions de l'Amateur, 1985– .

Approximately 55,000 paintings, all periods, international. Provides basic biographical data, average price of painting in French francs, record price, title of the work, and the author's name of a "reliable catalogue" (in most cases, the author or editor of the most highly regarded catalogue raisonné). Description based on 1997 edition.

Gordon's Print Price Annual. New York: M. Gordon, 1978– .

Gordon's Print Price Annual is the most extensive guide to auction sale prices for prints and multiples. Each year, approximately 50,000 sales are recorded. Old Master, modern and contemporary, decorative, historical, sporting and other types of prints are included, as are selected multiples (e.g., Picasso ceramics). Entries are arranged alphabetically by title, and each includes full description, edition size, name of auction house, high and low estimates, and price realized. Prices realized are reported in US dollars, the Euro, and British pounds. Many works are keyed to their artist's associated catalogue raisonné, a very useful feature particularly for prolific artists who have produced prints in series.

Le Guidargus de la Peinture du XIXe Siècle à Nos Jours. Paris: Editions de l'amateur, 1980– .

Brief entries record auction sales, include signature/date information, date of sale, auction house, prices in pounds or French francs.

Lawrence's Dealer Print Prices. Phoenix, Ariz.: Gordon's Art Reference, 1992– . Annual. CD-ROM version: covers January 1, 1990 through October 1, 2004 dealer prices.

Presents a compilation of retail prices derived from dealers' catalogs and inventories. Each entry includes description of the work including dimensions, title, and edition size, asking price, and information on the source dealer.

Payne, Christopher. *Animals in Bronze: Reference and Price Guide*. Woodbridge, Suffolk, England: Antique Collectors' Club, 1986. Reprinted 1993. 424p.

Surveys the modeling and casting process of the primarily 19th century sculptors of animals. Index of sculptors includes some marks and signatures. Individual works arranged by subject matter (horses, etc.).

Polsky, Richard. *Art Market Guide: Contemporary American Art*. San Francisco: Marlin Press, 1998. 207p.

Somewhat dated now, this guide to the market for works by major contemporary artist offers a good analysis of individual artists' careers. Each of the 50 artist profiles includes gallery or estate representation, top prices at auction, and a brief "market analysis" comprising work recommendations (media, periods, etc.) and the author's opinion on the artist's status as a "buy," "sell," or "hold." More current information is presented in the author's column "Art Market Guide," in the free-of-charge *artnet Magazine*. See entry to *artnet* on page (188).

Photographic Art Market. New York: Falk-Leeds, 1981/82– .

One of the very best sources for prices on photographic works. Includes all of the major photography auctions with complete information, including negative and print dates, in many cases.

Weidmann, Dieter. *Altmeistergemälde*. Munich and Berlin: Deutscher Kunstverlag, 1999.

German auction sales, offers market trends and tips, pricing, quality, provenance, etc. Higher-end sales of works noted.

Geographical Focus

Art Auction Trends: Major 19th Century American Artists. Shrewsbury, Pa: Connemara-Coleman, 1992.

Focus on major artists of the 19th century. Partial contents: General market analysis; Regional markets; Styles & subject matter; Artist rankings; Artist performance charts.

El Arte: A Precio de Martillo: De 1977 a Junio de 1997. Mexico, D.F.: Lomas, 1997. 420p.

Two-decade inventory of auction prices realized, includes prints, paintings, works on paper, and three-dimensional media. Data sources include Sotheby's and Christie's New York, Louis C. Morton and Rafael Matos (Mexico).

Australian Art Sales Digest: A Survey of Australian and New Zealand Sales of Art at Auction from 1988 to 1997. Compiled by John Furphy. Armadale, Victoria, Australia: Acorn Antiques Pty., 1998. See also: *Australian Art Sales Digest* (electronic resource.)

Records Australian and New Zealand sales. Works included if price realized exceeds $100. Entries include artist name, dates, media, number of works offered, number sold, average price, price range, highest price. Includes index of aboriginal artists.

Belgian Artists in the World's Salerooms. Brussels: Arts Antiques Auctions, 1989– .

International sales records of Belgian artists. Entries include name, dates, title, media and dimensions, sale number and price realized.

A Buyer's Guide to Irish Art. Compiled and edited by Roberta Reeners; foreword by Dorothy Walker. Dublin: Ashville Media, 1999. 414p.

Records sales dating from 1994 through 1999, all in Ireland or U.K. Basic details on each lot, including signature, auction house, place. Records withdrawn and bought-in works. Focus is on painting.

The Canadian Art Sales Index. Vancouver: Westbridge, [1980]– .

(Description based on 2005 edition.) Price information on approximately 4,700 works by over 1,100 artists. Entries include basic auction information along with signature/inscription details. Media covered include oil, watercolor, drawings, prints, sculpture and art books. Partial contents: Chronological list of auction sales; Market analysis; Top 100 Canadian paintings at auction; Top 100 Canadian artists' auction records.

Catalogo dell'Arte Italiana dell'Ottocento. Milan: G. Mondadori, 1983– . Continuation of *Catalog della Pittura Italiana dell'Ottocento.*

Approximately 1,000 primarily Italian artists surveyed. Signature/monogram example for most entries. Brief biography, including education and notable works; bibliographic sources; media; prices for some works.

Currier's Price Guide to American Artists, 1645–1945, at Auction. Brockton, Mass.: Currier, 1988.

Approximately 8,000 American artists, many lesser known, low valued works. Price entries include artist's name, subject matter, and price. Separate "record price" index for higher value works. Partial contents: Determining value: seven important factors; Outside influences on value; Period frame; The frame: an aesthetic statement; How period frames are affecting the value of paintings.

I Dipinti dell'Ottocento Italiano: Il Valore nell'Analisi Critica, Storica ed Economica. Turin: Umberto Allemandi, 1983. 551p. (Series: *Annuari di Economica dell'Arte.*)

Biography and sales information for Italian painters. Most entries include signature or monogram. Some color, primarily black and white illustrations. Entries include brief biography of subject artist, prices realized for selected works.

Franklin and James Decade Review: American Artists at Auction. Mansfield, Ohio: Franklin & James, Edition 1993 (covers 1/83–1/93); 1998 (covers 5/88–7/98); 2001 (covers 5/91–5/01). Other title: *The Franklin & James Review of American Artists at Auction, 5/85–5/90.*

Provides auction sale information on American artists. One of the best sources for sales data on unknown artists, and sales conducted at smaller, regional auction houses.

The James Adam Price Guide to Irish Art: List of Works by Irish Artists Sold Through These Rooms, 1999 & 2000. Dublin: James Adam Salerooms.

Records sales data for primarily oils, also includes watercolors, pastels, some mixed media. Auction catalog/exhibition price report includes only items sold, no buy-ins.

Leonard's Price Index of Latin American Art at Auction. Newton, Mass: Auction Index, 1999.

Provides basic auction sales information for Latin American artists' works from 1969 through 1998. Entries include price realized, title, dimensions, auction house, date of sale. Partial contents: Latin American auction market; Twentieth century art of Latin America; Latin American art; Artists' biographies; Auction prices.

Mackenzie, Ian. *British Prints: Dictionary and Price Guide.* Woodbridge, Suffolk: Antique Collectors' Club, 1998.

A comprehensive guide to the works of British printmakers, including "foreign printmakers who either worked in Britain during that period or who worked abroad but reproduced paintings by British artists" (Introduction). Entries include names, dates, media, primary subject matter, reproductions of other artists' works, reference to catalogue raisonné and other data. Prices above £5 are noted.

Prices of Victorian Paintings, Drawings and Watercolours: From the Records of Sotheby's Belgravia. London: Carter Nash Cameron; Distributed by Barrie and Jenkins, 1976. 400p.

Records Sotheby's Belgravia sales of (c. 1840–1900) oil paintings, watercolors, drawings, including lower-end to major works. No illustrations or descriptions, basic sale information (description of lot, catalog information and price realized).

Gallery Research: Finding Artists, Finding Artworks

Most of the sources discussed so far apply only to the secondary (auction) market because, as noted earlier, auctions sales are well documented. The commercial gallery is the other major venue for the sale of art, and various sources, both print and electronic, can assist the researcher in locating galleries that represent a sought-after artist, or that have examples of an artist's work. We begin this section with the major online sources, and follow with some standard print tools that can be used to determine which of the world's many thousands of commercial galleries handle the works of individual artists.

Online Directories

Art In Context. http://www.artincontext.com.

Excellent, free resource. "Provides free public access to information that is added by curators, dealers, artists, writers and others from around the world. On the Web since 1995, now serving over 700,000 images per month and viewed by over 50,000,000 visitors."

artprice.com. http://www.*artprice*.com.

Biographies include list of representatives, up-to-date listing of exhibitions (group and solo). Use this source last for dealer searches after the free sources have been exhausted.

artnet. http://www.*artnet*.com.

artnet, described earlier on pages 188–191 provides an easy-to-use index of artists. Over 16,000 artists are indexed to date. Entries provide full gallery contact information, along with some good images of available pieces.

AskART. http://www.*AskART*.com.

"Hit-or-miss" coverage of art dealers, retrievable by artist name. Useful for identifying galleries that sell works by obscure artists. Free of charge. (See full description of *AskART* on pages 192–193)

Google. http://www.google.com.

Never underestimate the power of search engines. Google, and other search engines, can be very effective tools for identifying galleries that represent artists—particularly artists who are unknown or have no formal gallery representation. I recently purchased a small painting that was included in a large group exhibition, and found numerous references, and additional examples of the artist's work, on the Internet. A recent MFA graduate, the artist does not yet have gallery representation, and so is not listed in any of the major published directories.

Print Directories

The following sources can be used to locate galleries (commercial and nonprofit), auction houses, museums and other art exhibition venues.

Art Diary International. Milan, Italy: G. Politi, 1990– (Annual).

International in scope. Provides contact information for artists, often including telephone number and email address.

Art in America. Annual Guide to Galleries, Museums, Artists. [New York]: Art in America, 1982– .

Arranged by state and indexed by artists' names, this annual reference tool provides contact information on galleries, museums, university galleries, nonprofit exhibition spaces, corporate consultants, private dealers and dealers who specialize in prints.

International Directory of Arts = Internationales Kunst-Adressbuch = Annuaire International des Beaux-Arts. Berlin: Kaupterverlag, 1952– .

Global directory of museums and galleries, colleges, universities, associations, art and antique dealers, art and antique fairs, restorers, publishers, periodicals, antiquarian and art booksellers.

Printworld Directory. West Chester, Pa: Printworld International, 1985– . Irregular.

Up-to-date indexing of printmakers, most useful for its index to print publishers and galleries specializing in prints.

SEVEN

Resources for Establishing the Value of Decorative Arts

In recent years, public interest in the decorative arts and collectible objects has grown immensely. Perhaps in response to the runaway hit PBS program, *Antiques Roadshow*, librarians find themselves fielding ever-increasing numbers of questions from their users about the value of what they hope might turn out to be "treasures"—furniture, porcelain, silver, and the like. Thankfully, several established and emerging information resources are available to assist the researcher seeking value information in these areas. We'll survey these sources in the following pages.

While the number of major discoveries hidden in attics or basements is probably miniscule, many people probably own pieces that have at least a modest value on the auction or retail market. At the other extreme—at the *very* high end of the auction market—record six- and seven-figure prices for major works are garnering considerable attention in the major news media, which in turn is likely fueling the popular fantasy of finding that lost million dollar urn, vase, chair, or other object.

It is probably safe to assume that there are many more people who collect the decorative arts than there are collectors of fine art. Just about everyone has furniture, for example, and some might even own pieces that would achieve a decent price if offered for sale at auction or consigned to a retail dealer of antiques. Furniture, ceramics, glassware, lighting, to name just a few of the many categories that comprise the decorative arts, can be found just about everywhere we look—including our own homes and offices.

Not everything that we own is, or ever will be, considered to be "collectible." With very few exceptions, the manufactured chair purchased at a major department store 10 years ago, with some visible wear and tear, has certainly not appreciated in value. Rather, like most utilitarian objects, it began to lose value the minute it left the store or showroom. Unless it is kept in near pristine condition, and a "retro" trend occurs years after its purchase, it will most likely find its final home in the garbage heap or junkyard.

But before relegating anything that might possibly be of value to the garbage heap, it is a good idea to do a little research. The author experienced this firsthand several years ago. A friend, who was in the process of moving, was about to put a funny looking white plaster lamp out for the trash collector on moving day. The odd piece, previously owned by her father (a decorator — another clue that the piece was worth investigating!) turned out to be selling on the auction market in the $5,000–$9,000 range! Today it can fetch as much as $15,000 at auction, since works by designer Jean-Michel Frank have skyrocketed in value. Neither of us knew, but a little detective work saved this mid-century modern classic from a terrible fate.

In the preceding chapter, we saw that researching the value of artworks can be quite straightforward, particularly in cases in which the identity of the artist is known — that is, when the work in question is signed. Decorative arts information sources are much less straightforward and can, in fact, be quite cumbersome to use. Most objects cannot be easily organized under the name of their maker, because in most cases there is no personal name, or even manufacturer, to be used as the indexing term. Rather, some published guides focus on materials (e.g., porcelain), period (e.g., 20th century furniture), country of origin, style, or producer (usually workshop or manufacturer, but sometimes individual designer).

Before we begin our investigation of subscription-based online sources and print publications for decorative arts market research, let's survey some of the best tools for locating galleries, flea markets and auctions, and some powerful Internet-based sources that are available free.

Decorative Arts Gallery Research

The following directories are helpful tools for finding dealers, designers, artisans and their works. To find additional sources of this type, in libraries that utilize the Library of Congress Classification System, conduct a subject search using the heading "Antiques — Exhibitions — Directories."

Collectors.org. http://www.collectors.org.

This free-of-charge site includes geographically-arranged databases of flea markets, auction houses, and collectors' clubs and associations.

Flea Market Info and Directory. http://www.keysfleamarket.com.

This free-of-charge Internet site provides up-to-date information on flea markets, arranged by state.

The International Guide to Art Fairs and Antiques Show. New York: Artmediaco, 2002– . Semi-annual. http://www.artandantiquesfairguide.com.

Lists and describes forthcoming art and antique fairs, including date of establishment, average attendance, whether or not "vetted," hours, admission price, etc. Includes indexes: Fairs and shows listed alphabetically; Fairs and shows by place; Fairs and shows chronologically.

Kovel, Ralph, and Terry Kovel. *Kovels' Yellow Pages: A Collector's Directory of Names, Addresses, Telephone and Fax Numbers, Email and Internet Addresses to Make Selling, Fixing, and Pricing Your Antiques and Collectibles Easy.* New York: Random House Reference, 2003. 560p.

This handy and inexpensive directory provides thousands of entries for collectors of all kinds of decorative and collectible objects. Partial contents: How to sell your antiques and collectibles; Collectibles A-Z; General information & source lists: Clubs & their publications; Archives and museums; Selling through auction houses; Conservators and restorers, and more!

Kovels Online features offers a good deal of directory information — including listings for appraisers, auctions, clubs and publications, matching services, museums and archives, conservators, and much more. *Kovels Online Yellow Pages* can be found at http://www.tias.com/stores/kovelsyellow.

Maloney, David J., ed. *Maloney's Antiques and Collectibles.* 7th ed. Iola, Wis.: Krause, 2003. 862p.

Maloney's is probably the most comprehensive directory of resources for the antiques, fine art and collectibles industries. The latest edition includes nearly 3,200 categories of art, antiques and collectibles, and provides over 20,000 listings of professionals, specialists, dealers, and art, design and antique institutions.

Maloney's Online: Antiques and Collectibles Resource Directory is freely available on the web. It provides a good deal of information, but is not nearly as comprehensive as its print counterpart. http://www.maloneysonline.com.

Rinker, Harry L. *Official Guide to Flea Market Prices.* New York: House of Collectibles, 2001. 502p.

Practical advice for the flea market shopper, with price guidance. Partial contents: Finding and evaluating flea markets; Top U.S. flea markets; Flea market survival guide. Includes good selection of flea market guides, trade newspapers, other additional sources for research.

Selected Internet Auctions and Retail Stores

The Internet has ushered in an enormous range of opportunities for both buyers and sellers of everything from antique furniture to works of fine art. Some very well-established auction houses have gotten into the business; others, like eBay, were actually born on the Internet and have surprised the nay-sayers who questioned the viability of their business model. Today, new online auctions as well as retail "stores" appear on the Internet each day. The availability of many easy-to-navigate stores and auctions has injected a new level of competition in the market for many classes of object, from works of art to books. Because they are in the business of selling, these dealers and auction houses make all of their data available to the researcher;[1] the collective offerings and recorded sales price information made available on the Internet is unprecedented, and represents a very important resource for the collector, dealer, or other researcher interested in valuation data on objects.

The following entries include some of the most important of the online auction and retail vendors of the decorative arts and represent very good starting points for retail and auction sales information on a vast array of objects. These sites are highly selective, of course; they have been chosen primarily for their use in identifying items and their asking prices or prices realized.

eBay. http://www.eBay.com.

With the emergence of eBay as a major force in the online auction world, collectors of all kinds of objects have been given instant access to tens of thousands of items, 24 hours a day. Some of eBay's off-beat sales have garnered considerable media attention, but today, some serious collectors look to eBay as a legitimate venue in which they can find good deals on works of decorative art, antiques, and collectible objects. Some very knowledgeable dealers utilize eBay as their online showroom, and because of this, eBay has become a valuable resource for the researcher.

As a librarian who specializes in research in fine and decorative artworks, I have frequently used eBay to identify porcelain, glass, furniture and other works. eBay offers tens of thousands of items in these categories, and increasingly, items for sale are very professionally illustrated. As an aid to identifying marks or monograms alone, eBay is a superlative source. Remember, however, that eBay changes constantly, so print out those examples that you plan to use in your research — they might not be there for long!

GoAntiques.com. http://www.goantiques.com.

GoAntiques is a unique and well-established e-commerce site that includes the collective offerings of some 1,700 dealers from 24 countries; individual works are cataloged by broad subject (e.g., "furniture"), and even broader "channels" (e.g., antiques, collectibles, etc.). Here, the researcher can browse several hundreds of thousands of fine and decorative art works offered for sale and at auction. GoAntique's innovative virtual shopping service (called F.I.N.D.) will even send out an email notification when a sought-after item appears in one of GoAntique's shops or auction sales.

Like much Internet-based information (especially commercial data), items and their associated sales data tend to appear and disappear rather quickly. Once an item has been sold, dealers and auctioneers have little incentive to maintain accessible archives of sales data. Recently, GoAntiques launched *PriceMiner.com*, a most innovative database of price information culled from a variety of sources. Because *PriceMiner.com* is subscription-based, its description is included below (page 213) with other fee-based information sources.

Newel. http://www.newel.com.

Newel Art Galleries, Inc., is one of the largest galleries of major decorative arts objects in the nation. Founded in 1939, its spacious showroom on New York City's upper east side includes thousands of pieces spanning the past five centuries.

The galleries' website provides a wealth of information for the researcher of high-end furniture, lighting, statuary, arms and armor, and other decorative and collectible items. This easy-to-navigate site allows the user to perform keyword searches, or to browse among hundreds of offerings arranged by style (e.g., art deco) or object category (e.g., lighting). An online glossary of terms provides succinct definitions to a wide range of terms, from techniques to periods and styles.

TIAS. http://www.tias.com.

TIAS is a well-established Internet-based "mall" that brings together, in one easy-to-navigate, searchable site several hundreds of thousands of items, ranging from lower-end and mid-range pieces and reproductions to a very few high priced original works of fine and decorative art.

Decorative Arts at Auction

SCIPIO, the online database of auction sales catalogs, was discussed in some detail in the preceding chapter, but some of its features make it particularly useful for decorative arts research. We begin this section, therefore, with an overview of the auction market for decorative arts objects and offer some tips for using *SCIPIO* to pinpoint the large number of catalogs that will be germane to the decorative arts market research project.

Decorative arts, antiques, and increasingly, "collectibles" comprise a great deal of most auctioneers' offerings. Collectibles, by the way, can include just about everything else in the world that would not be included under the headings "fine" or "decorative arts," including fountain pens, walking sticks, Disneyana and the like.

The larger, international auction houses hold hundreds, if not thousands of auctions each year that are either devoted to, or that include, what would be considered decorative arts objects. Just as the major sales of certain categories of fine art (e.g., Impressionism, contemporary) are held at specific times during the year, so are their decorative arts counterparts.

These sales might feature major works by Louis Comfort Tiffany, Frank Lloyd Wright, or museum quality furniture, porcelain, or silver works.

For the reasons set forth in chapter four in the discussion of decorative arts research, identifying sales that feature a certain type of object can be a daunting task. *SCIPIO*, discussed in the preceding chapter, can be a tremendous aid to the researcher attempting to identify the catalog or catalogs featuring certain types of objects. Refer to pages 184–185 for a review of *SCIPIO* basics; here, we'll review certain data elements that can assist in the search for specific objects in the auction catalog literature.

We saw in the preceding chapter that most libraries with significant runs of auction catalogs store them in one of two ways: either chronologically, subdivided by auction house name, or vice-versa. In closed-stack libraries, where patrons request materials rather then browse shelves independently, this can pose a problem, particularly for decorative arts research. Few, if any libraries have the staff to fulfill a request for, say, all of the French furniture catalogs of the past two years, for the simple reason that these indispensable tools are not organized by object type. Rather, the reader is expected to identify relevant dates and auction house names. This is where *SCIPIO* can be most useful.

Databases for Establishing Value

Compared with the fine arts, the decorative arts auction literature is served by fewer auction sales databases. The following represent some of the best and most powerful of the commercial systems featuring decorative arts and collectible objects.

Artfact. http://www.artfact.com.

Artfact offers about 10 different subscription options and terms, ranging from one-day access to the entire database for the infrequent market researcher, to annual access to the last five years of data intended for the budget-conscious professional.

Founded in 1989, *Artfact* is one of the oldest and largest of the digital art market information sources, and differs from its competitors in some very important ways. First, recall from our discussion of auction catalogs that many individual entries include a great deal of information beyond the "bare-bones" descriptive cataloging data (title, dimensions, media, price, etc.) found in most market sources, whether online or in print. At the higher end of the auction market, the catalog entry for a single work of art might run several pages, and will often include a lengthy bibliography, exhibition history, provenance, and critical essay. Unlike the other systems described in this section, *Artfact* includes all of this important documentation; it is, in fact, "the only antiques or art market information service that has the legal authority to publish online complete auction catalogs and sale results."[2]

The inclusion of information on decorative arts and collectible objects also sets *Artfact* apart from most of the other art market information providers described in this section. For a number of reasons, it is often more difficult to research the decorative arts than the fine arts, because the latter can usually be organized by the artist's name. By contrast the decorative arts—furniture, porcelain, etc.—do not share a single "indexable" characteristic, but rather must be classed by style, country of origin, designer, manufacturer, etc. It is here that the ability to search full entries by keyword proves most valuable.

In addition to its subscription-based services, *Artfact* offers free access to registered users that allows collectors, students and other researchers to view items to be included in upcoming auctions. *Artfact* registered users may also search the entire database, but are blocked from "prices realized" and "Illustration" for pieces that have appeared in past sales. Registered users are also eligible to receive auction market updates including the weekly *Artfact Auction Newsletter*, written and edited by Jonathan Fairbanks, curator emeritus of the Museum of Fine Arts, Boston.

Because the system predates the Internet era,[3] many of *Artfact*'s earliest catalog entries lack illustrations. The company is making great strides toward retrospective digitization of its earlier catalogs by scanning thousands of images monthly. As this vast repository of images expands, *Artfact* will undoubtedly emerge as the pre-eminent art market research tool.

Other useful features of *Artfact* include:

- **Artist Directory.** *Artfact* provides a very useful online directory of approximately 50,000 international artists representing all periods and styles. Most entries feature biographical data (brief, ranging from a few sentences to two paragraphs in length); selected art works from the Artfact database; auction houses that recently sold works by the artist; pricing metrics, including recent highest price paid, recent average price paid, and recent "transaction count," i.e., number of sales or offerings; related artists; and links to other valuable free resources online.
- ***Artfact*'s Fine Art Style Guide.** *Artfact* provides a list of 40 popular international art styles complete with a brief description of the movement; selected works from the *Artfact* database; auction houses that specialize in the particular style; and artists associated with each movement (including links to the artists' pages on *Artfact*).

Kovels Online. http://www.kovels.com.

Ralph and Terry Kovel have been avid collectors of antiques and collectible objects for decades. Their website offers a good deal of information for collectors, including a free database of prices. Interested users simply register for a password, which is valid for 50 price look-ups. The prices are a bit out-of-date, and little descriptive information is provided for individual items. However, depending upon the specificity of the sought-after item's description, this handy source can be very useful for establishing price estimates for thousands of pieces, from porcelain to furniture and other decorative arts categories. Many prices provide a link to a sales form for one of the Kovels' recent price guides; these sources, very reasonably priced, will provide much more current prices along with images and description of the subject pieces.

PriceMiner.com. http://www.priceminer.com.

This enormous database of price information is one of the most comprehensive and powerful, but least expensive of the fine and decorative arts subscription services. It contains data from eBay, GoAntiques, and TIAS, all described in the preceding section on Internet auction and retail sites. *PriceMiner* affords the collector, dealer or other market researcher instant access to millions of prices, all searchable by object category and keyword.

A *PriceMiner* search for a specific object will yield historical as well as current price data. Searches may be limited to auction or retail, broad category (e.g., animation art), items sold or unsold (or both). The ability to perform a keyword search alongside these delimiting categories allows the user to pinpoint comparable works. Individual items are very often illustrated and are usually well described.

PriceMiner does more than record prices. Subscribers may construct an "Analysis" by selecting individual items. For the serious collector or dealer, this feature will prove to be a great boon. Because the analyses can be saved and new items or examples added later, serious researchers can employ this powerful tool to track specific pieces or object types.

PriceMiner has announced its soon-to-be-released wireless version, which will be compatible with all browser-based PDAs (including both Palm and Microsoft systems, as well as all Smartphones). The wireless version holds great promise for the collector, who will be able to check millions of prices while strolling through galleries, antique shows, and flea markets.

My searches for a number of lower-end and mid-level items retrieved many, many directly relevant sales records, most complete with prices realized or actual retail values attained. Still a relatively new service, *PriceMiner* holds great promise, and in fact surpasses several of the much more expensive tools described in this section.

p4A.com. http://www.p4a.com.

p4A.com is an excellent source for researching decorative arts, collectibles and works of fine art. The vendors have wisely chosen to focus on the many regional auction sales that frequently go unrecorded elsewhere. Each entry is illustrated, and offers a good deal of textual content from its sales catalog.

Several very simple search options make this one of the most easy-to-use of the online sources. A "browse" feature allows the searcher to select from a broad range of categories, e.g., "glass," or "furniture." Once selected, the browse can be further delimited by "type," e.g., furniture>>cabinet. If desired, the resulting list may be further limited by geographical area. Finally, a distinctive keyword may be entered in order to retrieve only items germane to the research project at hand. This final feature is most effective in instances in which the researcher might know the name of a designer, type of glass work, etc. Take, for example, a research problem like this: "I need to find prices for some 1950s pieces of furniture that were designed by Frank Lloyd Wright. I only know the time period, and the fact that they were manufactured by Henredon."

A search of "furniture" with the keywords "Wright" and "Henredon" provides 20 relevant, detailed auction records with images— several of which are directly comparable to the subject piece.

p4A.com offers one of the most useful of the subscription-based price databases, and for the researcher of decorative arts in particular, is an essential source of regional American auction house sales data.

Price Guides to Decorative Arts Market Information

Many of these guides offer similar guidance to their users. Usually, they note that the prices recorded will vary, depending upon a number of factors— primarily, condition and location of the sale's transaction. Some offer general price ranges that are vetted by dealers and other professionals with expertise in the object category. Price guides with explicit criteria for inclusion are identified as such.

This bibliography is highly selective, largely because an all-inclusive list of price guides would comprise multiple volumes, and many of the price guides available are simply not very useful or well-produced. Further, the world of "decorative arts" is currently very expansive. For the collector or researcher of highly specialized decorative arts and collectible objects (cork screws, walking sticks, lunch boxes and the like), the following publishers are well-known producers of hundreds of high quality, well-illustrated guides:

Collector Books
  http://www.collectorbooks.com
  P.O. Box 3009, Paducah, KY 42002–3009
  Phone: (270) 898–6211
  Fax: (270) 898–8890

Collector Books produces a great many price guides each year, many focusing on highly specialized, lower end categories including collectible objects. For the collector of anything from Matchbox toys to fishing lures, the Collector Books' website is well worth searching.

Krause Publications
  http://www.collect.com
  700 East State Street
  Iola, WI 54990

Krause publishes the many highly-regarded "Antique Trader" titles (several described in this section), along with many more highly-specialized books and magazines geared toward collectors of everything from traditional antiques to comic books, records, firearms and other collectibles. The Collect.com website serves not only as the firm's e-bookstore, but offers a number of additional features of interest to collectors, including dealer directories and classified ads for buyers and sellers.

Miller's (Mitchell Beazley)
http://www.mitchell-beazley.co.uk/mbeazley/home.htm
2–4 Heron Quays
London, England E14 4JP
Phone: 020 7531 8400
Fax: 020 7531 8650

Founded in 1979 with its first title, *Miller's Antiques Price Guide* (now in its 23rd year), Miller's is a highly-regarded publisher of antiques reference books for both novice and experienced collectors and dealers. Miller's titles represent some of the best in the areas of glass, pottery and porcelain, furniture, and other traditional collecting specialties. The website includes some additional features, including a discussion forum and selected links to Internet sources for the collector.

General Price Guides

The following titles represent a selection of the most valuable price guides. All include a wide variety of objects and media. Specialized guides (e.g., glass, silver) are identified and described in the subject-specific lists that follow.

Gaston, Mary Frank. *Collectors Guide to Art Deco: Identification & Values.* Paducah, Ky.: Collector Books. 1997. 223p.

While the prices included here are dated, the introductory material and the many very good reproductions make this an excellent source for identification. Objects covered include: Barware; Clocks; Dresser accessories; Lamps; Smoking items; Statues; Tableware; Vases.

Hammond, Dorothy. *Pictorial Price Guide to American Antiques: And Objects Made for the American Market.* Woodbridge: Antique Collectors' Club, 2002. 256p.

This encyclopedic price guide includes a vast range of traditional antiques and collectible objects. Good black and white illustrations of hundreds of objects make this a useful tool for identifying styles, patterns, etc. Prices reflect auction market. Partial contents: Banks; Boxes; Folk art; Furniture; Glass; Lighting; Metals; Paintings and pictures; Pottery and porcelain.

Husfloen, Kyle. *Antique Trader Antiques & Collectibles Price Guide.* Dubuque, Iowa: Antique Trader Books. Annual.

This guide is one of the basics for any serious collector of antiques, decorative arts or collectible object category. The latest edition includes thousands of illustrated items, including a great many low-end pieces and contemporary collectibles, toys, and ephemera.

Huxford, Sharon, and Bob Huxford. *Schroeder's Antiques Price Guide.* 23rd ed. Paducah, Ky.: Collector Books, 2005. 602p.

Provides values for over 50,000 items, particularly useful for lower-end collectible objects. Essential background information on the object precedes prices for specific examples.

Kerr, Ann. *Collector's Encyclopedia of Russel Wright: Identification & Values.* 3rd ed. Paducah, Ky.: Collector Books, 2002. 301p.

Surveys the designs of Russel Wright — not only the well-known dinnerware but also furniture, metalwork and other products sought-after by the collector. The 3rd edition of this standard reference works includes a good number of primary source materials and hundreds of very good photographs of representative pieces, with values.

Knowles, Eric. *Miller's Art Deco.* Tenterden, Eng.: Miller's, 2001. 192p. (Series: *Miller's Antiques Checklist.*)

Intended for the beginning collector, provides concise overview of a great variety of objects. Well organized and illustrated.

_____. *Miller's Art Nouveau.* London: Miller's, 2000. 192p. (Series: *Miller's Antiques Checklist.*)

This series' useful Q&A format guides the novice collector through the identification process with a wide range of representative objects. Partial contents: Furniture; Glass; Ceramics; Sculpture; Silver, jewelry & metalwork; Posters; Glossary of terms.

Kovel, Ralph, and Terry Kovel. *Kovels' American Antiques, 1750 to 1900.* New York: Random House Reference, 2004. 384p.

Collectors' guide to American antiques, includes valuable information for collectors of potter and porcelain, glass, furniture, silvers, and other decorative arts objects. Provides information on factories and designers, including dates, locations and identifying marks.

_____, and_____. *Kovels' Antiques & Collectibles Price List: For the 2003 Market, Illustrated.* 35th ed. New York: Three Rivers Press, 2003. 894p.

Provides recent retail prices culled from galleries, antique shows, and other sales venues. Includes a good deal of reference material, including company histories, marks and monograms. See also the entry on various Kovels' online tools and products, pages 208 and 212.

_____, and_____. *Kovels' Know Your Collectibles.* New York: Crown, 1992. 404p.

Practical advice for the novice collector. Focuses on 19th and 20th century furniture, pottery, glass and other collectible objects.

Lyle Official Antiques Review. New York: Perigee Books; Berkeley, [1972?]– . Annual.

Provides current values, descriptions, and over 5,000 photographs of a wide range of antiques and collectibles. Classified arrangement and a detailed index make *Lyle* an indispensable source for all levels of collecting. Prices reported are drawn from the preceding year's auction and retail sales. Available in many hundreds of libraries in the U.S. and abroad.

Mascarelli, Gloria, and Robert Mascarelli. *Warman's Oriental Antiques.* Radnor, Pa.: Wallace-Homestead Book, 1992. 385p. (Series: *Encyclopedia of Antiques and Collectibles.*)

Survey of Chinese, Japanese and Korean antiques includes paintings, prints, porcelain, ceramics. Appendices include: Chinese pottery and porcelain marks; Glass interior-painted snuff bottle marks; Japanese pottery and porcelain marks; Netsuke artists' signatures; Woodblock artists' signatures; Woodblock publishers' seals.

Mayer, Enrique. *Dictionnaire des Meubles et Objets d'Art: 8000 Prix en Ventes Publiques dan le Monde Entiere.* 1994 ed. Paris: Albin Michel, 1993. 771p.

While over 10 years out-of-date, this handy source is included here because it provides prices, but more importantly, it is an excellent source for identifying particular works. While the emphasis is on the decorative arts of Europe, some American works are included. Lots of decent illustrations, prices keyed to specific sales at a number of American, British and Continental European auction houses. Partial contents: Meubles; Céramiques; Tapisseries; Art nouveau, Art deco, Art moderne; Art Africain.

Miller, Judith. *Antiques Price Guide 2004.* New York: DK, 2003. 752p.

Contents: Porcelain; Pottery; American and Canadian folk art; Oriental; Furniture; Glass; Silver & metalware; Clocks, watches & scientific instruments; Jewelry & costume jewelry; Objects of vertu; Textiles; Toys & dolls; Tribal art; Decorative arts; Modern furniture; American paintings.

Raycraft, Don, and Carol Raycraft. *Wallace-Homestead Price Guide to American Country Antiques.* Iola, Wis.: Krause. Annual. 1978– .

Well-illustrated annual price guide to antiques and collectibles, including an overview of shops, shows, auctions and galleries, hot country antiques. Good for "lower-end" of the market. [16th ed, 1999].

Rennie, Paul. *Miller's 20th Century Design Buyer's Guide.* London: Miller's, 2003. 304p.

Partial contents: Furniture; Ceramic; Glass; Lighting; Metalware; Silver; Sculpture; Clocks & watches; Jewellery; Textiles; Posters; Designers: Sir Ambrose Heal; Alvar Aalto; Jean Prouve; George Nelson; Charles & Ray Eames; Robin & Lucienne Day; Piero Fornasetti; Arne Jacobsen; Hans Wegner; Verner Panton; Memphis Group.

Rosson, Joe. *Price It Yourself! The Definitive, Down-to-Earth Guide to Appraising Antiques and Collectibles in Your Home, at Auctions, Estate Sales, Shops and Yard Sales.* New York: HarperResource, 2003. 369p.

Presents the basic concepts of appraisal in an easy-to-understand, practical fashion. Glass, ceramics, furniture, other categories of collectible objects included.

Seton, Alistair. *Collecting Japanese Antiques.* Boston: Tuttle, 2004. 303p.

Some price guidance, along with serious advice for the connoisseur of Japanese antiques and decorative arts. Partial contents: Ukiyo-e and other prints; Sagemono; Ceramics; Furniture; Textiles; Lacquerware; Cloisonné; Sculpture and metalwork; Swords and armor; Tea ceremony utensils.

Zoglin, Ron, and Deborah Shouse. *Antiquing for Dummies.* Foster City, Calif.: IDG Books, 1999. 352p.

Primer for the beginning collector of decorative arts offers practical tips on identifying, evaluating and acquiring antiques, as well as information on care and maintenance, various sales venues (auction, flea market, retail shop), etc.

Furniture: Price Guides

American Manufactured Furniture: A Complete Guide to Furniture Produced in the 1920s. 5th rev. ed. Atglen, Pa.: Schiffer, 1996. 407p.

Reference guide to hundreds of furniture manufacturers, complete with indexes to manufacturers, geographical index, and classified index of products.

Andrews, John. *British Antique Furniture: Price Guide & Reasons for Values*. 4th ed. Woodbridge, Suffolk : Antique Collectors Club, 2001. 431p.

Excellent source for the serious collector. Illustrates nearly 1,500 examples of British furniture produced between 1650 and 1860. Serves as an update to the original volume, published in 1968. Partial contents: Furniture buying—principles and precautions; Glossary of technical terms, description of woods. Each piece is referenced to a price list. Price lists and charts include: Oak; Walnut; Early mahogany; Late mahogany; Regency; Early Victorian; Country.

_____. *Victorian and Edwardian Furniture: Price Guide and Reason for Values*. Woodbridge: Antique Collectors' Club, 2001.

Collectors' guide to British furniture, includes a brief overview of British furniture styles from 1860 through 1930, including Elizabethan, Rococo, Gothic, the Aesthetic Movement, Anglo-Japanese, Arts and Crafts, Art Nouveau, Queen Anne, Georgian Revival and Edwardian Sheraton. Very well-illustrated chapters on various types of furniture (bookcases, cabinets, etc.) make this an essential tool for identifying and pricing British furniture of the period.

Curtis, Tony. *Lyle Price Guide to American Furniture*. New York: Berkley, 1998. 510p.

Handy slim-format pocket guide for the antique show aficionado, items conveniently arranged by object type. Very well illustrated, provides thousands of examples from Colonial through mid–20th century. Prices based on auction sales.

Davidson, Richard, consultant. *Furniture*. 2000. 192p. (Tenterden: *Miller's Antiques Checklist*.)

Like other titles in the *Checklist* series, Davidson's *Furniture* provides the basics of connoisseurship and pricing guidance for the beginning to intermediate level collector.

Field, Rachael. *Collector's Guide to Buying Antique Furniture*. London: Little, Brown, 1998. 176p.

Excellent source for the serious collector of English antique furniture. Profile of each work (e.g., Adam round-back chair) includes historical background, signs of authenticity, likely restoration and repair, construction and materials, variations, reproductions and price ranges. Partial contents: The history of English furniture: An introduction; Woods: Characteristics and use; Cleaning and care; Repairs and restorations: Trade practices; English antique furniture: The classic styles.

Furniture of the Arts & Crafts Period: "Stickley," Limbert, Mission Oak, Roycroft, Frank Lloyd Wright, and Others with Prices. Gas City, Ind.: L-W Book Sales, 1992. 133p.

Illustrated (black and white, some color) catalog with descriptive cataloging of various pieces, conveniently arranged by type of furniture (rockers, tables, etc.). Prices recorded relate to pieces in excellent condition, derived from recorded sales at Treadway Galleries, specialists in Arts and Crafts furniture. Treadway-Toomey's website is one of the very best sources for pricing furniture of the Arts & Crafts Period. See Appendix B for description.

Gilham, Leslie, and Judith H. Miller. *Miller's Late Georgian to Edwardian Furniture Buyer's Guide*. Tenterden, Eng.: Miller's, 1998. 400p.

Guide to identifying styles and variations in furniture, arranged by type of furniture. Includes materials on identification of woods, maintenance of furniture, restoration, etc.

Hill, Conover. *Antique Oak Furniture: An Illustrated Value Guide.* Paducah, Ky.: Collector Books, 2003. 125p.

The popularity of oak furniture has increased among collectors over the past decade; this guide provides 2003 values, along with hundreds of photographs to aid in the identification of oak chairs, tables, cabinets, and other types of furniture.

Jenkins, Emyl. *Emyl Jenkins' Appraisal Book: Identifying, Understanding, and Valuing Your Treasures.* New York: Three Rivers Press, 1995. 326p.

This handy manual provides a good deal of information for the novice object researcher. Provides a great many tips for evaluating the quality of silver, China, crystal and other glassware, furniture, etc., evaluating insurance needs, and the like. The author correctly cautions the reader to seek the services of a professional appraiser, the advice of dealers and others in the professional decorative arts world.

Ketchum, William C., et al. *Antique Hunter's Guide to American Furniture: Chests, Cupboards, Desks & Other Pieces.* New York: Black Dog & Leventhal, 2000.

While its prices are now out-of-date, this is an excellent source for the connoisseur of American furniture. Partial contents: Simple way to identify furniture; American furniture styles; Parts of furniture; Hardware. Collecting tools: Checklist for identifying styles; List of plates by style; Construction and connoisseurship; General types of wood; Woods by stylistic period.

Koon, Larry. *Stickley Brothers Furniture Identification and Value Guide.* Paducah, Ky.: Collector Books, 2004. 238p.

Important reference source for the Stickley collector. Important background information on the Stickley Company precedes survey of individual pieces, complete with description, dimensions, prices, etc. Partial contents: Gustav Stickley's American Mission; Gustav Stickley Museum; Buying and selling resources; Reproduction Stickley furniture.

Lindquist, David P., and Caroline C. Warren. *The Big Book of Antique Furniture: Featuring English & Continental, Colonial Revival, and Victorian Furniture.* Iola, Wis.: Krause, 2002. 648p.

Well illustrated and indexed reference guide to collectible antique furniture, with prices. Each major section includes a survey of styles, their history, and relevant facts for the serious collector.

_____, and_____. *Victorian Furniture: With Prices.* Iola, Wis.: Krause, 1995. 200p.

Introduction to the market for Victorian furniture, well-illustrated and indexed. Partial contents: Gothic revival: 1830–1850; Cottage furniture: 1840–1890; Rococo revival: 1840–1865; Renaissance revival: 1860–1880; Victorian ingenuity: patents and progress: 1850–1900; Furniture of reform: Eastlake and the Aesthetic Movement: 1870–1890; Mail-order opulence: 1890–1900.

McNerney, Kathryn. *American Oak Furniture: Book II.* Paducah, Ky.: Collector Books, 2001. 223p.

Updates the author's 1984 guide with new examples of the increasingly popular American oak furniture. Well illustrated, with relatively recent values assigned to each piece.

_____. *Victorian Furniture: Our American Heritage*. Paducah, Ky.: Collector Books, 1999. 253p.

Illustrated price guide arranged by type of furniture; one or more editions widely held in libraries across the nation.

Miller's Pine & Country Furniture Buyer's Guide. Rev. ed. Tenterden, Eng.: Miller's, 2001.

Very extensive reference guide to pine and oak country furniture, arranged by furniture type. Value ranges in British pounds.

Modern Furniture Price Guide: A Comprehensive Collection of Auction Results 1991–1999. Cincinnati, Ohio: Treadway Gallery, in association with the John Toomey Gallery of Oak Park, Ill., 1999. 2 vols.

Treadway Gallery is one of the largest auction houses specializing in postwar furniture and design. This very well-illustrated, two-volume guide is an excellent reference source for modern furniture. Volume 1: Charles Eames, John Risley; Harry Bertoia; Alexander Girard; Samuel Marx; Gio Ponti; Jean Prouvé; George Nelson; Florence Knoll; Fornasetti; Norman Cherner; Dunbar; Paul McCobb; Kem Webber. Vol. 2: Edward Wormley; Alvar Alto; Arne Jacobsen; Art Deco; Donald Deskey; Eero & Eliel Saarinen; Frank Gehry; George Nakashima; Gilbert Rohde; Isamu Noguchi; Mies van der Rohe; Paul Frankl; Pierre Paulin; Heywood Wakefield; Robsjohn-Gibbings; Vladimir Kagan; Warren Platner; Warren McArthur.

Moran, Mark. *Antique Trader Furniture Price Guide*. Iola, Wis.: Antique Trader Books/Krause, 2001– . (Triennial).

(2001 edition). Partial contents: Antique furniture in the new millennium; Furniture dating chart; American furniture terms; Price listings for 18th–mid–20th century furniture pieces, arranged by type (cabinets, chairs, etc.).

_____. *Furniture: Field Guide*. Iola, Wis.: Krause, 2002. 512p.

Its small format makes this reference work the perfect flea market companion. Each piece is illustrated, described in depth, and priced. Items are arranged by type (e.g., benches, bookcases). Some special features include a furniture style dating chart, furniture terms, construction details, and a glossary of terms.

_____. *Warman's Arts & Crafts Furniture: Identification and Price Guide*. Iola, Wis.: Krause, 2004. 207p.

Excellent source for researching the history and current prices of Arts & Crafts furniture. Includes significant amount of materials on major designers of the movement, including John Ruskin, Charles Rennie Mackintosh, William Morris, the Stickley Brothers, and others. Includes detailed information, including prices for over 1,500 items.

Neumann, George C. *Early American Antique Country Furnishings: Northeastern America, 1650–1800s*. New York: McGraw-Hill, 1984. 353p.

Encyclopedic survey of colonial through 19th century Americana. Excellent source for style and pattern identification. Partial contents: Country furniture: beds; chests; cupboards; desks and boxes; floor coverings; lighting; seating; tables, stands. Cooking and eating: cooking; woodenware; ceramic tableware;

pewter tableware; glassware. Glossary of terms, hundreds of good b/w reproductions.

Philip, Peter, and Walkling, Gillian. *Field Guide to Antique Furniture.* Boston: Houghton Mifflin, 1992. 336p.

This handy guide to antique furniture offers practical information for the collector, including "recognizing woods," "finishes," and "threats to woods." In-depth overview of British, Continental European, and New World furniture periods and styles provides descriptions of style and appearance, materials, construction, decoration, finish. Prices reflect primarily London auction sales.

Schiffer, Nancy. *The Best of Golden Oak Furniture: With Details and Prices.* Atglen, Pa.: Schiffer, 2000. 157p.

Beautifully illustrated reference work on 19th century oak furniture. Partial contents: Case furniture; Bookcases; Seating; China cabinets; Tables; Accent pieces. Prices reflect retail values.

Swedberg, Robert W. *Collector's Encyclopedia of American Furniture.* Paducah, Ky.: Collector Books, 1991. Vol. 1: *Dark Woods of the Nineteenth Century: Cherry, Mahogany, Rosewood and Walnut.* Vol. 2: *Furniture of the Twentieth Century.* Vol. 3: *Country Furniture of the Eighteenth and Nineteenth Centuries.*

(Only volume 3 available for review). Color reproductions illustrate good descriptive entries on various types of furniture and styles. Volume 3 includes price guide.

Warman's American Furniture. Edited by Ellen T. Schroy. Iola, Wis.: Krause, 2000. 352p.

Arranged by furniture type, provides an easy-to-use survey of hundreds of pieces of American furniture. Useful for determining style and period. Price listings, while somewhat dated, can still be useful for determining ballpark prices for a vast array of American furniture pieces.

Pottery and Porcelain: Collectors' Associations

Belleek Collectors' International Society. http://www.belleek.ie.

Membership organization for Belleek collectors. Maintains Collector's Hall of Fame and Belleek Museum. Membership includes subscription to *The Belleek Collector* (3 issues/year).

Membership Inquiries to: The Belleek Collectors International Society
P.O. Box 1498
Great Falls, VA 22066

International Nippon Collectors Club. http://www.nipponcollectorsclub.com.

Association for serious collectors of Nippon porcelain (hand-painted chinaware manufactured in Japan in the late 19th — early 20th century). Membership includes subscriptions to *INCC Journal* and *INCC News.*

Membership Inquiries to: Jennifer Cavedo
INCC Membership
8363 Dusty Lane
Mechanicsville, VA 23116

Pottery and Porcelain: Price Guides

General Pottery and Porcelain Price Guides

Atterbury, Paul, Ellen Paul Denker, and Maureen Batkin. *Miller's Twentieth-Century Ceramics: A Collector's Guide to British and North American Factory-Produced Ceramics.* London: Miller's, 1999. 256p.

Major producers of 20th–century ceramics are surveyed. Includes factory histories and marks, overviews of designs, major artists and designers, prices.

Bagdade, Susan D., and Allen D. Bagdade. *Warman's English & Continental Pottery & Porcelain.* 3rd ed. Iola, Wis.: Krause, 1998.

Well-indexed overview of the current market for approximately 200 categories and sub-categories of English and continental European pottery and porcelain. Over 10,000 price listings included. Brief histories of companies include some identifying marks.

Husfloen, Kyle. *Antique Trader American and European Art Pottery: Price Guide.* 2nd ed. Iola, Wis.: Antique Trader Books, 2002. 301p.

Very well-illustrated reference guide includes hundreds of good photographs to aid the collector in identifying and pricing works of art pottery produced during the late 19th and early 20th centuries. Thousands of works included, all major firms represented.

_____. *Antique Trader Ceramics: Pottery and Porcelain Price Guide.* 4th ed. Iola, Wis.: Iola, 2003. 779p.

Indispensable resource for the serious collector of pottery and porcelain. Includes a good number of photographs to aid the researcher in the identification of individual designers' and manufacturers' wares. Provides basic historical facts about manufacturers, offers good tips for collectors, and includes a very good subject index.

Kamm, Dorothy. *American Painted Porcelain.* Paducah, Ky.: Collector Books, 1999. 144p.

Color illustrations of individual pieces, some marks and signatures, with values from the 1990s. Some very useful research material, including tips on collecting, cataloging and maintaining a collection.

Lang, Gordon, consultant. *Pottery.* Judith Miller and Martin Miller, general editors. London: Miller's, 2000. 191p. (Series: *Miller's Antiques Checklist.*)

_____. *Porcelain.* Judith Miller and Martin Miller, general editors. London: Miller's, 2000. 192p. (Series: *Miller's Antiques Checklist.*)

Like other titles in the *Checklist* series, these guides present the basics of connoisseurship for the beginning to intermediate collector. Prices included.

Rago, David, and Suzanne Perrault. *How to Compare and Value American Art Pottery.* London: Octopus, 2001. 176p. (Series: *Miller's Treasure or Not?*)

Essentially a guide to connoisseurship for the beginning collector, this *How to* guide surveys the factors that contribute to the value of one piece over another, including age, rarity, provenance, and restoration, among others. Perrault and Rago, acknowledged experts in the field, convey a great deal of information in a most accessible style.

Sandon, John. *Miller's Collecting Porcelain.* Tenterden, Eng.: Miller's, 2002. 160p.

Partial contents: Forming a collection; Collecting by style; Collecting by decoration; Collecting by maker or country; Collecting by object or shape; Care & display.

Sigafoose, Richard. *American Art Pottery*. Paducah, Ky.: Collector Books, 2001. 272p.
Provides a well-illustrated survey of 48 art pottery manufacturers, including the best known and most highly sought-after (Roseville, Rockwood, etc.) as well as lesser-known companies. Company histories, individual pieces with prices, and interesting research material (e.g., original advertisements) make this an essential work for the collector of American art pottery.

Spencer, Christopher, and Jo Wood. *Miller's Ceramics Buyer's Guide*. London: Mitchell Beazley, 2000. 385p.
Hundreds of illustrated examples of pottery and porcelain, fully described, with values. Major sections (pottery, porcelain) arranged by type of item. Includes reference material of interest to collectors at all levels.

Specialized Pottery and Porcelain Price Guides

Abingdon Pottery

Paradis, Joe. *Abingdon Pottery Artware 1934–1950: Stepchild of the Great Depression*. Atglen, Pa.: Schiffer, 1997. 196p.
Somewhat dated pricing information, but this handy guide includes a great deal of reference material for the Abingdon collector in addition to good reproductions to assist in identification.

Belleek

Eng, Loman, and Petula Eng. *Collecting American Belleek*. Atglen, Pa.: Schiffer, 2003. 176p.

Dresden

Harran, Jim, and Susan Harran. *Dresden Porcelain Studios: Identification and Value Guide*. Paducah, Ky.: Collector Books, 2002. 240p.
Provides historical information on 19th and 20th century Dresden studios, including characteristic styles, manufacturing process details and production techniques. Tips for collectors, facsimile original catalogue pages, and a very detailed index make this an essential tool for the Dresden collector.

Fiesta

Huxford, Bob, and Sharon Huxford. *Collector's Encyclopedia of Fiesta, Plus Harlequin, Riviera and Kitchen Kraft*. 9th ed. Paducah, Ky.: Collector Books, 2001. 221p.
Hundreds of color photographs make this an excellent source for identification of old and more recent Fiesta. Provides values and practical advice for the serious collector.

Limoges

Gaston, Mary Frank. *Collector's Encyclopedia of Limoges Porcelain*. 3rd ed. Paducah, Ky.: Collector Books, 2000. 456p.
Presents the history, marks, and values of Limoges porcelain. Many color photographs make this an excellent identification tool. Partial contents: Identifying and collecting Limoges porcelain; Major Limoges companies; Other Limoges companies; Unidentified Limoges marks; Index and cross reference to companies, initials and symbols.

Waterbrook-Clyde, Keith, and Thomas Waterbrook-Clyde. *Art Deco Limoges: Camille Tharaud and Other Ceramists.* Atglen, Pa.: Schiffer, 2005. 222p.

Includes current value ranges, in addition to reference material for the serious collector. Partial contents: Photographs of the works of Camille Tharaud; Dating of porcelain and decorating marks for Camille Tharaud; Other art deco ceramics: Robj; Edouard Marcel Sandoz; Suzanne Lalique; Royal Limoges.

_____, and_____. *Distinctive Limoges Porcelain: Objets d'Art, Boxes and Dinnerware.* Atglen, Pa.: Schiffer, 2001. 248p.

Hundreds of good color photographs make this an excellent resource for Limoges porcelain identification and dating. Values, information on marks, and other reference material on both utilitarian and decorative objects.

McCoy

Hanson, Bob, Craig Nissen, and Margaret Hanson. *McCoy Pottery: Collector's Reference & Value Guide.* Paducah, Ky.: Collector Books, 1996–2002. 3 vols.

Presents an historical survey of the McCoy Pottery firm. Works well-documented, and arranged by type of object. Volume 3 includes index to the set, marks and labels directory.

Roseville

Bassett, Mark. *Understanding Roseville Pottery.* Atglen, Pa.: Schiffer, 2002. 302p.

From the late 19th through the mid–20th century, Roseville Pottery Company productions were sought by collectors of American art pottery, and the market for the best works continues to attract a great deal of interest. This very well-researched history of the company includes information on identifying marks and prices.

Moran, Mark. *Warman's Roseville Pottery: Identification and Price Guide.* Iola, Wis.: Krause, 2004. 255p.

One of the very best guides for Roseville art pottery identification. Each pattern illustrated with a generous sampling of good quality color images.

Royal Copenhagen

Pope, Caroline, and Nick Pope. *A Collector's Guide to Royal Copenhagen Porcelain.* Atglen, Pa.: Schiffer, 2001.

An essential reference source for collectors and other researchers of Royal Copenhagen. Historical material, good photos (many in color), information on marks, and price guide included.

Wedgwood Jasper Ware

Herman, Michael. *Wedgwood Jasper Ware: A Shape Book and Collector's Guide.* Atglen, Pa.: Schiffer, 2003. 189p.

Presents an historical survey of Wedgwood production from the 19th through early 20th century. The presentation of major pieces illustrating Wedgwood productions in good color reproductions makes this an excellent source for identification and dating. Includes information on marks and values.

Willow

Gaston, Mary Frank. *Gaston's Blue Willow: Identification & Value Guide.* 3rd ed. Paducah, Ky.: Collector Books, 2004.

Excellent reference source for the serious collector. Partial contents: Collecting Blue Willow; Marks; Traditional Blue Willow pattern; Other Willow patterns; Glossary; Index to manufacturers; Index to objects.

Lindbeck, Jennifer. *A Collector's Guide to Willow Ware.* Atglen, Pa.: Schiffer, 2000. 158p.

Good pictorial survey of Willow, with hundreds of good illustrations. Includes information of interest to the serious collector, including marks, price guide.

Glass: Collectors' Associations

American Carnival Glass Association

http://www.woodsland.com/acga

"The American Carnival Glass Association is a nonprofit, educational group, interested in encouraging enthusiasm for Carnival Glass. A member of the ACGA benefits by receiving a quarterly newsletter devoted to Carnival Glass. It includes such things as news on reproductions, how to distinguish the new from the old, and detailed information about individual pieces. Current auction price results are also printed in the newsletter."

Membership Inquiries to: Dolores Wagner
5951 Fredericksburg Road
Wooster, OH 44691

American Cut Glass Association

http://www.cutglass.org

The American Cut Glass Association is a non-profit organization devoted to the study and research of American Brilliant cut glass. Membership includes subscription to collectors' newsletter, the *Hobster.*

Membership Inquiries to: ACGA
Kathy Emmerson
Executive Secretary
P O Box 482
Ramona, CA 92065–0482

Fenton Art Glass Collectors of America

http://fagcainc.wirefire.com

Fenton Glass collectors association; membership includes subscription to bi-monthly newsletter, *The Butterfly Net.*

Membership Inquiries to: Fenton Art Glass Collectors of America, Inc.
P.O. Box 384
Williamstown, WV 26187

Fostoria Glass Collectors

http://www.fostoriacollectors.org

Membership includes subscription to *The Glass Works* (8 issues) newsletter.

Membership Inquiries to: Fostoria Glass Collectors, Inc.
P.O. Box 1625
Orange, CA 92856

Fostoria Glass Society of America

http://www.fostoriaglass.org

The Fostoria Glass Society of America is a nonprofit, tax-exempt corporation formed to acquire and disseminate detailed knowledge concerning Fostoria Glass, and to establish and maintain a museum for housing and displaying Fostoria glass. Membership includes subscription to *Facets of Fostoria* (8 issues).

Membership Inquiries to: Fostoria Glass Society of America
Box 826
Moundsville, WV 26041

Glass Art Society
http://www.glassart.org
Professional organization whose purpose is to encourage excellence, to advance education, to promote the appreciation and development of the glass arts, and to support the worldwide community of artists who work with glass. Membership includes subscription to *GAS News*, and *Journal.*
Membership Inquiries to: Glass Art Society
1305 — 4th Ave. Suite 711
Seattle, WA 98101–2401

International Carnival Glass Association
http://www.woodsland.com/ICGA
Membership includes quarterly newsletter, *The Carnival Pump.*
Membership Inquiries to: Lee Markley, ICGA Secretary
Box 306
Mentone, IN 46359

National American Glass Club
http://www.glassclub.org
Educational membership organization, involved in the study and research of glass, with an emphasis on American glass. Membership includes subscription to *Glass Club Bulletin* (3 issues).
Membership Inquiries to: NAGC Membership Chairman
P.O. Box 1497
Hagerstown, MD 21741–1497

National Depression Glass Association
http://www.ndga.net
Membership includes subscription to semi-monthly newsletter containing articles on glass and related topics.
Membership Inquiries to: NDGA, Inc.
PO Box 8264
Wichita, KS 67208–0264

National Fenton Glass Society
http://www.fentonglasssociety.org
Promotes the study and understanding of handmade glass, with emphasis on Fenton Art Glass Company. Membership includes subscription to *Fenton Flyer*, bimonthly newsletter.
Membership Inquiries to: National Fenton Glass Society
PO Box 4008
Marietta, Ohio 45750–7008

National Imperial Glass Collectors Society
http://www.imperialglass.org
Membership organization devoted to the study of American glass with emphasis on the Imperial Glass Corporation. Membership includes subscription to quarterly journal, *The Glasszette.*

Membership Inquiries to: National Imperial Glass Collectors Society
P.O. Box 534
Bellaire, OH 43906

Glass: Price Guides

General Glass Price Guides

Antique Trader American & European Decorative and Art Glass Price Guide. Edited by Kyle Husfloen; contributing editor, Louis O. St. Aubin, Jr. 2nd ed. Iola, Wis.: Antique Trader Books, 2000. 202p.

Manual and price guide for the serious glass collector. Includes descriptions (some with illustrations) and price information for over 3,000 19th and 20th century glass works, glossary of terms, directory of glass collectors' associations, and more.

Benson, Nigel. *Glass of the '50s & '60s: A Collector's Guide.* Tenterden, Eng.: Miller's, 2002. 64p.

Basic primer for the beginning collector. Brief introduction to various styles and glassmaking methods (e.g., mould-blown textured glass, engraved glass). Partial contents: Designers, glass-makers & marks; Glossary; Where to buy & see; What to read.

Bredehoft, Thomas H. *Fifty Years of Collectible Glass, 1920–1970: Easy Identification and Price Guide.* Dubuque, Iowa: ATB, 1997–2000. 2 vols. Volume 1: *Tableware, Kitchenware, Barware and Water Sets.* Volume 2: *Stemware, Decorations, Decorative Accessories.*

Hayhurst, Florence. *Miller's Glass Buyer's Guide.* Tenterden, Eng.: Miller's, 2001. 320p.

Excellent source for the identification of glass works; major sections arranged by type (e.g., bowls and dishes). Partial contents: Carnival glass; Gray-Stan; Legras; Loetz; Webb; Directory of specialists.

Higgins, Molly. *Antique Stained Glass for the Home.* Atglen, Pa.: Schiffer, 2001. 192p.

Guide to style identification and pricing of stained glass windows. Major chapters arranged by window type (e.g., "Arches and Round Windows"). Covers Victorian, John Lafarge and Louis Comfort Tiffany, Arts & Crafts movement, the Glasgow School, Frank Lloyd Wright and the Prairie School.

Luther, Louise. *Miller's Art Glass: How to Compare & Value.* Tenterden, Eng.: Miller's, 2002. 176p.

Miller's "Compare and Value" series presents examples side-by-side, and instructs the reader in the points of comparison that affect items' relative importance, and hence, relative values. Partial contents: Understanding the art glass market; Displaying and caring for art glass. Art glass primer; American art glass; European art glass; Contemporary international studio artists; Sources and references.

Official Price Guide to Glassware. 3rd edition. New York: House of Collectibles (Ballantine), 2002. 840p.

Indispensable handbook for the serious glass collector. Includes over 25,000 prices, and excellent descriptive information on each piece, including manufacturer's name, pattern, etc. Partial contents: Foreign glass and glassmaking—

the world history and evolution of glassmaking; Foreign glass price guide from the 19th and 20th centuries; Pressed glass—the early and middle American periods of glass, including the origin and history of glassmaking in America; Pressed glass price guide from the 19th and early 20th centuries; Cut glass—the Brilliant period of American glass. America's fine crystal and price guide from 1880–1915; American art glass—from Tiffany to Steuben. Art glass price guide from the late 19th and early 20th centuries; Carnival glass—America's fad; Depression glass—America's great depression; Modern and miscellaneous glass—American glassware and price guide from the 1940s; Museums; Glossary; Manufacturers' marks.

Reilly, Daryl, and Bill Jenks. *Early American Pattern Glass: Collector's Identification & Price Guide*. 2nd ed. Iola, Wis.: Krause, 2002. 512p.

For the serious collector of early American glass, provides extensive information on more than 350 patterns, including names, production numbers, references, etc., along with pricing information.

Schroy, Ellen Tischbein. *Warman's Pattern Glass: A Value and Identification Guide: An Illustrated Reference Guide to Nearly 450 Different Types of Pattern Glass*. 2nd ed. Iola, Wis.: Krause, 2001. 223p.

Provides descriptive information on thousands of pieces of glassware. Excellent indexing with numerous cross-references. Partial contents: History; Manufacturers; Reproductions; State of the market.

Shotwell, David J. *Glass A to Z*. Iola, Wis.: Krause, 2002. 638p.

Well-organized selection of useful resources intended for the serious glass researcher. Definitions of technical terms, styles, patterns, historical information on glass manufacturers and their marks.

Shuman, John A. *Art Glass Identification & Price Guide*. Iola, Wis.: Krause, 2003. 256p.

Hundreds of works are illustrated, identified and priced in this very useful guide to assembling a collection of fine art glass. Includes data for Baccarat, Durand, Kimball, Lalique, Tiffany and many more producers of art glass.

_____. *The Collector's Encyclopedia of American Art Glass: A Vivid Color Guide to Numerous Art Glass Types*. Paducah, Ky.: Collector Books, 1999. 336p.

Describes in great detail the various art glass offerings of major manufacturers. Works are illustrated in color, with 1999 values. Reference material includes advertisements, glossary of terms, locations of manufacturers, timeline, and some cut glass marks.

West, Mark. *Glass*. London: Miller's, 2000. 192p. (Series: *Miller's Antiques Checklist*.)

Like other titles in the *Checklist* series, provides very basic information on glass collecting and pricing, intended for the beginning collector.

Yates, Sarah, Mark West, and David McCarron. *Collecting Glass: The Facts at Your Fingertips*. London: Miller's, 2000. 176p.

Provides very basic, readable information for the beginning collector of glass. Hundreds of items, well-illustrated, with price ranges indicated for each object along with practical advice on acquiring and displaying objects.

Specialized Glass Price Guides

Anchor-Hocking

Florence, Gene. *Anchor Hocking's Fire-King & More: Identification & Value Guide, Including Early American Prescut and Wexford.* Paducah, Ky.: Collector Books, 1998. 223p.

Excellent source for identification of Fire-King glassware. Prices represent dealer (retail) prices.

Hopper, Philip L. *Anchor Hocking Decorated Pitcher and Glasses; The Fire King Years.* Atglen, Pa.: Schiffer, 127p.

Price guide to collectible 20th century glassware, includes section on company history, identification marks, identification methods.

Carnival Glass

Edwards, Bill, and Mike Carwile. *The Standard Encyclopedia of Carnival Glass.* 9th ed. Paducah, Ky.: Collector Books, 2004. 430p.

Partial contents: Basics of Carnival Glass collecting; Fenton story; Imperial story; Millersburg story; Northwood story; English Carnival Glass; Australian Carnival Glass; Old trademarks; New marks.

_____, and_____. *The Standard Encyclopedia of Carnival Glass: Price Guide.* 13th ed. Paducah, Ky.: Collector Books, 2004. 96p.

Current price guide, arranged by pattern name and/or manufacturer. Use with previous title for identification purposes.

Quintin-Baxendale, Marion. *Collecting Carnival Glass.* 2nd ed. London: Francis Joseph, 2002. 144p.

For the serious collector of Carnival Glass, hundreds of illustrated examples with prices. One of the best guides for identifying patterns and manufacturers.

Schroy, Ellen T. *Warman's Carnival Glass: Identification and Price Guide.* Iola, Wis.: Krause, 2004. 256p.

Hundred of good color photographs and other illustrations make this an essential source for the researcher of Carnival. Includes extensive current price data.

Cobalt Glass

Clements, Monica Lynn, and Patricia Rosser. *Cobalt Blue Glass.* Altglen, Pa.: Schiffer, 1998. 144p.

Brief history of cobalt glass production precedes well-illustrated chapters devoted to specific object types (e.g., jewelry, candlesticks, vases). Each work includes value range.

Cut Glass

Evers, Jo. *Evers' Standard Cut Glass Value Guide.* Paducah, Ky.: Collector Books, 2000. 156p.

Illustrates nearly 2000 pieces of cut glass from several of the leading distributors and manufacturers during the Brilliant Age (1875–1915). Entries include company and pattern name, and variant sizes along with current (2000) values. Entries arranged by object type.

Swan, Martha Louise. *American Cut and Engraved Glass: The Brilliant Period in Historical Perspective.* Iola, Wis.: Krause, 1998. 337p.

Encyclopedic overview of glassmaking in the United States. Partial contents: Cut glass in America: early and middle periods; Brilliant period cut glass;

Nomenclature of motifs and patterns; Evolution of a glass factory: Mount Washington/Pairpoint; Libbey cut glass; Dorflinger, Hawkes and Steuben; Tuthill, Meriden, Bergen, and Niland; Why and how to build a collection; American and Canadian trademarks or signatures; Value guide (based upon retail prices).

Depression Glass

Brenner, Robert. *Depression Glass for Collectors.* Atglen, Pa.: Schiffer, 1998. 175p.

Very well-illustrated guide for the serious collector. Includes prices and all major producers are well-represented. Partial contents: History of depression glass; Brief history of major depression glass manufacturers.

Florence, Gene. *Collectors Encyclopedia of Depression Glass.* 16th Edition. Paducah Ky.: Collector Books, 2003. 256p.

Reports retail prices for Depression glass in mint condition. Many good color images make this an effective source for identification. Brief profiles of patterns and manufacturers include production colors, along with item-by-item description with prices.

_____. *Very Rare Glass of the Depression Years: Identification and Values. Sixth Series.* Paducah, Ky.: Collector Books, 1999. 175p.

Well-illustrated collection of higher-end Depression glassworks. Arranged by name of manufacturer, price range included.

Kovel, Ralph M., and Terry Kovel. *Kovels' Depression Glass & Dinnerware Price List.* 8th ed. New York: Three Rivers Press, 2004. 272p.

Important, reliable reference source for serious collectors, includes over 8,000 prices; information on factories and marks; over 250 illustrated glass patterns; over 450 pottery and porcelain dinnerware patterns. Well indexed and cross-referenced.

Luckey, Carl F. *Depression Era Glassware: Identification & Value Guide.* 4th ed. Iola, Wis.: Krause, 2002. 224p.

Photographs and line drawings assist the collector in the identification of patterns and manufacturers. Includes thousands of prices.

Mauzy, Barbara E., and Jim Mauzy. *Mauzy's Comprehensive Handbook of Depression Glass Prices.* 5th ed. Atglen, Pa.: Schiffer, 2003. 224p.

Small guide to Depression glass, arranged by pattern type, useful for identification and value guidance.

_____, and_____. *Mauzy's Depression Glass: A Photographic Reference with Prices* [*A Schiffer Book for Collectors*]. Rev. & expanded 3rd ed. Atglen, Pa.: Schiffer, 2004. 256p.

This exhaustive reference work includes over one thousand color images of Depression glass works, including some that are newly discovered and previously undocumented. Full documentation, including dimensions, color and recent prices make this an essential tool for identifying and valuing Depression glass.

Fenton Glass

Heacock, William, and Eugene C. Murdock. *Fenton Glass: The Second Twenty-Five Years.* Marietta, Ohio: Glass Press, 1998. 118p.

Excellent identification tool for Fenton Art Glass company products. Prices updated in 1998 with the publication of Robert Eaton Jr.'s *Fenton Glass: The*

Second Twenty-Five Years: Comprehensive Price Guide, which is keyed to Heacock and Murdock's original work.

Fostoria

Kerr, Ann. *Fostoria.* Vol. *2: Identification and Value Guide to Etched, Carved and Cut Designs.* Paducah, Ky.: Collector Books, 1997. 357p

Illustrated with photographs and some line drawings, excellent source for identification of Fostoria glass works. Sections arranged alphabetically by design type and or product line number.

Lalique

Moran, Mark F. *Warman's Lalique Identification and Price Guide.* Iola, Wis.: Krause, 2004. 175p.

Illustrated price guide to several hundred works by important Art Nouveau glass artist. Biography and additional reference material on detecting fakes make this an important source for the serious collector of Lalique.

Milk Glass

Newbound, Betty, and Bill Newbound. *Collector's Encyclopedia of Milk Glass: Identification and Values.* Paducah, Ky.: Collector Books, 1995. 253p.

Standard price guide, works arranged by type (bowls, boxes, etc.). Partial contents: Telling old from new — the myths and the realities; What is a marriage and do I want one?; Early American pattern glass in milk; Glass company histories.

Seneca

Seneca: Stems, Etchings, Cuts and Patterns: A Guide to Catalogs and Prices. Altglen, Pa.: Schiffer, 2000. 240p.

Reference guide to Seneca Glass Company's wares as featured in its own catalogs. Prices are keyed to original catalog pages, and represent a good selection of early offerings through the early 1980s.

Metalwork: Price Guides

General Metalwork Price Guides

The following guides include value information for more than one type of metal (silver, copper, etc.).

Gaston, Mary Frank. *Antique Brass & Copper: Identification & Value Guide.* Paducah, Ky.: Collector Books, 2001. 206p.

Presents a brief historical survey of the brass and copper industries, with an emphasis on European and American works. Includes many photographs and value guide, useful for identifying lighting, fireplace, kitchen wares, and purely decorative pieces.

Husfloen, Kyle, and Mark F. Moran. *Antique Trader Metalwares Price Guide: Including Silver, Aluminum, Brass, Chrome, Copper, Pewter, & More.* Iola, Wis.: Krause, 2003. 304p.

Price guide to mid- and higher-level metalwares, arranged by metal. Many items illustrated, good descriptions provided for all. Partial contents: Aluminum; Brass; Chrome; Copper; Iron; Lead; Pewter; Sheffield; Silver; Spelter; Steel; Tin & tole.

Specialized Metalwork Price Guides

Aluminum

Grist, Everett. *Collectible Aluminum.* Paducah, Ky.: Collector Books, 2003. 157p.
Survey of various types of aluminum decorative and utilitarian objects, with prices.

Pewter

Scott, Jack L. *Pewter Wares from Sheffield.* Baltimore: Antiquary Press, 1980. 261p.
Partial contents: Sheffield, city of metals; History of the industry; James Dixon; Methods of construction; Characteristic features; Marks; Illustrations; Makers and their marks.

Silver

Bace, Jill, Juliet Nusser, and Alexis Butcher. *Collecting Silver: The Facts at Your Fingertips.* London: Miller's, 1999. 176p.
An essential primer for the silver collector. Practical information on connoisseurship, where to buy (from antique shops to flea markets), collection maintenance and care, identification (hallmarks) and more. Section on silverworks arranged by object type (e.g., drinking vessels, etc.).

Bexfield, Daniel. *Miller's Silver & Plate Buyer's Guide.* London: Mitchell Beazley, 2002. 320p.
Well-illustrated guide to silver and plate, arranged by object type. Individual items' value ranges are keyed to dealer or auction house names. "Miller's Compares" sections provide an exploration for variations in prices realized by pieces that appear similar. Includes various tips for care and restoration, identifying fakes and forgeries, and identifying marks.

Bones, Frances, and Lee Roy Fisher. *The Standard Encyclopedia of American Silverplate, Flatware and Hollow Ware: Identification and Value Guide.* Paducah, Ky.: Collector Books, 1998. 445p.
Price guide and identification tool for American silverplate works. Original catalog pages illustrate various patterns and works of flat and hollow ware. Arranged by name of American manufacturer.

Clayton, Michael. *Christie's Pictorial History of English and American Silver.* Oxford: Phaidon, 1985. 319p.
This encyclopedic survey of silver, from Elizabethan through Victorian, is an excellent source for identification of styles. Prices reflect primarily 1970s and 1980s New York and London auction sales prices realized.

Feild, Rachael. *Collector's Guide to Buying Antique Silver.* London: Greenwich Editions, 1998. 175p.
Contents: History of English silver, an introduction; Sheffield plate 1745–1840; Repairs and restoration; Value and price; Armorials and cartouches; Assay and hallmark glossary; Weights and measures; Principal silversmiths. Entries arranged by object type (e.g., candlesticks, ewers and jugs) and include tips on identifying reproductions, variations, etc.

Fennimore, Donald L., and Elizabeth von Habsburg. *Antique Hunter's Guide to American Silver & Pewter.* New York: Black Dog & Leventhal, 2000. 478p.
Guide for the serious collector of silver and pewter. Partial contents: A simple way to identify silver, silver plate, and pewter; Good, better and best:

silver and silver plate, pewter; Caring for your collection; Illustrated guide to American makers and marks; Price guide.

Hagan, Tere. *Sterling Flatware: An Identification and Value Guide.* Gas City, Ind.: L.W. Books Sales, 2002. 312p.

Well-indexed guide to major manufacturers' products. Arranged alphabetically by company name, includes indexes to patterns, manufacturers, and marks.

Waldron, Peter. *The Price Guide to Antique Silver.* Woodbridge: Antique Collectors' Club, 2001. 368p.

Well-illustrated, scholarly treatment for the serious collector of silverworks. Main section arranged by object type (boxes; candlesticks, etc.). Prices in British pounds and U.S. dollars.

Wilson, John. *Silver & Plate.* Tenterden, Eng.: Miller's 2001. 192p. (Series: *Miller's Antiques Checklist.*)

Like other titles in the *Checklist* series, this guide is intended for the beginning and intermediate level collector.

Rugs and Carpets: Price Guides

Azizollahoff, J.R. *The Illustrated Buyer's Guide to Oriental Carpets.* Atglen, Pa.: Schiffer, 2002. Rev. 2nd ed., 196p.

This beautifully illustrated guide to Oriental carpets uses good, clear line drawings and color photographs to illustrate aspects of rug design of interest to the beginning or intermediate collector. Value ranges reflect 2002 prices, but represent a good basis for extrapolating current values for both antique and more contemporary rug designs.

Eiland, Emmett. *Oriental Rugs Today: A Guide to the Best in New Carpets from the East.* Berkeley, Calif.: Berkeley Hills Books, 2000. 200p.

Excellent overview of the "newer" rugs of the East. Partial contents: Rugs and carpets from Turkey; Rugs and carpets of Nepal and Tibet; Rugs and carpets of Pakistan; Rugs and carpets of India; Rugs and carpets of Afghanistan; Rugs and carpets of China; Rugs and carpets of Iran, Egypt and Romania.

Ford, P. R. J. *Oriental Carpet Design: A Guide to Traditional Motifs, Patterns and Symbols.* Rev. ed. London: Thames and Hudson, 1992, 1989. 352p.

Practical information for the serious carpet collector and researcher. Partial contents: How to identify an Oriental carpet by its design; Structure; Colors; Values of Oriental carpets; Dates and signatures in carpets.

Ware, Joyce C. *Collecting Oriental Rugs.* New York: Random House, 2004. 164p. (Series: *Instant Expert.*)

Partial contents: First things first: an overview of rug history and today's market; How Oriental rugs are made; Rug formats; Rug motifs; Classical carpets and tribal weavings—1500–1800; Tribal weavings—1800–1925; Village rugs—1800–1925; Flat weaves—1800–1925; Commercial decorative rugs and carpets; Contemporary collectible rugs; Sampling of current market prices; Care, repair and maintenance.

EIGHT

Sources for the Study of Art Market History

The following sources include fine art sales price data that predate 1960. Many of the primary sources are out of print, but will be found in larger academic, museum and research libraries. Citations presented in this bibliography are limited to dictionaries, sales results compendia and other reference sources. Exhaustive periodical research can be conducted using the various databases discussed in chapter 2, and the more specialized tools identified at the end of this chapter. Note that unlike most of the sources selected for inclusion in this book, because of the historical nature of this chapter, many of the sources described here are relatively rare.

Auction Catalogs—Historical Research Tools

In previous chapters, we saw that the auction catalog is one of the primary sources of information for the contemporary buyer or seller of art. The modern auction catalog was actually "born during the seventeenth century in the northern provinces of the Netherlands in conjunction with the early development there of an art market that initially rivaled that of London, its greatest competitor, in both size and sophistication."[1] Auction sales catalogs comprise a vast store of information of interest not only to the art historian, but also to anyone researching social history, economics of art and related disciplines. The resources identified here represent a selection of some of the most important tools available to the historian of the art market.

Duplessis, Georges. *Les Ventes de Tableaux, Dessins, Estampes et Objets d'Art aux XVIIe et XVIIIe Siecles (1611–1800): Essai de Bibliographie.* Paris: Rapilly, 1874. 122p.

Bibliography of auction catalogues, listed chronologically. While it does not provide prices realized, serves as an excellent tool for identifying sales. The primary focus is on paintings and drawings, but also extends to decorative arts, books, etc. Emphasis on European artists.

IDC Art Sales Catalogs, 1600–1900.

See Lugt, Fritz, below.

Lancour, Harold. *American Art Auction Catalogues 1785–1942: A Union List.* New York: New York Public Library, 1944.

Chronologically arranged list of the sales catalogs held by 21 libraries. The entry numbers are frequently used in other tools—notably, they are searchable in the *SCIPIO* database (see description, pages 184–185).

Lugt, Frits. *Repertoire des Catalogues de Ventes Publiques, Interessant l'Aart ou la Curiosite, Tableaux, Dessins, Estampes, Miniatures, Sculptures, Bronzes, Emaux, Vitraux, Tapisseries, Ceramiques, Objets d'Art, Meubles, Antiquites, Monnaies Medailles, Camees, Intailles, Armes, Instruments, Curiosites Naturelles, etc.* La Haye : M. Nijhoff ; Paris: Foundation Custodia, 1938–1987. Vol. 1: Première période vers 1600–1825. Vol. 2: Deuxième période 1826–1860. Vol. 3: Troisième période 1861–1900. Vol. 4: Quatrième période 1901–1924.

Standard reference sources for the location of auction catalogs. Entries chronologically arranged by date of sale. Index to collectors of works sold. "Lugt" number frequently used in other publications, and searchable in the *SCIPIO* database.

The print version of Lugt's *Répertoire*, long out of print, has been digitized by IDC Publishers as *IDC Art Sales Catalogs, 1600–1900*, and is available in some larger academic and research libraries. The digital version of Lugt enables the researcher to perform complex searches, and serves as the "springboard" for IDC's ambitious historical art sales catalogue digitization project.

As this research guide goes to press, IDC Publishers is adding fully digitized versions of historical art sales catalogues to its *Art Sales Catalogues Online* project. Catalogs are searchable by:

- Lugt number
- Date
- Place of sale
- Provenance
- Auction house
- Content
- Copies

A recent enhancement allows the user to search the collections of libraries with extensive holdings of catalogs. IDC has further enhanced this powerful database with cross-references to the Provenance Index of the Getty Research Institute (see description, pages 176–178).

The IDC catalogues are also available on microfiche. The microfiche project is divided into three components:

- **Part I, 1600–1825.** More than 4,400 catalogs comprise this section. The microfiche represents the holdings of 13 libraries in the Netherlands, including the National Institute for Art History, one of the largest collections in the world. The IDC project includes several hundred catalogs that were unknown to Lugt, and hence not included in his *Répertoire*.

- **Part II, 1826–1860.** Part II of the IDC Collection includes over 8,000 catalogs, and like the previous set, includes a great many titles that are not included in Lugt.
- **Part III, 1861–1880.** Part III includes an additional 5,365 catalogs based on the third volume of Lugt.
- **Part IV, 1881–1900.** An additional 8,642 catalogs, also based on Lugt, are the most recent addition to the IDC Lugt microfiche program. The firm intends to continue filming these important historical sources, with the goal of developing a complete collection of catalogs published between 1600 and 1900.

M. Knoedler & Co. *Auction Catalogues on Microfiche.* New York: Knoedler, 1973. Ca. 2,000 microfiche.

Microform copies of some 26,000 volumes from the Knoedler Library, dating from the mid–18th century through the 1970s. Includes catalogues of the American Art Association (1884–1939), American Art Galleries (1886–1929) and Anderson Art Galleries (1911–1939).

Pre–1960 Price Guides and Monographs

American Art Sales. Washington, D.C.: American Federation of Arts, 1920–1932. Monthly (Dec.-June), 1922–1932; four numbers a year, 1920-June 1922.

Presents results of auctions held in American auction houses. Entries include artist name, title, dimensions, catalog number, buyer, and price.

Annuaire des Ventes de Tableaux, Dessins, Aquarelles, Pastels, Gouaches, Miniatures: Guide du Marchand, de l'Amateur. Paris: L.M. Lang, 1919–23. Cont'd. by *La Cote des Tableaux, ou, Annuaire des Ventes de Tableaux, Dessins, Aquarelles, Pastels, Gouaches, Miniatures: Guide du Marchand, de l'Amateur.* Paris: L.M. Lang, 1924–29.

Reports annual auction sale prices for works of art. Primarily French artists, all European. Includes dates of auction, types of objects sold, and experts' names. Entries, alphabetical by artist's name, include title, description, medium, prices in French francs.

Annuaire du Collectionneur: Répertoire des prix des tableaux: Peintures, Aquarelles, Pastels, Dessins, Miniatures Vendus de .... Paris: Diffusion Artistique et Documentaire, 1949– .

Prices realized reference source, includes retail gallery prices. Partial contents: Commissaires-priseurs au Département de la Seine; Répertoire alphabétique des galeries de Paris; Références, abbreviations d'experts; Renseignements généraux; Dimensions Françaises des tableaux; Répertoire des ventes; Répertoire des prix.

Annuaire Général des Ventes Publiques en France. Paris: Editions Art et Technique, [1942–43].

Presents an in-depth narrative survey of auction sales activity. Introductory essays precede chronologically-arranged section detailing individual sales.

Sales records for paintings, engravings, books and autographs, coins, ceramics, tapestry included.

Art and Auction: International Art Dealers and Collectors Guide. Rotterdam: Van Kouteren, 1957–1969. Continued by *International Art Market.*

In later years, featured very good illustrations; primarily 20th century art, some other periods and styles, and good coverage of high-end decorative arts. Partial contents: Marketfile: In brief: Record sales of furniture items; Auction reviews: completed auction house sales figures; Sales previews: upcoming offerings; Calendar.

Art Prices Current. [London: Dawson, 1907–1973].

Records sale prices for works of art sold at London auction houses. Earliest years recorded only sales conducted at Christie, Manson & Woods. Arranged by date of sale, artist/title index.

Art Sales of the Year...Being a Record of the Prices Obtained at Auction for Pictures and Prints Sold from October [Year] to the End of the Season. Edited by J.H. Slater. London: Hutchinson, 1901–02.

Short-lived annual inventory of paintings and prints offered for sale at auction. Each entry includes date of sale and name of auctioneer, artist's name, title, dimensions, and in the case of prints, often very detailed description of the work including "state," and some condition notes.

Auction Prices Weekly: Combined with Auction Digest. New York: Auction Digest, 1936–37.

Includes special reports on art, antiquities, decorative arts. Broad range of decorative arts, auction news, calendar of sales. Auction sale entries include lengthy description of lots along with sale prices. Buy-ins not recorded.

Auction Sale Prices. London: Otto, Limited, 1902–14. (Supplement to *The Connoisseur.*)

This monthly reports prices realized at auction sales of coins, paintings, etchings, engravings, medals; lace & needlework, miniatures, furniture, musical instruments, objets d'art, pottery & porcelain, silver, tapestry. (Approximately 50 percent decorative, 50 percent fine art). Records sales by type (i.e., books, etc.), further subdivided by artist or author name. Auctioneer, location, date and currency of sale.

Benezit, E. *Dictionnaire Critique et Documentaire des Peintres, Sculpteurs, Dessinateurs, et Graveurs ... de Tous les Temps et de Tous les Pays par un Groupe d'Écrivains Specialists Français et Étrangers.* Paris: Gründ, 1999. 3rd ed., 1976; New ed., 1966; 1st ed. Paris: R. Roger et F. Chernoviz [etc.], 1911-[23]

"Ventes publiques" (Public sales) for most entries include references to auction sales, some dating from the mid–19th century. See complete description of Benezit, an artists' biographical reference source, in chapter three [page 104].

Beurdeley, Michel. *Trois Siècles de Ventes Publiques.* Fribourg, Switzerland: Office du Livre, S.A., 1988. 234p.

Narrative overviews of major sales dating from 1650 to 1987. Includes sales of decorative artworks, works of fine arts, jewelry and other collectibles. Each sale description includes copious illustrations as well as prices attained for major works sold at auction internationally.

Blanc, Charles. *Le Tresor de la Curiosité: Tire des Catalogues de Ventes de Tableaux, Dessins, Estampes, Livres, Marbres, Bronzes, Ivoires, Terres Cuites, Vitraux, Medailles, Armes, Porcelaines, Meubles, Emaux, Lacques et Autres Objets d'Art.* Paris: Chez Ve J. Renouard, 1857–1858. 2 vols.

Analysis of a number of important auction sales, arranged chronologically. Important for the study of the history of connoisseurship and the market for art.

Bourcard, Gustave. *Dessins, Gouaches, Estampes et Tableaux du Dix-Huitième Siècle: Guide de l'Amateur.* Paris: D. Morgand, 1893.

Practical guidance for the 19th century collector of drawings, prints and paintings.

Burtin, François-Xavier de. *Traité Theorique et Pratique des Connoissances qui sont Necessaries à Tout Amateur de Tableaux, et à Tous Ceux qui Veulent Apprendre à Juger, Apprécier et Conserver les Productions de la Peinture; Suivi d'Observations sur les Collections Publiques et Particulières, et de la Description des Tableaux que Possède e ce Moment l'Auteur.* Brussels: Impr. De Weissenbuch, 1808.

Essentially a philosophical treatise on the practice of painting and aesthetics, along with practical advice for the collector. Some high quality engraved illustrations included.

Butler, John. *Art as Investment.* London: Economist Intelligence Unit, 1979. 85p. (Series: *Special Report* no. 74.)

Compares the "returns on investment in art, within the period 1960–79 with the earnings from ordinary industrial shares over the same time [report summery]." Surveys include: Old Master paintings; English 18th and 19th century paintings; Impressionist paintings; Modern paintings; American paintings; Modern prints; Manuscripts; Books; Porcelain and ceramics; Chinese ceramics; Glass; Antique and Victorian silver; Chinese jades; Furniture.

_____. *Art as Investment.* 1984 ed. London: Economist Intelligence Unit, 1984. 106p. (Series: *Special Report* no. 167.)

Compares "the returns on investment in art, within the period 1959–1983, with earning from ordinary industrial shares over the same years [report summary]." Surveys include: Old Master paintings; English 18th and 19th century paintings; European 19th century paintings; Impressionist paintings; Modern paintings; American painting; Portrait miniatures; Manuscripts; Books; Furniture; Ceramics; Chinese ceramics; English silver.

Catalogue de Tableaux, Vendus à Bruxelles, Depuis l'année 1773: Avec les Noms de Maîtres mis en Ordre Alphabetique, et la Désignation du Sujet, de la Grandeur et du Prix de Chaque pièce en Argent de Change, avec l'Extrait de la Vie de Chaque Peintre. Brussels: N. Alexandre, [1803?].

Records auction sales of paintings in Brussels from 1773 to 1803. List of sales, auctioneers, locations, etc. precedes listing by artists' names; some entries include brief biographical data. Basic descriptive information on each work, with prices in French francs.

Cowdrey, Mary Bartlett. *American Academy of Fine Arts and American Art-Union, 1816–1852.* New York: New York Historical Society, 1953. 2 vols.

This in-depth study traces the founding, development and eventual dissolution of the American Academy of Fine Arts and American Art-Union. Includes primary documents, including by-laws, administrative rosters, etc. Art sales information provided includes "Table of Art-Union Purchases with Total and Average Prices," as well as statistical information on prices realized at the auction sales of pictures owned by the American Art Union in 1852.

Darmon, J. E. *Repertoire des Estampes Japonaises; Les Artistes et Leurs Signatures, les Procedes, les Oeuvres et Leurs Prix dans les Ventes, Biographies et Bibliographies.* Paris: Editions Albert Morance [1922]. 152p.

Biographical sketches include bibliographical references, signatures, and some 1920 sales prices.

Defer, P. (Pierre). *Catalogue Général des Ventes Publiques de Tableaux et Estampes Depuis 1737 Jusqu'à Nos Jours : contenant 1. Les Prix des Plus Beaux Tableaux, Dessins, Miniatures, Estampes, ... 2. Des Notes Biographiques Formant un Dictionnaire des Peintres et des Graveurs les Plus Célèbres de Toutes les Écoles.* Paris: Chez Aubry, Clement, Rapilly, 1865–68.

Prices attained by paintings and prints at public auction. Basic biographical information, indications of sales (seller's name), prices realized.

De Marchi, Neil. *Rules for an Emergent Market: Selling Paintings in Late Seventeenth Century London.* Durham, N.C.: Duke University, Department of Economics, Working Paper 02–33, 2002.

Economic analysis of painting sales in the 17th century, provides references to a great many additional historical data sources.

Drugulin, Wilhelm Eduard. *Allgemeiner Portrait-Katalog: Verzeichniss einer Sammlung von 24,000 Portraits berühmter Personen aller Länder und Zeiten mit biographischen und chalkographischen Notizen, welche zu den beigesetzten billigen Preisen von dem Leipziger Kunst-Comptoir zu beziehen sind.* Nendeln, Liechtenstein: Kraus Reprint, 1981. Originally published: Leipzig: Kunst-Comptoir, 1860. 2 vol. in 1.

Lists approximately 24,000 portraits, including basic information on subject.

Eudel, Paul. *L'Hôtel Drouot et la Curiosité.* Paris: G. Charpentier, 1882–1891. 9 vols. Cont. by *La Gazette de l'Hôtel Drouot* (see entry below).

Overview of auction sales of works of art, jewelry, books, antiquities and other items. Volume nine is an index to names cited throughout the first eight (annual) volumes.

Fage, André. *Le Collectionneur de Peintures Modernes: Comment Acheter, Comment Vendre.* Paris: Editions Pittoresques, 1930.

Collectors' handbook, includes historical values of 19th and 20th century (primarily French) painters' works. Partial contents: La peinture moderne peut-elle etre un placement? Les peintures qui "montent' et ceux qui "baissent"; Notions élémentaires de peinture moderne; Comment composer une collection; Les galeries et les marchands; L'Hôtel des ventes; Les grandes ventes depuis 1922 et ce qui'l faut en retenir; Les salons, les foires et les brocanteurs; Prix comparatives des œuvres peintres en 1922–23 et en 1928–29.

La Gazette de l'Hôtel Drouot. Paris: *L'Hôtel Drouot.* Weekly (except Aug.), 1891– . Cont. of *L'Hôtel Drouot et la Curio sité* (see entry above).

Glossy but informative magazine featuring high-end decorative arts, and some antiquities and fine arts offered at auction. Includes sales results for major Drouot sales.

Graves, Algernon. *Art Sales From Early in the Eighteenth Century to Early in the Twentieth Century: (Mostly Old Master and Early English Pictures)*. London: A. Graves, 1918–21. Reprint: *Burt Franklin: Bibliography & Reference Series* #340; *Art & Art History Reference* #30; New York: Burt Franklin, 1970.

Major source for 18th and 19th century sales of artworks. Provides data of sale, auctioneer name, owner, lot no. and picture title, purchase (if available), and sale price. Buy-ins are included.

Herrmann, Frank. *Sotheby's: Portrait of an Auction House*. New York and London: W.W. Norton, 1981.

See description, page 14.

Hofstede de Groot, Cornelis. *Beschreibendes und Kritisches Verzeichnis der Werke der Hervorragendsten Holländischen Maler des XVII. Jahrhunderts; nach dem Muster von John Smith's Catalogue raisonné Zusammengestellt von Dr. C. Hofstede de Groot* ... Esslingen a.N., P. Neff; [etc.] 1907–28.

Descriptive and critical catalogue and history of specific German artists. Entries include detailed exhibition histories, descriptive cataloging of individual works, catalog numbers, limited price information.

Index of Paintings sold in the British Isles during the Nineteenth Century. Edited by Burton B. Fredericksen; assisted by Julia Armstrong and Doris Mendenhall.

Series title: *The Provenance Index of the Getty Art History Information Program*

Santa Barbara, Calif.: ABC-CLIO, 1988– . (Volume 3 published by Sauer, Munich.) Vol. I: 1801–1805, ed. Burton B. Fredericksen, 1988. Vol. II: 1806–1810, ed. Burton B. Fredericksen, 1990. Vol. III: 1811–1815, ed. Burton B. Fredericksen, 1990. Vol. IV: 1816–1820, ed. Burton B. Fredericksen, 1996.

This ambitious undertaking has as its goal the documentation of auction sales in the British Isles (primarily London) during the 19th century. The index of painting sales is preceded by very well annotated entries on individual sales catalogs. A great deal of valuable provenance information appears in the form of handwritten annotations, sometimes by the auctioneer.

James, Ralph N. *Painters and Their Works: A Dictionary of Great Artists Who are not now Alive Giving Their Names, Lives, and the Prices Paid for their Works at Auctions*. London: L. Upcott Gill, 1896–97. 3 vols.

Brief biographical essays precede chronologically-arranged auction sales results, dating from the 18th–19th centuries. Many works include title of individual sale name (often name of collector and estate), in addition to title of work.

Ketelsen, Thomas, and Tilmann von Stockhausen. *Verzeichniss der verkauften Gemälde im deutschsprachigen Raum vor 1800 / The Index of Paintings Sold in German-speaking Countries before 1800*. Edited by Burton B. Fredericksen and Julia I. Armstrong; assisted by Michael Müller. Munich: K.G. Saur, 2002.

Focus on paintings sold in German-speaking countries. Artists of all nationalities and schools included. Entries include date of sale, name of artist, place, title, auctioneer, auction house, buyer. Title, description and some biographical information on artists.

Learmount, Brian. *A History of the Auction*. [Iver, Bucks, UK]: Barnard & Learmount, 1985. 212p.

Historical survey of the auction market from its earliest recorded history through mid–20th century. Partial contents: 19th century auction wars in England and the United States; Sotheby's and Christie's 1745–1900; Auction methods and styles; Modern times 1900–1950.

Lejeune, Théodore Michel. *Guide Théorique et Pratique de l'Amateur de Tableaux; Études sur les Imitateurs et les Copistes des Maitres de Toutes les Écoles dont les Œuvres Forment la Base Ordinaire des Galeries.* Paris: Vve. Jules Renouard, 1864–65.

Collector's manual, provides practical advice on assembling, assessing and maintaining a collection of paintings by artists of the French, Italian, Spanish, German, Flemish, Dutch and English Schools. Individual artists' entries include brief biography, information on signatures, public collections and sale prices attained by representative works.

Mireur, H. *Dictionnaire des Ventes d'Art Faites en France et à l'Étranger Pendant les XVIIIme & XIXme Diècles: Tableaux, Dessins, Estampes, Aquarelles, Miniatures, Pastels, Gouaches, Sépias, Fusains, Émaux, Eventails Peints & Vitraux.* Paris: Maison d'Editions d'Oeuvres artistiques, Ch. De Vincenti, 1911–12. Reprint: France: *artprice*.com, 2001.

Major source of sales data for 18th and 19th century paintings, drawings, prints, watercolors, etc.

Parker, John. *Great Art Sales of the Century.* London: Pitman; New York: Watson-Guptill, 1975. 120p.

Arranged by decade from the 1920s, provides a lively account of some major sales at Christie's and Sotheby's. Primarily fine art, but some decorative arts and jewelry included, with prices realized.

Picture Prices Current: An Alphabetically Arranged Record of Pictures and Drawings Sold by Auction in Great Britain and America. London: F.L. & E.L. Wilder, 1936–37.

Records auction sales prices for paintings, drawings, and watercolors. Individual artist entries are keyed to auction sale date, prices realized noted. Sales of important collections are identified.

Print Prices Current. London: F.L. & E.L. Wilder, 1919–1939. Imprint varies. "Being a complete alphabetical record of all engravings and etchings sold by auction in London, each item annotated with the date of sale and price realized."

Provides an interesting preface detailing restrictions on removal of currency from Germany in World War II and the practice of using art as currency to circumvent restrictions (i.e., buying art in Germany and selling in another country). Entries include basic descriptive details, prices realized in pounds sterling. Includes lower-end works, sketches, etc. Index of author and engravers' names. (Vol. 21, October 1938-August 1939 reviewed).

Redford, George. *Art Sales: A History of Sales of Pictures and Other Works of Art ; with Notices of the Collections Sold, Names of Owners, Titles of Pictures, Prices and Purchasers, Arranged Under the Artists of the Different Schools in Order of Date ; Including the Purchases and Prices of Pictures for the National Gallery; Illustrated with Autotypes from Small Sketches of Great Pictures & Watercolour Drawings Sold, Portraits of Eminent Collectors and Views of their Residences, Objects of Ornamental Art, &c., &c.* London: Bradbury, Agnew, Printers: "Whitefriars" Press, 1888.

Volume 1 contains brief, narrative accounts of the sales of various collections, beginning with the sale of the collection of Charles I. A great deal of historical data, including inventories, prices, and buyers make Redford's *Art Sales* an indispensable source for the history of collecting from the 17th century through the third quarter of the 19th.

Volume 2 presents an overview of auction sales in the following categories: Modern painters—British School; Continental schools; Old Masters: Italian, Spanish; French; German, Flemish and Dutch. Individual entries arranged by artist's name, with price realized and in many instances, names of buyers as well as an indication of buy-ins.

_____. *Continuation of Redford's Art Sales, Commencing From 1887.* [London, 1887–1918?].

Rare, unpublished, handwritten manuscript records sales of paintings and drawings of "British Schools" and "Foreign Schools." Copies held by the Metropolitan Museum (New York), the Frick Collection, and Yale University. Entries include artist's name, date of sale, descriptive details of lot; some include name of purchaser.

Reitlinger, Gerald. *The Economics of Taste.* London: Barrie and Rockliff, 1961–1970. 3 vols.

Gerald Reitlinger's historical study of the market for works of art is one of the most often-cited in the secondary literature on the subject. Its data are frequently used by writers on the economics of art investment.

Volume 1: *The Rise and Fall of Picture Prices 1760–1960.* Includes sales analysis of most popular artists. Contents: Art collecting in the late eighteenth century, 1760–1792; Revolutionary and Napoleonic period, 1792–1815; Rewards of the living painter, the Georgians, 1760–1820; Rewards of the living painter, the Proto-Victorians, 1800–1860; Old Masters, 1815–1884; Golden age of the living painter, 1860–1914; Treasures depart, 1884–1929; Slump, war and inflation, 1929–1960. Index of artists; Index of collectors, dealers and others.

Volume 2: *The Rise and Fall of Objets d'Art Prices since 1750.* Partial contents: Genius and craftsmanship, a tale of two markets; Contemporary objets d'art, 1750–1820; Antiquarian and eclectic taste, 1741–1842; Romantic taste and the Victorian Age, 1791–1895; Return of the eighteenth century—furniture; Return of the eighteenth century—porcelain, tapestry and sculpture; Orient rediscovered, 1815–1915; Apogee and decline of ritzy taste, 1900–1929; Long Depression and the paper recovery, 1929–1963. Part Two comprises "Sales Analyses of selected types of objets d'art since 1750." Includes furniture, porcelain, glass, carpets, and other classes of decorative arts.

Volume 3: *The Art Market in the 1960s.* Composed largely of sales analyses including both fine and decorative arts. Partial contents: Paintings and drawings; Sales analysis of sculpture; Objets d'art, including, among others: Carpets; Chinese art; Furniture; Glass—European; Japanese art; Porcelain—English; Porcelain—Continental; Silver.

Provides prices for paintings, sculpture, and decorative arts, along with narrative analysis of the art market in England and the United States.

Répertoire des Tableaux Vendus en France au XIXe Siècle. Edited by Burton B. Fredericksen and Benjamin Peronnet; assisted by Julia Armstrong, Sophie Hauser, and Armell Jacquinot. Los Angeles: Provenance Index of the Getty Information Institute, 1998– .

One of the Getty Provenance Index projects, records 19th century sales results and includes an index, by artist's name, to the various sales. Includes discussion of sales in addition to raw data. Includes references to approximately 21,000 paintings. Extensive list of sales and auctions by date. Entries include artist's name, date of sale, place, "expert," title of work, annotations from sales catalog, signature/date information, price realized.

Reverdy, Anne. *L'École de Barbizon; Évolution du Prix des Tableaux de 1850 à 1960.* Paris: Mouton, [1973].

Surveys the prices attained by major and minor artists of the Barbizon School. Artists surveyed include Rousseau, Millet, Diaz, Daubigny, Corot, Troyon, Jacque, Dupré, Osabeu and Chintreuil.

Roberts, William. *Memorials of Christie's: A Record of Art Sales from 1766 to 1896.* London: Bell, 1897. 2 vols.

Surveys high-end sales of art, books, prints, etc. at Christie's London. Some very good reproductions. Entries arranged chronologically under chapter headings. "Journal" entry style, or narrative accounts of many important collections auctioned by Christie's over the course of the subject period.

Schurr, Gérald. *1820–1920, les Petits Maitres de la Peinture: Valeur de Demain.* Paris: Editions de la Gazette, 1969– . Vols. 2–7 have imprint: Editions de l'amateur, Paris.

Approximately 600 painters per volume, includes values for a good many minor painters. European artists. Entries include short biography, museum collections, highest price realized, recent sales. Organized by subject matter or style, e.g., countryside, symbolism, etc.

Seguier, Frederick Peter. *A Critical and Commercial Dictionary of the Works of Painters Comprising Eight Thousand Eight Hundred and Fifty Sale Notes of Pictures and Nine Hundred and Eighty Original Notes on the Subjects and Styles of Various Artists Who Have Painted in the Schools of Europe Between ... 1250 and 1850.* London: Longmans, Green, 1870.

Focus on "Schools of Europe." Entries include names, birth-death dates and places, "School" affiliation, year of sale, name of purchaser, price. Biography of some artists follows list of sold items.

Les Ventes Publiques en France: Répertoire General des Prix. Paris: Bureau International d'Édition et de Publicité, 1945– .

Records sales of paintings, watercolors, pastels, drawings, miniatures and gouaches. Entries include basic descriptive details, price realized.

Versteigerungsergebnisse. Leipzig: Klinkhardt & Biermann, 1919–1930. Monthly.

Records sale prices for works of art sold in Berlin, Cologne, Munich, Frankfurt, New York, Paris and London. Entries include basic description of lots, catalog number, and price realized in local currencies (marks, francs, U.S. dollars).

Verzeichniss der Kőniglichen Gemälde-Gallerie zu Dresden: Mit einer historischen Einleitung, Nortizen über die Erwerbung und Angabe der Bezeichnung der einzeinen Bilder. Dresden: Druck von B.G. Teubner, 1880.

Details sales of paintings sold in Dresden. Entries include school or artist's name, title, description of work, some biographical information, prices. Some monograms.

Watson, Peter. *From Manet to Manhattan: The Rise of the Modern Art Market.* New York: Random House, 1992. 558p.
See description, page 15.
Williamson, E. *La Curiosité: Revue des Ventes Publiques de Tableaux, Aquarelles, Pastels ... Faites en France et à l'Étranger.* Paris: Ch. Béranger, 1900.
Records sale prices of paintings, watercolors, pastels, drawings, engravings, sculpture, furniture, tapestries, etc. Entries provide collection owner's name, notable items by artist's name, title, price. For larger collections, catalogue number, descriptive data on individual lots, organized chronologically by auction date.

For Further Research

Over the course of the past decade, academic research in art market history has grown immensely. The trend toward interdisciplinary scholarship has been particularly fruitful in this area; in addition to the writings of art historians, many economists, sociologists, social historians and others have taken an interest in the history and development of various art markets.

Several databases, described in chapter two, can be particularly useful for the researcher attempting to identify scholarly articles on historical aspects of the art market. Some of the best of these include:

America: History and Life. Santa Barbara, Calif.: ABC-CLIO, 1964– .
America: History and Life is the primary bibliographic database for researchers of North American history. Published since 1964 in print, and now available in its entirety on the Web at subscribing institutions, the database includes close to 500,000 entries from scholarly journals dating from as early as 1954. Journal coverage includes more than 2,000 titles, including state and local history titles and some multi-disciplinary titles in the social sciences and humanities. In addition to its journal literature coverage, many citations to doctoral dissertations (with their abstracts) are included. For the art market researcher, *America: History and Life* includes many articles on historical topics that fall outside the traditional art history literature.

Dissertation Abstracts / ProQuest Digital Dissertations. UMI/*ProQuest*, 1861– .
Most academic libraries provide access to the online version of *Dissertation Abstracts.* This powerful database provides citations to doctoral dissertations dating from 1861. From 1980 to the present, lengthy abstracts are included.

EconLIT [see page 37]. Nashville: American Economic Association, 1969– . Coverage: 1969– .
The online version of the *Journal of Economic Literature* provides indexing to professional journals geared toward economists, economic historians, and others.

FRANCIS: *International Humanities and Social Sciences*. Vandoeuvre, France : Institut de l'information scientifique et technique (INIST), 1984– .

General social science and humanities database with significant coverage of journals published in Europe.

Historical Abstracts. Santa Barbara, Calif.: ABC-CLIO, 1955– .

Historical Abstracts is one of the primary databases for the researcher of world history (1450 to the present), excluding the United States and Canada. It offers citations with abstracts to more than a half million bibliographic items drawn from more than 2000 international journals. In addition to its journal literature coverage, *Historical Abstracts* includes references to many books on historical topics, as well as a significant number of doctoral dissertation abstracts; it is most useful for the researcher seeking data and analysis of patronage and the history of collecting.

Appendix A: Periodicals and Newsletters of Interest to the Art Market Researcher

The following titles represent some of the best art market periodicals and newsletters. Note that most of the print publications have corresponding websites that promote their respective titles, and in many cases also supplement the content found in their print counterparts. Some titles are included, full text, in various databases (like *ProQuest* Research Library, Factiva, and others discussed throughout this book).

The Antique Trader Weekly
Krause Publications, Inc.
700 E State St, Iola, WI 54990
ISSN: 0161-8342
1957– .
http://www.antiquetrader.com

Antique Trader Weekly is an excellent source for the latest news in the market for antiques and collectible objects. Collectors will find here a great deal of news on the current market, as well as a great classified section for buying and selling.

Antiques & Collecting Magazine
Lightner Publishing Corporation
1006 S. Michigan Ave., Chicago, IL 60605
ISSN: 1084-0818
Monthly; 1931– .
Indexed: Wilson Omni Full Text.

This magazine features articles of interest to all types of collectors. It is especially useful for the collector or researcher of decorative arts, antiques and collectible objects. Its calendar of events is most useful for identifying shows, exhibitions and fairs in the United States.

Apollo
Apollo Magazine Ltd.
20 Theobald's Rd, London WC1X 8PF
United Kingdom
0003-6536
Monthly; 1925– .
http://www.apollo-magazine.com/
Indexed: *Art Full Text*; *Art Index Retrospective*; *ArtBibliographies Modern*; *Bibliography of the History of Art* (*BHA*); *FRANCIS*.

Apollo is a beautifully produced journal with a good deal of information on the fine and decorative arts. Lengthy feature articles provide in-depth coverage of historical and contemporary subjects. Some of the magazine's regular features—notably, "Market Preview" and "Market Review"—offer very intelligent overviews of the higher-end markets for art, decorative arts, and, to a lesser extent, some categories of collectibles.

Art & Antiques

Trans World Publishing, Inc.
2100 Powers Ferry Rd, Ste 300, Atlanta, GA 30339
ISSN: 0195-8208
Monthly (except July and Aug.); 1984– .
http://www.artandantiques.net/
Indexed: *Art Full Text*; *ArtBibliographies Modern*; *Bibliography of the History of Art (BHA)*; *FRANCIS*; *Readers' Guide to Periodical Literature.*

Art and Antiques provides a great deal of practical information for the collector or researcher.

Art and Australia

Art and Australia Pty Ltd.
42 Chandos St, St Leonards, NSW 2065 Australia
ISSN: 0004-301X
Quarterly (Supplements accompany some issues); 1963– .
http://www.artaustralia.com/
Indexed: *Art Full Text*; *ArtBibliographies Modern*; *Bibliography of the History of Art (BHA).*

Art and Australia provides a great deal of information on the contemporary market for Australian art, and the Australian market for works of art in general. Particularly useful are the regularly featured "Market Profiles," as well as the lengthy feature articles on auction and gallery market issues. The magazine's Website provides a minimum of content, but does feature useful tables of contents to the past few years' issues.

Art in America

Brant Publications, Inc.
575 Broadway, 5th Fl, New York, NY 10012
ISSN: 0004-3214
Monthly; 1939– .
http://www.artinamericamagazine.com/
Indexed: *ABI/Inform*; *Art Full Text*; *Art Index Retrospective*; *ArtBibliographies Modern*; *Bibliography of the History of Art (BHA)*; *FRANCIS*; *ProQuest Research Library*; *Readers' Guide to Periodical Literature.*

Its inclusion in ABI/Inform attests to *Art in America's* value to the researcher of art market issues. The magazine focuses on the higher-end of the market, with particularly strong coverage of 20th century artists and their works.

Art Monthly

Britannia Art Publications
4th Fl., 28 Charing Cross Rd., London WC2H 0DB United Kingdom
ISSN: 0142-6702
Monthly; 1976– .
http://www.artmonthly.co.uk
Indexed: *Art Full Text*; *ArtBibliographies Modern*; *Bibliography of the History of Art (BHA)*; *Readers' Guide to Periodical Literature.*

The UK's leading journal of contemporary visual art, *Art Monthly* provides in-depth coverage of market issues. A number of regular or semi-regular features, including "ArtNotes" and "Salerooms" offer insight into the market for primarily contemporary works of art in British galleries and auction houses. The magazine's Website offers some content online, as well as a free table of contents alerting service.

Art Newspaper

Umberto Allemandi & Co.
70 South Lambeth Rd., London SW8 1RL United Kingdom
ISSN: 0960-6556
Monthly (except August); 1990– .
http://www.theartnewspaper.com/
Indexed: *Art Full Text*; *ArtBibliographies Modern.*

Art Newspaper is one of the very best sources for coverage of the art market, and for peripheral issues of interest to art lovers and art collectors worldwide. Intended for a professional audience, *Art Newspaper* provides up-to-date coverage of the international gallery, auction and museum world, along with very in-depth coverage of art law, conservation, archaeology and related fields. The Website offers a great deal of content, at no charge, to interested researchers.

Art Press

ArtPublications
8 Rue Francois Villon, Paris 75015 France
ISSN: 0245-5676
Monthly.
http://www.artpress.com/
Indexed: *Art Full Text*; *ArtBibliographies Modern*; *Bibliography of the History of Art (BHA)*; *Readers' Guide to Periodical Literature.*

This French language magazine provides up-to-date coverage of the international art market, with particular reference to French artists. Its Website provides free, full-text of several feature articles from latest issues.

ArtNews

ArtNews LLC
48 W 38th St., New York, NY 10018
ISSN: 0004-3273
Monthly (June–Aug. combined) 1923– .
New York: Artnews Associates.
http://www.artnewsonline.com
Indexed: *ABI/Inform*; *Art Full Text*; *Art Index Retrospective*; *ArtBibliographies Modern*; *Bibliography of the History of Art (BHA)*; *FRANCIS*; *ProQuest Research Library*; *Readers' Guide to Periodical Literature.*

The sheer number of indexing sources that have elected to include *ArtNews* attest to the magazine's value. Of particular interest to collectors and other market researchers, *ArtNews* includes a number of regular features—particularly, the "Art Market" report, that survey the auction and to a lesser extent, the retail gallery market for works of fine art.

Artnewsletter

ArtNews LLC
48 W 38th St., New York, NY 10018
ISSN: 0145-7241
Biweekly.
http://www.artnewsonline.com

Artnewsletter is an indispensable source for art world professionals, and serious collectors of art, with some content also of interest to the decorative arts researcher. The *Artnewsletter* Website provides a good amount of content, free of charge, on its Website.

Burlington Magazine

Burlington Magazine Publications Ltd.
14 Dukes Rd., London WC1H 9AD United Kingdom
ISSN: 0007-6287
Monthly; 1903– .
Indexed: *Art Full Text*; *ArtBibliographies Modern*; *Bibliography of the History of Art (BHA)*; *Design and Applied Arts Index.*

Burlington is one of the very best sources for the researcher of art market history, collecting, and patronage. All of its articles are lengthy, scholarly studies with excellent illustrations.

Christie's Magazine

(Continues *Christie's International Magazine* 1984–1998)
London: Christie, Manson & Woods Ltd.
ISSN: 0266-1217
Seven issues per year; 1998– .

Beautifully illustrated magazine surveys both fine and decorative arts. Features international art market news and articles by Christie's specialists.

Connaissance des Arts

Societe Francaise de Promotion Artistique
23 Rue des Jeuneurs, Paris 75002 France
ISSN: 0153-8055
Monthly; 1952– .
Indexed: *Art Full Text*; *Art Index Retrospective*; *ArtBibliographies Modern*; *Bibliography of the History of Art (BHA)*; *FRANCIS.*

Connaissance des Arts offers lengthy articles on the fine and decorative arts, along with some coverage of the French art market and related issues.

Flash Art International

Giancarlo Politi Editore
PO Box 95, Borgo Trevi 06032 PG Italy
Bimonthly.

http://www.flashartonline.com/
Indexed: *Art Full Text*; *Art Index Retrospective*; *ArtBibliographies Modern*; *Bibliography of the History of Art* (*BHA*); *FRANCIS*; *Readers' Guide to Periodical Literature*.

Flash Art International is an excellent source for researching contemporary art and its gallery and auction markets. The magazine's Website offers a substantial amount of free content. *Flash Art* is particularly valuable for its calendar of events, and its coverage of international art and design fairs.

La Gazette de l'Hotel Drouot

10 Rue du Faubourg Montmartre, Paris Cedex 9 75441 France
ISSN:1169-2294
Weekly.
http://www.gazette-drouot.com

News magazine on the international (primarily French) auction world. The magazine's Website provides a great amount of content.

IFAR Journal

International Foundation for Art Research (IFAR)
500 Fifth Ave., New York, NY 10110
ISSN: 1098-1195
Quarterly.
Indexed: *Art Index / Art Full Text*; *ArtBibliographies Modern*.
http://www.ifar.org

Quarterly, scholarly and professional journal devoted to issues of authentication, forgery, fraud, international cultural property issues, and art theft.

Magazine Antiques

Brant Publications, Inc.
575 Broadway, 5th Fl., New York, NY 10012
ISSN: 0161-9284
Monthly.
Indexed: *Art Full Text*; *Art Index Retrospective*.

Magazine Antiques is an important source for the researcher of art market history, patronage and the history of collecting. It is particularly valuable for its coverage of the decorative arts. Regular columns provide news on exhibitions, fairs and other art world events.

Maine Antique Digest

PO Box 1429, Waldoboro, ME 04572
ISSN: 0147-0639
Monthly; 1973– .
http://www.maineantiquedigest.com/

Monthly newspaper for the art market, the antiques professional and serious collector. Extensive coverage of regional sales and auctions. Free Website offers copious amounts of supplementary material.

New England Antiques Journal

24 Water Street, Palmer, MA 01069
ISSN: 0897-5795
Monthly.
http://www.antiquesjournal.com/

This monthly magazine includes substantial feature articles of interest to collectors. Primarily decorative arts-oriented, and with particular emphasis on furniture, glass, porcelain, and other works of fine and decorative arts of the northeastern Unites States. Regular columns include "Care and Repair Q & A," "Focus on Furniture," "Period Restorations" and "Auction Views."

L'Oeil

Editions Gallimard
15, Rue Sebastien-Bottin, Paris 75328 Cedex 07 France
ISSN: 0183-3014
Monthly; 1955– .
Indexed: *Art Full Text*; *Art Index Retrospective*; *ArtBibliographies Modern*; *Bibliography of the History of Art* (*BHA*).

L'Oeil is an excellent source that provides in-depth coverage of art market issues. Lengthy articles in most issues offer overviews of markets for specific periods, media and genre.

Southwest Art

Southwest Art Publishing
5444 Westheimer Ste 1400, Houston, TX 77056
ISSN: 0192-4214
Monthly.
http://www.southwestart.com

Indexed: *ABI/Inform*; *Art Full Text*; *ArtBibliographies Modern*; *ProQuest Research Library*.

This highly specialized magazine offers overviews of the arts of the Southwest and a good deal of market information. The magazine's Website provides substantial current content, including an artists' showcase, calendar of events and exhibitions, "news beat" and "artists to watch."

TIAS Collector's Newsletter

http://www.tias.com

This information-filled semi-monthly newsletter is available free to registered readers. *TIAS* offers a vast amount of practical information on antiques and collectibles, and, to a lesser extent, the market for works of fine art. Subscribers receive the newsletter via email. It can also be read on the Web (along with its keyword searchable backfile).

Die Weltkunst

Weltkunst Verlag GmbH
Nymphenburger St. 84, Munich 80636 Germany
0043-261X
Semi-monthly.
http://www.kunstbuecher-online.de/weltkunst/
Indexed: *Art Full Text*; *ArtBibliographies Modern*; *Bibliography of the History of Art* (*BHA*); *FRANCIS*.

This German-language periodical provides excellent coverage of the international art market, with particular reference to Germany but with a good deal of coverage of other Western European nations.

Appendix B: Auction Houses and Websites

Increasingly, auction houses large and small provide valuable information on their websites. The following list represents a selection of the most useful sites for sales research. Because many firms have multiple offices both here in the U.S. and abroad, only web addresses are provided. Main and regional office addresses, phone numbers, email contacts and more are easily located on each firm's website.

Art & Antiques Auctionhouse Michael Zeller
www.zeller.de
Zeller specializes in 19th and 20th century paintings, decorative arts, sculpture, jewelry, furniture, and other collectible objects. Founded in 1893, this German house now offers online bidding and expert appraisals. Auctions are held in April, September, and December of each year, with special auctions in June. Previous auction catalog covers are available in PDF format, while the actual listing of the contents has been converted to a searchable inventory including item listings, artist index, results, and categories.

Arthur James Galleries
www.arthurjames.com
Established in 1958, this Florida auction house specializes in upscale decorative arts, furniture, and art pieces. Arthur James Galleries has handled several notable estate sales and celebrity auctions and lists high-quality photographs and descriptions of current auction lots. Past auction results are not archived; however, the current listings include estimates, and the gallery does offer fee-based appraisal services.

Biddington's
www.biddingtons.com
Biddington's offers a wide variety of collectible items, primarily contemporary art, prints, and antiques. Auctions are held continuously online and are arranged by category. Biddington's also offers a low-cost art valuation service.

Bonhams
http://www.bonhams.com/
Established in 1793 by Thomas Dodd, antique print dealer, and Walter Bonham, rare book specialist, Bonhams conducts hundreds of sales not only in London, but in nine additional British salesrooms. Numerous sales are also held in various locations on the Continent. Bonhams & Butterfield is one of the largest auction houses on the West Coast, where it conducts more than 50 sales annually in San Francisco and Los Angeles.

The Bonhams website offers a number of features of interest to the market researcher. Recent sales results from all locations are conveniently listed in reverse chronological order. All include descriptions and prices realized, and many are illustrated. Bonhams is particularly useful for researching British, Irish and Australian works of fine and decorative arts, although its offerings are truly global.

Butterfield & Butterfield see ***Bonhams***

Casa d'Aste Babuino

http://www.astebabuino.it/

A large Italian auction house in Rome, Casa d'Aste Babuino deals in high-end paintings, antiques, and furnishings. Current auction listings are spare, but the archived auction descriptions are easily navigated despite being listed solely in Italian. Anyone with a passing familiarity with Latin or a Romance language should be able to understand the listings. The website lists many auction catalog lots in a searchable database; some knowledge of Italian is helpful in navigating this portion of the website. Certainly the best feature of the site is the high-quality photography of lots listed for auction. Extensive descriptions (in Italian) and artist information accompanies each photograph.

Christie's

http://www.christies.com

Founded in 1766 by James Christie, Christie's is one of the largest of the international auction houses, with branches in Europe, Asia and the Pacific, and the Americas. Christie's website offers a great deal of material for art market researchers; the very intuitive "Lotfinder" allows keyword searching of sales results, and in most instances results include the complete textual content included in the sales catalog, along with an image of the lot. Price realized lists, providing lot numbers and prices realized, are posted soon after each auction, and are easily found on Christie's website.

Doyle

http://www.doylenewyork.com/

Founded in 1963, Doyle's auction house handles a great variety of properties, including fine art, decorative art work, collectible objects, jewelry, books and manuscripts. The firm's website offers searchable access to recent auction catalogs, and the complete price realized lists of the past few years' sales. Many of the catalog entries include images.

East Australian Trading Company

www.guyearlsmith.com

Located in Australia, Guy Earl Smith's East Australian Trading Company specializes in international tribal and aboriginal art, artifacts, and antiquities. The focus of this small but international auction house is Australian and East Asian art. Although the website's contents are spare, there are some high-quality photographs and auction results are posted in PDF format.

Galerie Fischer Luzern Auction House

http://www.fischerauktionen.ch/

Galerie Fischer Luzern specializes in fine art, mostly paintings from the 19th and 20th centuries, decorative arts, and armor. Artists are listed separately, and high-quality photographs and descriptions are available for works being offered. Catalog covers and contents are posted online for viewers. Fischer Luzern also offers appraisal, valuation services and storage of art.

International Art Centre

www.internationalartcentre.com

Focusing on high-end European and New Zealand art and artists, this auction house's website features high-quality photographs of current offerings. Prior sales are archived for a few months, although not all of the photographs are retained. An artist index lists works sold by lot number, though it does not list final sale prices. Additionally, the gallery does a good deal of exhibiting, and there is an archive of news articles about the auction house and some notable pieces it has sold at auction that is useful for researching specific artists or sales. Some final sale auction price information is available through this feature.

Laurel Auction, Inc.

http://laurelauction.com

Laurel Auction, Inc. offers furniture, antiques, and collectibles. Of primary interest here are its detailed photographs of late 19th and early 20th century furnishings. Unfortunately, sale prices are not listed and sales are archived only for a few months.

Neal Auction Company

http://www.nealauction.com/indexie.html

The Neal Auction Company is a well-respected New Orleans-based auction house specializing in fine paintings, furniture, silver, and decorative arts. Its website highlights the auction house's record sales, and has a useful section on shipping works of art. The catalogs are not listed as such; current listings are found under the Artist Index. Some auctions are also handled through eBay's live auctions online listings. Upcoming auctions are listed by date. Condition reports for items offered are available online. Forms and information are available for both buying and selling through the auction house, including forms for establishing credit. Only current catalogs are available, but they are extensive and well-illustrated, including photographs of the work and price estimates.

New Orleans Auction

www.neworleansauction.com

New Orleans Auction offers paintings, decorative arts, furniture, and silver. This auction house is a great resource for antiques and furniture, and it provides high-quality photographs of current offerings, including the estimation value, on its website. Upcoming auctions and previewed items are available online. Instructions and forms for consigning items are also available online; at this time, the website does not offer online bidding. Extensive and detailed auction house catalog listings are available on the website, including provenance and price estimates. Results of previous auctions are listed only by lot number and hammer price.

Northeast Auctions

http://www.northeastauctions.com/

Northeast Auctions is a small but highly regarded auction house specializing in 18th and 19th century works of fine and decorative art. The firm holds several sales annually, and posts very high-quality, PDF-versions of the sales' catalogs on its website, along with basic information about the business and its personnel.

Peter Wilson Fine Art Valuers and Auctioneers

www.peterwilson.co.uk

Established in 1955, this British auction house offers a searchable catalog (by date) with photographs and illustrations of current and past auctions. Peter Wilson specializes in antiques, decorative arts, and paintings. Some entries offer a good deal of information about the artist and the item. Auction results are searchable through a separate database. Auction calendars are listed by month, and are ongoing.

Phillips de Pury & Company

http://www.phillipsdepury.com

Venerable Phillips de Pury & Company specializes in contemporary art, photography, design art and jewelry. Currently operating in Berlin, Geneva, London, Munich, New York, and Paris, Phillips holds regular sales at each location. A calendar on the site lists past and upcoming auctions for all of the Phillips locations. Forms are available online for bid and instructions for selling through Phillips. Online catalogs for upcoming auctions at various locations are also available online, as are PDF listings of the results of each lot at auction; not searchable. Phillips also offers appraisal services for a fee.

Quittenbaum Art Auctions

http://www.quittenbaum.de/index_e.php

This newcomer to the art auction house market specializes in Art Deco and Art Nouveau pieces, from paintings to pottery. It also deals in African tribal art and fine paintings and antiques. Auctions are listed by date, and only the highlights of each auction are listed. Result lists are archived and available in PDF format; prices are listed by lot number.

Samuel T. Freeman & Co.

www.freemansauction.com

Samuel T. Freeman & Co. has been offering fine arts and antiques sine 1805. Currently Freeman's also deals in jewelry and decorative arts and furniture. Based in Philadelphia, the website offers a comprehensive catalog of sale results, as well as an archive dating back approximately one year. Descriptions are terse, but photographs of the art are usually listed.

Skinner

http://www.skinnerinc.com

The Skinner auction house is based in Massachusetts and deals in everything from fine paintings to antique books, musical instruments, low-end collectibles and decorative arts. Perhaps best known for its association with the popular PBS program *Antiques Roadshow*, the staff at Skinner are broad-based in expertise and very accessible to the public. Skinner also conducts Appraisal Days, in which a team of experts offers appraisals of flea market finds and family heirlooms (most take place in Massachusetts).

Upcoming auctions are listed online, and the catalogs are available for download in PDF format. Auction results are archived for approximately one year; listed by lot and hammer price. If one is a frequent buyer or seller, the website also offers a way to track individual purchases or sales throughout the year. Appraisals are available, though estimates are not listed on the website unless items are being auctioned by the house. Try "The Expert's Eye" section for a brief explanation of how objects are evaluated.

Sotheby's

http://www.sothebys.com

Sotheby's is one of the world's largest auction houses, with offices in the U.S., Latin America, U.K. and Ireland, Europe, the Middle East, Asia and the Pacific. As such, its auction offerings are among the most diverse of any auction house in the world. The firm's website is extremely easy to navigate, and the "lot search" provides a variety of options for searching the site's thousands of illustrated sales offerings and prices. Recognizing the fact that increasing numbers of users are seeking estimates on particular items, Sotheby's has added a "What's It Worth?" page, with the following options. This feature will provide only estimates, of course, but as such it can be very helpful to the user seeking a "ballpark" value for an item. Here, the user receives actual "prices realized" for works sold. Link to Sotheby's fee-based appraisal service. Link to forms for requesting auction estimates for your property.

Swann Auction Galleries

http://www.swanngalleries.com

Founded in 1941, Swann Galleries has expanded from a rare books house to one of the largest auctioneers of prints, photographs, books, manuscripts, maps and other, largely paper-based, media. Its website offers a surprising number of very well-illustrated catalogs, including those for upcoming auctions as well as an impressive number of archives and past sales. For the researcher seeking recent values for books, photographs, and other works on paper, Swann is a likely first stop.

Treadway Toomey Galleries

http://www.treadwaygallery.com

Treadway Toomey specializes in 20th century American and European decorative art works. For anyone researching arts and crafts, 1950s modern, and other contemporary styles, Treadway Toomey is the very best! The firm maintains a good backfile of catalogs, with index pages hyperlinked to beautifully illustrated lots. From paintings to furniture, ceramics, porcelain and other decorative objets d'art, Treadway Toomey's richly illustrated site is one of the very best freely-available Internet sites for style, artist and designer identification.

Notes

Preface

1. One recent exception is the major collection of contemporary art amassed by Dorothy and Herbert Vogel. Since the early 1960s Dorothy, a librarian, and Herbert, a postal worker, acquired major works by emerging contemporary artists (in many cases, directly from the artists) for a fraction of their current value. The Vogels have bequeathed their massive collection to the National Gallery of Art in Washington, D.C.

2. A simple Internet search (using Google) for the terms "Andy Warhol" and "authentication" brings the researcher directly to the website describing the process required by the Andy Warhol Art Authentication Board, Inc.

3. The Comité Chagall is the recognized authority on works of art by Marc Chagall.

Chapter One

1. Dr. Elin Lake Ewald, ASA. "The Measure of Loss in Damage /Loss Appraisals, Part I." *Art World*, November 2004. http://www.otoole-ewald.com.

2. Treasury Regulation Sec. 20.2031–1[b].

3. *The Appraisal of Personal Property: Principles, Theories, and Practice Methods for the Professional Appraiser.* Patricia C. Soucy and Janella N. Smyth, ASA, co-editors. Washington, D.C.: American Society of Appraisers, 1994, p. 50.

4. *Ibid.* p. 52.

5. Learmount, Brian. *A History of the Auction.* [Iver, Bucks, UK]: Barnard & Learmount, 1985, p.1.

6. *New York Times*, Nov. 19, 1961, p. 1.

7. *New York Times*, Nov. 20, 1961, p. 33.

8. As a librarian, I can attest to the major change online book vendors have effected in the out-of-print book market. In the past, an o/p vendor could charge hundreds of dollars for a not-at-all-special imprint. Today, one can find in an instant numerous available copies of all but the rarest items.

Chapter Two

1. "History of OCLC." http://www.oclc.org/about/history

2. Dorment, Richard. "Dealers are the art world's real brains." *The Art Newspaper*, March 2004, p. 22.

3. Full document available online at: http://www.collegeart.org/caa/ethics/art_hist_ethics.html.

Chapter Three

1. The first catalogue raisonné of Pablo Picasso's work, *Pablo Picasso*, compiled by Christian Zervos (Paris: Cahiers d'Art, 1932–), comprises 33 very large volumes with many hundreds of reproductions.

2. Peter Kraus, "The Role of the Catalogue Raisonné in the Art Market," in *The Expert versus the Object: Judging Fakes and False Attributions in the Visual Arts* (Oxford; New York: Oxford University Press, 2004), p. 71.

3. Searches of both the Research Libraries

Information Network (RLIN) and OCLC *WorldCat* were used to assess the availability of titles. RLIN and OCLC are described in chapter two.

4. See also the *Art and Architecture Thesaurus Online*, page 120.

5. The Detroit Institute of Arts/Research Library and Archives website. Introductory statement to the digitized Exhibition Catalogues page.

Chapter Four

1. Reflects the result of a *SCIPIO* auction catalog search conducted on April 12, 2004.

2. One noteworthy exception is the Winterthur Program in American Culture, established in 1952 by the Henry Francis du Pont Winterthur Museum and the University of Delaware.

3. Including its electronic counterparts, *Art Index Retrospective*, and *Art Abstracts / Art Full Text*.

4. Getty Research Institute, *Art and Architecture Thesaurus Online*.

Chapter Five

1. Innes, Michael. *From London Far*. London: Victor Gollancz, 1946. p. 147.

2. *Ibid.*

3. Major discoveries often garner considerable attention in the media. Most recently, Leigh and Leslie Keno of *Antiques Roadshow* fame discovered a previously unknown, but authentic work by 19th century American artist Martin Johnson Heade. The Heade was "hammered down" on December 7, 2003, for just over $1 million.

4. McFarland-Taylor, Laura. "Comment: Tracking Stolen Artworks on the Internet: A New Standard for Due Diligence." *The John Marshall Journal of Computer & Information Law*, 16 (Summer 1998): 939.

5. *Ibid.*

6. "Stolen Works of Art." CD-ROM, http://www.interpol.org/Public/WorkOfArt/CDrom/default.asp.

7. From the "About Us" section of the Lost Art Internet Database.

Chapter Six

1. Some libraries' older sales catalogs are annotated, indicating the highest price offered for those works that did not meet their reserve, or were "bought-in." Art market professionals often attend auctions themselves, in order to develop a collection of catalogs with this type of unpublished market information.

2. Editioned, or numbered prints are essentially the same; the larger the edition, the more likely the sought-after print will have been sold at auction.

3. Reflects the result of a search conducted on February 1, 2004. Note that a search of this type will retrieve only those catalogs that happen to have "garden statuary" in their titles; many other sales (e.g., individual estate sales) will also include pieces of garden statuary, but in order to locate these, item-level indexes must be used.

4. The strength of the Art Institute of Chicago's collection is demonstrated by the number of international catalogs it holds. As this book goes to press, 13,999 Hôtel Drouot (Paris) catalogs are included in the online catalog!

5. Reflects the result of an *AskART* search conducted on February 8, 2004.

Chapter Seven

1. Online dealers generally do not maintain rich archives of past sales; these Internet-based sources are, therefore, constantly changing as new items arrive and sold works are deleted.

2. *Artfact* website, http://www.artfact.com/artfact/about.cfm

3. Like many of the sources described in this section, the earliest version of *Artfact* was in CD-ROM format.

Chapter Eight

1. *Corpus of Paintings Sold in the Netherlands During the Nineteenth Century: 1801–1805*. Edited by Burton B. Fredericksen, with Ruud Priem and Julia I. Armstrong. Los Angeles: Provenance Index of the Getty Information Institute, 1998, p. ix.

Index